To Rebuild the Empire

SUNY series in Chinese Philosophy and Culture

David L. Hall and Roger T. Ames, Editors

To Rebuild the Empire

Lu Chih's Confucian Pragmatist Approach to the Mid-T'ang Predicament

JOSEPHINE CHIU-DUKE

State University of New York Press

Published by
State University of New York Press, Albany

© 2000 State University of New York

For information, address State University of New York Press,
State University Plaza, Albany, N.Y., 12246

Production by Diane Ganeles
Marketing by Nancy Farrell

Library of Congress Cataloging-in-Publication Data

Chiu-Duke, Josephine,
    To rebuild the empire : Lu Chih's Confucian pragmatist approach to
the mid-T'ang predicament / Josephine Chiu-Duke.
        p. cm. — (SUNY series in Chinese philosophy and culture)
    Includes bibliographical references and index.
    ISBN 0-7914-4501-1 (alk. paper). — ISBN 0-7914-4502-X (pbk. :
alk. paper)
    1. Lu, Chih, 754–805. 2. China—History—T'ang dynasty, 618–907.
3. Confucianism. I. Title. II. Series.
DS749.42.L8C46   2000
951'.017—dc21   99-40512
                                                                    CIP

10 9 8 7 6 5 4 3 2 1

To the memory of my father
Chiu Shao-ying
and to my mother
Cheng Hsiu-ch'iung

Contents

Acknowledgments

Limited space allows me only briefly to express my sincere gratitude to those whom I owe very great intellectual debts. Since this book has evolved and developed from my doctoral dissertation, I would like first to thank my thesis supervisors: Professor Chen Jo-shui for his insightful comments and guidance and for his continuing support; and Professors Daniel Overmyer and Alexander Woodside for their many helpful suggestions and advice. Further gratitude goes to Professor Lin Yü-sheng for stimulating and nurturing my interest in Chinese intellectual history in 1980 and for his encouragement over the years, and to Professors Yü Ying-shih, Mao Han-kuang, Li Yu-ning, and Wang Zhen-ping who, without knowing me, have all kindly given me valuable instruction and supplied me with much needed information about Lu Chih. During the preparation of this present work, Professor David McMullen, also without knowing me, answered my inquiries about Lu Chih and generously shared with me his own research findings as well as many thoughtful comments on how to strengthen my earlier drafts. Professor C. T. Hsia, with his encyclopedic knowledge on many Chinese subjects, also gave me important suggestions for improving my manuscript.

I would like to offer my special thanks to Professor Denis Twitchett. Having read my dissertation as an external examiner almost a decade ago, Professor Twitchett has been unceasing in his encouragement to me to find "a home" for Lu Chih. I have long admired, as have so many, his important contributions and his devotion to the field of traditional Chinese studies; but his warm and humane support for a late comer is even more deeply appreciated by someone who has only met him thus far on the phone and through the post.

My friends Doctors Lo Jiu-jung, Li Hsiao-ti, Mr. Osabe Yoshihiro, and my sister Wei-wei, brother-in-law Tse-hua, and Tse-hua's father, Mr. Liu Shih-ching, all went through a great deal of trouble to help me locate precious materials and archive documents in Taiwan and Japan, as for many years did the dedicated staff of the University of British Columbia Asian Library—Mr. Yim Tse, Mrs. Jean Tsai, and the late Mrs. Marcia Hsiao. My heartfelt thanks to every one of them. I am especially grateful to Lo Jiu-jung for giving me a rare edition of Lu Chih's works from her family library, and to Mr. Yim Tse for his beautiful calligraphy that adorns the front cover.

I owe an enormous debt as well to the three anonymous readers for SUNY Press. Their perceptive comments and criticisms led to important revisions without which this book would be less than it is. I am equally indebted to Professor Charles Hartman for introducing me to SUNY Press and for his encouragement and advice in my final preparation of this work. My thanks also to Ms. Nancy Ellegate, Dr. James P. Gubbins, Ms. Diane Ganeles, and Ms. Nancy Farrell at SUNY Press. This book has greatly profited from their meticulous editorial expertise.

I must thank my parents for their unique way of upbringing. I only wish that my father could have lived to see the coming of this book.

Finally, my inexpressible gratitude goes to Michael S. Duke. His never failing assistance and support, and above all, his loving care and joyful companionship have sustained me throughout to bring Lu Chih to life.

Needless to say, I am responsible for any errors that may remain in this book.

Abbreviations

AM	*Asia Major*
BSOAS	*Bulletin of the School of Oriental and African Studies*
CHC	*The Cambridge History of China, Volume 3, Sui and T'ang China,* Part 1
CTS	*Chiu T'ang-shu*
CTShih	*Ch'üan T'ang-shih*
CTW	*Ch'üan T'ang-wen*
CYKCC	*Ch'en Yin-k'o hsien-sheng ch'üan-chi*
CYYY	*Chung-yang yen-chiu-yüan li-shih yü-yen yen-chiu-so chi-k'an*
HHS	*Hou-Han shu*
HJAS	*Harvard Journal of Asiatic Studies*
HCLCC	*Han Ch'ang-li ch'üan-chi*
HTS	*Hsin T'ang-shu*
HYCC	*Han-yüan chi-chu*
LHSWC	*Lü Ho-shu wen-chi*
LHTCC	*Liu Ho-tung ch'üan-chi*
LWKC	*Li Wen-kung chi*
LYPWC	*Li Yüan-pin wen-chi*
PCIC	*Po Chü-i chi*
PLC	*P'i ling chi*
SKSC	*Sung kao-seng chuan*
SL	*Shun-tsung shih-lu*
SPPY	*Ssu-pu pei-yao*
SPTK	*Ssu-pu ts'ung-k'an*
SS	*Sung shih*
TCTC	*Tzu-chih t'ung-chien*
TFYK	*Ts'e-fu yüan-kuei*

THY	*T'ang hui-yao*
TKCK	*Teng-k'o chi-k'ao*
TTCLC	*T'ang ta-chao-ling chi*
TT	*T'ung-tien*
WYYH	*Wen-yüan ying-hua*
YHCHTC	*Yüan-ho chün-hsien t'u-chih*
YHHT	*Yüan-ho hsing-tsuan*
YHHTSCC	*Yüan-ho hsing-tsuan ssu-chiao chi*
YTSC	*Yüan Tz'u-shan chi*

T'ang Provinces in 780

T'ang Provinces in 780

Introduction

In the first half of the eighth century, T'ang China (618–907) stood out as the world's unrivaled empire.[1] As the second half of that century proceeded, however, this once splendid dynasty was pushed to the brink of collapse by a major rebellion and a series of subsequent military uprisings. Born one year before that great rebellion, Lu Chih (754–805), better known by his canonical name Lu Hsüan-kung, became a pivotal figure during an age of dynastic decline. This study concerns him and his efforts to rebuild the T'ang Empire from around 780 to 795. It is intended to be not only a narrative analysis of the man and his time, but also an exploration of Lu Chih's significance in that time and the implications of that significance in the Chinese political and intellectual tradition. I hope that placing Lu Chih in a larger context will allow readers to see how his political endeavors are relevant both to his own particular historical moment and to Chinese history as a whole.

Lu Chih rendered his most important political service first as a Han-lin scholar and then as a chief minister. In the former role, his work was crucial at a time when the T'ang state was in crisis. His responses to contemporary social and political problems brought to him by Emperor Te-tsung (r. 779–805) made a substantial contribution to the restoration of political stability. This success and his close relationship with Te-tsung led to his rapid rise to the position of chief minister at a relatively young age. As chief minister, he attempted to carry out a number of related reforms, but they had only limited impact. The breakdown of his intimate relationship with Te-tsung resulted in a precipitous fall from power and a complete withdrawal from the mid-T'ang political stage.

1

The dramatic changes in Lu Chih's short political life entail a poignant story, which is important in several ways. From the viewpoint of social and economic history, the rise of his family in the T'ang is an early symptom of the incipient decline of the medieval Chinese aristocracy.² His financial policies, though not completely carried out, represent the most powerful and farsighted contemporary critique of the famous two-tax system. They also contain a practical suggestion, unprecedented in Confucian economic history, to realize the *Chou li* (The Rites of Chou) ideal of "pacifying the rich while relieving the poor."³ Lu's activities as a Han-lin scholar testify to an institutional erosion of regular bureaucratic power by imperial personal attendants.⁴ His once close but later soured relationship with Te-tsung throws into sharp relief a fundamental problem inherent in the traditional Chinese political structure. Most important, Lu Chih's approach to the mid-T'ang predicament and his pursuit of the ideals implicit in that approach give him a stature that is unique in T'ang intellectual development and rare in the entire Confucian tradition. In my opinion, Lu Chih comes close to being a traditional Chinese exemplar of the Weberian concept of a true statesman.

Lu's approach to government underpins his efforts to restore dynastic stability. It also opens a new vista that enables us to reevaluate the usual categorization of Confucian scholar officials based on the standard *Ta Hsüeh* (Great Learning) polarity. The two ends of this polarity are not necessarily mutually exclusive, but on the basis of their political inclinations, Confucian scholar officials have generally been placed either at one end where they are seen to advocate personal cultivation as the key to government, or at the other end where they are perceived to stress the importance of practical administrative changes. That is, they are either placed in the category of "idealistic Confucian," or that of "pragmatic Confucian."⁵

This categorization has served modern scholarship well in our understanding of the Confucian tradition, and its validity has been widely accepted. However, it does not appear to offer the proper framework to characterize someone who can be placed at both ends and for whom neither end can sufficiently encompass the nature of his political approach, as is the case with Lu Chih. Lu's approach reveals another heretofore unexplored area of the rich Confucian landscape. It discloses the diversity and complexity of mid-T'ang intellectual predilections, and helps us distinguish the dominant characteristic of the Confucian political outlook in this period from that of Sung Neo-Confucianism.

These salient aspects of Lu Chih's political life constitute a challenging subject that deserves a critical study of some length, but such a work has thus far not been forthcoming. Two factors probably account for this: the intrinsic difficulty of an examination of Lu Chih's political endeavors due to the truncated nature of his literary remains, and his being overshadowed by the myth of Wei Cheng (580–643).

Lu Chih is not a household name to the majority of educated modern Chinese. Unlike the great T'ang poets Tu Fu (712–770) and Po Chü-i (772–846), or the eminent T'ang prose masters Han Yü (768–824) and Liu Tsung-yüan (773–819), he left little imaginative poetry and no literary or philosophical essays, the very assets that give most of his contemporaries a larger readership in modern China. As a court official, Lu Chih is also not a familiar figure in the collective memory of educated modern Chinese. Compared with the early T'ang Chief Minister Wei Cheng, Lu's crucial service in the mid-T'ang rarely receives the kind of recognition commonly accorded Wei in modern Chinese intellectual circles.

For centuries Wei Cheng was hailed as a paragon of Confucian ministers whose moral rectitude helped to ensure Emperor T'ai-tsung's good rule, but this traditional Chinese myth was deconstructed over two decades ago. Wei did fervently proclaim the Confucian principle of benevolent rule in his remonstrances to T'ai-tsung, but most of the court officials in T'ai-tsung's reign (627–649) shared Wei's views and presented similar suggestions to the throne.[6] After this period, as Lu Chih's service at court illustrates, such intense and frequent remonstrance was not widely practiced by most officials under later T'ang emperors. Lu himself conscientiously observed this tradition of remonstrance, but he found no T'ai-tsung as Wei Cheng and his colleagues had in their times.

With T'ai-tsung, Wei Cheng served under a comparatively enlightened ruler who was largely responsible for making him a celebrated Confucian hero in Chinese historiography. T'ai-tsung's personality and his obsession with his place in history created an unusually favorable context in which Wei was induced to exercise his Confucian duty. The ideal relationship that Wei Cheng and T'ai-tsung are often depicted as having is atypical, and Lu Chih's official life serves as a better reflection of the essential ruler-minister relationship in traditional Chinese political reality.

Lu Chih's political endeavors did earn him high respect from several important literati and scholar officials of subsequent dynasties. In 945 when the Later Chin dynasty historians finished compiling the *Old T'ang History*, Lu Chih was one of only four T'ang ministers whose lives and deeds were given an entire chapter in the biographical section. A passage in this work says that in recent times Lu has been considered an honest and public-spirited minister. It also laments the fact that Lu was a chief minister who "fought alone to eliminate every evil, and tried single-handedly to prevent all villainy, but his emperor did not trust his sincerity" (CTS, 139: 3818).

By 1093, the eminent Sung dynasty *ku-wen* (ancient prose) writer and poet Su Shih (1037–1101) and some other court officials collected Lu's extant works and presented them to the throne. They commended Lu's advice to Te-tsung, stating that his memorials "bring together the seminal essence of ancient and contemporary [writings], and [constitute] a genuine mirror for government."[7]

The well-known early Ming Confucian scholar official, Hsüeh Hsüan (1389–1464), also had high praise for Lu Chih:

> As for someone whose learning was pure and honest; who regarded correcting [his majesty's] mind as the first priority in serving the ruler, and practicing rightness as imperative in discussing [governmental] affairs; and who obviously had the talent to be a state minister—I can only find one such person in [all of] mid-T'ang [history]. This person is none other than Lu Hsüan-kung. . . . If the ruler at that time (Te-tsung) had adopted his suggestions, the order of the Three Dynasties could have been restored, not to mention the good rule of the Chen-kuan and K'ai-yüan periods.[8]

Huang Tsung-hsi (1610–1695), one of the most critical Confucian thinkers of the late Ming or in all traditional Chinese history, included Lu Chih in his list of *the* seven model Confucian scholar officials in Chinese history.[9] In a 1692 essay written to refute the contemporary idea that the honor of being enshrined in the Confucian temple should be limited to orthodox neo-Confucian scholars such as Ch'eng I (1033–1107), Ch'eng Hao (1032–1085) and Chu Hsi (1130–1200) or their intellectual heirs, Huang explained why he held Lu Chih and six others in such high regard:

> But if an age is disordered, the scholar-official must strictly guard his honor, and be determined not to sacrifice the high standards to which he has dedicated his life, no matter what tortures and punishments are visited on him by the ruler. For him, simply to write commentaries on the Four

Books, compile philosophical dialogues, or open a school and gather students does not suffice to fulfill his [Confucian] duty.

Throughout the ages, past and present, there have been those like . . . Lu Chih of the T'ang, . . . who actually practiced the teachings of Confucius.[10]

Allowing for some probable exaggeration, it is evident that the compilers of the *Old T'ang History*, Su Shih, Hsüeh Hsüan and Huang Tsung-hsi all considered Lu Chih's type of political activity crucial to an ordered government. Hsüeh Hsüan found Lu Chih the sole Confucian minister in the mid-T'ang. Huang Tsung-hsi even ranked Lu as one of only seven exemplary scholar officials in Chinese history who genuinely practiced the Confucian teachings. These assessments call our attention to Lu Chih's official life, and challenge us to test the validity of Huang Tsung-hsi's statement and explore the implied complexity of the Confucian tradition.

Lu Chih emerged on the mid-T'ang political stage in the perilous times created by the An Lu-shan rebellion and the second Ho-pei rebellion. The An Lu-shan rebellion (755–763) was a major turning point in T'ang history. It permanently divided the empire but for a short period of restoration, and left behind a legacy of rampant and chronic militarism throughout the second half of the dynasty.[11] The Ho-pei region, where the An Lu-shan rebellion first started, became semi-independent after the T'ang court settled the rebellion through a policy of compromise. When Te-tsung attempted to exert central control over this region soon after ascending the throne in 779, his actions precipitated the second Ho-pei rebellion, and again plunged the T'ang court into a grave crisis. Lu's political life is significant first of all due to the policies he advocated and their successes and failures in this chaotic era.

Faced with the catastrophic social and political changes brought about by the An Lu-shan rebellion, many concerned T'ang scholar officials felt compelled to find a way to restore their state to its previous order. Their undertakings gave rise to the mid-T'ang Confucian revival, a revival that valued Confucianism mainly as a political rather than as a moral and metaphysical philosophy.[12] Lu Chih's political life gains equal significance due to its parallels with this most crucial development in T'ang intellectual history.

The mid-T'ang Confucian revival is a comparatively unexplored area of T'ang history, though some critical studies have recently become available.[13] These studies all see Lu Chih as an important mid-T'ang figure, but he is discussed only parenthetically, and not as a main representative of this revival. This made me wonder why Huang Tsung-hsi selected Lu Chih, rather than any other mid-T'ang Confucian revivalist, as one of only seven exemplary Confucians in Chinese history. It also made me curious to know whether Lu Chih played some sort of role in, or had some kind of bearing on, the mid-T'ang Confucian revival. Recent scholarship has enormously enriched our present knowledge of the revival. Discovering Lu Chih's place in it will bring us one step closer to the goal of producing a complete and well-rounded picture of its development.

Although Lu Chih does not figure prominently in recent studies of the mid-T'ang Confucian revival, he is by no means a complete stranger to Western students of T'ang history. Some parts of his extant works were translated into French in 1735 and into German early in the third decade of the twentieth century.[14] In his 1949 study of Po Chü-i, Arthur Waley commented that Lu Chih was "the most able and fearless statesman of the period."[15] By 1960, a small portion of Lu's criticism of the two-tax system was translated for English readers. In this same year, E. G. Pulleyblank also dealt briefly with Lu's political orientation in a pioneering article on mid-T'ang intellectual activities. Denis Twitchett's 1962 essay was, however, the first systematic study of Lu Chih in English.[16] No further research specifically concerned with Lu Chih has been published in English during the intervening, almost forty, years.

Lu Chih is also held in high regard by some concerned modern Chinese scholars. Hu Shih (1891–1962), one of China's most influential twentieth-century intellectual leaders, wrote in 1940, in a manner reminiscent of Huang Tsung-hsi, that Lu Chih, along with twenty-two other historical figures, should be singled out as a model character for the Chinese nation.[17] When the Nationalist government regained control after the Japanese surrender in 1945, trials were held in Shanghai of those who had served under the Japanese puppet government in the occupied territories. At one such trial, Lu Chih's 783 suggestion to Te-tsung—that the throne should adopt a lenient policy toward the rebellious governors and especially toward their subordinate soldiers—was specifically cited by a military trial lawyer urging a judge to issue a less severe sentence to a chief collaborator who had served as leader of the Japanese southeastern regional puppet government in 1938.[18]

Interest in Lu Chih has continued among Chinese scholars. A number of short articles on his political views and financial policies have been published—since the late 1950s in Taiwan, and in China after 1980. Three book-length studies of Lu's life and works also became available in 1975, 1978, and 1985.[19] The short Chinese articles certainly enhance our knowledge of some aspects of Lu Chih's approach to government, but their limited scope prohibits an overall investigation of the subject. The three lengthy studies of Lu Chih, on the other hand, tend to be descriptive and do not undertake a critical analysis of Lu's responses to the mid-T'ang crisis. They also fail to reconstruct an accurate account of Lu's earlier career and his family background.

By comparison, Twitchett's 1962 essay continues to stand out as a major study. It provides an analysis of Lu Chih's views on mid-T'ang political reality during his two periods of service at the court. It offers an explanation for the deterioration of the close relationship between Lu Chih and Te-tsung. What is more important, it emphasizes that Lu Chih was not a conservative Confucian, but a professional court official whose primary concern was to solve practical problems confronting the T'ang state during the late eighth century.[20]

Nevertheless, many questions still remain. Twitchett's essay is not intended to be an overall study. Because of this, various aspects of Lu Chih's life and the implications of his family's rise in the T'ang are not discussed. Like all the other available Chinese and Japanese studies of Lu Chih, Twitchett's article contains similar inaccurate views concerning the development of Lu's provincial and central government service.[21] Furthermore, Twitchett's exposition is primarily focused on the mid-T'ang political situation and Lu Chih's critique of the two-tax system, and thus offers no intellectual framework either for understanding Lu's concrete contribution to the restoration of dynastic stability or for exploring his possible role in the mid-T'ang Confucian revival. The suggestions Lu made to the court while serving as a Han-lin scholar, and his reform efforts as chief minister to carry out a series of policies aimed at rebuilding the T'ang empire also do not receive complete scrutiny. The breakdown of a relationship as complex as the one between Lu Chih and Te-tsung would equally seem to have involved more factors than the three given prominence by Twitchett: Lu Chih's outspoken personality, his change of role, and Te-tsung's autocratic rule. Finally, the position Twitchett maintained almost four decades ago that Lu Chih was primarily a pragmatist whose orthodox Confucian beliefs were of secondary importance has been challenged. David McMullen's 1988 book provides a contrary view. In McMullen's

brief discussion of Lu, he treats him not as a pragmatist, but as a
Confucian statesman who insisted on the cultivation of personal
morality, and was devoid of appreciation of the need to employ
expediency in government.[22] Because of these two conflicting views,
similar to the *Ta Hsüeh* polarity, the exact nature of Lu Chih's
approach to government has eluded our grasp. Not only do his
political convictions and his political commitment remain unknown
to us, his significance in mid-T'ang intellectual history is also left
undefined.

Without giving satisfactory solutions to the above problems,
Lu Chih's life and his political approach remain tantalizingly unclear. Our understanding of a segment of mid-T'ang history, and of
the complexities of the Confucian tradition at that time, also continue to be less than adequate. This work represents a new attempt to solve these problems by redefining Lu Chih's approach to
government, recuperating his political convictions and ideals, and
establishing his place in the mid-T'ang intellectual milieu.

The central difficulty I had to face in conducting this study was
the insufficiency of existing traditional sources concerning Lu Chih.[23]
Lu Chih's extant works serve as my fundamental source throughout, but they are not complete and may be somewhat biased due to
the personal preferences of their chief compiler.[24] Lu's surviving
works, numerous as they are, consist of mainly the imperial edicts
he drafted for the throne and his memorials to Te-tsung during his
two periods of service at court.

Any study of Lu Chih then must rely exclusively on his memorials—his responses to particular historical situations and to a
particular ruler at a particular time. This presents several meth-
odological problems. How is one to reconstruct Lu Chih's political
approach, given the occasional nature of his extant works?[25] Even
after contextualizing each and every one of Lu's memorials, can we
identify a theme to unify all these contextualized but not necessarily related texts? Assuming a successful reconstruction, how are we
to establish Lu's place in his time? This would inevitably involve
making comparisons between him and his contemporaries, while
the available sources work against claims of conspicuous influence
by Lu on them, or vice versa. Comparisons of course need not be
limited to tracing mutual influences. They can be carried out to
establish parallels. And it should suffice if our comparisons between Lu Chih and his contemporaries are confined only to the
area of political perspective. Careful scholars may still be concerned
about the validity of any attempt to make legitimate comparisons

between Lu Chih's political approach, reconstructed without the benefit of informal writings, and those of his contemporaries, whose extant works may or may not include memorial writings.

A close reading of Lu Chih's collected works and other available sources seems to offer positive solutions to these problems. One important fact is that all the memorials presented by Lu Chih to Te-tsung during his early service as a Han-lin scholar were private documents. Even though they are about Lu's views on public matters, they are all personal exchanges between Lu and Te-tsung. They are the fruits of Lu's private reflections on all the social and political problems brought to him by the throne. They reveal his "conscious responses to the situations in which he [found] himself."[26]

As a form of communication between minister and ruler, memorial writings unavoidably adopt a certain degree of rhetoric, ranging from normal expressions of excessive self-depreciation to extreme protestations of one's loyalty. Lu Chih's memorials are no exception, but there is a significant difference between Lu's memorials and those of previous T'ang chief ministers. Due to Lu's unusual relationship with Te-tsung, his memorials are frequently more personal than theirs.[27] He mentions his family, his preferences in friends, his social life or lack thereof, his self-evaluation, and his personal reasons for taking particular positions. Most importantly, he persistently maintains his own principled views. The issue here is still whether we can even identify these principled views, and most crucially, whether his proclaimed principles can be sustained by his actual political behavior. A comparison of his words with his deeds, though simplistic as it may seem, is a basic and inescapable criterion for evaluating a political figure no matter what historical period we are discussing. It is one way we distinguish principles from platitudes or individual positions from rhetoric. I make such a comparison in this study.

Lu Chih's early memorials do reveal certain fundamental principles that underlie all his responses during his service as a Han-lin scholar. Under the rubric of these basic principles, his memorials no longer appear to be mere disconnected individual items. They begin to form a coherent and meaningful whole in which a definite political approach begins to loom large.

Having formed a notion of Lu's political approach, the question becomes: Did Lu Chih consistently apply this approach to government in the second stage of his court service—during his tenure as chief minister? All the memorials Lu presented to the throne during this period indicate a positive answer. They continue to represent his conscious responses to the problems currently confronting Te-tsung's court. The chief difference is that Lu Chih presented most of the memorials in this period, not as private exchanges with the emperor, but as public documents. What matters is whether Lu Chih's early political approach, as manifested in his private exchanges with Te-tsung, is consistently matched by the approach that emerges from a reading of his later public memorials. If his early and later, private and public, political approaches remain the same, or, if his private advice to the emperor was congruous with his public policy proposals, we are justified in believing that these writings represent Lu Chih's authentic approach to government. We then have equally good reason to affirm that Lu's political behavior is a reflection of his political convictions and ideals. With our knowledge secure in this respect, we can also substantiate the legitimacy of comparing Lu's political ideas and actions with those of his contemporaries, even those whose extant works contain no memorial writings.

Of course there may be other possibilities for dealing with these same difficult problems, but the nature of Lu Chih's extant works is such that I found it crucial first to reconstruct and validate his political approach. Through the process of reconstruction, a solid logical foundation for comparisons between Lu Chih and his contemporaries was built and firm grounds were established to explore Lu's significance in mid-T'ang intellectual history.

While recent studies of the mid-T'ang Confucian revival focus essentially on intellectual changes in this period and try to clarify the relationship between the revival and Sung Neo-Confucianism, they do not particularly emphasize the political approach of the major revival leaders. This is unfortunate because the political approach seems to offer another key to characterize the revival and distinguish it from Sung Neo-Confucianism. Concern to bring out this aspect also played a role in my decision to present the comparisons between Lu Chih and his contemporaries the way I have.

In addition to discussing the larger social implications of the rise of Lu Chih's family in T'ang history, the first three chapters of this work also clarify and revise our view of Lu's earlier career, some facets of his personality, and his immediate family. In the fourth chapter I attempt both to define the exact nature of Lu Chih's political approach, and to delineate how Lu relied on his approach to help Te-tsung resolve the social and political crisis that occurred during his tenure as a Han-lin scholar.

Twitchett's position that Lu Chih was primarily a pragmatist and McMullen's view that Lu was a conservative Confucian leave us with two paradigms of polarization. It has seemed more fruitful in my reexamination of Lu's political approach, however, to try to transcend any such polarization paradigm, and allow Lu's own expressed views and his efforts to realize these views to lead us to their most logical conclusions. Lu Chih's writings and recorded actions demonstrate that he considered moral cultivation and practical administrative changes equally necessary in governing a state. For this reason I characterize his political approach as a *Confucian pragmatist approach* in contrast to the conventionally applied term *pragmatic Confucian.*

The next two chapters explore whether or not Lu continued to apply the same consistent approach to government throughout his official service. These chapters analyze Lu's reform policies and conceptualize his political convictions and ideals. This allows us to see whether Lu Chih was merely a bureaucrat, or whether he represented something different in the sense that he aspired to go beyond his prescribed duty and fulfill some higher goal. At this point, I offer some reflections on the final breakdown of Lu Chih's close relationship with Te-tsung.

Building on this foundation, the last two chapters investigate Lu's significance in mid-T'ang history. To assess Lu Chih in a broader perspective, I compare his approach to government first with that of two notable chief ministers during his time, and then with that of the leading mid-T'ang Confucian revivalists. These comparisons serve both to establish Lu Chih's place in his time, and to disclose the dominant characteristic of the political approach favored by a majority of leading Confucian revivalists. They also further my discussion of the implications of Lu's political life in the epilogue.

Of the two chief ministers, I pay particular attention to Tu Yu (735–812) for two reasons. For decades Tu Yu has been regarded as the direct opposite of Lu Chih. Such a view neglects the many similarities and confuses the essential differences both between Tu Yu and Lu Chih and between Tu Yu and other leading Confucian revivalists.[28] Moreover, a comparison of Lu and Tu's approaches to government makes apparent why I feel it necessary to employ the term Confucian pragmatist approach instead of adopting the conventionally used term *pragmatic Confucian.* Since our knowledge of Lu Chih and Tu Yu and even some other major mid-T'ang intellectuals has been flawed, missing much of the complexity of the mid-T'ang intellectual scene, it would seem more reasonable to provide a more accurate picture of them by offering a new category for comparison than to use the conventional term to cover all the

Confucians who have pragmatic tendencies while in fact ignoring the substantial nuances and differences in their political approaches. This also explains why I borrow the term *utilitarian Confucian* to contrast Tu Yu's approach to government with Lu Chih's Confucian pragmatist approach. In the field of Chinese intellectual history, as our understanding of Confucianism deepened, scholars, in order to bring out the subtle nuances in different concepts as accurately as possible on the basis of the existing documentary evidence, have from time to time invented additional terms or adopted traditional Chinese terms to characterize different forms of Confucianism. My term Confucian pragmatist approach is intended to be an example of this type of intellectual investigation.

The final aim of this inquiry is to demonstrate the unique nature of Lu Chih's contribution to the mid-T'ang Confucian revival. Anyone who studies the life and work of a particular historical figure must have a genuine interest in that person, and there is always the danger of making that person appear larger than life. I have been fully conscious of these pitfalls throughout my research. Thus, in chapters two and three, I exhaust as far as possible all the extant writings on Lu Chih in order to record and examine any negative comments about his life and work. I point out how he disposed of two officials he did not like, and I suggest both self-serving and principled reasons for this and other similar actions. I also discuss in chapters five and six whatever problematic areas I discover in Lu's policy suggestions. None of these problems alter my major findings about Lu Chih based on his writings and all the other available historical evidence. I hope these findings will help place him in a proper historical perspective. I also hope that my elucidation of Lu's political approach and the new vista it provides will ultimately reveal the diversity and complexity of mid-T'ang Confucian predispositions and their possible latent influence on the Chinese intellectual tradition.

I begin with Lu Chih's life and family background.

CHAPTER ONE

A Bureaucratized
Aristocratic Lineage

Lu Chih was born in the thirteenth year of the T'ien-pao era (754 C.E.), the second reign period of emperor Hsüan-tsung, just before the An Lu-shan rebellion shattered the unity of the empire and reduced the "golden age" of the T'ang to the status of a bygone memory. We do not know exactly how Lu Chih was brought up in this turbulent age, but it is possible to establish a reasonably complete and reliable account of his family history, an account that also illustrates a significant aspect of T'ang social and political history—the bureaucratization of aristocratic lineages.[1]

The Lu Lineage and T'ang Social Hierarchy

It is well understood that early and middle T'ang society, like the previous Six Dynasties and the Sui, was marked by clearly observed social segregation and stratification. An enormous gap existed between commoners (*shu-min*) and the elite class (*shih ta-fu*),[2] but within the elite class there were different categorizations to define the place of a lineage or a clan in that social hierarchy.[3] Most members of the T'ang elite class belonged to the category of illustrious provincial lineages, but at the top of this class, a very small number of lineages made up what some modern historians call the "aristocratic families." What made these families aristocratic was their "hereditary high social status, independent of full court control."[4] They were a super elite with national recognition.[5] Most of

13

them began to emerge from the early fourth century on when north China was taken over by non-Chinese rulers.

Education and culture, economic wealth, local power based upon accumulated landed property and clan solidarity, the practice of marriage exclusivity, and ingrained social respect for birth all amounted to valuable assets for the rise of these aristocratic lineages. Local property ownership seems to have been the most important of these assets for ensuring their survival during dynastic changes.[6] Such lineages enjoyed high esteem and great influence in society; this enormous social prestige usually guaranteed them high ranks in the nine-tiered system of official recruitment, thus allowing successive members of these great families to dominate most top government positions during the Six Dynasties.[7] Their participation in government further perpetuated their overall socioeconomic power, and they survived into the T'ang despite the rise and fall of dynasties.[8]

Liu Fang (fl. ca. 740–765), a mid-eighth-century historian and genealogist, singled out four regionally based groups of aristocratic lineages as the most eminent families in T'ang China.[9] Two of these groups were in the north and two were in the south. In the north were the Shan-tung aristocratic families (*east of the mountains*, included modern Hopei, Honan, and central Shansi), the most prestigious group among the four elite groups, and the so-called Kuan-lung block to which the T'ang ruling house belonged. The Kuan–lung group was formed by an alliance of Kuan-chung (modern southern Shansi and modern Shensi) and Tai-pei (modern northern Shansi) aristocratic families. The two groups holding local power in southeast China were defined as the southern aristocracy. One of them consisted of emigré clans, and the other constituted a native aristocracy. The native aristocracy in the south seems to be culturally closer to the northern aristocracy than to the southern emigré clans. They paid serious attention to Confucian classical education as did the northern aristocratic families, while belles lettres and Buddhism occupied a much more important place in the cultural consciousness of their aristocratic neighbors.[10]

Lu Chih's family belonged to the Wu *chün* Lu lineage (the Lu lineage of Wu commandery), one of the four most prestigious representatives of the native southeast aristocracy.[11] This makes his family culturally more in line with the tradition of support for Confucian classical education than that of literary writing. Of course, it does not follow that literary pursuits would have had no place in the education of the Lu lineage, and although Lu Chih considered himself primarily a follower of the Confucian teaching, he also excelled in literary composition.

Comparatively speaking, due to the suffering and losses inflicted on the southern aristocracy by repeated military uprisings in the sixth century, their power and prestige could not rival that of the northern aristocratic groups. Ch'ang-an being the T'ang capital and the center of cultural and political activities also put the southern aristocratic families in an inferior position vis-à-vis the northern aristocracy. Nevertheless, in Liu Fang's view, this did not alter their superior social position in the T'ang elite class as a whole. In short, though Lu Chih's southeastern lineage held a less prominent position than the northern aristocratic families, it still occupied the highest levels of T'ang social structure.

The presence of powerful aristocratic clans was one of the main characteristics of T'ang social structure, but, ironically, it was precisely during this era that the bureaucratization of the aristocracy began to take place through the examination system (*k'o-chü chih-tu*). In the process of being bureaucratized, a process that was not complete until near the very end of the dynasty, members of the aristocratic clans always had a better chance to enter and advance in the T'ang bureaucracy.[12] Before the collapse of the T'ang, no matter how the aristocracy was transformed, the standing in social and political life of a person like Lu Chih was always closely related to his family background.

A Profile of the Lu Lineage

Wu *chün*, home region of the Lu lineage, was an administrative district that included the southeast and the northeast areas of modern Kiangsu and Chekiang provinces. In 758 the T'ang court replaced the old Han name of Wu *chün* with Su-chou,[13] but both names were used interchangeably throughout the later half of the dynasty. Altogether there were seven counties included in Su-chou or Wu *chün* under T'ang rule.[14] Situated in the lower reaches of the Yangtze River, it constituted one of the most important economic areas of the T'ang state, especially after the An Lu-shan rebellion.

Both the *New T'ang History* genealogy (HTS *tsai-hsiang shih-hsi piao*) and a preface to the recompiled genealogy of the forty-nine branches written in 812 by Lu Shu[15] agree that one Lu Lieh initiated the history of the Lu lineage in Wu county (Wu *hsien*) of Wu *chün*.[16] We do not know when this took place, but it seems certain that before the Eastern Han (25–220), the Lu lineage was already firmly established in that area. The *History of the Eastern Han (Hou Han shu)* unmistakably refers to the Lus of Wu *chün* as "a prominent surname for generations" (*shih wei tsu-hsing*).[17] Early in 634, the Lu family already appeared in an imperially approved list of "notable clans" (*wang-shih*).[18] Even in the late tenth century it was still recognized as one of the illustrious "four surnames" in the southeast.[19] Apparently, the Lu family developed into a very large kinship organization several centuries before the T'ang.

Up to the Eastern Chin dynasty (317–420) the Lu clan contained at least eight branch groups.[20] By the mid-T'ang, the clan became so large that it expanded to forty-nine branches which were acknowledged by the imperial ruling house. Lu Shu's 812 Preface advises each subgroup of the Lu clan to establish a separate genealogy; otherwise, he warns, the lineage history might be lost due to demographic expansion.[21]

Despite this proliferation of Lu subgroups, only three branches are mentioned in the *New T'ang History*, presumably because they produced six chief ministers during the T'ang. These three subgroups included the Tan-t'u branch, the T'ai-wei (Defender in Chief) branch and the Shih-lang (Vice Director) branch, which Lu Chih's immediate family belonged to.[22] Tan-t'u was the name of a county (modern Chen-kiang in Kiangsu); the other two clan names referred to the official titles assumed by their branch ancestors.

Of these three subgroups, only the activities of the T'ai-wei branch is continuously documented in pre-T'ang dynastic histories.[23] Only the T'ai-wei branch, with its regional base in Wu *hsien* of Wu *chün*, was considered one of the four prominent aristocratic lineages in the southeast area. This is largely due to its enormous social prestige and its members' powerful positions in government.[24] Compared with the T'ai-wei branch, information about members of the pre-T'ang Tan-t'u and Shih-lang branches is quite limited.[25] It was only in the T'ang that members of the Tan-t'u and Shih-lang families began to make their lineages well known.

Its accumulated social esteem and powerful influence and its geographically concentrated local base sustained the Lu lineage during the military rebellions and political chaos at the end of the Six Dynasties. But how did it maintain power and continue its reputation for being a member of the national elite in the T'ang, an era when the social and political stage was mainly dominated by the northern aristocracy, and the imperial rulers attempted to build a strong and effective bureaucracy? Tracing the emergence of members of the three major Lu branches in T'ang history reveals how the Lu lineage acquired its super elite position in the T'ang social hierarchy, and demonstrates the process of radical transformation of a prominent T'ang aristocratic clan.

The Tan-t'u Branch

Lu Te-ming (original name: Yüan-lang, ca. 560–630) carried the line of the Tan-t'u subgroup into the T'ang. His erudition won him respect and office in both the Ch'en (557–589) and Sui (581–617) dynasties. When T'ai-tsung, then Prince of Ch'in, recruited him to be an Academician of the Institute of Education (or Academy of Literary Study, *Ch'in-fu wen-hsüeh-kuan hsüeh-shih*) in his palace, Te-ming had already achieved a reputation as a renowned classical scholar. He was also known for his loyalty because he refused to serve the rebel general Wang Shih-ch'ung.[26] In 624, Lu Te-ming greatly enhanced his reputation as a Confucian scholar in a debate on Confucianism, Taoism, and Buddhism.[27] He was subsequently promoted to the rank of Erudite of the National University (*Kuo-tzu po-shih*), and ennobled as Baron of Wu-*hsien* (*Wu-hsien nan*).[28] Te-ming's erudition confirms the general consensus that the native southern aristocracy had an intense interest in Confucian classical education. Te-ming was one of only two members of the entire Lu lineage to serve in the governments of the first two T'ang emperors,[29] and his rise in T'ang officialdom depended not so much on his family background as on his prestige as a learned Confucian scholar.[30] Lu Te-ming himself never seems to have acquired substantial political power, but it is significant that one of his two sons, Lu Tun-hsin, rose to be chief minister from 665 to 666 under Emperor Kao-tsung (r. 649–683).[31]

By the late months of 660, Kao-tsung's court was firmly controlled by his favorite consort, Empress Wu Tse-t'ien.[32] In spite of her recent victory in liquidating all her enemies in the top echelons of government, Empress Wu continued to amass all the support she could within the bureaucracy to pave the way for a future takeover of the imperial throne.[33] To promote someone from a southern aristocratic lineage whose immediate family had become more recognizable under T'ang rule would both maintain the previous policy of balancing the power of regional aristocratic groups and cultivate her own power base.[34] It is very likely that the elevation of Lu Tun-hsin to the post of chief minister was engineered by Empress Wu for just those reasons.

Descendants of the Tan-t'u branch continued to serve in the T'ang bureaucracy until the end of the dynasty. Most of them occupied either high- or middle-rank positions.[35] In all, there were twenty-one male members in the Tan-t'u branch during the T'ang era. Fifteen of them served in the government; most of their appointments seem to have been concentrated in the metropolitan area far away from Wu *chün*.[36] While their active participation in the bureaucracy apparently helped them sustain their branch's elite status in society, it simultaneously increased their dependence on the T'ang state.

The T'ai-wei Branch

The T'ai-wei branch was the largest subgroup of the Lu lineage. During the T'ang period alone, it produced one hundred and fourteen male offspring, eighty-one of whom served in the government, three of them as chief minister.[37] The earliest T'ang member of this branch was Lu Shan-jen who served as a local official early in the dynasty.[38] We do not know how Shan-jen became an official, but his eldest son, Lu Chien-chih, was famous for calligraphy, and this talent most certainly earned him access to the bureaucracy.[39] Still, the T'ai-wei branch does not seem to have regained its powerful pre-T'ang position in the government until Chien Chih's nephew, Lu Yüan-fang (639–701), rose to be chief minister during Empress Wu's reign (690–705).[40]

Lu Yüan-fang entered the bureaucracy through the doctoral examination system. He passed the *ming-ching* (enlightening the classics) examination and special decree examinations, probably around 659.[41] At this time, the *ming-ching*, with its emphasis on classical scholarship, still had much greater prestige than the *chin-shih* (advanced scholar) examination. This situation was reversed after 681 when Kao-tsung, under the influence of Empress Wu, made literary composition a required subject in the *chin-shih* examination, and made it much more difficult than the *ming-ching*. From then on, the *chin-shih* examination gradually became the most prestigious and important channel for acquiring official status.[42]

Another early member of the T'ai-wei branch who also entered the civil service by means of the doctoral examination was Yüan-fang's uncle, Lu Yü-ch'ing. He did not take the *ming-ching* examination, but rather obtained the *chin-shih* degree sometime during

Kao-tsung's reign.[43] If this was after 681, it would be apparent that he chose the more difficult and more highly regarded route to enter the bureaucracy just as Yüan-fang had done by taking the *mingching* examination before 681.

Lu Yüan-fang and Lu Yü-ch'ing had similar careers. They were the first two T'ai-wei Lus to pass the doctoral examinations to acquire a nominal official status. This shows that their classical scholarship and writing ability reached a certain recognizable standard, and it implies that their decisions to take the examinations could have been influenced by Kao-tsung's new, 659, emphasis on the importance of the examination system.[44] The examination system was not the only access to nominal official status,[45] but it gradually became a necessary route for officials who had ambitions for the highest positions in the court.[46] It was then no coincidence that both Yüan-fang and Yü-ch'ing chose to join the bureaucracy through the doctoral examinations. They must have realized that passing the most prestigious doctoral examination in their time was the surest way to enter and advance in the bureaucracy. What is more important, they must also have believed that it was the safest channel to preserve their families' traditional power. It would perhaps not be far-fetched to assume that the increasingly close relationship between the *chin-shih* examination and bureaucratic advancement gave some of the Lus a great incentive to strive for literary excellence.

Both Yüan-fang and Yü-ch'ing's promotions to high-ranking posts were conferred by Empress Wu as rewards for their accomplishments in the border regions.[47] This again demonstrates that to consolidate her own power, Empress Wu apparently preferred to promote men who were not likely to get involved in factional intrigues and whose immediate families had just begun to participate in the government.[48]

The power and prestige of the T'ai-wei branch was reassured by Yüan-fang and Yü-ch'ing's performance in government and was continued by that of their descendants. Their official accomplishments even allowed some of their sons to enter the bureaucracy through the protective *yin* privilege.[49] As far as we know, at least six members of the T'ai-wei branch occupied different official posts during Hsüan-tsung's reign (712–756). Their achievement must have helped to establish a powerful position in the bureaucracy. Ironically, the bureaucratic success of the T'ai-wei Lus loosened their ties with their local property base in Wu *chün*. Thus, either in the late eighth or the ninth century, the descendants of Lu Yüan-fang began gradually to sell off their local property.[50]

This sale of local property seems to have been a logical result of their success in the T'ang bureaucracy. Living a bureaucratic life at court and in different parts of the T'ang empire must have made it difficult for the T'ai-wei Lus to care for their local holdings in Wu *chün*. In the late ninth century, Lu Yüan-fang's seventh-generation grandson, Lu Kuei-meng (d. ca. 881), considered himself impoverished even though he is said to have owned several hundred Chinese acres (*mou*) of farm land and thirty houses in the southeast.[51] If this was the case, then their property holdings in the eighth century must have been even larger. Maintaining such a large amount of landed property far from Ch'ang-an would become a burden for the Lus if they wanted to succeed in a government that increasingly tended toward the bureaucratization of pretentious aristocratic families.

Once the T'ai-wei Lus sold their local property, they could always buy land near the capital or in the popular Lo-yang region. This was exactly what many other aristocratic families did during the T'ang. In so doing, these aristocratic families became more and more centralized as a metropolitan elite and gradually lost their local ties.[52] As a result, the power base supporting their aristocratic cachet was also in danger. From the point of view of the aristocratic families as a whole, the sale of property by the T'ai-wei Lus testifies to the ever accelerating trend toward bureaucratic transformation of the aristocracy.

There were also some members of the T'ai-wei branch who stayed in Wu *chün* and gained fame through scholarship or a Taoistic lifestyle without entering the bureaucracy. One was the above mentioned Lu Kuei-meng, a late T'ang *chin-shih* and a renowned classical scholar.[53] On the other hand, Lu Kuei-meng's uncle, Lu Hsi-sheng (d. ca. 895) and his descendants do not seem to have given up the pursuit of official appointments. Lu Hsi-sheng was even appointed to the position of chief minister in 895, though he only served for a short while.[54] Compared with the bureaucratic path taken by the majority of the T'ai-wei Lus, or for that matter the Tan-t'u Lus, Lu Kuei-meng's case is an exception to the general trend of Lu clan development during the T'ang.

The Shih-lang Branch and Lu Chih's Immediate Family

This general trend of active government service applied equally to the evolution of the Shih-lang branch. Because there is some confusion about this branch, and because this is the branch to which

Lu Chih's immediate family belonged, I offer here a revised picture of the Shih-lang branch.

Unlike the T'ai-wei and Tan-t'u Lus whose sub-choronym was always represented by Wu *hsien* of Wu *chün*, the geographic base of the Shih-lang branch was in Chia-hsing county of Wu *chün*.[55] It is not clear when the Shih-lang group became established in Chia-hsing but, like the Tan-t'u branch, it could not match the T'ai-wei branch for prestige and power either before or during the T'ang.[56]

The founder of the Shih-lang branch was Lu Kuan. The only information we have about him is that he occupied the post of vice director of the secretariat (*Chung-shu shih-lang*) in the Eastern Chin dynasty. Lu Kuan's seventh-generation grandson, Lu Hsün, acquired an important position in the southern Ch'en dynasty.[57] From the Ch'en dynasty to the early T'ang, the Shih-lang Lus do not seem to have obtained any position in the bureaucracy. It is only during the K'ai-yüan era (713–741) that we find Lu Hsün's ninth-generation grandson, Lu Ch'i-wang, serving as director of the Palace Library (*Pi-shu-chien*).[58] This position was usually conferred upon officials who had outstanding literary talents,[59] and it is most probable that Lu Ch'i-wang also relied upon such gifts to enter the bureaucracy. The *New T'ang History* genealogy records that Ch'i-wang had eight sons, and all of them received official appointment. The same source states that one of his sons, Lu Pa, was Lu Chih's father, thus making Lu Ch'i-wang Lu Chih's grandfather.[60]

This genealogical attribution for the Shih-lang branch has created a certain amount of confusion, especially in relation to Lu Chih's direct family. Instead of eight sons as listed in the *New T'ang History* genealogy, Lu Ch'i-wang had only six sons. The eldest son named in this genealogy was Lu Mi, and he really belonged to a Lu clan in Honan that was of foreign origin. This explains why Lu Mi was not included as Lu Ch'i-wang's son in the *Yüan-ho hsing-tsuan*.[61] The two Lu Ch'ans listed in the genealogy refer to the same person, two different characters for Ch'an being used interchangeably during the T'ang.[62] From a contemporary essay, we know that Ch'i-wang's six sons should very likely be listed in the following order of seniority: Lu Wei, Lu Feng (or Lu Li), Lu Pa, Lu Jun (or Lu Chien), Lu Huai, and Lu Ch'an.[63] Meanwhile, contrary to the *New T'ang History* genealogy, it seems that among Lu Ch'i-wang's six sons only Lu Feng's (or Lu Li's), not Lu Ch'an's, family line extended into the last years of the T'ang.[64]

Lu Pa, Ch'i-wang's third son, was not Lu Chih's father. Lu Chih's father was named Lu K'an.[65] The name provided by Ch'üan

Te-yü (759–818) in his preface to Lu Chih's collected works is Lu K'an-ju,[66] but it is quite certain that these two names refer to the same person, and that Lu Chih's father was Lu K'an or Lu K'an-ju.[67] Were Lu Pa and Lu K'an also the same person? The answer is no. Ch'üan Te-yü was Lu Pa's friend. He once composed a rhapsody (*fu*) to see Lu Pa off for Ching-chou (modern Hupei).[68] If Lu Pa were indeed Lu Chih's father, or if Lu Pa and Lu K'an were the same person, it would seem very unreasonable for Ch'üan Te-yü not to have mentioned any of these "facts" in his preface to Lu's extant works. Furthermore, since Lu Chih's father died long before Lu reached adulthood, and since Ch'üan Te-yü was five years younger than Lu Chih, it would have been virtually impossible for Ch'üan Te-yü to have befriended Lu Pa if Lu Pa were Lu Chih's father. Evidently, Lu Pa and Lu K'an were two different people; Lu Pa was Lu Ch'i-wang's third son and definitely not Lu Chih's father. Lu Chih belonged to another family under the Shih-lang branch.

As listed in the *Yüan-ho hsing-tsuan*, Lu Chih's grandfather was Lu Ch'i-cheng, Ch'i-wang's cousin. He served as a district magistrate, probably during the K'ai-yüan era when Ch'i-wang was a director in the Palace Library. Lu Ch'i-cheng had only one son whose name, as mentioned above, was Lu K'an or Lu K'an-ju. Like his father, Lu K'an's only official position was also as magistrate, either of Li-yang or Li-shui county (near modern Nanking).[69] We don't have the slightest idea how Lu K'an and his father started their careers, but their descendant, Lu Chih, certainly acquired his official status through the *chin-shih* examination.

The *Yüan-ho hsing-tsuan* says that Lu K'an had two other sons besides Lu Chih: Lu Shang and Lu Keng.[70] This contradicts the *New T'ang History* genealogy which lists Lu Wei as Lu Shang's father and says nothing about Lu Keng.[71] Since this genealogy is often mistaken,[72] as has already been shown by its incorrect identification of Lu Pa as Lu Chih's father, it seems more reasonable to believe that Lu Shang and Lu Keng were Lu Chih's brothers, even though we have no way to prove it. In any event, as far as we know, their family line seems to have been transmitted only by Lu Chih's son Lu Chien-li. Aside from knowing that Chien-li obtained his *chin-shih* degree no earlier than 816, his life remains a complete blank.[73]

Having established a more accurate genealogy of the Shih-lang branch, and gained a better understanding of the connection between Lu Chih's immediate family and Lu Ch'i-wang's family, I can now discuss the most important characteristics the Shih-lang branch shared with the other two subgroups within the Lu lineage.

Most Important Shared Characteristics

The first distinct feature of the Shih-lang branch, also enjoyed by members of the Tan-t'u and T'ai-wei branches, is their cultivated background. One of their contemporaries once described Lu Ch'i-wang's sons in this way: "Lu Feng and his younger brothers Lu Pa, Lu Jun, and Lu Huai were all famous for their literary abilities and virtuous conduct (*wen-hsing*)."[74] This was the image of the Lu brothers, Lu Chih's uncles, among their contemporaries. The Lu brothers' circle of friends also included many illustrious literary figures of the time. Lu Wei, the eldest or second eldest of the six sons, was highly regarded by the notable prose stylist Hsiao Ying-shih (717–759).[75] His younger or elder brother, Lu Feng (or Lu Li), was a close friend of another literary talent, Hsiao Ts'un (739–800), Hsiao Ying-shih's son.[76] He had many other famous literati friends besides Hsiao Ts'un. They ranged from poets like Lu Lun and Ch'ien Ch'i, members of the Ten Literary Talents of the Ta-li Era (766–779, *Ta-li shih ts'ai-tzu*) to the renowned Buddhist monk Chiao-jan. The poems exchanged between Lu Feng and his literati friends confirm his own reputation for poesy.[77] This literary tradition of the Lu brothers was continued by Lu Feng's great grandson, Lu I, in the late-T'ang.[78]

The next characteristic of the Shih-lang branch which constituted a common denominator of the Lu lineage is their active participation in the T'ang bureaucracy. Like the other two major subgroups, the great majority of the Shih-lang branch members also engaged in government service. So far as we know, Lu Ch'i-wang's six sons all served in the government, as did all the male members of Lu Chih's immediate family.

We cannot be certain about the exact means through which some of the Shih-lang Lus entered the bureaucracy, but their literary skills were clearly a facilitating factor. In other words, education and culture, two of the most important attributes of the aristocracy, still served as stepping stones to their official careers. For example, we do not know Lu Wei's exact official position,[79] but he seems to have attained it with Hsiao Ying-shih's recommendation due to Hsiao's high regard for his literary accomplishments.[80] Lu Feng, who was still at court in 800, also seems to have relied upon his literary reputation to acquire official appointment.[81] His service in the government was contemporaneous with Lu Chih's career as was that of all of Lu Ch'i-wang's sons. Lu Huai's literary abilities may have won him a good grade in the examination system and led to an appointment as editor in the Palace Library (*Pi-shu sheng chiao-shu-lang*) in 790.[82] At the very beginning of the T'ang bureaucratic system, this position was considered by T'ang scholars a good starting point for a promising career.[83] Since Lu Chih enjoyed tremendous imperial favor in 790, it is possible that he helped Lu Huai obtain this starting position. Both Lu Chih and his son also acquired official rank through their literary talent. The manner in which the Shih-lang Lus entered and rose in the T'ang bureaucracy clearly demonstrates that literary excellence was crucial in their pursuit of a bureaucratic career.

The final characteristic shared by the Shih-lang branch and the other two Lu subgroups is that their willingness to participate in bureaucratic life also led to gradual alienation from their local base. This can be seen in the careers of Lu Feng's descendants and in Lu Chih's own official life. Lu Chih's political life will soon be explored in detail; one example is sufficient to illustrate this point here.

Lu Feng's great grandson, Lu I, passed the *chin-shih* examination in 886. Inheriting his family's chief traits, Lu I's talent for literature also won high praise from his contemporaries; largely on that account he soon rose to be chief minister in 896 under Emperor Chao-tsung (888–904). Lu I was considered a native of Shan-chou (northwest of Lo-yang, in modern Honan) instead of Wu *chün* because his family moved there from Wu *chün*, presumably when his father acquired an official position in Shan-chou. Their bureaucratic service entailed closer ties with the state. As a result, when the T'ang central government was on the verge of collapse, Lu I also had to spend his political life in the shadow of imminent chaos. He met a tragic death at the end of Chao-tsung's reign.[84]

Since all of these three main characteristics will be equally reflected in Lu Chih's political life, it is time to determine what status Lu Chih's immediate family assumed within the Shih-lang branch.

The Status of Lu Chih's Immediate Family

Most of Lu Chih's uncles, Lu Ch'i-wang's six sons, served at court when he did, but the exact relationship between Lu Chih and them remains quite unclear. We do know that the two well-known poets Lu Lun and Ch'ien Ch'i,[85] authors of the only poems to Lu Chih now extant, were good friends of Lu Feng. Because of the early death of Lu Chih's father, his older uncles probably introduced him to the literary world during his childhood. Moreover, in 791, when Lu Ch'i-wang's wife (née either Cheng or Ho-lan) died, Lu Chih composed her tomb inscription.[86] There must have been other similar instances to demonstrate the relationship between Lu Chih and his uncles, but the available sources do not permit speculation.

Lu Chih shared some experiences with his uncles' families, but his immediate family's status seems to have been inferior to that of Lu Ch'i-wang's, at least before Lu Chih became chief minister in 792. Lu Chih himself once said "my family has been very poor."[87] He might have been exaggerating, but his statement does imply that they were probably not very affluent. Of course, lack of wealth was never the only factor determining the inferior status of a family. The comparatively low-ranking official positions occupied by Lu Chih's grandfather and father, the early death of his father, and the small number of male offspring from his family participating in the government would all have contributed to his family's status. It is true that Lu Chih's mother was a member of the prominent Wei clan from the Kuan-chung aristocracy, but how high his mother's immediate family stood within the Wei clan, and to what extent the influence of his mother's family could have reached to the Shih-lang branch remain unknown. The aristocratic background of Lu Chih's mother could certainly have made it easier for her to provide her children with education and culture, absolutely necessary accomplishments for members of a prominent lineage and key prerequisites for a bureaucratic career.

To put it plainly, the status of Lu Chih's immediate family does not seem to have matched that of his uncles, and the Shih-lang branch in turn was not as powerful as the T'ai-wei branch, though it might have enjoyed equal status with the Tan-t'u subgroup. In other words, Lu Chih's own family occupied a secondary position within the Shih-lang branch, and, at most, a third-class standing within the three major Lu branches.

In the process of reconstructing Lu Chih's immediate family background, and examining the overall development of the three major Lu branches, two important points emerge. First, although family background was not the exact basis upon which Lu Chih and the other Lus entered the T'ang bureaucracy, their aristocratic family upbringing provided them with all the skills needed to join the bureaucratic competition. Admittedly, Lu Chih's immediate family ranked only third within the three major Lu subgroups, but being a member of the Wu *chün* Lu lineage would have already given Lu Chih's family assured status among the illustrious aristocratic families of the T'ang. In short, the relatively inferior position of Lu Chih's immediate family within the Lu clan did not change the overall superior status of his larger family in T'ang society, nor did it alter his status as an aristocratic member of that society.

Second, the development of the Wu *chün* Lu lineage unequivocally demonstrates that a southern aristocratic lineage, though surviving dynastic changes in the pre-T'ang period, could no longer preserve its previous independence in a unified T'ang empire. The emphasis on the examination system as the major channel for entrance into the bureaucracy and especially for rising to the highest official positions, definitely led many Lus to take the examinations. Their willingness to seek official positions and their settlement in the metropolitan area to preserve those positions played an even more significant role in their bureaucratization. Since their bureaucratic success entailed the gradual loss of their local power to sustain themselves during times of violent dynastic change, it seems unavoidable that when the collapse of the T'ang state grew imminent, their fate as the medieval aristocracy was also sealed.

The sad future of the Wu *chün* Lu lineage is outside the scope of this study, and so I now turn to Lu Chih's own life.

CHAPTER TWO

Into the Limelight

Lu Chih's private life is largely an enigma, but the attitudes and feelings made known in his memorials to Te-tsung, insufficient as they are, help to reveal some aspects of his inner landscape, and, used in conjunction with other available sources, also provide a more complete profile of the man.

An Independent Young Man

We do not know Lu Chih's exact birthplace, but it is reasonable to assume that he was a native of Chia-hsing county.[1] Besides stating that he lost his father while quite young, his *Old T'ang History* biography also tells us that he was an independent and outstanding young man (*t'e-li pu-ch'ün*). It particularly points out that Lu studied Confucianism diligently (*p'o ch'in ju-hsüeh*).[2] Since the general intellectual climate of the T'ang "valued literature and slighted Confucianism" (*chung-wen ch'ing-ju*), especially before the An Lu-shan rebellion,[3] this comment seems to indicate that Lu Chih demonstrated independence of mind early in life by taking Confucianism seriously, rather than conforming to the currently dominant trend of "valuing literature."

Lu Chih was well aware of the important function of literature in his time, but he accorded this function a different level of significance. In one of his seven surviving rhapsodies (*fu*), Lu said that "those who think, set their minds on the Way; those who advance, cultivate literary style."[4] He evidently recognized the utilitarian value of literature as a necessary vehicle for any one who wanted to enter and advance in the bureaucracy. Without diminishing the practical function of literature, Lu Chih emphasized another realm for "those who think"—that is, the Way, or *Tao*. He did not explain what he meant by *Tao* in this rhapsody, but he did say "those who have thoroughly grasped the Way are morally superior men (*t'ung yü tao che shih wei chün-tzu*)."[5]

Lu Chih's idea of a morally superior man with its underlying ethical principles is conflated with his image of a genuine Confucian scholar, a title he clearly claimed for himself.[6] Aspiring to be a *chün-tzu*, his notion of a Confucian scholar differed from the current T'ang idea of a Confucianist. While most T'ang Confucian scholars were primarily concerned with exhaustive exegetical scholarship on the five canons and state ritual programs, such studies were never central to Lu Chih's Confucian learning.[7] Rather, he often described himself as "a man who has the greatest respect for benevolence and rightness [*tsun-mu jen i*]" (12: 13a),[8] implying that a *chün-tzu* would at least have to understand and practice these two fundamental Confucian principles.

Striving to achieve the lofty ethical status of a *chün-tzu* sustained by Confucian principles, Lu Chih also pursued the practical goal of entering the bureaucracy through the examination system. In 773, at the age of nineteen (twenty *sui*), Lu proved his literary excellence by obtaining the *chin-shih* degree with a respectable sixth place among thirty-four successful candidates.[9]

First Official Appointment

To gain immediate appointment, Lu Chih did not wait for the usual placement process, which required completing another four steps of assessment (*k'ao*),[10] but took the "vast erudition and grand composition" (*po-hsüeh hung-tz'u*) examination instead. This and the "outstanding judgment on court affairs" (*shu-p'an pa-ts'ui*) were the two highest placement examinations at the time. They were reserved for candidates who had already obtained nominal official status, and had excellent literary talent and a good understanding of court affairs.[11] Lu Chih passed the *po-hsüeh hung-tz'u* examination either in 773, the same year that he obtained his *chin-shih* degree, or, more likely, in the following year.[12] After passing this examination, Lu was appointed district defender (*hsien-wei*) of Cheng county in Hua-chou near Ch'ang-an.[13] He continued his first service there as a minor official for no more than three years.

Most sources assert that Lu Chih never took his first appointment in Cheng county because he did not like this position, and that he visited Chang I, prefect of Shou-chou, right after he resigned from the proffered position around 774.[14] A closer examination proves otherwise. It confirms that Lu Chih most certainly did take his first office in Cheng county in 774, that he did resign out of dislike for the position, but that he hoped to receive another appointment. When this hope evaporated in 777, he chose to return to Wu *chün*.[15]

First Mentor and Friend

In 777, Lu Chih resigned from his Cheng county appointment and returned to Wu *chün*. On his way home, he stopped at Shou-chou (in modern Anhui) to visit the newly appointed Prefect Chang I (d. 783). A member of one of the most eminent native aristocratic families in Wu *chün*, Chang I entered officialdom through the protective *yin* privilege.[16] Before serving in Shou-chou, Chang I was prefect of Hao-chou (also in modern Anhui) for two years.[17] During his tenure there, he acquired a good reputation as a successful local administrator and an erudite classical scholar. A recent study has placed him in the category of "*hsing ming* scholars" due to his phonologically based interpretative work on the *Meng tzu* (Mencius) and his practice of government according to the Mencian principles of "benevolence and rightness."[18] His administration of Hao-chou earned him high praise as one of the three best provincial administrators in the middle years of the Ta-li era.[19] From what we know of Chang I, Lu Chih's purpose in visiting him might well have been as much to pay his respects to an esteemed classical scholar as to seek a job offer from a celebrated Confucian administrator.

Probably because he had never heard Lu Chih's name mentioned before, Chang I at first did not pay too much attention to him. When he finally talked to Lu Chih three days later, he was so impressed that he was even willing to accept him as a friend regardless of their age difference (*wang-nien chiao*).[20] When Lu Chih bade him farewell, Chang I presented him with many gifts and a large sum of money. He told Lu to use them as expenditure for a day's meal for his mother. Lu only accepted a bundle of newly prepared tea leaves as a token of Chang's appreciation.[21] This early manifestation of ethical precision would be typical of the way Lu dealt with financial matters throughout his career. It is not clear how the relationship between Chang I and Lu Chih actually developed, but Chang's later career as chief minister from 781 to 782 probably helped facilitate Lu Chih's rapid rise to Te-tsung's favor.

A Close Friendship in Ch'ang-chou

Chang I was Lu's first significant friend, but his acquaintance with Hsiao Fu (732–788) was destined to become even more important. After his visit with Chang I in 777, Lu Chih did not stay in Wu *chün* too long. We know that he spent the next two years in Ch'ang-chou, but he never mentioned when and why he went there. Chang I probably recommended him to Tu-ku Chi (725–777), prefect of Ch'ang-chou, for a minor post on the provincial staff. Whether or not Lu Chih actually met Tu-ku Chi depends entirely upon when he arrived at Ch'ang-chou, and of this we cannot be certain. He definitely did meet and form a close and lasting friendship with Hsiao Fu, the prefect who succeeded Tu-ku Chi.[22]

Lu Chih wrote that he "became acquainted with Hsiao Fu through [two years'] observation of his government and conduct,"[23] presumably while serving as a minor official in Hsiao Fu's Ch'ang-chou administration. The seeds of friendship were sown then and, as far as we know, Hsiao Fu is the only person whom Lu Chih ever described as a close friend. Their relationship grew more intimate when they were both stationed in the capital later in the 780s; they met quite frequently, and, Lu wrote, their "mutual affection deepened as time went by." He even claimed that he completely understood Hsiao Fu's intention and temperament (*chih-hsing*).[24]

But who was Hsiao Fu? He was, like Chang I, another well-known provincial administrator in the middle of the Ta-li era. His ancestors founded the Southern Liang dynasty (502–557). His family belonged to the highest aristocracy. His grandfather, Hsiao Sung, was chief minister from 728 to 733 during Hsüan-tsung's reign. In addition, his father, Hsiao Heng, was even married to Hsüan-tsung's daughter, the Hsin-ch'ang princess; and his cousin, Hsiao Sheng, was also married to Su-tsung's daughter.[25] Most of his cousins led a luxurious life, but Hsiao Fu himself was known both for his frugality and his pursuit of scholarship.[26] Like Lu Chih's other friend, Chang I, Hsiao Fu was much older than Lu Chih. We do not know Chang I's actual age, but Hsiao Fu was at least twenty-two years older than Lu Chih.[27] Also in common with Chang I, Hsiao Fu was very particular about his choice of friends. He did not like the "current fashion [*liu-su*]", and did not like to make friends with people unless they were "poets or Confucian scholars."[28]

Hsiao Fu's family background and his determination to be a man of integrity made him Te-tsung's loyal but critical subject. In 783, Hsiao Fu was appointed chief minister. At that time, Lu Chih was already one of Te-tsung's private advisors. As a court official, Hsiao Fu's unsociable and straightforward personality is said to have often alienated his colleagues. His criticism of the appointment of eunuchs as army supervisors, and of Te-tsung's sycophantic favorite minister Lu Ch'i (d. 785) also offended the emperor. As a result, Te-tsung was determined to send him to the south as pacification commissioner (*hsüan-fu*),[29] but he heard that Hsiao Fu would refuse to accept this appointment. Thus displeased Te-tsung asked Lu Chih about Hsiao Fu's character.

In his protest against the arrangement of Hsiao Fu's "send down," Lu Chih made what appears to be an objective evaluation of his friend to his superior. He told Te-tsung that Hsiao Fu had always been inspired by upright men and hence had been determined to cultivate his own moral character. Lu Chih believed, though, that this moral conviction sometimes made Hsiao Fu "go to extremes." Because Hsiao Fu intended to accomplish everything with perfection, he could be inflexible; in Lu's delicate phrase, he "lacked the ability to adapt to changing circumstances." Sometimes his perfectionist attitude was said by Lu Chih to have incurred the criticism that he longed for fame. Nevertheless, Lu Chih continued, a man like Hsiao Fu who always maintained that to understand the meaning of the classics was to "tenaciously guard the good Way unto death without any regret" might very well have various personality flaws, but they would not make him a capricious or treacherous man unworthy of imperial trust.[30]

Lu Chih's assessment of Hsiao Fu is rather revealing. As his own career developed, his judgment of Hsiao Fu as someone who "tenaciously guarded the good Way" could be taken equally to reflect his own ideal personal character. We may regard Lu's portrait of Hsiao Fu as offering emperor Te-tsung a conscious or unconscious self-disclosure.

Second Official Appointment

In the fifth month of 779, Te-tsung succeeded his father Tai-tsung to the throne. Hsiao Fu was then given a new position in T'an-chou (modern Hunan). Lu Chih had already left Ch'ang-chou at the end

of 778 or right before the fifth month of 779 in order to take the
shu-p'an pa-ts'ui placement examination in the capital for a new
position.[31] Since Lu had already qualified for another appointment
by passing the *po-hsüeh hung-tz'u* examination, it is noteworthy
that he also took this extremely difficult and highly competitive
examination. Apparently he was not satisfied merely being a man
of literary talent. He aspired to be a *chün-tzu* who set his mind on
the Way of government, and taking the *shu-p'an pa-ts'ui* examination was a reasonable way to prove his excellent potential for conducting government affairs.

Lu Chih's new position was one of assistant magistrate (*chu-pu*)
of Wei-nan county (modern Shansi not far from Sian). It was still a
beginning position with a rank of either 9a2 or 9b1, but he was able
to assist in county government. During his service in Wei-nan, Lu
Lun wrote a poem to him.[32] In this poem, Lu Lun expressed sad
resignation toward himself for aging without any prospects for success, and he took aim at Lu Chih's new responsibility by satirizing
the onerous burdens assumed by low ranking officials in general.

Like Chang I and Hsiao Fu, Lu Chih's two poet friends, Lu
Lun and Ch'ien Ch'i, were also much older than he.[33] Thus all four
of Lu Chih's known friends were his elders. They either came from
the same southeastern region as he did, or else had spent some
time in the south, and this geographical background probably
influenced Lu's choice of them as friends. To a certain extent, all
four of them seem to have acted more like father figures than
friends. Whereas Lu Lun and Ch'ien Ch'i might have influenced
him in the literary realm, Chang I and Hsiao Fu likely served as
models of exemplary scholar officials.

First Central Government Appointment

As Lu Chih continued his service in Wei-nan county, the newly
enthroned Te-tsung launched several measures to restore imperial
authority. One of the most significant policies Te-tsung put forward
was the two-tax system (*liang-shui fa*).[34] In the second month of 780,
Te-tsung dispatched eleven personnel evaluation commissioners (*ch'u-
chih shih*) to the eleven major regions of the empire to initiate the
new tax system and to negotiate quotas with local authorities. One
Yü Ho was the commissioner dispatched to the capital area.[35]

Lu Chih had a discussion with Commissioner Yü Ho, and this
discussion most likely led to Lu Chih's first appointment in the

central government.[36] Lu made some suggestions for the conduct of government, including how to understand the customs of the general population, how to distinguish a capable and just local government from its opposite, how to select local talents, and the importance of providing welfare for the needy, eliminating unnecessary official positions and tedious laws, and the abolition of redundant food supplies to the armies.

The most interesting of these proposals involve Lu's ideas on managing a sound financial administration, something he would be deeply involved in later, and his suggestions were well received at this time. Lu Chih served in provincial office no more than five years, but his knowledge of these different administrative methods indicates his concern for and understanding of local affairs. Probably on this account he was soon promoted to be an investigating censor (*chien-ch'a yü-shih*, rank 8a1) in the capital, no earlier than the second month of 780.[37]

Lu Chih remained in this position for some time. In a memorial to Te-tsung presented at the end of 783, he stated plainly that he had been given an imperial audience during the first half year of his service at the Censorate, but was never again asked for.[38] As an investigating censor Lu was at the beginning of a promising career pattern such as any T'ang civil servant would have envied.[39] He would shortly acquire another appointment that would make him a cynosure on the mid-T'ang political stage and circumvent the many years usually required to climb to the top of the bureaucracy. Before that, the T'ang state was faced with a grave threat—in the first month of 781, rebellion broke out in the Ho-pei region.

The background of the second Ho-pei rebellion is complicated and will be analyzed in a later chapter. The rebellion spread as far as the Huai-hsi region (Ho-nan area); another army revolt and a popular uprising at the capital also broke out in the late months of 783. Te-tsung was then forced into exile in Feng-t'ien west of Ch'ang-an.

It was against this background that Lu Chih's new appointment as a Han-lin scholar changed his personal fate and left a significant imprint on mid-T'ang political history.

The Han-lin Scholars

The T'ang practice of gathering a group of talented young poets, calligraphers, artists, scholars of classical studies, and even masters of chess around the ruler began as early as T'ai-tsung's time. The unifying title of Han-lin scholars (*Han-lin hsüeh-shih*) of the Han-lin Academy (*Han-lin yüan*) first appeared in 738 during Hsüan-tsung's reign. As personal attendants to Hsüan-tsung, most of them held other concurrent titles for the purpose of grading their ranks and salaries.[40]

Hsüan-tsung originally kept the Han-lin scholars on hand more for personal pleasure than political decision making, but this changed abruptly after the An Lu-shan rebellion. The chaos brought about by the rebellion may have forced Su-tsung (r. 756–762) to rely heavily upon Han-lin scholars to draft imperial edicts since they were always close at hand. This made the emperor easily susceptible to their influence. The same situation continued in the post-rebellion era. When Te-tsung came to the throne, the scholars' role as private secretariat to the emperor had been firmly established.

This transformation of the Han-lin scholars' functions demonstrates how they could be used as a convenient and trustworthy means for emperors to circumvent regular bureaucratic procedures, especially during chaotic periods. Their existence, like that of the eunuchs, may be seen as another instance of the recurrent struggle in traditional Chinese history between the so-called "inner court" and the "outer court." Unlike the eunuch situation, the conflict between the Han-lin scholars and the regular bureaucracy must not be overstated; the highest official positions always remained the logical place for the extension of a Han-lin scholar's career, especially after Te-tsung's reign.[41] Lu Chih's career development is itself a conspicuous example.

Appointment as Han-lin Scholar—A Turning Point

Lu's new appointment as Han-lin scholar had a profound effect on his political life. Despite some confusion surrounding the exact date when he assumed this position, Lu Chih's career development and an 837 T'ang source convince me to place it in the third month of 783.[42]

When Lu Chih first set in as a Han-lin scholar, he accompanied Te-tsung from morning till night, reciting poems, singing songs, and entertaining him.[43] Two of his three remaining poems seem to have been composed during this period. The first is entitled "Passing the Southern Palace at Dawn, I Heard the Imperial Music."

Passing the Southern Palace, I heard the ancient music;
The sound first heard at daybreak amazed me.
Through the mist from that far secluded spot,
I recognized the silk-wood zither's strains:
Its rhythms modulated by each new scale,
The melody grew light on the lingering breeze;
In elegance enough to transform the vulgar,
In harmony calling forth genuine emotions.
As the distant strains saturated the morning,
An echo trailed through the city in spring.
With the coda came the first rays of sunlight,
Illuminating the vastness of Heaven and Earth.
                    (WYYH, 184: 3; CTShih, 5: 4: 1744.)

While serving as Han-lin scholar, Lu Chih also held the position of vice director at the Bureau of Sacrifices. "Southern Palace" (*Nan-kung*) refers to the Ministry of Rites, and it is likely that sometime during this period when he was on his way to the Bureau of Sacrifices, the music on an early spring morning inspired him to compose this poem. Compared with the masterpieces of the T'ang poetic tradition, this poem is pedantic and ordinary, but it does indicate that Lu Chih had some knowledge and understanding of music. Besides being able to detect the musical instrument by listening to the melody, his attitude reflects a typical Confucian interpretation of the social function of music.[44]

This entertainment duty did not fulfill Lu Chih's ambitions, as can be seen from the following poem—"On Receiving a Fragrant Plant from the Imperial Garden."

Deeply secluded in the Imperial Garden,
Jade grasses grow under the sun's light.
In mist and fog they bend in the wind,
Seem to be tinged with evening glow.
Tender shoots, ever more luxuriant after the rain,
Their stalks grow sweet when the wind is warm.
Like ceremonial escorts, they line the imperial highway
As the royal carriage enters the Chien-chang Palace.
Sodden with mist, they are not shaken,
Though slender shadows are broken and shapeless.
Always afraid the spring sun will shine too late:
No one will appreciate their virgin fragrance.
                    (WYYH, 188: 7; CTShih, 5: 4: 1744.)

A sense of understated discontent permeates this poem in which a fragrant plant from the imperial garden provides an allegorical link to Lu Chih's early Han-lin service. We do not know exactly when this poem was composed, but judging by the rapid advance of Lu Chih's later career, it is quite unlikely that he should have given vent to such a lament while he was moving closer to the political center. This poem unmistakably reaffirms Lu's higher expectations of himself. With his mind set upon the Way of government, he was not satisfied with the life of a Han-lin scholar whose chief duty was entertaining the emperor like "a fragrant plant in the imperial garden." His ambitions would soon be realized.

On the Rise

In the tenth month of 783, Te-tsung, joined by Lu Chih and a small group of officials, was forced by the uprising at the capital to escape to Feng-t'ien. The T'ang court was on the verge of collapse, but Lu Chih's personal career experienced a rapid rise. During their exile, Te-tsung entrusted Lu Chih with the duty of drafting all state papers. The court was in great peril, and it needed someone who was both reliable and capable of accomplishing these tasks within a pressing time limit. Lu Chih proved to be an ideal candidate. His competence in composing and managing all the state documents won high praise from his biographers:

> The whole empire was in turmoil and beset with difficulties. Affairs of state piled up; mobilization and exactions had to be carried out near and far. The policies of state had to follow up innumerable lines of action. Each day several tens of edicts had to be promulgated. All these came from Lu Chih's hand. Wielding the brush and holding the paper he completed his drafts in an instant, and yet he never needed to rewrite anything. It would appear that he had given no thought to the matter at hand, but when it was completed there was never a detail of the affair that had not been covered, and it was exactly what was needed for the circumstances. The clerks making copies of these documents had no rest, while his colleagues just sat with folded arms and sighed, unable to assist in any way (CTS, 139: 3791–92).[45]

This passage shows how Lu Chih became Te-tsung's indispensable formulator of state documents, affirms that Lu had a deep understanding of current affairs of state, and confirms his unusual literary talent.

I should note parenthetically that not only Lu's views on government, but also his writing style inspired Su Shih; and even the distinguished Sung Neo-Confucian philosopher Chu Hsi held Lu's prose style in high regard.[46] Lu Chih's memorials, though written in the parallel prose (*p'ien-wen*) format of four- and six-syllable lines, had already assumed some attributes similar to the *ku-wen* writing—a simple and vigorous classic style of composition intentionally opposed to the ornate and rhetorical parallel prose.[47] He does not employ heavy literary or historical allusions, the usual practice in writing parallel prose, but concentrates on necessary details and important principles. In other words, his writing is oriented towards substance rather than fixated on embellishment.

Both the artistry of Lu's style and the cogency of his political views no doubt contributed to his influence on Te-tsung. His role as a Han-lin scholar was on this account not merely confined to that of private secretary. Throughout the period of exile, he presented more than thirty memorials to the throne, almost all of them direct replies to Te-tsung's consultation. Te-tsung did not entirely follow Lu Chih's advice, but Lu's suggestions often became guidelines for court policies. His influence on the imperial decisions and his ability to manage state papers led his contemporaries to call him an "inner chief minister" (*nei-hsiang*).[48]

Toward the end of 783, Te-tsung promoted Lu Chih to be director of the Bureau of Evaluation (*k'ao-kung lang-chung*) with a rank of 5b1, and still kept him on as a Han-lin scholar. Lu Chih at first declined this promotion, telling Te-tsung that "rewards should start with distant officials of low position, and then reach to those near officials of high position; thus deeds of merit will not be overlooked" (13: 9a).[49] As a Han-lin scholar close to the emperor, Lu meant to say that he should be the last to be promoted. To all appearances, Lu had no intention of abusing his "inner" advisor's power at the risk of the regular bureaucracy.

In the meantime, because the rebels in the capital delayed their efforts to take Feng-t'ien, it became possible for loyalist commanders such as Li Sheng (727–793) and Li Huai-kuang (729–785) to redeploy their forces to relieve Feng-t'ien.[50] A new and dangerous tension then developed between these two loyalist generals. Li

Huai-kuang went into rebellion, forcing Te-tsung in the second month of 784 to escape to Liang-chou, on the border between Szechwan and the Wei valley. Huai-kuang and the rebels in the capital were soon defeated, and Te-tsung's exile came to an end.

Te-tsung returned to the capital in the seventh month of 784. At the same time, Lu Chih was again promoted to be grand master of remonstrance (*chien-i ta-fu*) with a rank of 5a1. This post was soon followed at the end of 784 by another important position as drafter in the secretariat (*chung-shu she-jen*) with the same rank. His position as Han-lin scholar remained unchanged, but his services in the palace were no longer very much in contradiction with his duties in the bureaucracy.[51]

Limited Circle of Friends

Although Lu Chih's public role became increasingly important, his circle of friends seems to have remained limited. This was especially so after the deaths of Hsiao Fu and Chang I. Chang I was murdered as a result of an army revolt just as Te-tsung was escaping to Feng-t'ien in the tenth month of 783.[52] Chang I's death must have brought some grief to Lu Chih, but he still enjoyed a close friendship with Hsiao Fu, who also accompanied the emperor to Feng-t'ien. After Hsiao Fu offended Te-tsung and was sent to the south at the beginning of 784, Lu Chih was probably left without any close friends. This would seem to have been a result of conscious choice.

In his memorial pleading for a reevaluation of Hsiao Fu, Lu Chih mentioned that ever since he accompanied Te-tsung to Feng-t'ien, he had spent most of his time in the palace in exile, and lost all contact with the world outside the imperial residence.[53] With some exaggeration, Lu Chih meant that he deliberately chose not to be associated with the other court officials. As a personal attendant to the emperor, a Han-lin scholar was not expected to have too much communication with the outside world, and Lu seems to have carefully observed this unwritten law. This job requirement would seem partially to account for the scarcity of source materials for his private life.

At the beginning of 793, after Lu had been chief minister for eight months, Te-tsung sent an envoy to express his displeasure. He had resumed the old practice of accepting gifts and money as "tribute" (bribes) from provincial governors, but Lu Chih was opposed to this practice. Displeased by his opposition, Te-tsung told Lu that being "unsociable and upright" he had become "unnecessarily careful and pure." Te-tsung said if he was not willing to receive monetary presents from the local governors, he should at least accept some small gifts as a gesture of good will.[54]

Lu Chih's reply was quite forceful:

> My nature is ordinary and vulgar; how could I not attend to selfish concerns? My family has always been poor; how could I not have desires? The reason that I severely practice self-restraint and diligently cultivate personal integrity is because I carry a great responsibility [as Chief Minister] but have not yet reduced the tax burden or relieved the suffering of the poor. If I shamelessly open the door to bribery, it will betray my sincere concerns for the state, and increase the speed of my personal disaster. Therefore, I have practiced independent integrity and completely rejected private relationships (20:6b).

The purpose of Lu's memorial was, of course, to advise Te-tsung not to accept bribes, but it also suggests that his distance from contemporary social and intellectual life was a deliberate choice. With such high expectations for his own conduct, Lu was probably not a terribly popular figure among his colleagues, and he may have quite naturally preferred to be a rather isolated character. Here we see that Hsiao Fu's role as a close friend might have exerted some influence upon him, but Lu's own choice seems to have played a deciding role in his self-imposed "unsociable" lifestyle. This asserted unsociability may also help partially explain why "there is a curious lack of reference to [Lu Chih] both in the writings of his contemporaries and in the unofficial histories and collections of historical anecdotes, which are very rich for his period."[55]

Even though he was a self-proclaimed loner, Lu Chih did not sever all communication with his colleagues. Quite the contrary, while serving the court in exile, he seems to have developed a certain relationship with Chiang Kung-fu.

A former Han-lin colleague, Chiang Kung-fu, like Hsiao Fu, rose to be chief minister at Feng-t'ien toward the end of 783.[56] Unlike Hsiao Fu or Lu Chih, Chiang was not a member of the highest aristocracy. He seems to have come from a comparatively humble family. Except for the fact that he was a native of Jih-nan county of Ai-chou (in today's Vietnam), we know little about his family background.[57] Coming from a southern border province, Kung-fu entered the bureaucracy through the *chin-shih* examination. He later received a high mark in a special decree examination that led to a promotion. His literary gifts also won him the position of Han-lin scholar.[58]

Chiang Kung-fu did not last long as chief minister. When the court was forced to escape to Liang-chou in the second month of 784, Te-tsung's favorite daughter, princess T'ang-an, died on the road. Concerned more with the urgent financial needs of the military, Chiang Kung-fu opposed the emperor's plan to build a pagoda as a temporary burial for the deceased princess.[59] Offended and furious, Te-tsung asked for Lu Chih's advice on how to deal with the situation.

Knowing that Te-tsung intended to punish Chiang, Lu Chih admitted that Chiang Kung-fu was his long-time colleague but nevertheless expressed his disapproval of the idea. He defended Chiang in these words: "Who would dare offend the imperial countenance and violate the taboo if he were not one who forgets his family for the state and harms his person for the sake of the ruler?"(15: 1b–2a). Lu obviously implies that Chiang Kung-fu's concern with military expenses was reasonable. He also stated that even if Chiang might have given inappropriate advice, the emperor should have forgiven him due to his efforts to perform the duty of a chief minister.[60] Lu's advice was in vain. Chiang was demoted to the post of advisor to the heir apparent, and Lu himself had to compose the rescript ordering his demotion.[61]

Lu Chih probably would have made the same protest for other colleagues as long as he believed they acted out of a sense of duty. His relationship with Chiang Kung-fu, however, seems to have been more than that of a mere colleague. It is even possible that their relationship led Lu to divulge an imperial secret to him.

In 792, when Lu Chih first took up his duties as chief minister, Chiang asked him to arrange a promotion for him. Explaining why he could not do so, Lu told Chiang Kung-fu that he learned from the previous chief minister, Tou Shen (734–793), that Te-tsung would no longer approve any promotions for him. This secret frightened Chiang, and he immediately pleaded to be allowed to leave office for a Taoist post. Te-tsung demanded his reasons and he revealed what he had heard, but "dared not" give out Lu Chih's name as his informant. Enraged by Chiang's reply, Te-tsung demoted him again and banished him to the south in the eleventh month of 792. Tou Shen was blamed for divulging the secret; this incident is said to have become a catalyst leading to Tou's subsequent death sentence.[62]

Lu Chih seems to have had few other friends. At the end of 783, Te-tsung wanted him to recommend some competent local officials to the court. He was supposed to make a recommendation according to a list of names prepared by the Secretariat. Among the thirteen names, Lu Chih thought ten of them deserved his recommendation. Besides "public opinion" about them, he said he chose them because he "had always known them well" (*su so an-chih*).[63] No evidence exists to assure a close personal connection with any of these candidates. It is also possible that Lu Chih's statement only implies that he knew them not as "friends," but rather as public figures.

One thing is clear: the list of these thirteen candidates was not prepared by Lu Chih, and most of them were either known for their classical scholarship or their upright conduct.[64] Many of them were subsequently given positions at court. Ts'ui Tsao (737–787), a member of the so-called "Four K'uei" group, even became chief minister in 786.[65] Without excluding the possibility that they might have been his personal friends, Lu Chih's recommendations were apparently based as much on objective evaluations as partisan considerations.

The background of a few of these candidates does suggest that they probably had some relationship with Lu Chih. Lu Ch'un (d. 805) was a fellow member of the Wu *chün* Lu clan. Shen Chi-chi, though not a member of the Lu clan, came from Wu *chün* as well. Both of them were banished in 781 after the downfall of Chief Minister Yang Yen (726–781).[66] Li Chou had no geographical affinity with Lu Chih, but he was close to Chang I, Lu Chih's first significant friend; he was also Yang Yen's confidant, and may have been banished to the south around this same time.[67] Perhaps, Lu Chih's concern for his fellow prefecturals, for Chang I's protégé, and his sympathy for exiled but worthy officials caused him to recommend them to the throne. Perhaps this same concern also led him to arrange a court position for Lu Ch'un later in 785,[68] at a time when Te-tsung still greatly appreciated his service as the "inner Chief Minister." Unfortunately, no extant sources can substantiate our speculation. If Lu Chih did play the role of a political patron to his fellow clan member and Chang I's protégé, we still cannot be certain that a close private relationship existed between them. Neither can we be sure that such patronage contradicts Lu Chih's self-proclaimed unsociable private lifestyle. That Ch'üan Te-yü, a friend of Lu Chih's uncle and an active participant in mid-T'ang social and intellectual life, wrote a preface to Lu's collected works, but never indicated a particularly close friendship with Lu, as he did with his personal friends like Li Chou, would seem to demonstrate that Ch'üan did not regard Lu Chih as a member of his inner circle, thus indirectly supporting Lu's own claim of unsociability.[69]

During his entire official life, Lu Chih did constantly communicate with at least one person: Emperor Te-tsung. Before the court fled to Feng-t'ien, Lu was already his close attendant. In exile, his relationship with Te-tsung grew more intimate. Ch'üan Te-yü writes that Te-tsung often called him "Lu Chiu" (Lu the Ninth), expressing his rank among family members as well as imperial fondness.[70] He had audiences with Te-tsung every morning and every night at Feng-t'ien; Te-tsung relied so heavily upon him that Lu had to assist in dressing and undressing him.[71] When Te-tsung was forced to take refuge at Liang-chou, Lu Chih and some other officials fell behind. When the emperor arrived at a post house in the mountains and learned that Lu was not there, he "wept and wailed in the forbidden lodge," and issued a handsome reward for anyone who could find him. When Lu Chih finally arrived, the imperial heir apparent and other princes all came out to greet him.[72] Such favorable treatment demonstrates the unusually intimate relationship that existed between Te-tsung and his personal attendant, at least during this tumultuous time.

Years of Silence

Between 785 and 787, Lu Chih seems to have presented only one memorial to the throne;[73] he continued to compose edicts throughout this period. He was still a Han-lin scholar, but his status seems to have been more like that of a regular court official than a private attendant of the emperor.[74]

Lu Chih's near silence during this period would seem to be partly related to the fact that two competent chief ministers were in charge of the administration from 786 to 789. They were Ts'ui Tsao, whom Lu Chih had previously recommended, and Li Mi (722–789), a "most fascinating, unconventional figure."[75]

Ts'ui and Li both tried to carry out some reforms, but were unsuccessful due primarily to Te-tsung's unwillingness to commit himself to long-term reform. Their deeds help us to understand why Lu Chih had no conspicuous voice in the years between 786 and 789. He probably respected their competence and reformist efforts and thus observed the regular bureaucratic routine by not acting as an "inner minister." Lu had already said as early as 783 that as a Han-lin scholar, it was his duty not to interfere with court affairs unless he was inquired of by the emperor.[76] With these capable ministers in court, it is also likely that Te-tsung no longer felt the need to consult Lu Chih.

Lu's comparative silence during these years must also be related to his mother's death during the latter part of Li Mi's tenure as chief minister. Sometime before 787, Te-tsung dispatched a eunuch to Wu *chün* to help Lu Chih bring his mother to the capital where he could directly care for her. She died in the winter of 787 at the capital, and Lu Chih resigned his office to observe the traditional three-year mourning ritual.[77]

In Mourning at Lo-yang

Burying his mother in Lo-yang, Lu Chih also wanted to re-inter his father from the south to Lo-yang so that his parents could be buried together. Te-tsung again sent a eunuch to escort Lu's father's hearse to Lo-yang for him. Such honorable treatment from the emperor was greatly admired by other court officials,[78] and shows that Lu Chih continued to enjoy imperial favor.

Why did Lu Chih not bury his mother in Wu *chün*? Certainly, with Te-tsung's trust and support, he could have easily arranged his mother's burial in the southeast without disturbing his deceased father's grave. Like members of other Lu families, a strong sense of being close to the political and cultural center must have prevailed over Lu's need to preserve local ties. His decision to observe the mourning ritual in Lo-yang is another sign of aristocratic bureaucratization.[79]

When Lu Chih was leaving the court, some provincial governors provided him with a great deal of money and gifts for burial expenses and his monthly expenditure. He rejected all but one of these offers. Reporting first to the throne, he only accepted the monthly tribute money from Wei Kao, the military governor of Chien-nan (Szechwan). Wei Kao was known to Lu Chih long before he began his official career.[80] He very likely had some close connection with Lu's mother's family,[81] and thus Lu accepted his financial support. Lu soon took up temporary residence in the Feng-lo Ssu, a Buddhist temple on Sung-shan, a popular Buddhist mountain resort outside Lo-yang.[82]

Lu Chih seems to have been continually occupied with state affairs before he came to Sung-shan, and he would become even more so after he returned to the court. It seems that this mourning period was a perfect time for him to engage in scholarship. Several of his scholarly works, such as the *Pei-chü wen-yen*, a sort of administrative encyclopedia, and *Hsüan-tsung pien-i lu*, historical accounts of events during Hsüan-tsung's reign,[83] were most likely completed during these quiet years. It is also interesting that, although he had "studied medical books in his youth," he does not appear to have compiled any such works at this stage of his life.[84] That most of his early works dealt with political history and administration rather than subjects like medicine that are often associated with Taoist reclusion, reflects his deep concern for the conduct of government.

In the fifth month of 788, Lu Chih's close friend Hsiao Fu passed away in his southern residence.[85] It is unfortunate that we do not know how this sad news affected Lu. Had his literary *Pieh-chi* been preserved, we would definitely be able to learn more about his inner feelings toward this intimate friend.[86] Since Lu was a self-proclaimed loner, and since he is hardly ever mentioned in the extant writings of his contemporaries, one wonders to what extent his lost works might have contained information that would greatly enhance our knowledge of his detached attitude toward personal relations. At any rate, the quiet years of mourning reached an end toward 790. Lu Chih was undoubtedly ready to resume his official life after three years on the periphery.

CHAPTER THREE

Untimely Exit

Lu Chih returned to the capital at the beginning of 790, six years after the T'ang court settled the second Ho-pei rebellion. Ho-pei was semi-independent just as before the rebellion, but its military governors evinced no further intention to replace the court. They continued to fight among themselves, often relying upon the T'ang court's approval to strengthen their positions. As long as they felt secure in their spheres of power, they were nominally submissive to the court, and Ho-pei remained quite stable throughout the rest of Te-tsung's reign.[1]

In comparison, from 793 to 805, many individual army uprisings broke out, frequently in the border provinces of Kuan-chung and simultaneously in the Ho-nan region. The court's main concern became to maintain the stability of these strategically important regions. Te-tsung's bitter experience during the second Ho-pei rebellion brought his earlier ambition to control the disobedient areas to an end; he resumed his father's appeasement policy, and generally just gave in to the demands of these provinces.[2] This reflects the continuous eclipse of T'ang imperial authority by regional forces. The second stage of Lu Chih's political life began in this context.

In the second month of 790, as Lu resumed his position as Han-lin scholar, Te-tsung also promoted him to temporary vice minister of the Ministry of War (*Ping-pu shih-lang*) with a rank of 4a.[3] When Lu Chih was given an audience to express his gratitude to the emperor, he "prostrated himself and wept" at which point Te-tsung's countenance softened and he began to console him.[4]

With the conspicuous psychological and material benefits to be derived from this new phase of his life, Lu Chih's extravagant emotional gesture is perfectly understandable. In the post–An Lu-shan

45

era, the position of vice minister became considerably more important than that of minister of the Six Ministries under the Department of State Affairs. The vice ministers were now responsible for administrative decisions, while the position of minister became a nominal rank given for reward and promotion.[5] Once appointed vice minister, the possibility of becoming chief minister was definitely within Lu's reach. This new promotion would certainly change the status of Lu Chih's family among the wider circle of their relatives.[6]

That Te-tsung not only did not become estranged from Lu Chih during his three year absence from court, but also appointed him to such a crucial position must have been a reassuring sign of imperial favor. Now that he had lost both his parents and his close friends, this continuous intimate relationship with Te-tsung seems to have become more meaningful to Lu Chih.[7] Lu's personal feelings toward Te-tsung must also have been quite complex. After all, Te-tsung was his ruler, but he also played the roles of benevolent elder and sometime frustrated friend in need of advice.

This new appointment made Lu's return to the capital a pleasant one, but he was soon ensnared in a power struggle.

First Power Struggle

Two of Lu Chih's former colleagues in the Han-lin Academy, Wu T'ung-hsüan (d. 792) and his brother T'ung-wei, had always competed with Lu for imperial favor. Coming from the south, both Wu brothers started their service in the Academy in 783.[8] Their Taoist father had taught Te-tsung before he ascended the throne. Through this connection, they became the heir apparent's favorites. Their literary abilities subsequently won them both the position of Han-lin scholar.[9]

The Wu brothers, especially T'ung-hsüan, seem to have become quite dissatisfied when Lu Chih began to dominate imperial attention in Feng-t'ien. They began frequently to criticize Lu in front of Te-tsung. Due to their interference, Lu was even passed over for chief minister when people with inferior backgrounds and abilities such as Chiang Kung-fu rose to that position.[10] Their mutual antipathy grew apace, and Lu Chih treated the Wu brothers in a similarly haughty manner.[11]

In an early 788 memorial, Lu Chih advised Te-tsung to return the responsibility for edict formulation to the Secretariat's drafters because it was only expedient to assign Han-lin scholars such functions during times of chaos.[12] This memorial was no doubt intended to strip the Wu brothers of the power to formulate rescripts, and to prevent them from forming a faction in the palace to remove him from the position of Han-lin scholar.[13] It is perfectly probable that Lu was motivated by purely selfish interests, but we should recall that shortly after he assumed the position of Han-lin scholar in 783, he already stated that it was the Han-lin scholars' duty not to interfere with the regular bureaucratic operations. Moreover, at the end of 783, he was also opposed to his own special imperial promotion. This 788 memorial can thus be regarded as a logical extension of his earlier convictions. On the other hand, that he himself was about to leave the service makes this memorial appear more self-serving and less seriously concerned with the proper function of the regular bureaucracy. As often happens in politics, principle and self-interest were not necessarily in contradiction. In any event, Te-tsung did not accept his suggestion at the time.[14]

After Lu Chih received his vice ministerial promotion, Wu T'ung-hsüan was appointed to the position of grand master of Remonstrance (Chien-i ta-fu) in 791. Expecting a much more important position, T'ung-hsüan was bitterly disappointed.[15] His discontent exacerbated the already existing antagonism between Lu Chih and himself, and he soon found supporters willing to assist him in his intrigues against Lu.

One of Wu T'ung-hsüan's supporters was a favorite nephew of then Chief Minister Tou Shen. Tou Shen was recommended in 789 to be chief minister and to head the financial office by his predecessor, Li Mi.[16] Scion of an illustrious lineage, Tou Shen made his name as a competent and impartial official in a succession of legal posts.[17] He did not have the literary polish shared by most of the scholar officials in high governmental office, but Te-tsung valued his ability in judging legal cases and gave him several audiences to discuss state affairs before he became chief minister.[18]

When Lu Chih returned to the court at the beginning of 790, Tou Shen had been chief minister for a year. During his administration, he was notorious for accepting bribes in the guise of "tribute money" from provincial governors and indulging his favorite nephew's corruption.[19] Considering this unsavory political conduct, it is understandable that Lu Chih informed Te-tsung that "Tou Shen and Your subject (myself) are always at odds" (19: 19b). Neither is it surprising to learn that Lu Chih soon began to criticize Tou Shen's misconduct.

Under these circumstances, the Wu brothers found Tou Shen's nephew a willing partner in their schemes for an attack on their common enemy.[20] Through their combined efforts, Lu Chih was eventually removed from the position of Han-lin scholar which he had occupied for at least eight years. Although he lost his constant access to Te-tsung, Lu still seems to have enjoyed his trust. By the eighth month of 791, he was formally designated to take up the office of vice minister of the Ministry of War.[21]

The *Dragon and Tiger List*

In the winter of 791, Lu Chih was placed in charge of the administration of the doctoral examinations for the coming year. The examination results were quite remarkable; many of the graduates became prominent political and intellectual figures in decades to come. Not only were the famous *ku-wen* writers Han Yü, Li Kuan (766?–794?) and Ou-yang Chan on the list; the future statesmen Li Chiang (724–830) and Ts'ui Ch'ün were also among those who received their degrees in 792.[22] No wonder that these 792 graduates were later referred to as ascended to the *dragon and tiger list (lung-hu pang)*.[23] Lu Chih chose these candidates following suggestions given by his examination advisor Liang Su (753–793).[24] A decade later, when Han Yü mentioned this astonishing examination, he praised Lu Chih's rigorous evaluation of the candidates' essays, especially his unwavering trust of Liang Su's recommendations.[25]

When Liang Su assisted Lu Chih in managing these examinations, he was a Han-lin scholar who concurrently held the position of right rectifier of omissions (*Yu Pu-ch'üeh*) in the Secretariat.[26] His gift for literary composition, especially in *ku-wen* style writing, is said to have been nonpareil among his contemporaries. Like his teacher, Tu-ku Chi, Liang Su also had a lively interest in Taoism and Buddhism. He wrote an important essay on meditation from a lay Buddhist perspective.[27] His intellectual caliber might easily have impressed Lu Chih, but Lu's preference for Liang, a man of roughly his own age, instead of Liang's friend Ts'ui Yüan-han, a much older man with a good reputation for literary composition, was probably also related to other factors.[28]

According to Liang Su's own account, he was a long-time friend of Hsiao Fu.[29] This connection probably began in 777 when Hsiao Fu succeeded Tu-ku Chi as prefect of Ch'ang-chou. As a disciple of Tu-ku Chi, Liang Su stayed in Ch'ang-chou for four years during Tu-ku Chi's administration.[30] When Hsiao Fu took over the administration after Tu-ku Chi's sudden death, Liang Su must have acquired a minor post on Hsiao Fu's staff, and the two became good friends. It is very likely that Lu Chih met Liang Su when they both served under Hsiao Fu in Ch'ang-chou. Lu Chih's trust in Liang Su did not, then, depend purely on Liang's personal talent, even though that was a necessary condition.[31] Liang Su, like Ch'üan Te-yü, enjoyed an active social and intellectual life, but does not seem to have had any private communication with Lu Chih. This indicates that their shared experience in Ch'ang-chou did not lead to a very intimate relationship.[32] It also implies that Lu Chih was already a rather unsociable character even before serving in the central government.

Liang Su's recommendations were an essential part of Lu Chih's evaluation of the candidates for the 792 examination, but the final decision could only be made by Lu Chih himself.[33] Among the twenty-three *chin-shih* graduates, many of them came from the highest stratum of T'ang society; many of them also, like Lu Chih, came from the south.[34] The unusual presence of southerners in this list suggests that the *chin-shih* examination provided a chance for provincial elite members to enter the bureaucracy.

Judged by the customary practice of candidates presenting scrolls (*hsing-chüan*) to influential scholars and officials while in the capital waiting to take the examinations, it is difficult to imagine that geographical background played no role in Lu Chih's evaluation of these southern graduates.[35] As we have stated, his limited number of friends all shared a similar southern provenance, or else had living experience in the south. On the other hand, the role of this geographical background should not be overemphasized. It was at most a contributing factor. After all, Lu's enemies also shared the same geographical background as his friends. Nevertheless, the unusual presence of the southern graduates probably gave the Wu brothers an excuse to use the administration of the 792 examination as the basis of their attack on Lu Chih.

His Opponents Fall

When Lu Chih was engaged in the examination details, the Wu brothers and Tou Shen's nephew were busy plotting against him. They accused Lu of accepting bribes in his administration of the examinations. A thorough investigation proved the accusation unfounded. At this juncture, Te-tsung discovered that Wu T'ung-hsüan had taken an imperial princess as his concubine. Obviously enraged by T'ung-hsüan's conduct and the intrigue he and his supporters plotted against Lu Chih, Te-tsung banished them to the south. On the way south, T'ung-hsüan was executed. Due to his indulgence of his nephew's corruption, Tou Shen lost his post as chief minister and was banished to Ch'en-chou (modern Hunan) in the fourth month of 792.[36]

Tou Shen's problems were not over yet. He went right on accepting lavish gifts from a local military governor. This was reported to the throne around the end of 792 by Li Sun (737–800), then the surveillance commissioner in Hunan. Li Sun's report was clearly motivated by his dislike of Tou Shen because Tou, during his tenure as chief minister, had sent him to the south. Li was summoned back to the capital only due to Lu Chih's recommendation in the seventh month of 792.[37] Believing that Tou Shen was now secretly dealing with some local military governors, Te-tsung was ready to order the death penalty for him.

At the time of Tou Shen's death, current opinion (*shih-i*) blamed Lu Chih because if he had not revealed that imperial secret to Chiang Kung-fu Tou might not have received the death penalty. A T'ang short story even accused Lu of sending an assassin to murder Tou Shen before Tou fell from power.[38] When Te-tsung was about to pronounce the death sentence on Tou Shen, it was Lu Chih, however, who presented several memorials asking him to reconsider. In his first memorial, Lu made it clear that since he was never on good terms with Tou Shen he did not have any private interests in rescuing him. He was simply concerned that no evidence had proven Tou Shen guilty of sedition. Were he given the death penalty, Lu said, the public would be shocked and would criticize it as an unjust verdict even though they all knew Tou Shen was guilty of forming a private *faction* (*tang*) and taking bribes.[39] Lu's arguments persuaded Te-tsung to change his verdict. Tou Shen was banished to the far south in the third month of 793. For the time being, the emperor did not press for Tou Shen's death, but he was determined to confiscate all his property, including his maids and concubines.[40] Lu Chih again remonstrated with him not to take such action. He argued that because Tou Shen was not guilty of treason (*p'an-ni*), it would be against the law to confiscate his property.[41]

Te-tsung changed his mind, but he later had Tou Shen executed on his way into exile due to his personal distrust of Tou Shen, and eunuch resentment toward him. A few years earlier, Tou Shen had slandered Wu Ts'ou, a reputable surveillance commissioner at Fu-chien and a brother of Te-tsung's grandmother. An investigation demonstrated Wu Ts'ou's innocence. It also laid a foundation for Te-tsung's distrust of Tou Shen.[42] Tou's nephew's involvement in the attack against Lu Chih only hastened his downfall.

Lu Chih certainly should not be blamed for Tou Shen's death, but he was responsible for the imperial punishment of Yü Kung-i. Like Lu Chih, Yü Kung-i also came from the southeast. He acquired the *chin-shih* degree in 781, but is said to have disagreed with Lu Chih when he first took the *chin-shih* examination.[43] During the Feng-t'ien exile, he served as secretary under General Li Sheng's command. Later when Lu Chih became chief minister in 792, Yü was the vice director of the Ministry of Sacrifice (*Tz'u-pu yüan-wai-lang*) under the Ministry of Rites.[44] Yü's literary compositions were greatly admired by his contemporaries. In the fifth month of 784, when the imperial forces finally recaptured the capital, it was Yü Kung-i who composed the victory announcement from General Li Sheng to the emperor. Te-tsung was extremely impressed by his literary polish and gave him a strong commendation. This greatly displeased Lu Chih.

While Yü Kung-i was highly regarded by his contemporaries for his literary abilities, he was, at the same time, criticized for his unfilial behavior toward his stepmother. After Lu Chih became chief minister, he reported Yü's unfilial conduct to Te-tsung, suggesting that he rescind Yü's official appointment; Te-tsung agreed. Yü was then issued a copy of the *Hsiao ching* (*Classic of Filial Piety*) and returned to the southeast. Thus stigmatized by this punishment for unfilial behavior, Yü Kung-i never again acquired an official appointment; he died in frustration. Those who sympathized with Yü blamed Lu Chih for his narrow and imperious personality (*pien-chi*).[45] A Sung dynasty scholar even believed that Lu's later downfall was the "scourge of Heaven" (*t'ien-ch'ien*) against him to avenge Yü Kung-i.[46]

Compared with his well-reasoned defense of Tou Shen, one cannot help wondering why Lu Chih bore such a grudge against Yü Kung-i. Perhaps his bitter feud with the Wu brothers had such an unnerving effect upon him that he was resolved to eliminate all potential opponents during his reign as chief minister. This still does not explain why he needed to take such extreme measures. After all, he had only followed the usual practice of banishing his opponent Yü Shao, whose literary competence was no less impressive than that of Yü Kung-i.[47] We need to consider some other factors.

Ever since the third century, Confucian values such as filial piety and brotherliness had become the prime cohesive forces of

Chinese family life.[48] For this reason, T'ang emperors always upheld the virtue of filial piety as the essence of Confucian teaching. The imperial endeavor to popularize the *Hsiao ching* during Hsüan-tsung's reign is an obvious example.[49] During Tai-tsung's reign (762–779), officials began to argue that understanding the Confucian classics was more relevant to the restoration of order in a shattered empire than skill at frivolous and impractical literary compositions. They also asked Tai-tsung to include the *Hsiao ching* in the doctoral examinations.[50] That unfilial behavior constituted one of the unforgivable ten abominations (*shih e*) during the T'ang demonstrates the extent to which filial virtue was regarded as a force for social stability.[51]

We may explain Lu Chih's treatment of Yü Kung-i as reflecting his genuine belief in the necessity for officials to maintain exemplary conduct, but it is also possible that he used Yü's "unfilial" behavior as a good pretext to eliminate a personal contender. Lu Chih successfully induced Te-tsung to remove Yü Kung-i from office, but he failed to persuade the emperor to disqualify P'ei Yen-ling (728–796) from the most important financial office in the realm; P'ei Yen-ling proved to be Lu's undoing.

Tenure as Chief Minister—Second Turning Point

In the fourth month of 792, right after Tou Shen's removal, Lu Chih was promoted to the position of chief minister. It seemed that Lu Chih finally had his chance to put his vision of government into practice, but ensuing personnel problems foreshadowed the unhappy fate of his reformist efforts.

The prelude began in the seventh month of 792 when Pan Hung, head of the Ministry of Revenue (*Hu-pu shang-shu*), passed away. Before his death, Pan Hung had developed a bitter conflict with Salt Commissioner Chang P'ang, a man he had originally recommended to serve as vice minister of the National Granaries (*Ssu-nung shao-ch'ing*).[52]

During Tai-tsung's reign, the state finances operated on two separate authorities with the Department of Public Revenue controlling the north and the Salt and Iron Commission controlling the south.[53] Two factors forced the government to rely heavily on the income from salt: the deterioration of the Ministry of Revenue (*Hu-pu*) to the extent that the court had to transfer its power to its subordinate but still functioning office, the Department of Public Revenue; and the second Ho-pei rebellion. Reliance on salt revenue inevitably refurbished the power of the Salt Commission, a situation that continued even after the complete suppression of the rebellion in 786.[54]

When Tou Shen became Chief Minister in 789, he was concurrently placed in charge of the Department of Public Revenue (ling Tu-chih).[55] Shortly before his demotion in the third month of 792, Tou Shen, knowing that Pan Hung was going to replace him and take control of the Department of Public Revenue (p'an Tu-chih),[56] arranged for Chang P'ang to become Salt Commissioner to circumscribe Pan's power over financial administration. Thus an unavoidable enmity developed between Chang P'ang and Pan Hung, heads of these two most important financial organs. When Lu Chih assumed the position of chief minister, they were wrangling openly and refused to cooperate. Lu then reported this administrative division and the personal feud to Te-tsung. He settled the problem only by reverting to the old practice of establishing dual financial authorities in northern and southern China.[57]

After Pan Hung's death, Lu Chih originally recommended four candidates to succeed him at the Department of Public Revenue. He said that these four candidates all had both experience and excellent records in financial administration.[58] The candidates included Tu Yu (735–812), author of the T'ung-tien (Comprehensive Compendium on Institutions), then governor of Huai-nan and a future statesman; Lu Cheng (737–800) and Li Heng, two previous assistants to the financial expert Liu Yen (716–781); and Li Sun, the man responsible for Tou Shen's second banishment.[59] Except for Li Heng, the other three candidates were apparently much older than Lu Chih.

The exact relationship between Lu Chih and these candidates is not clear, but his recommendation seems to have derived again more from objective knowledge of their financial expertise than from close private connections. Of course, it is possible that Lu Chih recommended Li Sun precisely because he had been an opponent of Tou Shen. In like manner, his choice of Tu Yu could be related to the fact that Tu Yu had been treated unjustly in 782 by Te-tsung's former favorite, Lu Ch'i.[60] In other words, Lu Chih's recommendation of these two may have been due to their suffering political injustice at the hands of his political opponents. Then again, if this was the case, it would be difficult to explain why Lu recommended Lu Cheng who had been Tou Shen's confidant.[61] Thus it seems that none of these candidates was definitely close to Lu Chih or his protégé.

Of the four candidates, Te-tsung rejected Tu Yu and Lu Cheng on the grounds that the former's position as governor of the Huai-nan

region was too important for him to be removed and that it would
be otiose to give the latter another appointment since he had recently obtained a new one. Te-tsung preferred Li Heng, then surveillance commissioner of Chiang-hsi, and he instructed Lu to send
an envoy to Chiang-hsi to summon him back to the capital.[62]

Lu Chih told Te-tsung that the function of the Department of
Public Revenue was too important to leave without a head during
the several months it would take Li Heng to return to the capital.
Lu asked Te-tsung to appoint the newly arrived Li Sun as supervising secretary (*Chi-shih chung*) while concomitantly making him
acting head of the Public Revenue Department. If Li Sun performed
his duty properly, Lu said, Te-tsung could then appoint him to the
position of vice president of the Ministry of Revenue (*Hu-pu shih-
lang*); if he failed to perform well, he could give him some other
position after Li Heng's return. In this manner, Lu Chih believed
the regular financial operations could continue while the court was
waiting for Li Heng's arrival from the south. Moreover, Li Sun's
ability to conduct financial affairs could also undergo a thorough
testing and evaluation.[63]

Te-tsung at first agreed with Lu Chih's suggestion, but he
changed his mind and insisted on replacing Li Sun with P'ei Yen-
ling (728–796), an old protégé of his former favorite Lu Ch'i. P'ei
also had close connections with Tou Shen.[64] Te-tsung feared that Li
Sun might not be an appropriate candidate to head up the Public
Revenue Department.[65] Later events would prove him mistaken.[66]
For the time being, P'ei Yen-ling retained his position as vice minister of the Court of National Granaries (*Ssu-nung shao-ch'ing*),
and was placed in temporary control of the Department of Public
Revenue (*ch'üan ling Tu-chih*).[67]

Archantagonist—P'ei Yen-ling

The exact relationship between Te-tsung and P'ei Yen-ling before
P'ei received this new appointment is not clear. P'ei came from one
of the most prominent clans in Ho-tung, but his immediate family
does not seem to have enjoyed high status within the lineage due
to its lackluster political achievements. After the outbreak of the
An Lu-shan rebellion, P'ei's family joined the tide of intellectual
migration to southern China, settling in the middle Yangtze region.[68] P'ei soon acquired some reputation as a scholar of the *Shih*

chi (*The Records of the Grand Historian*), a reputation that later justified his position in the Academy of Scholarly Worthies (*Chi-hsien yüan*) as assistant scholar under Lu Ch'i's patronage.[69]

P'ei Yen-ling was not banished after his patron Lu Ch'i fell from power at the end of 783, and it is possible that he had already gained some imperial favor before that time. Since P'ei was demoted in 787, however, his connection with Te-tsung at that time could not have been very intimate. He offended then Chief Minister Chang Yen-shang, and was demoted to the post of local magistrate in a district near the capital. He did not return to court until Tou Shen daringly took his side against Li Mi, who became chief minister in the sixth month of that year. Later on when Tou Shen took over as chief minister in 789, he made P'ei first vice minister of the Court of Imperial Treasury (*T'ai-fu shao-ch'ing*) and later vice minister of the Court of National Granaries (*Ssu-nung shao-ch'ing*), both appointments closely related to state finances.[70] It may have been through these positions that P'ei started to form a more intimate connection with Te-tsung.

Te-tsung's insistence upon replacing Li Sun with P'ei Yen-ling in the Public Revenue Department was in part due to his belief that P'ei's seniority and experience in financial administration would outshine that of Li Sun. Compared with Li Sun, the sixty-four year old P'ei Yen-ling was more experienced, having been in charge of the Public Revenue Department's branch office at Lo-yang in 786.[71] Another strong reason for appointing P'ei was that Te-tsung knew P'ei would not interfere with his acceptance of provincial tribute money; he could even depend upon P'ei to enrich his personal treasury.[72] If this was indeed what Te-tsung had in mind, events to come would testify to his financial prescience, at least concerning his own pocket.

Lu Chih's reaction to P'ei Yen-ling's appointment was completely negative. He gave two reasons for his strong opposition. First, he emphasized the crucial importance of this office to the survival of the state and the people's welfare. One could not afford to appoint the head of such a critical office lightly. Lu Chih told Te-tsung that "if the Head tended to be parsimonious, it might cause trouble [in the armies]; if he was too generous, fraud would then ensue." Second, Lu said that P'ei Yen-ling was an "eccentric, perverse, reckless, impetuous, arrogant, and loquacious" person, and was definitely not the right candidate for that position. Even so, he urged Te-tsung to solicit the opinion of Chao Ching, the second chief minister.[73]

P'ei Yen-ling was made temporary Head of the Public Revenue Department in the beginning of the seventh month of 792, only three months after Lu Chih became chief minister. From then on, Lu could not avoid direct conflict with him, and that conflict served as a catalyst for Lu's political downfall.

Declining Fortunes

Once in control of the Public Revenue Department, P'ei Yen-ling relied on experienced clerks of the department for various financial devices. From 793 to 794, he implemented a number of measures to increase state revenues, but they do not seem to have had the intended results.[74] They only created extra paper work and wasted human resources. At the same time, P'ei also advised Te-tsung not to refill vacant official positions any more so that the state could use these emoluments as revenue.[75]

Under these conditions, Lu Chih repeatedly appealed to Te-tsung to replace P'ei Yen-ling. Te-tsung neglected his requests and thought he was discriminating against P'ei; this only increased his trust in P'ei Yen-ling.[76] Lu Chih was not the only one during this period who advised Te-tsung to replace P'ei. Ch'üan Te-yü, then the left rectifier of Omissions (*Tso pu-ch'üeh*) in the Chancellery (*Men-hsia sheng*), also presented anti-P'ei memorials to the throne toward the end of 792 and in the seventh month of 793.[77]

Ch'üan Te-yü wanted to let Te-tsung know that the general opinion among the court officials was that P'ei Yen-ling had not performed his duties properly. He specified P'ei's misdeeds, such as claiming the unfinished regular tax revenues as surplus (hence attributing success to his own policies), and delaying food supplies to the border armies. He pleaded with Te-tsung to conduct an investigation to find out whether criticism against P'ei was due to his being a "lone, faithful and independent" official or his mismanagement of state finances.[78]

Ch'üan Te-yü's memorials presented no threat to P'ei Yen-ling. The main point of his advice was nevertheless incorporated into Lu Chih's later memorials to the throne. Neither Ch'üan nor Lu ever wrote that they were close friends, but the former's respect for Lu is evident in his preface to Lu's collected works. That Lu used Ch'üan's criticism of P'ei Yen-ling in his own memorials also indicates that they shared certain common principles and probably had some mutual communication.[79]

In the autumn of 794, P'ei Yen-ling intended to have hay and fodder substituted for the usual grain as tax payment from the metropolitan district around the capital. He was very likely to have believed this device could provide sufficient supplies for the palace army cavalry. It has been suggested that P'ei's plan was not without justification since the state pasturage had been ruined by frequent Tibetan invasions of Kansu even before the An Lu-shan rebellion.[80] The problem was that P'ei had not considered the complicated labor-procurement system, nor had he thought about the potential deficiency in tax income in the capital if this device was really put into practice. These were the reasons why Lu Chih made a strong objection to Te-tsung.[81]

Knowing that his plan had been obstructed, P'ei Yen-ling then told Te-tsung that the state should take over as summer pasture for the cavalry horses several hundred hectares of vacant land he claimed to have discovered in the capital region. Te-tsung believed him at first and told Lu Chih about this suggestion. Objections from Lu and other chief ministers forced the emperor to investigate the existence of this vacant land. The result confirmed their assertions that P'ei's report was false; there was no vacant land.[82] This incident still did not diminish Te-tsung's trust in P'ei Yen-ling.

Confronted with such frustration, Lu Chih must have realized the prospects for him to carry out any real reforms were indeed bleak. In the eleventh month of 794, he finally presented Te-tsung with a long memorial launching a serious indictment against P'ei Yen-ling. He not only criticized P'ei's inept management of finances, but also specifically attacked his personal conduct.[83]

First condemning P'ei Yen-ling as a shameless *small man* (*hsiao jen*), Lu Chih then gave specific examples of P'ei's "crimes" in managing state finances. To a large extent, Lu Chih's criticism was directly aimed at Te-tsung. He blamed him for accepting P'ei's absurd claim that he had retrieved a large sum of money and commodities from a pile of night soil. It was actually from the regular revenues. When this caused a controversy, Te-tsung would not allow any investigation; he acted as if nothing irregular had taken place. In this way, Lu said, Te-tsung himself had allowed "truth and falsehood to coexist" while "law and morality grew lax" (24: 6b).

To demonstrate that Te-tsung's trust in P'ei Yen-ling was misplaced, Lu further reminded him of P'ei's inexcusable delay of the food supplies to the border armies in the strategic outposts of Yen-chou (modern Ninghsia) and P'ing-liang (modern Kansu).[84] Lu's criticism clearly echoed Ch'üan Te-yü's previous attack on P'ei, but

by this time Lu was the only official who dared to protest directly
against Te-tsung's trust in P'ei Yen-ling. When provincial military
governors sent envoys to inquire about these food supplies, Lu
continued, P'ei Yen-ling always slandered and insulted them. If any
subordinate official disagreed with him, P'ei not only cursed him,
but vilified his ancestors or his whole clan. Lu Chih regarded such
profanity as "unbearable to the ears of morally respectable men"
(24: 13b). To show his confidence in these charges, Lu Chih again
asked Te-tsung to carry out a public investigation of P'ei's conduct.
If his criticism of P'ei was proven false, he would be willing to
accept whatever consequences should be inflicted upon him.[85]

Lu's account of P'ei's misdeeds was obviously intended to persuade Te-tsung to remove him from control of the Department of
Public Revenue. Lu might have succeeded if he had not misjudged
his fellow chief minister, Chao Ching (736–796).

When Lu Chih was appointed chief minister in the fourth month
of 792, Chao Ching was also promoted to chief minister, perhaps
even on Lu's recommendation.[86] His relationship with Lu Chih seems
to have gone well until he was transferred to the post of second
chief minister and placed under Lu's authority in the fifth month
of 793. Chao Ching deeply resented Lu Chih because he believed
Lu had arranged his transfer to a substantially inferior position.[87]

It is most likely that Chao Ching's transfer was in accord with
Te-tsung's instructions. A few months before his transfer, Te-tsung
told Lu Chih that if he had something important to report, he
should not tell Chao Ching. He should just have it written down
and presented to him secretly.[88] In reply, Lu Chih told him that
since both Chao Ching and he were in charge of a pivotal position
in the administration, he had never concealed any state secrets
from him. He also advised Te-tsung not to damage "the virtue of
impartiality" by hiding certain things from his ministers.[89] From
Te-tsung's remarks, it seems that, for whatever reason, he did not
completely trust Chao Ching. It is thus reasonable to believe that
Chao Ching's transfer was more an imperial decision than Lu Chih's
initiative. Nevertheless, Lu Chih was still the one against whom
Chao Ching bore a bitter grudge, but Lu did not even know it.

Demotion

By the time Lu Chih presented his indictment against P'ei Yen-
ling, Chao Ching had already revealed many of Lu's criticisms to

P'ei. This intelligence made it easy for P'ei to counter Lu's arguments and convince Te-tsung of his own trustworthiness.[90] A few days either before or after Lu Chih presented the memorial to the throne, he obtained Chao Ching's promise that he would join him in attacking P'ei Yen-ling in a conference before Te-tsung. Lu does not seem to have realized that Chao Ching felt offended for his earlier transfer. Lu obviously hoped to rely on Chao for confirmation that his criticism of P'ei Yen-ling was intended to improve the public welfare. He must have felt certain of Chao Ching's support since Chao himself had tried to save some officials from a frame-up engineered by P'ei.[91] In addition, Lu most likely thought the public investigation would confirm his correctness even if Chao Ching did not back him up, but this confidence proved to be mistaken. When Lu completed his criticism at the court conference, Te-tsung already appeared displeased. At this juncture, Chao Ching betrayed his promise by remaining completely silent.[92] This silence seems to have provided Te-tsung with a timely excuse to remove the now overly troublesome Lu from the position of chief minister.

In the twelfth month of 794, Lu Chih was demoted to the post of advisor to the heir apparent (*T'ai-tzu pin-k'o*). From then on he lived behind his own house doors. Except for going to court audiences, in his fear and caution, he refused to see any visitors or relatives.[93] P'ei Yen-ling was still not quite satisfied with this result. At the beginning of 795, he started to slander some officials who had criticized his financial administration, including Salt Commissioner Chang P'ang and Metropolitan Governor Li Ch'ung. In his plot against the metropolitan governor, P'ei obtained support from the director of the Review Bureau (*Pi-pu lang-chung*) who was willing to say that Lu Chih and the governor were involved together in several incidents of bribery. This director was none other than Ts'ui Yüan-han, the man whom Lu Chih rejected as an assistant in the 792 doctoral examinations, and his support of P'ei Yen-ling was evidently motivated by his resentment toward Lu.[94] This intrigue did not, however, immediately threaten Lu's life.

To achieve his goal of having Lu Chih executed, P'ei Yen-ling did not stop with accusations of bribery and factionalism. He also charged Lu Chih, Chang P'ang, and Li Ch'ung with trying to instigate a military uprising by criticizing his office for not providing fodder to the cavalry forces. At that point someone from the palace army told Te-tsung that P'ei Yen-ling had indeed delayed the fodder supplies. Te-tsung's reaction was not to blame P'ei, but rather to become convinced of what P'ei had said about Lu Chih's faction intriguing in the army. The emperor decided without hesitation to execute Lu Chih and his so-called faction.[95]

That almost no official dared to protest against this imperial decision demonstrates P'ei Yen-ling's dominance at court. It also shows that Lu Chih's conscious unsociability left him alone in this complicated political struggle with P'ei Yen-ling. Had Yang Ch'eng, the grand master of remonstrance (*Chien-i ta-fu*), not taken the risk of speaking up for him then, Lu would have been sentenced to death in the early months of 795 at the age of forty-one. Yang Ch'eng's protest against Te-tsung's punishment of an "innocent minister" almost cost him his own life, but the heir apparent's intercession saved both him and Lu.[96]

Banishment

Having escaped a death sentence, Lu Chih could no longer preserve his position in the capital. In the fourth month of 795, he was banished to Chung-chou (near modern Chungking in Szechwan) as an administrative aid (*Pieh-chia*) to the Prefect of that region. He remained there for ten years, and led his usual or perhaps an even more isolated life, so much so that the local population never saw his face.[97] Lu's friend or maternal relative, Wei Kao, appealed repeatedly to Te-tsung to let Lu replace him as governor of the Chien-nan area (Szechwan), but we do not know whether Lu had any communication with Wei during this time.[98] The only friend he might have had during this period was Li Chi-fu (758–814), then prefect of Chung-chou, author of the *Yüan-ho chün-hsien t'u-chih*, an important work of T'ang administrative geography, and a future statesman in Hsien-tsung's reign.[99] Sometime towards 800 when a new prefect was dispatched to replace Li Chi-fu in Chung-chou, Te-tsung told this official to send his regards to Lu Chih, but he never again summoned Lu back to the capital.[100]

Due to his fear of slander, Lu Chih deliberately refrained from composing any historical or literary works during his last ten years, but he did complete a fifty-chapter work on medicine entitled *Lu-shih chi-yen fang*. The purpose of this study was to find some relief for local residents suffering from diseases caused by pernicious miasmas. It is just possible that Lu Chih's devotion to this work on medicine was a desperate attempt to win back Te-tsung's attention since the emperor also had a strong interest in medicine.[101] Even so, his concern for the local people's suffering seems to have motivated him, more than his now crushed political ambitions, to return to this topic of his youthful studies. In any case, his medical studies did not appreciably improve his own physical condition.

Emperor Shun-tsung ascended the throne and summoned Lu Chih back to court in 805, but Lu died shortly before the imperial edict reached Chung-chou. Lu was buried in Chung-chou near a Taoist temple; he may have been re-interred later in Wu *chün*.[102] He was given the posthumous official title of Minister of War (*Ping-pu shang-shu*) as well as the canonical name *Hsüan,* and has been subsequently remembered primarily by the name Lu Hsüan-kung.[103]

From the time he became a Han-lin scholar to the day he lost his position as chief minister, Lu Chih was always close to the imperial power. This proximity to central power had two main consequences. Intimacy with the imperial power reinforced his chances of rising in the bureaucracy. Further, as happened with members of the other Lu branches and other aristocratic families, bureaucratic success increased his dependence upon the state. Such dependence nevertheless did not prevent him from trying to do what he believed ought to be done even at the risk of committing *lèse majesté*.

If Lu had not fought his losing battle against P'ei Yen-ling, he might have continued to enjoy both imperial favor and his own sphere of power in the court. Why was a man repeatedly described as "cautious" willing to risk all he had in such a battle? He had seen the rise and fall of various ministers, including that of his intimate friend Hsiao Fu. Would not the rapid changes in their political fates have made him realize the difficulty of the task he was engaged in? In the following chapters I hope to provide answers to these questions, but here let us listen to Lu Chih's own voice.

Before he decided to present his massive indictment of P'ei Yen-ling, some of Lu's friends [perhaps Ch'üan Te-yü or his uncles] urged him not to be too severe in his criticism and advice to Te-tsung. Lu Chih replied with elegant simplicity: "I have not betrayed the Son of Heaven on high and I have not betrayed what I have learned in this world; nothing else troubles me [*Wu shang pu-fu T'ien-tzu, hsia pu-fu wu so-hsüeh, pu-hsü ch'i-t'a*]."[104] To explain what Lu Chih meant by this, I have to explore the foundation of "what [he] learned" and explain how "what [he] learned" guided him in the service of Emperor Te-tsung. In short, I have to explain what his political approach is and how this approach helped rebuild the T'ang empire.

CHAPTER FOUR

A Confucian Pragmatist Approach

At the beginning of 785, six months since Te-tsung's return from exile, the Chao-i military governor, Li Pao-chen, came to court to report that the imperial Acts of Grace and Amnesty issued during the emperor's exile had moved all the Shan-tung area soldiers to tears. This display of public sentiment convinced Li that the court would soon suppress the rebels.[1] Lu Chih wrote in similar words about the emotional public response to these imperial edicts, and they may indeed have had a powerful impact on their audience.[2] As the person responsible for drafting these edicts and whose advice to the throne served as their guiding principle, Lu Chih played a significant role in the court's settlement with the rebels. Lu's contemporaries recognized this fact in their comments that in Te-tsung's suppression of the second Ho-pei rebellion he relied not only on the might of the military, but also on "the help of his virtuous and literary confidant" Lu Chih.[3]

Because Lu Chih's approach to reestablishing T'ang stability evolved through his conscious responses to concrete historical circumstances, I need first to discuss exactly how and why the second Ho-pei rebellion broke out.

The Second Ho-pei Rebellion

Te-tsung's early policies aimed at restoring imperial authority were its direct cause, but the political conditions under which Te-tsung came to power indirectly set the stage for this second Ho-pei rebellion.

When the An Lu-shan rebellion was settled in 763, the T'ang court lost effective control over Ho-pei, one of its richest and most populous provinces. Divided into four provinces after the rebellion, its leaders and their powerful military machines refused to carry out their financial obligations to the court and usurped the court's power to establish its own candidates as governors.[4] Local governors became just as powerful and equally difficult to control in several other provinces.[5]

At this point, the northwestern border provinces of Kuan-chung and the small provinces in Ho-nan became strategically important. They either had to confront the Tibetan threat from Kansu, or served as a new "buffer zone" between the Ho-pei provinces in the northeast and the court. The Ho-nan region was also critical because the vital Pien river supply line to the capital ran through it. Their complex strategic importance made heavily garrisoned forces in these two regions absolutely necessary, and these large forces themselves constituted another potential danger to the T'ang court. Provincial power in these two regions put the court at risk during the second Ho-pei rebellion.

The threat from the south was primarily economic. After the An Lu-shan rebellion, the survival of the T'ang central government became more than ever dependent on supplies from the provinces in the Huai and Yangtze valleys. The rich Ho-pei region was virtually independent from the court, and Ho-nan was transformed into a frontier zone that no longer served its agricultural function.

The economic importance of the southeastern region is even more obvious when we consider that the salt monopoly levies came from this area. An irregular exaction levied out of urgent need during the An Lu-shan rebellion, the salt monopoly continued in the post-rebellion era, and provided nearly half of the state's cash revenues on the eve of Te-tsung's accession. The T'ang court was extremely sensitive to the potential economic threat from the south. It implemented various highly successful measures to guarantee its control and the general stability of this region. As a result, this key area remained loyal before Te-tsung's ascent to power. It continued to be so even during the second Ho-pei rebellion.

It is nonetheless clear that when the thirty-seven-year-old Te-tsung took the throne in the fifth month of 779, the T'ang central authority was gravely eroded under the pressure of powerful regional forces. A young and ambitious monarch, Te-tsung was determined to restore central control over the potentially threatening regions, and even over the semi-independent Ho-pei provinces. To remind the Ho-pei provinces of their regular financial obligations toward the court, he transferred the gifts and money given to the throne as "tribute" for imperial birthdays by the governors of P'ing-lu (part of Shantung and northern Kiangsu) and Wei-po (southern Hopei, northwest Shantung and a corner of northeast Honan) to the state treasury as regular tax revenue. He also refused to follow the by then customary compromise policy of accepting and confirming the usurper Liu Wen-hsi as governor of the northwestern Ching-yüan region.[6] These policies sent a warning signal to the Ho-pei governors.

Meanwhile the two-tax system, reflecting a new centralized financial policy, was set for implementation. In the second month of 780, Te-tsung dispatched one of eleven commissioners to the Ho-pei region to negotiate the two-tax quotas with local authorities. He ordered the Wei-po military governor, T'ien Yüeh, to reduce the size of his armies and convert the disbanded troops back into taxpaying peasants. T'ien Yüeh tried to enhance his personal prestige among the soldiers by blaming the court for threatening their welfare. This unquestionably intensified centrifugal forces in Ho-pei, but the death of governor Li Pao-ch'en in Ch'eng-te (western Hopei) in the first month of 781 ultimately brought the court and Ho-pei's military governors into direct confrontation. When Te-tsung refused to accept Li Wei-yüeh, son of Li Pao-ch'en, as the succeeding governor of Ch'eng-te, the provinces of P'ing-lu and Wei-po joined Ch'eng-te in open rebellion. Worse still, they were supported by the governor of Hsiang-yang (Hupei area), who blocked the vital Han valley supply route from the capital to the middle Yangtze.[7]

In the ensuing conflict, the court achieved some initial successes owing to the loyal support of Chu T'ao, governor of Lu-lung province (near modern Beijing), and the assassination of Li Wei-yüeh by his subordinate, Wang Wu-chün, who then submitted himself to the court. The rewards Te-tsung bestowed upon Chu T'ao and Wang Wu-chün did not meet their expectations, and they turned against the court in 782. By that time, the northeast region was again in total rebellion. The subsequent revolt of the powerful Huai-hsi (Honan area) governor, Li Hsi-lieh, exacerbated an already bleak situation by cutting the Pien canal route through which the court received its major supplies from the south.[8] With two crucial economic lifelines under rebel control, and with each rebel leader assuming the title either of king or grand generalissimo at the end of 782, the T'ang court was indeed caught in a grave predicament.

Since all his supplies from the south were beyond reach, and his depleted treasury was yet to benefit from the newly implemented two-tax system, Te-tsung was forced to exact all kinds of irregular taxes from the capital population. The capital was soon teeming with popular resentment and discontent. At the same time, the loyalist troops were soundly defeated in Ho-pei and the prospect of victory appeared remote.[9]

By the ninth month of 783, Li Hsi-lieh had completely paralyzed the imperial armies in Huai-hsi. The court was forced to summon a detachment of crack troops from the northwestern province of Ching-yüan to break the stalemate. When these troops arrived at the capital a month later, after a long and exhausting march, Te-tsung repeated the same mistake he made in the previous year. He failed to reward them to the level of their expectations. An army revolt ensued and a popular uprising began in the capital. The rebellious troops established the previous governor of Ching-yüan, Chu Tz'u, elder brother of the Ho-pei rebel Chu T'ao, as their leader. This capital rebellion ultimately forced Te-tsung into exile in Feng-t'ien.[10]

In Feng-t'ien, Te-tsung's favorite chief minister Lu Ch'i (d. 785) deliberately prevented an imperial audience with the loyalist commander Li Huai-kuang whose armies had just marched a great distance from Ho-pei to save the court from imminent danger. Lu Ch'i knew that Li Huai-kuang had openly criticized his abuse of power and various intrigues against capable ministers; he feared that Huai-kuang's successful defense of Feng-t'ien would cause the emperor to listen to him.[11] Thus Lu Ch'i advised Te-tsung to send Huai-kuang away immediately to fight Chu Tz'u in Ch'ang-an. Te-tsung's consent alienated this loyal commander, and indirectly contributed to his later rebellion.

Li Huai-kuang's rebellion was due primarily to his resentment of the unfair treatment between Li Sheng's Shen-ts'e armies (Palace armies) and his provincial forces.[12] If Lu Ch'i had advised him to grant an audience with Li Huai-kuang, Te-tsung might have had a chance to placate Li in person and induce him willingly to endure his straitened financial conditions together with the court. Lu Ch'i's failure to do so led traditional Chinese historians to hold him responsible for Li's subsequent rebellion.[13] Due to public pressure, Te-tsung finally demoted Lu Ch'i in the twelfth month of 783, but he

was unable, or probably unwilling, to correct the unequal treatment between the Palace armies and Huai-kuang's forces. The result
was Huai-kuang's eventual rebellion and Te-tsung's further exile to
Liang-chou in the second month of 784.[14]

At this difficult and dangerous juncture, Lu Chih was thrust
into a position where his writing skills and his vision of how to deal
with the empire's pressing problems brought him into the center of
mid-T'ang political life. We see his approach to government take
shape through his responses to the court's predicament.

I and Ch'üan

Lu Chih presented more than thirty memorials to the throne between the eighth month of 783 and the eighth month of 785. He
also formulated more than eighty state rescripts. The guiding spirit
behind these publicly propagated edicts was in complete accord
with Lu's private memorials to the throne.

The two central principles that emerge from Lu Chih's memorials to Te-tsung are the notions of *rightness* and *expediency* (*I*
and *Ch'üan*). In a memorial advising Te-tsung how to reward some
peasants who presented melons to him during his exile, Lu said:

> The way to establish a state lies only in rightness [*i*] and
> expediency [*ch'üan*]. The method to lead people lies only in
> honor [*ming*] and profit [*li*]. Honor is close to emptiness,
> but is important in moral teaching; profit is close to sub-
> stance, but is light in virtue.

> All those measures used to consider and decide right and
> wrong and to set up legal institutions are dependent upon
> rightness.

> As for considering when to employ honor (emptiness) or
> profit (substance), judging the degree of their moral impor-
> tance, making them (honor and profit) coexist without
> harming each other, adopting them alternately without con-
> tradiction, following the multitude's desire, estimating the
> appropriateness of the time and hence practicing proper
> administration in prosperous or declining times so as not
> to exhaust the people—all of these things depend upon
> expediency.

If the ruler relies exclusively on substantial profits without the aid of emptiness (honors), these profits will then be wasted and deficient, and the [state's] resources will be insufficient. If the ruler relies exclusively on empty honors without supplementing them with substance (profits), these honors will then be absurd and deceptive and people will not be motivated to pursue them. The reason the state formulates a code of awards, grants money, and goods, and bestows grain emoluments is to make manifest the substance (profits); the reason it differentiates between official ranks and makes distinctions in the adornment of their clothes is to beautify the emptiness (honors).

The ruler has to understand the significance [of profits and honors], be skillful in alternating them, make them depend upon each other as the inside and outside [of a garment], and cause the people to employ them daily without realization. In this way, [the ruler] will consummate the principle of expediency in governing a state. (14: 17b–18a.)

Lu Chih upheld *I*, or rightness, as the moral foundation of a state. Without this foundation, there would be no standard upon which moral judgments and an institutional framework could be based. He put forward *Ch'üan*, or expediency, as a *complementary* principle by means of which the institutions of the state could be successfully operated within the moral framework established by the *I* principle. Without *I* , one would not know *why* certain actions should be taken, and without *Ch'üan* one would not know *how* to take appropriate actions. Both principles are equally necessary in Lu Chih's approach to government.

What is important here is that to Lu Chih the idea of expediency did not mean political trickery. According to his definition, expediency, or *ch'üan*, was a kind of keen ability to know when to apply the least harmful, or when to adopt the most helpful policies to preserve and increase the welfare of the state. This can be illustrated in his advice to Te-tsung not to displace Li Ch'u-lin as military governor of Feng-hsiang (western Shensi).

Li Ch'u-lin was not a loyal governor. In the tenth month of 783 he staged the murder of Lu Chih's mentor and friend Chang I when Chang was replacing the rebel Chu Tz'u as the governor of Feng-hsiang. Li Ch'u-lin surrendered to his former commander Chu Tz'u immediately after this murder.[15] When Chu Tz'u was defeated,

Li quickly sent tribute goods to the throne to show his support. Of course, Te-tsung resented Li Ch'u-lin's opportunistic behavior, but to keep Li as a supporter, though a superficial one, he was forced to accept him as military governor of Feng-hsiang.[16]

Nevertheless, when Te-tsung's compromise policy gradually soothed the Ho-pei rebels, he was ready to follow the general opinion among his ministers and strip Li Ch'u-lin of his military power. He refused to receive Li's envoys, retained them in his capital in exile, and tried to find a decisive way to deprive Li of his military power. To avoid suspicion, Te-tsung planned to grant Li the honor of escorting him on his return to the capital, at the same time intending to revoke his Feng-hsiang governorship. Considering his plan to be a form of expediency (ch'üan), Te-tsung asked Lu Chih for his opinion.[17]

Lu Chih advised him not to accept opinions arising from "the small loyalty of pedantic Confucian scholars [shu-ju hsiao-chung]" (16: 5a) because this would only obstruct the important task of restoring stability. Lu's argument was twofold. First, rebels still controlled the Huai-hsi area, and Te-tsung should placate Li Ch'u-lin by accepting his professed loyalty so as to concentrate the court's forces against them. Second, even though Li had earlier betrayed the court, he had just reaffirmed his loyalty. The court could now rely on his local armies to reinforce the loyalist forces, or at least to prevent him from becoming another threat to the court. Lu Chih quoted Confucius as a warning: "lack of self-restraint in small matters will bring ruin to great plans" (16: 4b–5a).[18] Lu alluded to the conduct of Duke Huan of Ch'i in the Spring and Autumn period (722–481 B.C.E.) as an exemplum of this Confucian proverb.

In the Tso-chuan story, Duke Huan wisely appoints Kuan Chung his chief minister, even though Kuan had once attempted to assassinate him, and Kuan becomes the Duke's main support in gaining the position of first hegemon.[19] Using Duke Huan as a model, Lu advised Te-tsung to relinquish short term gains for the sake of the greater needs of the state. Lu's own behavior in this instance was consistent with his suggestion. He personally could not possibly feel any goodwill toward Li Ch'u-lin, the man responsible for Chang I's murder; but when the well-being of the state was the main concern, Lu did not let personal animosity "ruin" what he believed to be "great plans."

Lu Chih stated that the imperial plan to withdraw Li Ch'u-lin's military power was not expediency but political scheming designed to trap Ch'u-lin. If Te-tsung carried out this scheme, he

could not morally justify his conduct to other military governors
who had betrayed the court before, but were ready to proclaim
their renewed loyalty. Those who had already been placated by the
court might even begin to distrust the court and cease to appreciate the policy of placation.[20]

Lu then clarified his idea of expediency:

> As for the meaning of expediency [*ch'üan*], it is derived from
> an analogy with *ch'üan* and *heng*. *Heng* is the steelyard;
> *ch'üan* is the weight. When the weight lies in the steelyard
> (or when the weight is hanging), the amount of things [one
> obtains] will be accurate. If you apply [the principle of] ex-
> pediency to human affairs, the lightness or heaviness of their
> rightness will not be missed. When using it to approach
> [moral] principles, one will definitely select the major ones
> and discard the minor ones; when using it to distance [your-
> self from] calamities, one will definitely choose to [endure]
> the lesser ones and avoid the greater ones. If you are not an
> enlightened person, it is difficult to exhaust the essence and
> subtlety of expediency. Therefore, the sage (Confucius) val-
> ued it. (17: 7b–8a.)

As Lu then recalled, Confucius once said that "a man good enough
as a partner in a common stand need not be good enough as a
partner *in the exercise of moral discretion* [*ch'üan*]" (17: 8a). To Lu,
the point of Confucius's statement was to show "how difficult it is to
know the incipient beginnings of a right opportunity [or an opportune moment—*chih chi chih nan ye*]" (ibid.).[21] From Lu's point of
view, the expediency principle can minimize this difficulty.[22]

It is not surprising to find Lu Chih telling Te-tsung that the
imperial plan to remove Li Ch'u-lin's military power at that particular time was not only inappropriate, but in opposition to
Confucius's way of practicing the expediency principle. In Lu's
view, if Te-tsung had carried out his plan, the court would have
gained only one region, but it would have lost the trust of all
the other military governors. How, wondered Lu, could one
consider something in opposition to Confucius's teaching to be
expedient? And how could one regard such political machina-
tions as wise?[23] Convinced by Lu Chih's advice, Te-tsung eventually abandoned his original plan, and Li Ch'u-lin also retained
his Feng-hsiang governorship.[24]

It is clear that Lu Chih's rejection of political trickery (*shu*, or *ch'üan shu*) as an example of expediency is not a general "condemnation of 'expediency.' "[25] His explanation of expediency demonstrates his search for a farsighted, and morally responsible policy to protect the well-being of the state. *Ch'üan* is the principle that makes it possible for the state to obtain the maximum possible amount of moral correctness with the minimum possible amount of damage at a specific time and under specific circumstances. For Lu Chih, expediency requires the emperor to adopt policies that would satisfy the greater needs of the general population. Its operation depends on a ruler's restraint of his personal desires for the sake of public welfare. The public spiritedness involved in the practice of expediency represents politically responsible behavior guided by a higher ethical standard, and does not contradict the principle of rightness. As Lu Chih explained them, these two principles ought to function alternately in the same spectrum.

How and under what conditions did Lu Chih ask Te-tsung to apply these two principles?

The Emperor's Role

Lu Chih advised Te-tsung how to govern the state, but the chief responsibility for carrying out that advice fell solely on the emperor's shoulders. This being the case, the imperial conduct was crucial for Lu since in traditional Chinese politics the emperor was ultimately responsible for the destiny of his state and his people.

Situated at the apogee of the entire social and political structure, Chinese emperors were not merely political rulers; they also assumed the role of moral leaders. The ideal ruler set out in Confucian political theory was one who governed without interfering action (*wu-wei*) and through delegating responsibility to his chief ministers. In reality, with the exception of those who were dominated by eunuchs or imperial relatives, emperors were fiercely protective of their ruling power.[26] As a consequence, the power of the chief ministers often suffered under a strong and ambitious emperor. Moreover, since emperors were the ultimate arbitrators of all bureaucratic decisions, their trust and respect for the bureaucracy became necessary if it was to operate on a reasonably objective basis. Under these conditions, the key to good government often resided more in the emperor than in the bureaucracy.

The enormous scope of Chinese imperial power was already theoretically established in the ancient political doctrine of the Mandate of Heaven (*t'ien-ming*). Its central idea is that the moral virtue of the ruler is the foundation of his legitimacy, but it also considers the person who becomes the supreme political ruler the Son of Heaven (*t'ien-tzu*), and ruler of all under Heaven (*t'ien-hsia*).[27] Once the position of emperor became institutionalized in the Ch'in (221–207 B.C.E.), although individual emperors still had to pay lip service to the moral teachings of the doctrine, they honored more its sanction of their political rule over the entire human world as divine descendants of Heaven.[28]

That emperors could not completely neglect the moral legitimacy of their rule bears witness to whatever limited effect the doctrine of the Mandate of Heaven still had on them. It is within this framework that we find many Confucian officials repeatedly relying on this doctrine, perhaps their only weapon within the imperial system, to circumscribe the imperial power and ideally to establish a benevolent government. In this respect Lu Chih consciously observed these Confucian norms.

Applying the Principle of Rightness

Since benevolent imperial rule was believed to be the source of the state's cohesion and stability, one major aspect of Lu Chih's approach to the problems faced by the T'ang court naturally focused upon the emperor's conduct. His application of the principle of rightness in this context can be examined in three closely related categories: raising the emperor's consciousness of benevolent rule, prescribing proper measures for the imperial treatment of court ministers, and urging the emperor to value the common people.

Raising the Imperial Consciousness

Strictly speaking, all of Lu Chih's memorials were intended to raise Te-tsung's awareness of how to be a benevolent monarch. His most conspicuous and specific discussion in this vein was on the Mandate of Heaven.

In the tenth month of 783, in exile in Feng-t'ien, Te-tsung was dismayed by the popular pressure to demote his favorite chief minister Lu Ch'i. In exculpation, he told Lu Chih that the prosperity or decline of the state had always been decided by Heavenly predestination (also *t'ien-ming*); the court's current predicament was predetermined, and his ministers (meaning Lu Ch'i) were not to be blamed.[29] Te-tsung was trying to clear Lu Ch'i of blame, but he seems to have actually believed that the present crisis was predestined because it reminded him of an earlier prediction made by a soothsayer (*shu-shih*).[30]

In reply, Lu Chih first discussed what he believed to be the causes of the court's predicament. While skillfully praising Te-tsung's early determination to restore imperial authority, Lu simultaneously pointed out that his impatience in carrying out his strong policies was the direct cause of the Ho-pei rebellion. He particularly blamed the emergency tax exactions for the popular uprising in the capital. Lu commented that his majesty's ministers (also referring to Lu Ch'i) had prevented him from learning of the popular and official discontent, and that Te-tsung's increasingly unforgiving and suspicious disposition was the real cause of "the perfunctory and careless [*kou-ch'ieh*]" behavior of his ministers.[31] Implying that Te-tsung failed to fulfill his responsibility as a benevolent ruler, Lu then attempted to reorient the imperial understanding of the Mandate of Heaven.

Before his reorientation, Lu Chih emphasized that he never dabbled in studies of divination or esoteric methods (*chan-suan mi-shu*), but from his study of the ancient classics, he understood that the Mandate of Heaven was neither constant nor predetermined. Its bestowal depended rather on human conduct or the ruler's behavior. Lu offered two classical citations to support his argument: "Heaven sees as my people see; Heaven hears as my people hear," and "It is difficult to rely on Heaven; its Mandate is not constant. If the sovereign sees to it that his virtue be constant, he will preserve his throne; if his virtue be not constant, the nine provinces will be lost by him."[32] Heaven's judgment is unquestionably derived from popular inclinations, and Te-tsung must realize that "there is no Mandate of Heaven beyond the realm of human affairs (*fei yü jen-shih chih wai, pieh yu t'ien-ming ye*)" (12: 5b).[33]

Even *The Book of Changes*, a classic Lu Chih believed to grasp the essence of changes in human destiny, upheld virtuous human conduct as the basis for granting the Mandate of Heaven. Lu reminded Te-tsung to heed a comment in the *Changes* traditionally attributed to Confucius:

> *Yu* [numinous help] means help. One whom Heaven helps is someone who is in accord with it. One whom people

> help is someone who is trustworthy. Such a one treads the
> Tao of trustworthiness, keeps his thoughts in accord [with
> Heaven], and also thereby holds the worthy in esteem. This
> is why "Heaven will help him as a matter of course; this is
> good fortune, and nothing will be to his disadvantage."(12:
> 5b–6a.)[34]

In the same manner, Lu also emphasized that none of the other
ancient classics maintain that prosperity and decline are determined by fate. On the contrary, they all agree that human conduct
is responsible for both calamity and good fortune. From this perspective, Lu told Te-tsung that "to win the multitude is to win the
state [*te-chung tse te-kuo*]" (12: 6b). He warned Te-tsung that good
government was the only key to winning popular support, which in
turn would lead to the prosperity of the state.

If Te-tsung still insisted that the present predicament was
predetermined, Lu Chih suggested his majesty consider that before
the army revolt broke out at the capital, the capital population,
though they did not understand soothsaying or divination, had
been worried about a potential threat caused by the emergency tax
measures. They certainly did not think that the subsequent uprising at the capital was predetermined by Heaven. Te-tsung should
understand that there was no causal connection between the
soothsayer's message and his exile in Feng-t'ien. Clearly, Lu was
saying that the emperor should be concerned with the practical
matter of good worldly government and not some unreliable divination. When such good government was practiced, Heaven's assistance would naturally follow.[35] In short, Lu's entire argument was
based on the Confucian belief that the Mandate of Heaven is predicated upon human governance [*t'ien-ming yu-jen*].

Lu Chih's discussion of the Mandate of Heaven was primarily
derived from classical Confucianism, but it was somewhat influenced
by the theory of the correlation between Heaven (or nature) and
human conduct. For example, we find Lu asserting that the present
crisis of the T'ang court was a Heavenly reprimand (*t'ien-chieh*)
due to Te-tsung's inappropriate policies.[36] In a later memorial, he
also stated that a disastrous flood was "perhaps" Heaven's warning
against the harsh imperial treatment of a former chief minister's
relatives.[37] These statements reflect the central tenet of the Han
correlative cosmology. Considering the important place the correlative cosmology of Han Confucianism occupied in T'ang Confucian
ideology, its influence on Lu Chih was quite natural.[38] Neverthe-

less, one suspects that Lu only appropriated the central intention of the Han correlative cosmology to restrain imperial conduct. The main emphasis of his advice to Te-tsung always fell on the importance of human agency—striving for virtuous rule. The idea of Heaven's warning only appeared in a subsidiary and peripheral manner.[39]

After he refuted Te-tsung's fatalism, Lu Chih urged him to "observe the Way [tsun Tao]" on the grounds that the Way was all he had to guarantee safe passage through the present ordeal.[40] Lu said, the Way was easy to understand and easy to carry out. It included,

> disregarding oneself to follow the multitude; disobeying one's own desire to follow the Way; distancing sycophants so as to be close to loyal and honest [subjects]; treating [subjects with] the utmost sincerity to be rid of swindling; stopping the road of flattery and extending the door of remonstrance; sweeping away all methods of seeking after [personal] profits; concentrating on measures for soothing the people; recording a small virtue and a small ability so as to exhaust the talents of every [minister]; forgetting small defects and small complaints so that no one is neglected. (12:8a.)

Two points are essential in his advice: the necessity of establishing a just, honest, and capable bureaucracy, and the importance of putting the people's welfare ahead of imperial desires. For Lu, to observe the Way was first to ensure the public well-being.

Lu Chih's prescriptions were not difficult to understand, but they were certainly not easy for Te-tsung to put into practice.

Sincerity toward Court Officials

In the eleventh month of 783, one month after Lu Chih admonished him to "observe the Way," Te-tsung asked Lu what the urgent tasks were at present. Lu Ch'i had just prevented the imperial audience with the originally loyal Li Huai-kuang. Aware of Li Huai-kuang's discontent and the public resentment of Lu Ch'i's obstruction of imperial contact with the regular officials, Lu Chih told Te-tsung that he believed the most urgent task was to "examine and investigate the public sentiment [shen-ch'a ch'ün-ch'ing]. What public sentiment desires most, your majesty should carry out first; what it resents most, your majesty should eliminate first" (12: 9b). This was so because "the root of order or chaos lies in the hearts of the people (*jen-hsin*)," and "to win the people is to win the state" (12: 9b–10a). In another memorial directly following, Lu cited a passage from the *Li chi* (*The Records of Rites*) to strengthen his position: "public feelings were the fields [cultivated by] the sage kings" (12: 13b).[41] Lu urged Te-tsung sincerely to accept ministerial remonstrance, and ensure that this channel—the only way public sentiment could be transmitted to his majesty—was not obstructed.[42]

Te-tsung praised Lu Chih for his "exhausting loyalty [*chin-chung*]" to the throne, but he also told Lu that the real cause of his present exile was nothing but his already "sincere treatment [*t'ui-ch'eng*] of [his court subjects]" (13: 10a).[43] He said he originally liked to accept ministerial advice and remonstrance and he also treated his subjects sincerely. Unfortunately his ministers were seldom loyal; their discussion of current affairs rarely went to the heart of the matter; they were simply showing off and blaming him for everything to win themselves a good name. Because he felt that his ministers had manipulated and betrayed him, and could not contribute anything significant to his administration, he had recently refused to accept their advice and remonstrance.[44]

Te-tsung's statement may have indeed reflected certain real problems among his ministers; Lu Chih had earlier mentioned their "perfunctory and careless behavior." He had also stated that Te-tsung's unforgiving and suspicious disposition was chiefly responsible for this state of affairs. Now that Te-tsung voiced his dislike of his officials and admitted his deliberate rejection of remonstrance, Lu challenged him.

He first defined what he believed to be exhausting loyalty: "to speak everything one knows is exhausting [*chin*], and to serve the ruler with rightness is loyalty [*chung*]" (13: 10b).[45] Lu Chih intended both to express his own principle for serving his ruler, and to urge Te-tsung to extend the sincere imperial treatment granted him to other court officials and forget their shortcomings. If he could accomplish this, Lu maintained, his officials would all exhaust their loyalty to the throne. But why should Te-tsung treat his ministers sincerely and forget their shortcomings, especially when he believed that they were not loyal to him?

Lu Chih answered: "the way of the Son of Heaven is the same as [the way of] Heaven. Since Heaven does not eliminate all growth because there are bad trees on earth, the Son of Heaven should not abandon [the practice of] listening to remonstrance" (13: 11a). Rejecting remonstrance was similar to "giving up eating for fear of choking." In Lu's view, as long as Te-tsung occupied the position of the Son of Heaven, he should live up to his title. Lu Chih also warned Te-tsung to be aware that "once [an emperor] is insincere, he can not hold [his people's] hearts; once he is untrustworthy, his words can no longer be carried out" (13: 11b). This was also why a passage from the *Chung yung* (*The Doctrine of the Mean*) in the *Li chi* particularly stated: "Sincerity is the end and beginning of affairs; without sincerity no affairs can be carried out" (ibid.).[46] Having indicated the inseparable relation between sincerity, the people's trust, and government, Lu asked Te-tsung how he could expect to consolidate the state without treating his ministers sincerely.

Lu Chih was not advising Te-tsung to behave naively. While accepting remonstrance and advice, Lu made it clear that he also needed to test their validity. Lu's argument implies that so long as Te-tsung did not act out of pure suspicion and self-assumed justice, being discreet and cautious did not contradict the principle of sincerity. Once Te-tsung treated his officials sincerely, the reverse would also take place, and the consolidation of the state would not be beyond reach. Lu believed that this was also the rationale behind the *Chung yung* teaching that "it is only he who possesses the most complete sincerity that exists under Heaven who can give full development to his nature. Able to give the full development to his own nature, he can do the same to the nature of other people" (13: 12b).[47] Thus, Lu asserted: "if you (the ruler) do not give full development to your own nature, but expect to give full development to other people's nature, the multitude will definitely suspect [your integrity] and not follow you. If you are not sincere in the beginning but say that you will be sincere later, the multitude will definitely doubt [your sincerity] and not trust you" (ibid.).

At this point, Lu Chih raised a basic question touching upon one essential aspect of his approach to governing a state. He asked Te-tsung:

Now if there were provincial governors who were not sincere to the state, your majesty would then send armed forces to attack them; if there were ministers and commoners who betrayed your majesty's trust, your majesty would then issue orders to have them killed. The reason the officials obey the orders to kill and attack and would not dare to release [those people] is that they rely upon what your majesty has (sincerity) to condemn those people [for their lack of trust-worthiness]. Now if your majesty becomes insincere in [managing] things, and not trustworthy to the people, people will criticize [your majesty]. What would your majesty then rely upon to suppress them? (12b–13a.)

With this statement, Lu Chih seems to have brought out the funda-mental issue of legitimacy in Confucianism. For one thing, his state-ment reaffirms the central belief of classical Confucianism that the relationship between a ruler and his subjects is reciprocal. If a ruler does not treat his subjects in the proper manner, his subjects may equally abandon their duty to him. As Confucius once said: "Let the ruler be a ruler, the subject a subject. . . ." Mencius later elaborated this principle: "If a prince treats his subjects as his hands and feet, they will treat him as their belly and heart. . . . If he treats them as mud and weeds, they will treat him as an enemy."[48] It follows for Lu that if a ruler failed to observe this type of reciprocity, it would effectively undermine the foundation of his legitimacy.

Lu Chih did not intend to weaken Te-tsung's rule, but he did intend to guide him back to the right Way, and to persuade him to accept advice and remonstrance again from his ministers.[49] He said that *nine maladies* (*chiu pi*) must first be eliminated to guaran-tee the practice of accepting remonstrance. As he put it:

Of the so-called "nine maladies," the rulers suffer from six and the subjects suffer from three. Preference for winning, embarrassment at hearing of [one's] mistakes, indulgence in sophistic debates, showing off one's intel-ligence, increasing one's authority, and failure to restrain one's strong will—these are the six [maladies] infecting the rulers. Flattery, taking a wait and see attitude, and cowardice—these are the three [maladies] infecting their subjects. (13:17b.)

Three of these nine maladies were not the rulers' fault, but Lu believed that the rulers' six maladies created an environment for the growth of wrongdoing by their subjects. Lu did not think "the original minds [*ch'u-hsin*]" of rulers were necessarily "wan-ton and violent [*yin pao*]," but once they contracted these six maladies, they subsequently refused to accept remonstrance from their subjects. When public feelings were no longer trans-mitted to the rulers, the seeds of chaos would soon be sown.

If Te-tsung intended to restore order in the state, Lu Chih suggested he follow the conduct of the six ancient sage kings—Yao, Shun, Yü, T'ang, and kings Wen and Wu—because they were exemplary rulers who had earnestly sought ministerial remonstrance.[50] Otherwise, Lu advised him at least to imitate the closest example of the great T'ang emperor T'ai-tsung.[51] Lu may have idealized T'ai-tsung's virtue, but if we compare T'ai-tsung's relative openness to remonstrance with that of other T'ang emperors, his advice seems justifiable. Lu Chih understood that not all remonstrances were significant, but he believed Te-tsung should treat every remonstrator with equal sincerity to understand the genuine sentiments of his subjects. Through such right conduct, Lu said, Te-tsung and his remonstrators would all acquire a good name.

These utilitarian reasons for accepting ministerial remonstrance do not seem to have convinced Te-tsung to follow his advice. Four months later, Te-tsung again displayed his suspicious inclinations. He told Lu Chih that recently there had been many low-ranking officials claiming to have escaped to the exiled court in Liang-chou from the capital to express their loyalty to the throne. He said he thought these sorts of people were usually no good, and might even harbor some evil plots against him. He wanted Lu Chih to do something about them.[52] Under the pressure of consecutive revolts by his subjects, Te-tsung probably had a heightened sense of insecurity. Believing that Te-tsung's poor attitude toward his subjects was the main reason for the present crisis, however, Lu was determined to reenlighten the emperor.

Lu Chih told Te-tsung that because he had a contemptuous attitude toward his ministers, he attempted to rule without consulting them and became exceedingly defensive against them. As a result, "those who were capable complained about not being employed, those who were loyal worried about being suspected, those who had accomplished notable deeds [for the state] feared that they would not be accepted [by the emperor], . . . these things led to treason and disaster" (15: 16a-b). Now if Te-tsung still held these low-ranking officials in contempt and tried to rely on schemes to govern them, they would never become close to his majesty; but if he exhibited warm feelings toward them, even if they harbored ill feelings toward the throne, they would become confidants. The capital was still occupied at the time by the rebels, and the road from Ch'ang-an to the exiled court was mountainous and dangerous. How many, Lu asked, have trudged over such a route to come to the exiled court as did those low-ranking officials? Even treating those low-ranking officials as sincerely as possible might not be good enough under the circumstances. If his majesty was suspicious of their motivation, who would dare talk about loyalty any more?

Lu Chih's own commitment to ministerial remonstrance was obvious enough, but Te-tsung still could not commit himself to Lu's prescription. Exactly around this time he insisted on demoting Lu's intimate friend Hsiao Fu and banishing Lu's colleague Chiang Kung-fu due to his resentment of their remonstrance. This testifies to the ineffectiveness of Lu's suggestions in this particular regard, but Te-tsung did adopt Lu's advice to apply the notions of sincerity and forgiveness in other respects. Before discussing that, I would like to examine how Lu demanded that Te-tsung value the common people more highly.

Winning the People's Hearts

Lu Chih repeatedly reminded Te-tsung that "the root of establishing a state lies in winning the multitude" (12: 13b).[53] He also encouraged him to imitate the ancient sage kings: "Follow the hearts of all under Heaven, but dare not ask all the people under Heaven to follow [your majesty's] desire" (12: 14b). What were the people's desires? Lu's answer to this question was based on his observation of much public suffering, and his understanding that the rebellion still posed a grave threat.

Ever since the rebellion broke out, military conscription had greatly disturbed the towns and villages. It had made "fathers and sons part; husbands and wives separate; one man is drafted, ten households have to provide him with financial support. Those who stay [at home] suffer from this financial burden; those who leave [for the battlefield] worry about [dying by] the sword." Furthermore, the emergency tax exactions and their accompanying harsh regulations are so great in number that "the clerks cannot bear [to carry them out], and the people have no means of livelihood. In the midst of conscription, the farmlands and the mulberry fields are abandoned; the people's flesh and blood are exhausted by floggings [to exact taxes]. Towns and market-places are distressed; households and families are resentful, all the multitude are screaming with pain, and the prefectures and counties are restless" (12: 2b–3a). Witnessing this general suffering, Lu Chih told Te-tsung that it should be clear that "what all under Heaven now desire is to put the weapons to rest, and to work in peace; what all under Heaven resent is the heavy taxes and levies, and the harsh regulations" (12: 10a).

As early as the eighth month of 783 Lu Chih had already exhorted Te-tsung to abolish all the irregular taxes imposed upon the capital population, and adopt a policy of compromise toward the Ho-pei rebels to reduce the size of the conscript levies.[54] His advice was to no avail, presumably because Te-tsung did not expect to be forced into exile. While the immediate danger to the court had passed, the capital city of Ch'ang-an was still under rebel occupation. Lu Chih understood that it was impossible and impractical to stop the war and all its accompanying measures at this particular time. He did not encourage Te-tsung merely to announce his intention to follow what the people really wished without putting in motion some concrete actions to back up his words. On the contrary, he said that empty talk would only violate the sincerity of the imperial repentance. To avoid such a situation, he told Te-tsung that he must "restrain his own desires to do what is difficult; extend his sincerity for the sake of eliminating what people criticize. Then his majesty's repentance can be made clear for all to see, and correspond with his discussion of [political] renewal" (12: 10b). The following examples serve to elucidate Lu's advice.

Toward the end of 783, there were discussions among Te-tsung's ministers about adding a few words in the coming year to the previously proposed imperial title of "Divinely Spiritual Civil and Military."[55] The divination officials believed that the T'ang state had lasted more than one hundred and sixty-six years, and there ought to be some changes to correspond with this number as well as to indicate the beginning of a new era.[56] The suggested change would have Te-tsung accept his ministers' advice and add even more exalted words to the resplendent title already proposed.[57] Te-tsung asked for Lu Chih's opinion, and as expected, Lu did not endorse what he called a "nonessential suggestion [mo-i]" (13:2a). He offered some clear and simple reasons why Te-tsung should not follow it.

Lu told him that it was not an ancient practice to adopt such a splendid title. He said that "the lightness and heaviness of a ruler lies not in his title. Making his title sublime does not help increase the goodness of his rule; decreasing his title does not damage the beauty of his virtue" (13: 3b). To adopt such a lofty title at such a perilous time would violate the sincerity of Te-tsung's repentance and lose the people's support. If Te-tsung felt he must follow the idea of correspondence between numbers and a new era, he should simply abandon the overly pretentious title previously proposed rather than adding more words to it. He really should restrain his own desires, humbly criticize himself, and publicly demonstrate the sincerity of his repentance by properly refusing to adopt this excessively exalted title. In conclusion, Lu stressed that the Taoist classic, *Tao te ching* also mentioned that "lords and princes refer to themselves as 'solitary,' 'desolate,' and 'hapless.'" This was meant to emphasize that rulers should take "the inferior as [the] root."[58] Just as Lu Chih could not possibly ignore the Han Confucian correlative cosmology due to its dominant position in the official T'ang ideology, he might have made this brief reference to a Taoist concept because the Taoist religion was greatly favored by the T'ang ruling house, and Te-tsung was extremely interested in Taoist medical works.[59] As with Han correlativism, Lu's appropriation of Taoist teachings was limited to the transformation of imperial conduct.

Besides behaving humbly, Lu Chih also asked Te-tsung not to deposit the public funds in his own private treasuries.[60] This was in the first month of 784, by which time the exiled court was no longer besieged by the rebels. Some loyal provincial governors, at the same time, had managed to send tribute and taxes to the throne.[61] His straitened financial conditions in previous months, and not necessarily his avaricious nature, perhaps motivated the frightened Te-tsung to keep these provincial tributes and taxes in his personal treasuries.[62] Strongly opposed to this selfish act, Lu Chih explained why it was necessary to discontinue the practice.

He told Te-tsung that "in handling affairs, if the ruler takes the public [interests] into his heart, the people will definitely be happy to follow him; but if he takes personal gain (tributes) into his heart, the people will definitely oppose and rebel against him" (14: 4b). Laying down the principle that the public welfare is the ultimate concern of the state, Lu reminded Te-tsung that when the court was first exiled to Feng-t'ien, he had endured the attendant hardships together with his subjects, and no one complained about the suffering.

Imminent danger had been just recently removed, but rebels still occupied the capital; injured troops still groaned and moaned on the roads; and his loyalist forces had still received no rewards. In the face of such miseries, how could his majesty bear to keep provincial tribute and taxes in his personal treasuries, and not pay the expenses of the court? Making the people suffer with the ruler during difficult periods, but refusing to share benefits with them during happy and fortunate times would certainly cause complaints and criticism. To avoid such resentment, Lu asked Te-tsung to restore the honest and unblemished governance practiced at the beginning of his reign, to abolish his personal treasuries, and to use the funds to reward the army and his meritorious subjects. "Having the same desires as the people" would prove the sincerity of his repentance and gain the support of the public (14:2b–6a).

These two examples bring out what Lu Chih believed Te-tsung should do to gain the sympathy and support of the people. Apparently, before any genuine measures of public relief could be put into practice, Lu insisted that virtuous imperial conduct was the key to winning the people's hearts. Te-tsung did not completely follow Lu's advice in the treatment of his ministers, but he acquiesced with regard to obtaining public support.[63] Te-tsung announced, in the famous Act of Grace and Amnesty formulated by Lu and issued at this time (the first month of 784), that from then on no one should address him with the overblown title of "Divinely Spiritual Civil and Military." He also blamed himself for the public suffering brought on by the war measures. In showing his repentance, he promised that he would practice frugal government, but would reward meritorious subjects. To rectify his previous mistakes he would treat his ministers with sincerity and forgiveness.[64]

Given that later on Te-tsung did not keep his promise concerning the treatment of his ministers, and that he also resumed the practice of keeping provincial tributes in his personal treasuries, this decision to abolish the unnecessarily resplendent title and personal treasuries can be regarded as a purely tactical necessity during a time of emergency.[65] The same cannot be said, however, about Lu Chih's advice.

Lu asserted that it was precisely because Te-tsung had deviated from the Confucian norm of benevolent rule in the first place that the state had been thrust into its present catastrophe. In Lu's view, virtuous imperial conduct was not to be practiced only in cases of emergency; it was the rightful duty of the emperor to realize at all times for the people's sake.[66] The only difference was that during times of crisis, when the emperor could not end the public suffering quickly, his virtuous conduct became even more absolutely indispensable. Exemplary conduct was the emperor's only remaining asset to convince the public that he was still a redeemable ruler. In short, virtuous imperial conduct was not a manipulative variable applied only in emergency situations—it was a basic constant never to be neglected.

During the last month of 783, based upon Lu Chih's earlier suggestions, Te-tsung finally decided to adopt a compromise policy to deal with the Ho-pei rebels.[67] When he was getting ready to issue the Act of Grace and Amnesty to placate the rebel forces as well as gain public support, he again consulted Lu on how to formulate this edict. In response, Lu again told him that sincerity is the key to winning the people's hearts, and sincerity requires a ruler to be consistent in words and deeds.[68] Even though Te-tsung only followed Lu's advice for a short while, the principle behind Lu's suggestions became the guiding spirit, not only for this particular edict, but for the later imperial Acts of Grace and Amnesty.

Besides exhorting Te-tsung to cultivate his personal conduct, Lu Chih also suggested other concrete measures for dealing with the rebels and for ameliorating public suffering. These measures involve the application of his principle of expediency.

Applying the Expediency Principle

While Lu Chih maintained that Te-tsung's cultivation of sincerity and virtuous conduct was the most necessary ingredient in the application of the principle of rightness, the improvement of the imperial perception and judgment became a parallel element in the exercise of expediency. Expediency was defined as a keen ability to recognize the opportune moment for applying the most appropriate policy to maximize the public well-being. Thus a correct perception of the changes of time and circumstances, and the judgment derived from such perception occupied a central place in Lu's advice to Te-tsung. Indeed, in his discourse with the throne, Lu frequently told Te-tsung to "examine the changes of the times," and to "understand the changes of the times" (12: 7b; 16: 16a). How to adapt to and appropriate the changed times and circumstances became another motif of his approach to the problems faced by the T'ang court. Lu exhorted Te-tsung to exercise his principle of expediency in dealing with the rebels as well as with loyal subjects in the chaotic circumstances of the day.

Expediency in Handling the Rebels

In the eighth month of 783, Lu Chih presented his two earliest extant memorials analyzing situations in the Ho-pei, Huai-hsi and Kuan-chung (capital) regions.[69] At this time, the T'ang capital had not yet fallen into rebel hands, but the fighting in Ho-pei offered very little reason to be optimistic about victory. These bleak prospects propelled Te-tsung for the first time to consult his favorite Han-lin scholar. This is also the first time that we find Lu holding forth on his particular notion of expediency.

The main thrust of Lu Chih's response was to encourage Te-tsung to "compare the degree of seriousness of the disasters and distinguish the order of importance and urgency in offense and defense" (11: 21a). He suggested a concentration of all imperial forces to recover the Huai-hsi region, loss of which posed a real threat to the economic survival of the court. Defeat of the Ho-pei rebels, Lu said, was only a secondary priority. The Huai-hsi rebels controlled the key economic supply line from the south to the capital, but the Ho-pei military governors were less of a threat due to their penchant for internecine fighting.[70] Lu also recommended strengthening the defense of the Kuan-chung region so that the heart of the empire would not be exposed to sudden invasions either from within or without.[71] He advised Te-tsung as a necessary exercise of expediency in government always to consider Kuan-chung's stability as his first priority.[72] To concentrate the fighting in the Huai-hsi region, and end the war soon, Lu proposed an offer of amnesty to the rebels. He said that "only four or five fierce people" were the leaders of the Ho-pei and Huai-hsi rebel forces; the rest of them were doubtless forced to join the rebellion either out of fear or by mistake. If they knew that Te-tsung was willing to offer them amnesty, most of them would rather preserve their lives than remain as traitors.[73]

In retrospect, Lu Chih's advice proved insightful, but Te-tsung was unable to appropriate his vision until two months later; after the fall of the capital he finally gave in to circumstances. In the first month of 784, the above-mentioned Act of Grace and Amnesty was issued, and Lu's suggestions became imperial policies to be put into practice. Besides terminating all the irregular taxes, and making an imperial self-criticism, Te-tsung also offered amnesty to all the rebel governors in Ho-pei and Huai-hsi, and confirmed their positions as governors in these provinces. All their subordinates were also to be pardoned accordingly.[74] Chu Tz'u was the only rebel leader who received no amnesty, possibly because he established himself as "emperor" and conducted his own court in the T'ang capital.[75]

The anticipated effects of this edict were not completely realized because Chu Tz'u and the Huai-hsi governor Li Hsi-lieh remained unmoved, but the majority of the Ho-pei rebel governors did show their appreciation for the imperial amnesty.[76] This led to their eventual acceptance of the court's compromise policies allowing them to continue as semi-independent provincial forces. This edict also set the tone for the next three Acts of Grace and Amnesty.[77] Since this policy of extending amnesty to all the subordinate rebels was repeatedly emphasized during the fighting against Li Huai-kuang and Li Hsi-lieh, it must have helped to weaken the rebel troops' will to fight, and consequently contributed to the suppression of these two rebel generals.[78]

It was not an easy task for Lu Chih to persuade Te-tsung to pardon all the subordinates of the rebel leaders. In fact, he frequently had to stress the importance of expediency so that Te-tsung would perceive the necessity of its application. Besides the above-noted example of retaining Li Ch'u-lin's military governorship, Lu's advice to release Chao Kuei-hsien is another case in point.[79]

After the defeat of Chu Tz'u and the court's return to Ch'ang-an, Te-tsung was in the process of issuing the second Act of Grace and Amnesty.[80] At this time, he told Lu Chih that most of his generals agreed that Chao Kuei-hsien, a court subject who supposedly surrendered to Chu Tz'u during the capital uprising, should be sentenced to death without leniency. Lu disagreed. He said that "it is a minister's usual intention to eliminate the evil ones for the ruler according to the law;" but insisted that "it is in the ruler's exercise of an important expediency that he pacifies the people's fear by examining the actual circumstances [of evil behavior]" (17: 3b–4a).

Lu explained that Chao was originally a subordinate general stationed in Feng-hsiang; when Te-tsung was forced into exile in Feng-t'ien, Chao was on the road to fight the rebels in Hsiang-ch'eng (in modern Honan). Chao was left alone when his immediate superior went back to Feng-hsiang. At this juncture, Chu Tz'u tricked him into going to the capital to await Te-tsung's return. Unaware that Chu had already betrayed the court, Chao followed him and became his captive, but he refused to accept Chu's appointment to serve under him. Judging from the above information, Lu said, Chao's case definitely deserved sympathy. The only crime that Chao was guilty of was that he did not preserve his integrity by committing suicide. If he had done so, he would have become a loyal martyr. Evidently, Lu was implying that even though Chao lacked the courage to become a martyr, his passive resistance to Chu's appointment already indicated that he had not voluntarily joined the rebels.[81]

Lu went on to argue that since the capital had only been recently recovered, it was time to extend the imperial virtue, and Te-tsung needed to be extremely cautious in the application of the penal code. If he sentenced those guilty ones strictly according to the letter of the law, it would cause those who, despite their fears, still intended to return to court to give up the idea, and so strengthen the rebels' position. If to follow the generals' suggestion and sentence Chao might well prolong the fighting, Lu asked, what benefit could the court get out of it? While urging Te-tsung to draw lessons from recent history, Lu also hoped that, with the exception of the principal culprits, he would sentence his fallen subjects leniently.[82]

We do not know what finally happened to Chao Kuei-hsien. In the Act of Grace and Amnesty issued immediately afterwards, Te-tsung did admit that it was his loss of virtue that brought suffering to the people and caused them to commit crimes of treason or bribery to keep alive during the crisis. It would, therefore, violate the sincerity of imperial repentance and the principle of increasing harmony if death sentences were given to the guilty ones.[83] In this context, it is likely that Te-tsung finally perceived the importance of Lu's form of expediency, and pardoned Chao Kuei-hsien in the hope that his generosity would encourage rebel defections. If this was indeed the case, Te-tsung's optimism was certainly justified because the two Acts of Grace and Amnesty he issued then greatly mollified the Ho-pei rebel governors, and pacified the population in the capital.

When Li Huai-kuang committed suicide and brought the fighting between the Ho-chung rebels and the court to an end, Lu Chih again felt compelled to remind Te-tsung of the expediency principle. This was in the eighth month of 785 when Te-tsung asked him how to handle this new situation.

Worried that Te-tsung would follow some reckless suggestions to exploit the victory over Ho-chung and push on fighting against the last rebel governor Li Hsi-lieh, Lu Chih told him that this was a time to distribute imperial favor (*hui*), not to show off imperial power (*wei*).[84] Te-tsung had already demonstrated his power by eliminating Chu Tz'u and Li Huai-kuang. What he should do now was offer amnesty to all the subordinate rebels in the Ho-chung region and to Li Hsi-lieh's forces as well. In this way Li Hsi-lieh would be left with no excuse to impugn Te-tsung's sincerity. If Te-tsung "extended the favor of his sympathy to add to his imperial power, and took advantage of the power [recently] gained from eliminating [the Ho-chung] rebels to distribute imperial favors," Li

Hsi-lieh would also have no excuse to persuade his close followers to fight the court and no distant cohorts to rely upon. Most of all, Te-tsung did not need to fight against Li because it was only a matter of time before either a man or a demon would dispatch him.[85]

Lu Chih's prediction concerning Li Hsi-lieh's fate was as dramatic as it was accurate. Li was poisoned by a subordinate general, Ch'en Hsien-ch'i, in the third month of 786. This not only forced the Huai-hsi rebels to surrender to the throne, but also concluded the last phase of a rebellion by military governors that had lasted nearly five years.[86] For the time being, Te-tsung willingly adopted Lu's suggestions. He offered a general amnesty to the Ho-chung and Huai-hsi rebels, probably right after Lu submitted his memorial.[87] Lu's specific suggestions for dealing with the rebels, derived from his principle of expediency, were eventually accepted by Te-tsung as the basis of his decision making.

Expediency toward Loyal Subjects

Lu Chih's memorials concerning loyal subjects do not specifically contain the term *ch'üan* (expediency), but they may be analyzed as examples of his expediency principle.

To relate how Lu Chih persuaded Te-tsung to apply expediency to situations involving loyal subjects, we have to switch our focus back to the time when Li Huai-kuang was on the verge of revolt. Before he joined the rebel camp, Huai-kuang had repeatedly refused the order to fight the rebel Chu Tz'u, and was in secret contact with him. On the alert for such activities, general Li Sheng pleaded with Te-tsung for permission to encamp his troops a short distance further away from Huai-kuang's armies at nearby Hsien-yang. Still hoping that he could keep Huai-kuang in line, Te-tsung refused to grant Li Sheng's request. In the meantime, since he did not intend to grant Huai-kuang a personal audience, he sent Lu Chih to Huai-kuang's encampment to placate him.[88] After returning from this mission, Lu immediately counseled Te-tsung to grant permission for the redeployment of Li Sheng's forces.[89]

Lu Chih contended that Huai-kuang had repeatedly disobeyed imperial orders, and if Te-tsung continued to appease him without taking some precautions, the consequences would be hard to predict. At this point when the court's very existence was in peril, Te-tsung must not treat this matter in any ordinary way. Lu told him that Huai-kuang himself even said with contempt that he did not care if Li Sheng's troops were shifted away from his armies. Under these circumstances, granting Li Sheng's request should not cause Huai-kuang to complain. As Lu said,

> when I first received your majesty's order to be an envoy and proclaim your majesty's instructions [to Li Huai-kuang], it was [originally] because the grain rations were unequal. [Quite] by chance [Li Sheng also wanted to] redeploy his troops. The two things occurred at the same time. Fortunately, Huai-kuang did not say anything to obstruct this (Li Sheng's) plan, but gave me a disingenuous reply; the event and the opportunity presented themselves together as if some hidden assistance had revealed itself. If your majesty loses this convenient opportunity, later repentance will not be able to recapture it. I only hope that your sage wisdom will come to an expeditious judgment and decision. (14: 12b–13a.)

In this manner, Lu urged Te-tsung to exploit this opportune moment and shift the palace armies as soon as possible. As events unfolded, it was precisely due to Lu's astute advice that Te-tsung was able in good time to save the palace armies from direct confrontation with Huai-kuang's forces. When a similar situation occurred later, Te-tsung, however, failed to heed Lu's suggestion; he procrastinated until the situation deteriorated. Te-tsung's failure to follow Lu's advice eventually led to the loss of two armies.[90] Had he also refused or hesitated to grasp the earlier opportunity to move Li Sheng's troops to safety, mid-T'ang history might well have run a different course.[91]

When Li Huai-kuang finally revolted, forcing Te-tsung to escape further to Liang-chou, Li Sheng's army was the only loyalist force that stayed near the capital region to fight the rebels.[92] Apparently frightened by Li Huai-kuang's mutiny, Te-tsung, however, told Lu Chih that Li Sheng and other commanders' armies had to be regulated and instructed by the court so that they would march forward. He told Lu he would send "an envoy" to proclaim the imperial decree to them.[93] Knowing that it was imperial practice to dispatch eunuch envoys to represent Te-tsung in the field, and to "supervise" military affairs, Lu expressed his strong disagreement in a memorial submitted in the fifth month of 784.[94]

He began his statement by demanding that Te-tsung compare the advantages and disadvantages between having field command-

ers make their own decisions in the middle of battle, and controlling them from a far-off central court or by an imperial delegate
with little understanding of military maneuvers. Discouraging Te-
tsung from controlling his field commanders from a distance, Lu
insisted that the device of sending eunuchs to spy on his commanders would only make things worse. The commanders would either
disobey imperial orders for the sake of strategic necessity, or follow
orders and lose a golden opportunity to win a battle. So impeded,
it would be only natural that no one would risk his life to fight for
the court. Lu then asked Te-tsung to "consolidate [your field com-
manders] by bestowing your trust upon them; delegate flexible
[decision-making] power to them; grant them unusual rewards,
and disregard all [other] trivial matters." Lu's rationale was that
"the emperor's power is very different from that of his ministers, and
only when he does not hold to his own views can he then adopt the
views of others. The most important thing about the use of this
power is to be in accord with people's desires; the key to using it lies
in fully understanding the changes of time and circumstances" (16:
16a). Lu never mentioned the word eunuch in this memorial, but his
critique of eunuch deployment as army supervisors is obvious.[95]

Lu's advice to Te-tsung regarding this particular practice seems
to have been given in vain.[96] Te-tsung was unwilling to employ Lu
Chih's idea of expediency in delegating authority to field commanders, but he did accept his suggestion to reward these generals and
their subordinates, as shown in the case of general Ch'ü Huan (726–
799).[97] Lu convinced Te-tsung to grant Ch'ü a special reward with all
dispatch because he was a rare exemplar of the loyal subject.[98] Ch'ü
Huan and his army later contributed a great deal in the fighting
against Li Hsi-lieh. After the war, Ch'ü became a capable local governor and reconstructed some devastated provinces near Huai-hsi.[99]

In the third month of 784, Lu Chih also convinced Te-tsung to
reward some peasants near the exiled court in a more appropriate
manner than originally intended. Te-tsung planned to grant honorific
official titles to these peasants for presenting melons and various
fruits to him on his way to Liang-chou. He wanted to please the
people by bestowing what he regarded as meaningless empty titles
that did not cost him a thing.[100] Lu was against this idea. He
explained that it was not suitable to grant honorific official titles
to ordinary peasants because "only those who make eminent contributions and possess [outstanding] talents and virtue are qualified"
(14: 15b–16a) to receive them, and too many such titles had already been awarded during the An Lu-shan rebellion.[101] These ir-

regular and wholesale grants only served to degrade further the value of these awards, thus rendering them worthless in gaining support from people who made genuine contributions to the defense of the empire. Lu concluded with the common sense assertion that what the peasants really valued was food and clothing not empty titles. Te-tsung should simply give them some money and goods. In this way, the peasants would not loose any benefits, and the state would not violate the expediency principle.[102]

In another situation, Lu Chih also argued, on the basis of his expediency principle, against Te-tsung's plan to dispatch one of his generals to round up his lost palace messenger girls.[103] Lu Chih maintained that Te-tsung's pursuit of personal pleasure should not come before his regard for the public welfare. He told Te-tsung that looking for palace maids was not necessary because he already owned an exceedingly great number of this type of female servant. He should be aware that although the capital had recently been recovered, the empire was still inundated with wounded soldiers and emaciated people. Looking for palace maids under these conditions would openly exhibit his indifference to the people's sufferings, and could easily cause public complaints and criticism. Furthermore, since these palace maids had been lost for months, it was likely that some generals or soldiers had already taken them as their private possessions. An imperial search could only cause suspicion and panic among these generals and soldiers because they never intended to return the maids. Giving his palace maids up for the time being would demonstrate that Te-tsung understood that "there are orders of priority for state affairs, and degrees of seriousness for rightful duties" (16: 18a). It would also show that he would not "let small matters obstruct the accomplishment of important tasks" (16: 19b). Te-tsung did not dispatch a general, but, still unwilling to forsake these prize personal possessions, he sent some eunuchs out to find them instead.[104]

This revealing little incident illustrates the fundamental difference between Te-tsung and his Han-lin scholar. Lu Chih regarded expediency as a responsible approach to be exercised both in emergencies and in normal times when one must abandon personal profits to achieve public well-being. Te-tsung was willing to apply Lu's expediency principle only when he considered it a useful scheme for the restoration of his state. If the application of expediency jeopardized his personal enjoyment at a time when there was no clear and present danger, he was unwilling to sacrifice his personal pleasures for the advancement of the public welfare.

A Confucian Pragmatist Approach

This analysis of Lu Chih's memorials to the throne, predicated upon his principles of rightness and expediency, indicates that his approach to all the problems faced by the T'ang court during this chaotic period was both moralistic and pragmatic. Lu believed that neither imperial moral conduct nor practical administrative policy was sufficient in itself to govern a state. This interdependent relationship he perceived between the moralistic and pragmatic aspects of his approach to government leads me to characterize it as a *Confucian pragmatist approach*.

In his striving to help Te-tsung reestablish the T'ang court, Lu Chih repeatedly reminded him that the people, not the ruler, were "the foundation of the state." It was the ruler's responsibility to ensure that the foundation of the state was stable and secure; the realization of public desires always came first, before satisfaction of the ruler's wants. This, of course, reflected the quintessential belief in "the importance of the people [*min wei kuei*]" sustained by the classical Confucians, especially by Mencius.[105] It was within this context that Lu constantly expressed his great concern for virtuous rule. This concern was the core of the moralistic aspect of his approach.

Lu Chih also steadily advised Te-tsung that a pragmatic sensibility was necessary when situational judgment was required to bring a maximum of moral correctness and a minimum of damage to the state. Clearly Lu perceived the application of expediency as a political necessity because it helped to achieve the greatest possible benefit for the state during a specific time and under specific conditions. It would not compromise the principle of rightness precisely because it was rightly aimed to achieve a higher ethical standard. From this we can see that Lu was neither conservative in the sense of refusing to adapt to changes of time and circumstances, nor a pure pragmatist whose proclaimed value system was secondary to practical concerns.[106] On the contrary, his emphasis on the complementary relationship between the principles of rightness and expediency shows that he placed equal weight on both the moralistic and the pragmatic sides of his political approach.

Unlike his Confucian scholar contemporaries whom he considered "pedantic," Lu Chih regarded the Confucian classics as the repository of living principles for imperial conduct. His interpretive framework for the concept of expediency was based on his understanding of Confucius's teaching of higher ethical standards as embodied in the *Analects* and other ancient classics.[107] Within this framework, the pursuit of a higher ethical goal became the prerequisite for realizing his pragmatism.

I should note that Lu Chih was not the first mid-T'ang scholar official to discuss the application of expediency in government.[108] He was, as far as can be ascertained, the first in the post-An Lu-shan rebellion era to assert unequivocally the complementary relationship between the principle of expediency and the principle of rightness. He also seems to be the earliest to clarify the boundary between exercising expediency and practicing political trickery, and consequently to place an even greater ethical responsibility on political leadership.

Lu Chih's emphasis on the ethical responsibilities of political leaders reminds one of the familiar Weberian idea of political ethics. Some parallels seem to exist between Lu's exhortations to Te-tsung and Weber's "ethics of intention" and "ethics of responsibility."[109] When he discussed these two kinds of ethical standards in politics, Weber viewed politicians who believe in the ethics of intentions as basically cosmic rationalists. They sincerely believe that only good results can come from good intentions and bad results from bad intentions. The only logical course open for them, then, is to reject using any morally dangerous means in their every political activity. When they actually face the unexpected evil consequences of their good intentions, they frequently blame them on someone else's stupidity or even on the will of God instead of taking responsibility for their own political actions. Worse still, logically convinced that the degree of intensity between good intentions and results is positively related, the cosmic rationalists in the empirical world can easily turn into millenarian prophets advocating the necessity of sanctifying immoral means for great moral ends. From this point of view, Weber warned that there are only two kinds of ultimate mortal sin in politics: lack of realism and lack of responsibility. To minimize these two kinds of mortal sin, Weber suggested that politicians should all have an "ethics of responsibility." That is, they should constantly base their political actions upon the foreseeable consequences for which they take full responsibility as long as the foreseeable consequences are parts of their desirable moral ends.

In our analysis of Lu Chih's application of expediency, we see that, like Weber, Lu insisted that political decisions had to be based on the "foreseeable consequences." Lu's advice to Te-tsung indicates that he believed that the ruler had to be fully responsible for the feasibility of political decisions. This means political decisions had to be derived from a realistic estimation of all the possible results. Only then would political decisions lead to desirable moral ends. In short, "realism" and "responsibility," the two ultimate criteria in Weber's idea of political ethics, were also the two essential ingredients in the *pragmatic* aspect of Lu's approach to government.

Lu Chih was of course concerned with the ethical intentions of political leadership. He maintained that Te-tsung's sincerity and his virtuous conduct were important assets to win back popular support. It must be noted, however, that during this period of chaos Lu always asked Te-tsung to provide concrete and realistic policies to substantiate his good intentions. In his application of the principle of rightness, Lu never forgot to urge Te-tsung to be responsible for the potential results of his intentions and his actions. In other words, Lu demonstrated that he did not believe that ethical intentions per se would necessarily bring forth desirable ends. In a strict sense then, the *moralistic* aspect of Lu's approach did not correspond exactly to Weber's "ethics of intention" that, as Weber explained, when applied to political activities, was often obsessed with the purity of intentions, and thus completely ignored the possible "consequences" of political actions.[110]

Contribution to Mid-T'ang Stability

Lu Chih made a seminal contribution to the restoration of T'ang stability by means of his Confucian pragmatist approach to government. Through the interplay of his two complementary principles of rightness and expediency, he helped the T'ang court consolidate its stability and exerted a key influence on the court's military policy decisions.

In the application of his principle of rightness, Lu served as a spokesman for both the court officials and the general population. He admonished Te-tsung to emulate sincerely the ancient sage kings by cultivating virtuous conduct and "restraining his personal desires." Believing that virtuous governance was the *sine qua non* for winning public sympathy and support, Lu urged Te-tsung to show his self-criticism and repentance to his subjects and accompany them with concrete policies to relieve the people's financial burdens. In so doing, he helped Te-tsung mollify the people and stabilize the vacillating public mind.

In the same manner, but operating on his principle of expediency, Lu helped the court lower the rebels' fighting morale by demanding that Te-tsung offer amnesty not only to the rebel governors but also to their subordinates. To a certain extent, the ensuing emotional impact of this policy on rebel psychology necessarily reduced the centrifugal forces away from the court, and correspondingly increased the court's chances of winning their military campaigns. In addition, Lu also prompted Te-tsung in good time to forestall a direct confrontation between the palace troops and Li Huai-kuang's armies, and dissolved several potential military threats by instructing Te-tsung to be generous toward military subjects who either committed or were alleged to have committed treason. Likewise, it was at his urging that the court finally took unusual measures to preserve the strength of the loyal general who made a difference fighting against the Huai-hsi rebels.

Although Te-tsung was always the final arbitrator in every decision that he made, this examination of Lu's approach to every problem Te-tsung brought to him shows that it was Lu Chih, not Te-tsung, who played the role of behind-the-scenes mastermind of many crucial imperial policies. From this perspective, he undoubtedly made an indispensable contribution to mid-T'ang stability even though the court's military campaigns were primarily responsible for the reassertion of T'ang power.

As a Han-lin scholar, or rather as an "inner chief minister," Lu Chih indeed served the court well through his Confucian pragmatist approach. While the T'ang court was in the process of gradual recovery, Lu was receding from the center to the periphery. When we next hear his voice, he will again be in the limelight on the mid-T'ang stage for a brief but significant performance.

CHAPTER FIVE

Road to Reform

Early in 793, eight months after Lu Chih assumed the responsibilities of chief minister, he presented a memorial to the throne containing the following passage:

> I, the lowly, have received your majesty's kindness in frequently sending [me] profound decrees expressing sympathy and comforting regards one after another. Your majesty's teaching and instructions are so comprehensive and complete that the loving-kindness between one's own flesh and blood can not even surpass them. . . .
>
> I suppose that since my abilities are ordinary and mediocre, I have not produced unusual and outstanding results. The only thing I must do is exhaust my loyalty and faithfulness to correct and assist your majesty's policies. What everybody feels it difficult to say, I will definitely not hide; where ordinary human feelings are easily covered up, I will definitely not retreat from mine. I hold my faithful heart in my hand to repay your majesty. My devotion is unchangeable. I only hope that my enlightened master will understand and tolerate me. (20: 2a.)[1]

Though expressed in a self-depreciating rhetoric, this memorial fairly represents Lu's sentiments and perception of his role as chief minister. He aspired to reenact the role of imperial adviser he played during the period of exile. He considered it his mission to "correct and assist" Te-tsung's policies, and urged Te-tsung here to accept him as a loyal but critical chief minister. He would now take the lead in putting forth his reformist policies rather than passively waiting for an imperial consultation to present his private advice.

As "inner chief minister," Lu made a crucial contribution to the reestablishment of stability, but his efforts to "correct and assist" the imperial policies suffered ultimately from the antagonism between him and his archopponent P'ei Yen-ling. Even so, during the two years he served as chief minister, Lu's reformist efforts were not a total failure. Some of his advice and suggestions were put into practice and produced beneficial results for the court. His approach to the contemporary tax situation was also applicable to problems created by the two-tax system. To understand his reformist efforts, I shall discuss the memorials Lu presented during his tenure as chief minister according to three main categories: reforming the bureaucracy, strengthening the power of the state, and improving the people's well-being.

Whereas these three categories constitute what may be called the public domain, another category that deserves equal if not more attention is part of the private sphere: Lu's continuing endeavors to transform Te-tsung's conduct. We need to look into these efforts in order to reinforce, from a different perspective, our understanding of his approach to government, and because his exertions gave rise to antagonistic forces that gradually jeopardized his entire reformist effort.

In this chapter, I shall only investigate the first two categories, leaving the other two for the following chapter. A brief discussion of Te-tsung's concerns during this time provides the necessary background for Lu's policy suggestions.

Te-tsung's Main Concerns

When Lu Chih became chief minister in the fourth month of 792, Te-tsung had already reinstated his father's appeasement policy towards provincial governor generals. He was most interested in preserving the status quo, and had resumed his former practice of accepting "tributes" from provincial governors to enrich his personal treasuries.[2]

A well-defended border capable of resisting foreign invasion was indispensable to the maintenance of the dynasty's newly restored stability. With the recent rebellions at an end, two western military governors induced the state of Nan-chao to renew its relationship with the T'ang court, consequently reducing to a considerable degree the Tibetan threat. An alliance with the Uighurs also eliminated a potential enemy from the north.[3] Without certain financial arrangements and an adequate border defense these successes would hardly have been attainable. Defense and finance dominated Te-tsung's concerns, and became in turn the main challenge for officials called upon to serve as chief minister.[4]

As chief minister, Ts'ui Tsao and Li Mi both tried to carry out some policies to improve border defenses and state finances. Ts'ui Tsao's financial reforms were fruitless, but Li Mi had some limited success. For example, his defense policies provided greater protection for vital economic regions in the Huai and Yangtze valleys, and also restored the alliance with the Uighur Turks against the Tibetans.[5] When Lu Chih replaced Tou Shen and took over the responsibilities of chief minister, his first steps were, however, aimed at increasing the quality and efficiency of the bureaucracy.

Reforming the Bureaucracy:
Capable Officials and a Just System

Lu Chih proposed that the secondary heads of various central government offices be allowed to recommend their own candidates for subordinate posts within their departments.[6] Te-tsung first approved of this policy and issued a decree for its enforcement in the fifth month of 792, but immediately changed his mind.[7] In a private decree to Lu Chih, Te-tsung said that the opponents of this policy claimed that bribes had been involved in the process of recommendation, and the policy had failed to obtain men of true talent for the posts. He told Lu that as chief minister he should appoint officials himself and should not entrust the heads of various bureaus with such power.[8]

Lu Chih immediately presented a long memorial defending his position:

> The pressing matter of governance lies in obtaining the [right] persons, but the difficulty of recognizing the [right] persons is still a problem even for the sages and wise people. If [appointment is granted by] listening to candidates' words, one cannot guarantee [the moral correctness of] their conduct; [if by] examining their conduct, one may neglect their abilities; [if by] evaluating their

administrative efficacy, artful schemes and false devices will frequently arise, and faithful and honest candidates will rarely be advanced; [if by] following their reputation, [excess] competition will greatly increase; those who [have profound understanding] but do not seek to advance in official life will not be promoted.

Only when [recommendation relies upon] officials who always communicate closely with [potential] candidates, have thoroughly detailed knowledge concerning them, inquire after their conduct and ambition, and examine their abilities, can those who guard the Way but hide their talents be recognized, and hypocrites who fish for fame and [excessively] ornament their appearances be rejected. Therefore, Confucius said: "Look at the means a man employs, observe the path he takes and examine where he feels at home. In what way is a man's true character hidden from view?"(18: 2a.)[9]

Lu Chih told Te-tsung that the recommendation method had been practiced in previous dynasties, and had also been followed earlier by the T'ang. According to the T'ang rule, Lu went on, appointment of officials with a nominal sixth rank or below to a substantive post was carried out in the Ministry of Personnel; the chief minister and the emperor merely gave their endorsement. This practice was unlike the appointment of officials with a nominal fifth rank or above, which had to be recommended first by the chief minister, and then followed by an imperial edict to confirm the appointment.[10] As time went by, Lu lamented, some dominant chief ministers violated this rule. They concentrated on increasing their own power and took this appointment function away from the Ministry of Personnel. These chief ministers became the arbitrators of official appointments, and as the channels of appointment grew increasingly narrow, the bureaucratic machine failed to recruit true talents. Arguing that this practice should be rectified, Lu specifically indicated that broadening the channels of official appointment and establishing a capable bureaucracy were two things he could do to express his gratitude to Te-tsung.

Lu thought that this recommendation system could prevent bribes and other unfair practices because officials who made such recommendations would be lifelong sponsors of their candidates.

They had to present written documents to provide grounds for and to guarantee the validity of their recommendation. If their candidates proved to be capable officials, they could advance in the official ranks and receive salary increases. Otherwise, they would be demoted and lose their salary.

In addition, Lu maintained that it was common for human beings to treasure their honor and reputation. Since secondary heads of the various offices were all potential candidates for higher official posts; they would not want to damage their reputation and incur punishment by making dishonest and prejudiced recommendations. This policy would help the court provide a proper method for evaluating higher-ranking officials.[11] With these preconditions established, Lu was convinced of the superior applicability of his proffered recommendation system.

Now that Te-tsung wanted to revoke his original consent to this policy, and asked him to monopolize the power of appointment, Lu Chih said this would amount to "changing a public recommendation into a private one, and transforming overt praise into a private secret." Since a chief minister could not possibly know all the available candidates personally, he would have to rely on his relatives or friends for such candidates. It would be better to allow secondary heads to make their recommendations in public than to depend upon the chief ministers' personal appointments made on the basis of private recommendations.[12]

Furthermore, Lu insisted that different offices should have different functions:

> When the sages regulated affairs, they would certainly estimate the appropriateness of [various] things. They would not presume all talent to reside in one person, or expect something beyond a person's ability; they made officials in senior positions take charge of important affairs, and officials in junior positions responsible for details. Therefore, rulers select their chief ministers; chief ministers select heads for a multitude of offices, and heads select their subordinates.... If one wants to obtain the [right] candidates, there isn't any easier way than this [measure]....
>
> As for seeking out talented persons, the important thing is to broaden [the channels] for examining and evaluating [officials]; this is to make [the selection process]

accurate. Broadening channels lies in [allowing] officials to
recommend whomever they know well, and recommendations made by senior heads will [perform] this [function];
accurate evaluation consists in demanding that actual performance correspond to the titles of the [evaluated] officials,
and the order of advancement established by chief ministers will [fulfill] this [function]. If the [channels] for seeking
candidates are not broad, the lower-ranking officials will
rarely advance; . . . [and] capable candidates [to fill] the
appointments will often be lacking; . . . if evaluation of the
officials is not accurate, capable and incapable [officials]
will be undifferentiated, . . . [and] the merits of the wise
and the able ones will not be manifested. (18: 10b–11a.)

Several elements of this statement deserve our attention. First,
Lu stressed that delegated responsibility was essential to efficient
bureaucratic operation. Second, he demanded "that the actual performance correspond to the titles of the [evaluated] officials" to
ensure that the court would have capable officials and the bureaucracy would function effectively. Third, by rejecting Te-tsung's idea
that the chief minister should monopolize the powers of appointment, Lu continued to show no particular interest in enhancing his
own personal power. In his view, his job was "carefully to observe
the rule of examining and evaluating officials, report and praise
intelligent ones, and make certain that due rewards and punishments are meted out without fail so that no one will be passed over
and the court will not lack talented candidates" (18: 5b–6a).

Lu's emphasis on "rewards and punishments" may make him
sound like a Legalist, but this is not unusual.[13] Legalist methods
had been blended with Confucian practices in the imperial government since the Han dynasty. The pre-Ch'in Confucian philosopher
Hsün Tzu even considered "rewards and punishments" indispensable in governing the state, and his theories also contain a streak
of Legalism. The key distinction is that for Lu, just as for Hsün
Tzu, "rewards and punishments" were intended as measures leading to the establishment of a just and capable bureaucracy, not as
devices to reinforce the power of the ruler that all legalists ultimately sought.[14] The legalist goal of elevating the ruler was
most antithetical to Lu Chih's Confucian pragmatist approach to
government.

Either due to his own admiration for Empress Wu's abilities or
to personal considerations, in his final plea Lu urged Te-tsung to

follow her appointment policy.[15] He praised Empress Wu's encouragement of the recommendation method as the reason
many able officials were recruited during her reign. He admitted
that her policy had made official appointments too easy, but
insisted that her critical evaluation of officials had produced an
efficient bureaucracy. Te-tsung was not convinced by Lu's comparison of the benefits and defects of his proposed recommendation system and the one Te-tsung wanted. He still chose to
rescind his previous order of consent, and thus ended Lu's first
reformist proposal.[16]

Reforming the Bureaucracy: Filling Vacant Offices

Lu Chih continued his efforts to improve the bureaucracy despite this setback. In the fifth month of 794, almost exactly
two years after he presented the above memorial, he again set
out to "correct and assist" Te-tsung's appointment and promotion policies. He was motivated by two things: frustration at Te-
tsung's intention to follow some other advisor's suggestion to
allow vacant official posts to remain unfilled, and disagreement
with Te-tsung's slowdown of official transfer and advancement.[17]

Lu first reaffirmed the teaching of the ancient classics that an
ideal ruler should function as a figure head and only rule through
able officials. Within this context, he made it clear that vacant
offices must be filled:

> I have heard from the classics which say: "stately are
> the many officers; King Wen through them enjoys his
> repose;" they also say: "let him not allow his various
> officers to hinder their roles. The work is Heaven's; men
> must act for it!" This tells us that officials must be
> many, and offices must be filled; it also honors the prin-
> ciple of employing people according to their abilities, and
> expounds the practice of holding oneself (the ruler) in a
> respectful posture without interfering. These are the
> reasons for success and failure in governing the state.
> (22: 7a.)[18]

Furthermore, Lu Chih said that there were seven errors currently practiced at court that prevented Te-tsung from obtaining capable officials. They included such things as granting

promotions on the basis of his favorite chief minister's recommendations rather than on his officials' abilities, "not evaluating actual situations, but only searching widely for criticism of his officials," and being too harsh and unfair to his officials, thus reducing the number of capable officials serving at court and promoting opportunistic behavior among those who remained.[19]

Lu Chih contended that Te-tsung's overzealous search for criticisms gave small men (*hsiao-jen*) their chance to attack superior men (*chün-tzu*).[20] *Chün-tzu* and *hsiao-jen* are typical Confucian terms that often carry heavy moral connotations, but *hsiao-jen* in Lu's mind were not necessarily immoral characters. In the 792 memorial discussed above, Lu Chih actually defined *hsiao-jen* as those who "regard preventing discussion as an outstanding thing to do, acting eccentrically as [evidence of] not forming a clique. They only pursue interests close at hand, but neglect [to make] long-term plans; they practice small sincerity but injure the great Way. Thus, the *Analects* say: 'They are determined to be sincere in what they say, and to carry out what they do. They are obstinate little men.' "[21] Accepting Confucius's teaching, Lu believed that the small men's concern was too narrowly focused, and they often obstructed the work of superior men.

Lu Chih called the last and most interesting error "following tradition without considering its feasibility" (22: 9a). Here he specifically focused on the problems of not refilling vacant offices, and delaying official transfer and advancement. Lu shows that the argument for such policies was that they were standard practices in the past. Intending to continue this tradition, Te-tsung particularly called Lu's attention to the fact that his imperial father-in-law had even served in one position for more than ten years during the previous reign; such traditional precedents ought to be observed.[22]

Looking to the past for examples was a universal attitude among Confucian scholars in Lu's time.[23] Lu himself also frequently urged Te-tsung to model himself on the ancient sage kings and to imitate the good rule of Emperor T'ai-tsung and Empress Wu. Why was he now opposed to the continuation of those historical precedents regarding vacant offices and the policy of delayed official advancement? Was he not contradicting his own position of learning from the exemplary rules of the past? His discussion of the last error answers these questions.

Lu Chih first pointed out the implied difference between him and those who advocated not refilling the vacant offices and slowing down official transfer and advancement. He criticized their resort to the past as "reciting platitudes but not making inferences from changes of time [and circumstances]; preserving the dross of the old classics but not basing one's judgment on [the reality of] things" (22: 15b). Opposed to any mechanical imitation of historical standards, Lu implied that the criterion for employing a tradition should be a flexible selection according to circumstances and the changing needs of the times.

To consolidate his argument, Lu then wrote:

In ancient times, since people's habits and customs were simple, there were few official titles; only the able were distinguished from the incompetent. There also were no discussions on seniority and rank order, no demands for effective results in one day, and no disputes based on minute differences in performance....

In recent times, the established offices are gradually increasing, the number of [official] ranks is even more numerous.... they all require regular qualifications that all have to be observed....

In the administration of the three [ancient] dynasties (Hsia, Shang, and Chou), what they added to and what they omitted from [the practices of the past] were different. Surely this was not because they loved to change. It was only because *the times and circumstances forced* them to do so....

Whenever seeking for old precedents, one must distinguish the right ones from the wrong ones. The right ones need not be changed and the wrong ones need not be preserved. Besides, there are differences [caused by] contradictions in the old precedents themselves.

At the beginning of the previous sagely reign (of Te-tsung's father), a dominant minister was in power. He dealt with official appointments mostly according to personal favor. There were frequent promotions within one month, and there were no transfers for many years. By the middle of the reign, ill feelings arose between the ruler and the minister; for the time being, they simply [let things] remain undecided and everything was stagnant. Appointment became even more difficult; at the beginning fairness was lost because of prejudice and partiality; and doubt and distrust followed to block the operation [of the appointment process]. Consequently, the regular order lacked assessment, and [transfer and advancement] of officials were thus hindered. These [defects] should all be corrected. How can they be worthy to serve as [our] models? (22: 15b–19a.)[24]

In this long refutation, Lu Chih makes several interesting points. He indicates that he viewed history as an evolutionary process. He observes that bureaucratic structures evolve from a primitive stage to a much more complex one. Thus, past practices no longer meet the needs of the present. He stresses that the motive force behind this evolutionary change is not the human factor but rather impersonal time and circumstances (*shih-shih*). For Lu, objective conditions sometimes dictate historical development even though human subjective will does not wish it. He allows that not all traditional practices were correct, and there is no point in imitating harmful precedents. They should be critically examined and, if necessary revised, before being applied to current situations.

All this does not necessarily mean that Lu perceived history as a progressive development. It is evident, though, that he recognized that historical standards are changeable. Here we find that his attitude toward traditional practices continues to accord with his accustomed pragmatist sensibility. He was not opposed to learning from the past; he simply insisted that the applicability of past practices depended on their feasibility under present conditions.

Lu urged Te-tsung to take a middle way (*chung-tao*) that neither hastened nor delayed official transfer and advancement. It should be based on consideration of the long and harsh process required for a scholar to enter officialdom for the first time, the common human psychology of sticking to old ways if one remained in the same position too long, and the danger of growing opportunistic if transferred too soon. It would comprise three methods for evaluating and regulating officials: "using elevation and promotion to make manifest those who have unusual abilities"; "using demotion and dismissal to correct those who neglect their duties"; and "using assessment and advancement carefully to [note the records of] those who observe the regular norms" (22: 19a). Lu believed that once this middle way was put into practice, special talents would be recognized and the variously ranked offices would be regulated. In the end, however, Te-tsung again failed to support Lu's suggestions.[25]

Despite these two failures, Lu Chih did succeed in carrying out some bureaucratic reforms during this period. He managed to change the current custom of assembling candidates for official appointments once every three years into an annual practice, thus facilitating a more rapid circulation of official appointments by filling vacant offices with qualified candidates who had been waiting for years.[26] This particular achievement doubtless resulted from imperial consent to his advice that offices should not be left vacant. Still, his original intention to establish a capable and just bureaucratic machine remained largely unfulfilled. In comparison, his efforts to strengthen state power achieved more satisfactory results.

Strengthening the State: Filling the Frontier Granaries

While attempting to reform the bureaucracy, Lu also wanted to reinforce the border defenses. He was aware of Te-tsung's concern with this matter, but his efforts were not in direct response to an imperial call. They were rather a result of his own perception of the urgent problems involved in defending the frontiers. Lu maintained that two things were of paramount importance in establishing a strong border defense: sufficient grain reserves and dependable armed forces.[27]

Before proposing a detailed policy regarding the frontier grain reserves, Lu Chih had tried other reformist measures, but to no avail. He pointed out that Te-tsung had previously relied on the policy of "harmonious purchases [ho-ti]," that is "compulsory purchase of [grain] by the government at high prices" from peasants in the border regions.[28] This policy was intended to encourage grain cultivation in the frontier provinces and subsequently reduce the burden of transporting grain from the interior.[29] Lu believed it to be an effective measure, but he felt its goals had not been realized, mainly because the local officials in charge did not carry out their responsibilities:

> ... the officials in charge of [the harmonious purchases] are narrow and parsimonious; they cannot follow the demands of the times to finish the task; they neglect the [harmonious purchases] plan designed by the government for [emergency] use and practice improper mercantile [activities].

When there is a good harvest and the peasants are willing
to let [the government] purchase their grain, [the officials]
cut down the [purchase] price, and do not gather and store
[the grain] in time; when there is a famine and grain is
difficult to come by, they do not consider the grain shortage
but even make [the peasants continue to] accept harmonious purchases. This gives dominant families and grasping
officials the power to make [large] profits. They buy grain
at cheap prices, wait until the government and the people
are both short of [grain], and then take advantage of the
urgency of the times to sell it at a price ten times higher.

Some close relatives of influential people and some traveling scholars either rely on frontier generals or officials in
charge to make low price [grain] purchases in [frontier]
military towns and sell this grain at high prices in the
capital. There are indeed many such people who make large
profits with very little exertion. (19: 7a-b.)[30]

Such abuses, Lu lamented, not only brought more misery to
the peasants, but reserved little grain for the border provinces. If
any emergency occurred, it would be impossible to sustain the frontier forces. Frustrated by this situation, Lu said that he had asked
Te-tsung to send a special envoy to correct these pernicious practices, but Te-tsung had rejected his plea and insisted that "the most
reasonable thing to do is to follow the [current] practice" (19: 9a).
Lu also suggested increasing the reserves of the military requisi-
tions on the frontier when there were abundant harvests, but the
officials in charge insisted that there was no extra budget for that,
and so his suggestion was passed over. Despite Te-tsung's rejection,
Lu did not give up; he worked out another proposal and eventually
persuaded Te-tsung to put it into practice.

Lu assured Te-tsung that his new plan would "not disturb the
people, not change the [current] practice (the harmonious purchases
of grain), not increase taxes, not require [extra] government money,
not eliminate the [emperor's] entertainments, and not restrain the
amount [usually available] for extra nonessential expenditure"
(19: 9a-b). He obviously understood that if his plan was to gain
imperial support this time, he had to convince Te-tsung that it
would satisfy the court's needs, but would not disturb the
status quo. Lu's new proposal continues his emphasis on the
importance of using the expediency principle in the regulation of

state expenditures, and his pragmatist approach led him to conduct a thorough empirical study of past and current practices, the
harm they did to the general population, and the official abuses
that accompanied them.[31]

The basic idea of Lu's plan was to reduce greatly the annual
amount of grain transported to the capital by water from southern
China and the Ho-nan region because good harvests had already
provided the capital area with a seven-year surplus of grain.[32] After
reducing grain transportation, the government could first sell the
grain thus saved at a reasonably low price (harmonious sale, or *ho-
t'iao*) to victims in flooded provinces. The money obtained from this
sale could be added to the large sum of money to be saved from
reducing transport costs. Altogether the government would obtain
some 1.33 million strings of cash. Lu's final goal was to appropriate
more than 66 percent of this huge sum of money to finance
"harmonious purchases" of grain on the northwest frontier, and use
the rest of the money for the same purpose in the capital.[33] If
everything was carried out in this way, Lu's new proposal would
"not change the current practice," but would continue to rely on the
"harmonious purchases" of grain to fill the border granaries.

Lu Chih believed that his plan could both benefit the peasants
in the capital area and keep the state granary reserves intact
because the grain purchased from the capital area would make up
the grain deficiency caused by the reduced transport. Besides, if
emergencies should occur, the court could continue to rely on the
grain transportation system to obtain the necessary supplies from
the south. At the same time, according to his investigation of the
northwest frontier provinces, his plan could also establish a satisfactory level of grain reserves in those provinces without adding
any extra financial burden to the government. With so many tan-
gible benefits waiting to be garnered, Lu urged Te-tsung not to
miss this Heaven-sent opportunity of establishing grain reserves in
the border provinces.[34]

Lu Chih seems to have been quite confident of the feasibility
of his own policy. He told Te-tsung that his goal was to "obtain one
year's grain (about one million *shih* of grain, according to Lu) for
one hundred thousand soldiers on the frontier for use in times of
urgent difficulty." He even stated that if Te-tsung would truly listen
to his suggestions "without being impeded by slander," he would be
able to accomplish this task within a hundred days.[35] Lu was probably worried that whoever had previously attacked his policy of
reforming the bureaucracy might try to obstruct this one as well.

Nevertheless, his misgivings about possible obstruction turned out to be unnecessary. Te-tsung accepted his policy.

In the ninth month of 792, one month after Lu's memorial, an imperial edict ordered the northwest border provinces to carry out his proposal.[36] Another edict issued in the tenth month of that year states that the border provinces had already stored 330,000 *shih* of grain through the practice of "harmonious purchases." It further mentions that the funds for those purchases were allocated from the transportation cost savings.[37] It is very likely that Te-tsung rendered Lu his full support in this particular policy, and that the intended goal was achieved within a mere eight months. Also, just as Lu promised, no new burdens were added to the regular state expenditures.[38]

As effective as Lu's policy proved to be, it does not seem to have endured very long. In the autumn of 794, two years after this policy was put into practice, Lu Chih already had to present another memorial requesting that Te-tsung not allow the officials in charge on the frontier to use the grain reserves for regular monthly military provisions. He was not opposed to any emergency appropriation; after all, that was the purpose of his policy. What he was opposed to was leaving those granaries empty afterwards.[39] Lu's suggestion probably went for naught; he fell from power at the end of that year.

In any case, through the continuing application of his expediency principle, Lu Chih designed a policy that, for a short while, conspicuously benefited the border granaries. After this accomplishment, he was more than ready to tackle the problem of frontier defense.

Strengthening the State: Building Dependable Frontier Armies

In a memorial of 793, Lu said that from his reading of history he had learned all the strong and weak points of nearly every border defense method applied in the past to deal with the neighboring "barbarians." He divided these methods into five categories. He also indicated that none of these methods was as flawless as its advocates usually claimed. Those who argued for transforming the "uncultivated" through virtue did not realize that "if authority was not established, then virtue [alone] could not tame [them]." Those who preferred to suppress them by military force were unaware that "if virtue was not cultivated, then force [alone] could not be relied upon." And those who supported marriage alliances between Han Chinese and foreigners did not know that "we make the alliances but they break them" (21: 3b). He was well aware that marriage alliances with the "barbarians" were not intended to establish genuine friendship, but were only a convenient device to please the "barbarians" and avoid invasion.

Lu Chih's intention was to show that these methods all had certain valuable aspects, but their actual effects varied in different historical contexts because some rulers insisted on practicing certain measures while neglecting to consider their feasibility, and

> this was due to clinging to normal principles to manage unusual circumstances; [being] used to what one has seen [before], but ignorant of the times one lives in. The middle kingdom has its [times of] prosperity and decline; barbarians [also] have their ups and downs; there are good and bad opportunities, and there are safe and dangerous arrangements. Thus, there is no definite rule, and there is no method that will always win. (21: 5a-b.)

As always with Lu, rules and methods should be tested against the objective background of different times and circumstances.

From Lu's perspective, there was no perfect plan for managing "barbarian" affairs, but he still asserted that there was one general principle that should be followed:

> If [the emperor] employs talented people and follows the multitude then [the state] will definitely be preserved, [but] if [he] employs the wrong people and indulges in his own desires, then [the state] will definitely fail. . . . this is the one [constant principle] that underlies all [other] principles of affairs. (21: 9a.)[40]

Lu Chih's ultimate criteria were to employ the right people and make the public welfare the first priority. Only with these preconditions, could one decide which defense methods would be most appropriate to contemporary circumstances.

After clarifying his basic understanding of border defense issues, Lu Chih stated there were six problems that rendered the current T'ang border armies insufficient in defending the state.[41] Although contemporary defense strategy tried to take possible objective factors into consideration, these six deficiencies (*liu-shih*) prevented it from achieving its goals. All six came about through failure to pay attention to the requirements of time and circumstance, or lack of consideration for the ordinary human feelings of the frontier soldiers.

One of two related deficiencies was the problem of increasing the numbers of military governors in frontier provinces, and having them inspected by eunuch supervisors, thus weakening their command authority. The other was not granting the frontier generals the power to make on-the-spot decisions. As we recall, Lu voiced similar criticisms in 784, and in 792 he also protested against the dispatch of eunuch supervisors and blamed these two related problems for causing the border forces to be defeated by the Tibetans.[42] He now argued that the Tibetans constituted the strongest threat to the T'ang because they had a single and unified command while the T'ang command labored under various restraints. Lu singled out some of these restrains this way:

> [The court] divided the Shuo-fang region, and gave military commands to three [new] provincial governors. The number of the other generals also reached forty; they all received a commission by special edict, and [the court] sent eunuchs to inspect and supervise each one of them; [these generals and eunuchs] contend with each other and do not obey each other's instructions. [The court] orders [the generals] to meet and arrange military attacks only after receiving a notice from the frontier asking for emergency help. Since there is no chain of command from above, [our] generals treat each other with only normal courtesy [as equals]. This is just like trying to save the drowning without exertion, or rescue the burning by bowing complaisantly to each other; it would certainly be very difficult to hope to avoid grave danger [in this manner]. (21: 19b–20b.)[43]

Lu intended to show how increasing the number of frontier generals without establishing a commander-in-chief paralyzed their combat ability, and sending eunuchs as army supervisors introduced another source of contention for power that impeded the generals' willingness to take any active initiative.

As in 784 , Lu reminded Te-tsung that decisions made at court could only impede his field commanders' willingness to engage the enemy in the best possible manner:

Recently decisions relating to the frontier armies have mostly been made by your majesty. When selecting and appointing military officials, [you] first sought those who were easily controlled; [you] lessened their powers by dividing their troops into many sections; and [you] weakened their minds by reducing their responsibilities. This corrected [previous mistakes], but it also produced some drawbacks. It has led to the elimination of the principle of instructing them to fulfill their delegated responsibilities; to a decline in their determination to risk the responsibility of blame or their lives should they fail in their assignments. . . .

When two powerful armies meet and come to a stalemate, the arrival of an opportunity demands immediate action; . . . The barbarians' fast riding and sudden attack is as quick as a whirlwind, but the postal courier's report only reaches [the throne] ten days or a month later. Those who guard the territory do not dare fight the enemy because they only have a few troops; those who share their command will not attack because they do not receive an imperial order. . . .

After the brigands have plundered to their hearts' content and withdrawn, [our] generals [simply] relate their own meritorious deeds and report a victory. They reduce every hundred of their dead and wounded to one while they exaggerate every hundred of whatever they seize to a thousand. Since those generals rejoice that the chief [power to] command is in the court, they are not worried about being punished. Your majesty also thinks that the important power [and responsibility] resides with you and you do not investigate the whole affair. Managing military forces in this manner means losing an opportunity due to the remoteness of command. (21: 22b–24a.)

Lu Chih knew full well that Te-tsung's intention was to prevent any particular frontier general from amassing too much

power and becoming a threat to the court's security. Still Lu felt
the need to remind him that such measures could no longer properly accomplish the task of defending the frontiers; the present
time and circumstances demanded a different approach to this
problem. Since both Te-tsung's concern and Lu Chih's criticism were
justifiable, they were facing a genuine dilemma.

Lu's way out of this dilemma was to take every possible pre-
ventive measure beforehand. He suggested that whenever the court
planned to select generals and commanders, it should first examine
their conduct and abilities. After instructing them what their future tasks would be, they should be required to make a self-assess-
ment in which they had to estimate whether or not they were
capable of such tasks. If they felt they were, they should state how
they were going to accomplish these tasks, by what means and
within how much time they thought they could achieve their goals.
The court would in turn evaluate their designs and devices and
examine their feasibility.[44]

At this time, Lu Chih went on, the court could select the proper
candidates based on their demonstrated talents. If they failed to
measure up, they should be rejected right at the beginning, so the
court would not have to worry about them in the future. Once they
were actually appointed, they should be entrusted with delegated
power without being under suspicion. Only then, Lu believed, could
"[the court] examine their judgments, and carry out rewards and
punishments. Those who receive rewards will not consider them
indiscriminate; those who deserve punishments will be unable to
find excuses [to get out of them]. Since the power of commission is
concentrated [on them], naturally they will no longer act in a merely
perfunctory manner" (21: 22b).

The four other deficiencies that Lu said existed side by side
with these two related problems were the inappropriate dispatch of inland forces (chiefly from the Ho-nan and Chiang-huai
regions) to guard the frontier; the court's failure to conduct a
fair evaluation of frontier generals; exhaustion of the court's
finances by continuously increasing the number of troops; and
unequal treatment between inland troops dispatched to the
frontier, frontier troops claiming to be subordinate to the palace
armies, and the regular frontier troops.[45]

Lu was opposed to sending troops alternately from southern
provinces to defend the border because these troops could hardly
adjust to the severe climate and crude living conditions on the
northwest frontier. Moreover, stationed regularly in inland prov-

inces, they had never experienced an imminent threat of foreign invasion and were frightened by their new mission. Since the court treated them like spoiled children, and did not encourage them to accomplish their mission or warn them of punishments to follow if they failed, they started to calculate their day of return as soon as they arrived on the frontier. Lu lamented that this not only weakened morale, but was also a stumbling block in the event of actual combat.[46]

Lu pointed out the problems caused by the failure of the court's frontier evaluation policies:

> When the court intends to reward a general for his merit, it worries that those who have [demonstrated] no merit will rebel; when it intends to punish a general for committing a crime, it again worries that those who committed the same crime will become anxious. Because of tolerance and covering up, crimes are not made known; because of jealousy and suspicion, merits are not rewarded; the practice of appeasement has actually gone this far. It therefore causes those who neglect their own lives and devote themselves to the court to be ridiculed by their peers; those who lead their troops to advance first to be resented by their subordinates; those who lose their troops and endanger the state to feel no guilt or fear; and those who are slow in rescue and fail [to arrive on] time to consider themselves intelligent and capable.... This is why loyal officers feel sick at heart, and brave ones have become demoralized. (21:16a–17a.)

Lu Chih's discontent with Te-tsung's policy for dealing with the frontier armies is clear. His emphasis on using rewards and punishments to evaluate frontier generals, like his insistence on applying them to assess civil officials, was not intended to strengthen imperial power. Rather, it was oriented toward establishing a system in which Te-tsung would have to operate fairly and justly so that both civil and military officials would not feel alienated and would willingly carry out their duties for the court.

Under the prevailing conditions, exhausting the court's finances was almost unavoidable, because, as Lu Chih saw it, Te-tsung did not investigate the actual situation when frontier reports claimed a lack of sufficient troops. He simply levied more taxes and enlisted more conscripts. As a result, "villages and towns are drained and the court's levies are increased day by day" (21: 17b), creating an unnecessary and wasteful burden on both the public and the court.

Lu Chih's criticism of the unequal treatment between different troops stationed on the frontier reminds us of his reflections on Li Huai-kuang's similarly motivated 784 revolt. Lu does not seem to have made any comments then, but now that the same situation was occurring among the frontier armies, he wanted to establish a fair system of evaluation to avoid another revolt.[47] Under such a system, "the able ones will try to reach [the prescribed standard]; the incompetent ones will rest their mind [at what they can reach]; and although there will be a difference between high and low, there will be no strife due to discontent" (21: 20b). For Lu, actual individual performance was his consistent standard for advancement or demotion for both civil and military personnel.

Of the six problems dealing with frontier defense Lu Chih raised, he urged Te-tsung to correct three of them first. He believed that establishing a single and unified command, entrusting field commanders with the power to make on-the-spot decisions, and setting up military agricultural colonies (*t'un-t'ien*) to substitute volunteer soldiers for troops sent from inland provinces as the basis of the frontier armies were the most urgent tasks for the time being. Only after these priority missions were accomplished, could the other three deficiencies be dealt with.[48]

Lu Chih's criticisms and suggestions were well received by Te-tsung, but they were not put into practice.[49] Te-tsung might have been deeply concerned with the efficiency of his frontier armies, but, as Lu himself noticed, appeasement was now his policy toward frontier generals. Since Lu's suggestions for selecting trustworthy generals to lead the frontier armies could not guarantee their loyalty, it seems inevitable that Te-tsung would choose to maintain the status quo on the frontier rather than risk any uncertain consequences. Te-tsung's appeasement policy brought an end to Lu Chih's efforts at reforming the frontier armies.

It may also have cost the court an opportunity, toward the end of 793, to restore its control over the Hsüan-wu military governor stationed in Pien-chou (in modern Honan). When general Li Wan-jung expelled the unpopular governor, Liu Shih-ning, and seized military power himself, Lu Chih argued that Te-tsung should not simply accept Li as deputy governor (*Liu-hou*), but seize this opportunity and send his own capable appointee as governor of that region. He warned that a policy of appeasement would only encourage other men like Li to usurp other governorships. With the court no longer threatened by rebellion, Lu believed that no time could be more appropriate than the present to restore its authority over this region. Haunted by the experience of his previous exile, however, Te-tsung was not willing to risk his present stability for the sake of any unpredictable results. He refused to accept Lu's suggestion and the court was subsequently in no position to put the Hsüan-wu region under its control. Another military revolt eventually broke out there in 799.[50]

It is clear that as chief minister Lu Chih continued to apply the same Confucian pragmatist approach to government, and its core remained both moralistic and pragmatic.

Compared with his success at storing grain reserves in the border provinces, Lu Chih's suggestions for improving the efficiency of the frontier armies failed to gain imperial support. Te-tsung sanctioned Lu's plan to correct the system of grain reserves, and make certain improvements, but only if they did not disturb the status quo.

Operating within such constraints, it is not surprising that Lu's policies to reform the bureaucracy and strengthen the power of the state achieved only limited success. This again manifests the crucial role of the emperor. Even though Lu Chih was now the head of the bureaucracy, and even though he continued to employ the same Confucian pragmatist approach to government, Te-tsung still monopolized the ultimate decision-making power. In exile, Te-tsung had generally followed Lu's suggestions, but now his main concern with preserving the present stability allowed Lu, or any other chief minister for that matter, very little room to pursue reformist policies. Nonetheless, Lu Chih did not think of quitting. He still wanted to correct some abuses in the current tax system. Only this time he spoke not for the bureaucracy nor for the state, but on behalf of the common people.

CHAPTER SIX

A Lone Pursuit

Lu Chih's efforts to improve the material well-being of the common people were closely related both to his financial policies and to his continuous attempt to transform Te-tsung's conduct.

The People's Welfare: Background

There is no question that Lu's successful measure for storing grain reserves in the border provinces, just like his earlier suggestion to abolish emergency taxes, involved his concern for the people's welfare. This concern is also apparent in some of the imperial edicts he drafted during the second Ho-pei rebellion, a time when his advice often formed the basis of Te-tsung's policy decisions. For example, Lu's sympathy for the common people is reflected in this vivid description of their suffering:

> [People] are hard pressed by famine and starvation; they are distressed and worried and have nothing to depend upon. Some of them depart from their villages and become employed as workers; some of them become beggars on the road and die of exhaustion; their villages and towns are still there, but the smoke of [cooking] fires (human activities) has already disappeared. (4: 11b.)[1]

Lu's systematic plans for alleviating such popular misery only fully materialized in the middle of 794 with his well-known memorial suggesting some crucial financial reforms focused on improving the two-tax system (*liang-shui fa*), introduced a decade and a half

119

earlier to replace the old *tsu-yung-tiao* system.[2] His concern for the common people's plight led him to propose these reforms and his ultimate goal was to relieve their heavy tax burdens, not simply to increase government income. Even the title, "On making taxation equitable and thus showing pity for the common people,"[3] indicates his primary aspiration. But what was the two-tax system and why did it replace the old system?

The old *tsu-yung-tiao* system was a complex of head taxes levied on individual adult males throughout the T'ang empire from 618 to 780. A properly functioning *chün-t'ien* or equal field system, a state-controlled system of land tenure and allocation, was the necessary prerequisite for implementing such a system. It was assumed that each taxpayer received an equal land allotment, and the taxes were levied at a uniform rate without considering economic realities in different regions. There was a tax in grain (*tsu*), a tax in kind (*tiao*) paid in cloth and a *yung* tax that was a *corvée* exemption tax—hence the name *tsu-yung-tiao*.[4] The system was established for two reasons: to prohibit land accumulation and any illegal private land ownership, and more important, to maintain a stable source of revenue for the state.

Due to the close connection between the *chün-t'ien* and the *tsu-yung-tiao* systems, if the former collapsed, the latter would certainly be ruined as well. This was exactly what happened in the mid-T'ang. The problems of land shortage, land accumulation, vagrancy and staff shortages as well as corruption of the T'ang local administrative apparatus all contributed to the collapse of the *chün-t'ien* system; after the An Lu-shan rebellion destroyed the registration system, it became virtually impossible to enact.[5] As a result, the *tsu-yung-tiao* taxation also lost its raison d'être even though it continued to function in theory.

Long before the complete breakdown of the *tsu-yung-tiao* system, the T'ang government began to rely on various supplementary taxes, such as the household levy (*hu-shui*) and the land levy (*ti-shui*). The T'ang court also depended on various irregular taxes that both increased the tax burden on the general population and created a chaotic tax structure. After the An Lu-shan rebellion broke out, the government levied a tax on liquor and, most importantly, on salt to support its onerous military expenses. As noted above, the power of the salt commissioners gradually began to undermine the authority of the regular central financial institutions.[6]

When Te-tsung ascended the throne, he encouraged concerned officials like Yang Yen to work out a tax reform proposal to help restore central authority. Yang Yen's tax proposal was intended to do just that, and, at the same time, maintain a stable revenue for the state. It was very welcome to the throne. Against this background the two-tax system replaced the bankrupt *tsu-yung-tiao* system in 780.

Under the two-tax system, taxpayers had only two basic liabilities—the household levy and the land levy.[7] The household levy was a tax levied on a graduated scale of wealth and property. In addition, it now made all households rather than individuals the tax unit to prevent vagrants, landless townsmen, or traveling merchants from evading their tax shares. The land levy, a tax on all lands under actual cultivation, also forced great landowners to pay their taxes. This new system, in short, not only enlarged the tax base, but also established a form of progressive taxation.

The land levy fixed the rates of assessment in terms of grain, as was the previous practice, and the household levy still continued to employ cash for both tax assessment and tax payment. The government demanded payment in cash, but the household levy was often paid in goods. These taxes continued to be paid according to local conditions in two separate annual installments—once in summer and once in autumn, hence the name *liang-shui*.

Although the central government had to negotiate with local authorities,[8] the implementation of the two-tax system finally provided the court with a regular and practical way to receive fixed tax revenues from the provinces, even from those where it had little real authority. Te-tsung had abandoned the idea of reviving the central authority after the second Ho-pei rebellion, but the financial stability promised by this tax reform eventually contributed to a rejuvenation of the T'ang court under Hsien-tsung. The two-tax system, furthermore, continued to serve as the basic system of taxation until the late sixteenth century.

When the two-tax system was launched in the second month of 780, Lu Chih made his first surviving comment on financial administration: the government should "set tax standards according to agricultural crop inspection results, levy taxes based on property assessments, calculate the payment of a *corvée* exemption (*yung*) according to an estimate of the number of adult males, and equalize profits based on levies from merchants" (HTS, 157: 4911).[9] On the whole, Lu's suggestions for tax levies do not seem to contradict the principle of the two-tax system. He did not advocate a uniform rate of taxation, but allowed flexibility for local government. Nevertheless, his advocacy of the *yung* tax certainly was not included in the two-tax system. It seems that from the beginning Lu did not completely agree with the new system.

Because the 785 Act of Grace and Amnesty favoring the two-tax system was drafted by Lu Chih, we might assume that he agreed with the imperial position that it represented an improvement in fiscal administration. Even if he did, this document also points out that due to the Ho-pei rebellion, the two-tax system had been abused by corrupt officials:

> Formerly taxes were both onerous and multifarious, so that the people were hardly able to survive. Once they were combined into the *liang-shui*, quotas were established that were easy to follow. When the rising of the armies ensued, the original assessments were overstepped, and the letter of the law was not adhered to. Petty officials became increasingly corrupt and caused trouble to our people.
>
> The [people] should now be allowed some respite. All levies and labor services, except for the *liang-shui*, that have been instituted in provinces and prefectures under various circuits on an emergency basis must be abolished. (2: 6a-b.)[10]

A later Act of Grace and Amnesty drafted by Lu and promulgated in the eleventh month of 785 also states that abuses of the two-tax system occurred even at the beginning when tax quotas were negotiated between the court and local authorities.[11] It would seem that by the end of 785, if Lu Chih had not yet conceived of any concrete ideas for improving the two-tax system, he was at least conscious of the suffering these abuses caused the people.

Two years later, at the end of 787, peasants in the capital area still complained bitterly about the court's failure to relieve them from the heavy burden of taxation. In the twelfth month of that year, Te-tsung went hunting near the capital. Visiting a commoner's home, he asked him why he was not happy since this was a year of particularly good harvests, and the man replied:

> The edict's instructions are not trustworthy. Formerly it said that there would be no other tax levies except for the *liang-shui*; now the court's endless exorbitant demands already exceed the [regular] taxes. Later the edict also said to practice *ho-ti*, but this was equal to procuring our grain

by force, and we have never seen one cent. . . . We are impoverished and can no longer bear any more.

Distressed and hard-pressed like this, how can I be happy? Whenever there are edicts proclaiming special relief for us, they are mere scraps of paper. I'm afraid my sagely lord deeply secluded in the nine levels of Heaven (the palace) is totally unaware of these things. (TCTC, 233: 7508.)

Te-tsung ordered a tax exemption for this man, but did nothing to improve the overall situation.

As modern scholars point out and Lu himself noted, the two-tax system was put into operation during very unfortunate times.[12] Besides those problems already mentioned, from 780 to 786 T'ang China was in the last phase of a period of growing inflation that began around 763. Then it went through a stage of progressive deflation that lasted from 786 until almost 850. The inflation was no doubt mainly caused by the An Lu-shan rebellion, and the almost seventy-year-long deflation was caused by a combination of factors such as a fall in grain prices, a government reduction of copper coinage, a growing demand for cash money to conduct trade, and an outflow of copper cash to foreign countries. With all this, the launching of the two-tax system also seems to have played a major role in triggering the deflation.[13]

The interaction between inflation, deflation, and the two-tax system had a severe impact on the common people because when the tax quotas and tax rates were first assessed for the household levy in 780, they were fixed according to an over-inflated currency. After the problem of cash shortage intensified, the common people had no choice but to pay their household levies in goods, especially in silk cloth, and the government subsequently had to accept this as a compromise arrangement. When deflation began after 786, the government failed to readjust the previously fixed rates. This failure inevitably forced the people to pay out more and more goods to meet the tax demands.[14]

Operating under such unfortunate circumstances, it would be unfair to maintain, as Lu Chih later implied, that the two-tax system was inferior to the previous *tsu-yung-tiao* system. After all, at the beginning of its operation, the two-tax system brought in a sizable revenue for the state.[15] The practice of this system over time created abuses that greatly threatened the common people's welfare, and concerned criticism would seem to have been unavoidable. This was the context within which Lu attacked the two-tax system and proposed to reform it.

The People's Welfare: Reforming the Two-Tax System

Lu Chih's general criticism of the two-tax system was that its initial conception was problematic and its subsequent operation was careless. By contrast, he maintained that the previous *tsu-yung-tiao* tax system had more humane qualities. He believed that under the old system taxpayers were not taxed unless the state had first granted them a certain proportion of land.[16] Such a claim betrays Lu's misconception or idealization of the *tsu-yung-tiao* system, but it also reveals his position on taxation.[17] Apparently, he believed that taxation should be based on the premise that the state first ought to make certain that its people had some taxable resources. As he saw it:

> The purpose of establishing the state and its offices is to nourish the people; the purpose of taxing the people and obtaining wealth from them is to assist the state. An enlightened ruler will not increase what assists the state and harm what the state nourishes (the people). Therefore, he should first [let the people take care of] their affairs and then employ their strength when they have leisure; [first] ensure each family is provided for and then tax their surplus wealth. (23:40a.)

Lu's emphasis on the people's welfare as the first priority of the state continues to reflect his basic Confucian conception of an ideal government; he endorsed the Mencian idea of the importance of providing constant means of support for the people.[18] He believed the two-tax system failed to come up to the standard implicit in this Confucian ideal.

While vaguely acknowledging that the two-tax system had ameliorated some old imperfections, Lu Chih quickly pointed out that new and graver problems were nevertheless created. The situation was similar to "[making] a complete paralytic of a man who was before only lame" (23: 4b). In Lu's view, because the commissioners who were sent to negotiate the tax quotas with local authorities in 780 decided to "use the highest annual tax rate in each province during the Ta-li period as the fixed quota for the two-tax system" (23:6b), it failed completely to relieve the heavy exactions on the common people. Lu asked rhetorically, "Isn't it a case of incorrect conception to create a law but not take relieving and enriching the people as its foundation?" (23: 7a).[19]

Lu was most critical of the fact that the government never dealt with inequalities involved in the assessment of the household levy. Theoretically it was assessed according to a progressive rate, but, as Lu made clear, since the officials in charge did not bother to discover the actual values of different types of property, false assessments and gross inequalities were unavoidable.[20] The consequences of this were serious:

> Therefore, those who range over the land and traffic in commerce are often able to escape their share of the tax burden while those who devote themselves to the basic vocation [of agriculture] and establish fixed abodes are constantly harassed by [ever-increasing] demands. This amounts to tempting the people to engage in evil doing [to circumvent the tax law] and forcing them to avoid the corveé. It is inevitable that productivity should decline and morals deteriorate, depression come to the villages and towns, and the tax collections decrease. (23:8a–b.)[21]

Lu Chih also criticized the court for its failure to levy taxes in accordance with local differences, an ironic situation since that was precisely what the two-tax system called for. The new tax quotas were based on the highest annual rate during the Ta-li period, while the 20 percent increase in tax quotas caused by the rebellions in each province had become permanent. In Lu's view, these arrangements completely ignored the differential impact the military uprisings had on various localities and neglected the different demands and needs of those regions.

Under these conditions, even heavier emigrations occurred from those provinces where the residents had previously been taxed on the basis of high tax assessments. This in turn made the tax load much more onerous for the remaining residents because they still had to share the same tax quota. By contrast, the tax burden of the residents in those regions where the previous tax rate had been low grew lighter when newly arrived immigrants helped to share the tax quota. As a result, the distribution of the tax burden became increasingly inequitable.[22]

To make Te-tsung understand how much misery this new tax system had brought to the common people, Lu Chih delineated a series of abuses involved in its actual operation.[23] For example, he reiterated the losses the common people suffered due to the interaction of inflation and deflation:

> Previously, paying one roll of silk cloth [for taxes] was equal to three thousand and two or three hundred cash; nowadays, paying one roll of silk cloth is equal to one thousand and five or six hundred cash. What was one in the past has become two or more now. The government has not increased the tax rate, but the people already pay double taxes. (23: 10b.)

Further abuses arose from the fact that all sorts of other taxes were superimposed on top of the original land and household taxes. These included double taxation on land: once being assessed the regular land tax and again being subject to the household tax.[24] The provincial *tribute goods* for Te-tsung's private treasuries were an added burden for the local people. Lu sharply reminded Te-tsung that these "gorgeous ornaments and an abundance of fine white silk fabrics do not grow out of the earth, nor do they fall from Heaven, if they are not [extracted] from the hard labor and the flesh and blood of the people, where can [provincial governors] obtain them?" (23: 11a).

Lu was trying to persuade Te-tsung to stop accepting provincial tribute goods for his private treasuries so that local authorities could lessen their irregular levies on the people, and he strongly implied that imperial thrift would greatly relieve Te-tsung's subjects from these heavy tax burdens.

To illustrate this point of view , Lu Chih again cited a passage from the *Analects* in which Confucius's disciple Yu Jo advised Duke Ai of Lu to tax his people at the light rate of 10 percent. When the Duke responded that he did not have sufficient revenue at his current rate of 20 percent, Yu Jo replied that "when the people have enough, how can you not have enough? When the people do not have enough, how can you have enough?" (23: 12b).[25] Lu obviously supported the basic Confucian principle of light taxation, but his purpose here was also to remind Te-tsung that he should place the people's well-being before his concern with the size of his private treasuries.[26]

Lu Chih's suggestions for reform of the two-tax system aimed only at correcting the most damaging measures involved in its operation. Conscious that he could only try out reform measures within the limits of the existing two-tax system approved of by Te-tsung, he did not intend to launch an overall reform. While assuring Te-tsung that all these suggestions would neither disturb the people nor change the current system, he continued to push the limits to bring forth more corrective measures to that system. For instance, to prevent the common people from suffering further financial losses caused by a depreciation in the value of tax goods, he made the seemingly regressive request that the throne substitute rolls of cloth for cash money as the unit for assessing tax quotas.[27] Considering the contemporary conditions of deflation, however, Lu's suggestion may very well have represented a practical adjustment to relieve the people.[28]

Promising that he would not make radical changes in the two-tax system, Lu also proposed that the court and local authorities negotiate new tax quotas.[29] With these revised quotas, local populations could pay their taxes in silk or other types of cloth without worrying about losses caused by deflation. Lu said the result would be that

> when the value of goods becomes very low, the goods paid by the people will not increase; when the value becomes very high, the taxes received by the government will not decrease. Thus, each family will be provided for and the state will have a sufficiency; conditions will be equitable and the laws will be carried out. (23: 24a.)

Lu Chih stressed that he was only restoring some measures of the previous *tsu-yung-tiao* system, not inventing a new system to correct the defects in present tax practices. It is apparent, however, that this revised plan, intended to abolish the use of cash money as the basic unit of tax assessment, would undermine one of the most important changes caused by the two-tax system. Lu knew that he would be challenged and he listed some answers to possible criticisms, such as that abolishing cash as a basic unit of tax assessment would eliminate a reliable method of government accounting, or that the government would not have enough cash to conduct "harmonious purchases" of grain.[30] The first would not become a major problem because the biggest expenses of the government, such as military provisions and clothing, had always been paid for in goods. Lu's terse reply to the second was that the government controlled the minting of money and had the power to manipulate the amount of cash to stabilize the prices of goods.

A third possible criticism was more serious because Te-tsung might agree with it. Some officials might argue that even though the two-tax system had brought an increase to the state treasury, the government still felt itself in want; if the tax income was to remain approximately the same, how could the government sustain its annual expenditures?[31] Lu's answer reveals again his fundamental position on taxation. From his point of view, those who might present such an argument showed no sympathy for the people precisely because the revenue increase brought by the two-tax system was at the expense of the people's welfare. Furthermore, since the government still felt itself in want under the conditions of abundant harvest and relative peace prevailing in recent years, then even if tax levies were increased again, the result would be the same. Lu argued that the best solution was to eliminate all unnecessary and excessive expenses. He believed that only when the government knew how to be frugal could it have a sufficiency. Besides reemphasizing the passage in the *Analects* regarding the Confucian position on taxation, Lu expressed his own point of view in recognizably modern terms:

> As for growing things, soil fertility has a definite extreme; and for making things, human power has an utmost limit. If a limit is set on taking, and spending is restrained, then there will always be a sufficiency, but if there is no limit on taking and no restraint on spending, then there will always be a deficit.

> It is for Heaven to decide the abundance or failure of growing things, but it is for human beings to control the amount of things for use.

> Thus, the sage kings established the rule of *measuring expenditure by income*, so even though they encountered calamities, the people would not become impoverished. Since [their] rule and [their] teachings have declined, things have become just the opposite: *measuring income by expenditure*. There is no sympathy for the people who have nothing. (23: 30a-b, emphasis added.)

Lu Chih's refutation of these three possible criticisms shows him to be an advocate of frugal government managed according to the Confucian principle of benevolence. Because "measuring income by expenditure" was the operational principle of the two-tax system, and because Lu's criticism was that this very principle threatened the people's welfare, his reasons for disagreeing with this system are thus quite clear.[32] Lu sought what he believed to be the most realistic solution to this contemporary problem due precisely to the harm it did to the common people.[33]

The People's Welfare: Appropriating the Tea Tax

Around the middle of 794, Lu proposed two more important plans to ameliorate the economic plight of the common people. First, he pleaded with Te-tsung to allow the annual tea tax to be used as a fund for "harmonious purchases" of grain to fill the relief granaries and reduce the death toll during times of famine.[34]

Lu had repeatedly spoken about the disastrous impact military revolts and severe tax exactions had on the people, and his descriptions of the people's suffering during times of drought and flood explain why he considered it imperative to fill the relief granaries:

> Whenever unseasonable weather occurs and the annual harvest fails to be adequate, the government's stock of grain is only enough for military provisions. If supplies remain deficient, the government has to take still more from the people; how can it relieve the people from a severe famine?

> When the people suffer from small deficiencies, they only seek a loan with interest; when they suffer from extreme exhaustion, they sell their land and houses. If fortunately they happen to have a year of good harvest, they can pay their debts. If the harvest is just completed and their stock of grain is already depleted, they will then hold the [old] IOUs in their hands, carry bags on their shoulders, and go borrowing [grain] again. While their loan interests are calculated one on top of another, they still frequently lack sufficient food.

> If a severe famine occurs, they are forced to drift from place to place; husbands and wives desert each other, and parents and children separate. They plead to be slaves and servants but still cannot get themselves sold. Some of them drift as beggars in the villages and some of them hang themselves by the roads.

When natural calamities occur, some places always suffer. I estimated the number of victimized places and often found it to be around ten or twenty prefectures each year. If your majesty were to see those victimized prefectures in your capacity as the people's parent, you would certainly have great sympathy for them; and if there is fortunately a way to rescue them, how can you discard it without thinking about it?

Now the tax exactions are already numerous; man power is already exhausted; bad harvests never end and there is never a surplus. Driving the people out to gather grain will never succeed. Establishing a foundation for saving [grain] is a task that has to be achieved through the government's assistance. (23: 44b–45a.)

This long statement full of detailed observation is illustrative of Lu's acute awareness of the common people's lives. He frankly pointed out that it was impossible to fill the granaries by levying another tax on the people, and that it was the government's duty to store more relief grain. He probably knew that Te-tsung did not intend to make any concrete improvements and so he told him that he could accomplish the task of saving more grain without cutting into the government's regular expenditures, but by using the tea tax as a fund for "harmonious purchases" of grain.[35] This would do more than just help the government fill its relief granaries. Since the tea tax was to be used to purchase grain from the peasants when there was a surplus, it would also protect the peasants from huge losses by stabilizing grain prices.

The imposition of a tax on the tea merchants was earlier proposed to the throne in 792 by Salt Commissioner Chang P'ang, and was carried out at the beginning of 793.[36] Chang's intention was to use the tea tax to make up for the revenue losses incurred due to the emergency policy of reducing the regular tax load on flood victims in the summer of 792. Chang also suggested that the tea tax could be used for future relief purposes.[37] Given that Lu Chih was the one who had requested Te-tsung to relieve flood victims by reducing their tax load in 792, and that Chang's proposal could both balance the government's revenues and benefit the people in the future, Lu had every reason to support it.[38] Knowing the background of the imposition of the tea tax, we can understand why Lu Chih had to inform Te-tsung specifically that his request to use the tea tax as a fund for filling the relief granaries would not contradict the intended purpose of this tax.[39]

The People's Welfare:
Reducing the Gap between Rich and Poor

The second proposal Lu made at this time was also his last financial reform proposal aimed at improving the lives of the poor. It dealt with the problem of the disparity between rich and poor which, according to Lu, was primarily due to an excess accumulation of land by the rich.[40] He wanted to restrict the rich landlords' exploitation of the poor peasants, but had no intention to ruin the rich.

Lu Chih believed on principle that "families that live on official emoluments must not contend for profits with the common people" (23: 46a). He noted that this principle had unfortunately been violated both in previous dynasties and during the T'ang.[41] Members of the official bureaucracy and of the imperial clans had joined in a contention for land that brought great harm to the poor. In Lu's view, the situation surrounding land accumulation was growing even worse during his time. This was mainly because the *chün-t'ien* system had completely broken down, greatly exacerbating the problem of excess land accumulation.[42]

Besides their excessive land holding, Lu particularly indicated that it was the extraordinarily heavy rent collected by the rich that led to the huge gap between rich and poor:

> The rich accumulate land up to several tens of thousands of *mou* (1 *mou* is about 0.133 acres) while the poor have no shelter for their bodies. They subject themselves to the powerful families and function as their private chattel. They borrow seeds and food from the rich, rent their huts in the fields, and serve diligently all year round without a single day of rest to pay back all they have borrowed, and still they constantly worry about not having enough. The families who own the fields simply sit idle and live on rent. This is how much the extreme disparity between rich and poor has grown.
>
> The heavy rents charged by the rich and their forced deadlines for rent [payment] are worse than the government levies. At present within the metropolitan region, the government

taxes five *sheng* for one *mou* of arable land, but the rent charged by private families reaches to nearly one *shih* for one *mou;* this is twenty times higher than the government levy. Even at the middle [landlord] range, the rent is still half the above amount; that is [still] ten times more than the government levy. (23: 47b–48a.)[43]

Eager to correct this injustice being inflicted on the poor, and recognizing that the *chün-t'ien* system could not be restored, Lu was forced to find a solution that would be more pertinent to the present time and circumstances.[44]

His suggestion was to place all the land occupied by the rich under government regulation. This was to be accomplished by limiting the land holdings of the rich land owners and forcing them to lower their rents. He insisted that this rent reduction must be regulated in such a way that it would both benefit the poor and preserve the rich. He said that this measure would "slightly harm those who have a surplus and slightly favor those who do not have enough, [but] while the harm done will not make the rich lose their wealth, the benefit given will nonetheless aid the poor" (23: 48b). In Lu's view, this was an absolutely correct way for "pacifying the rich and relieving the poor (*an-fu hsü-p'in*)" (23: 48b), two goals of benevolent government recommended in the *Chou li* classic (*The Rites of Chou*).[45]

Lu Chih's suggestion to reduce land rents has been praised as an unprecedented method in the history of Chinese economic thought.[46] The interesting question is how did he come up with such a singular idea, and the answer lies in his Confucian pragmatist approach. On the one hand, his concern for the welfare of the poor drove him to search for a solution to the problems caused by excessive land accumulation. On the other hand, to design a feasible plan, he also had to recognize that it was impossible to restore the old *chün-t'ien* system, even though he maintained that such a system had provided land for the poor and prevented excess land accumulation in former times. As a consequence, he proposed a policy that he asserted was in agreement with the teaching of the canonical *Chou li*. Under the guidance of this Confucian classic, he worked out a plan that he insisted would not only relieve the poor, but also avoid alienating the rich. In short, through his Confucian pragmatist approach, he believed he had found a solution to the problem of excess land accumulation that was both benevolent and practical.

With this proposed solution to the problem of land accumulation, Lu Chih's reformist attempts to improve the well-being of the poor also came to an end. Lu's subsequent fall from power may explain why his suggestions to relieve the suffering of the poor had no lasting results, but we cannot exclude the possibility that Te-tsung did not appreciate his suggestions in the first place. Since all of Lu Chih's proposals indicate that he had no intention of increasing the government's tax income, but actually planned to make the government measure its expenditure by its income, it is difficult to imagine Te-tsung lending his support to such proposals at a time when he remained obsessed with the financial hardships of his exile. Most importantly, because the government could now exact regular revenues from the land levy stipulated by the two-tax system, Te-tsung might not have felt any urgent need to adopt Lu's solution to the problem of land accumulation no matter how feasible that solution seemed to be.[47] That Te-tsung never even tried Lu's suggestion to improve the land accumulation situation after Lu's fall implies that he probably did not appreciate Lu's policies to relieve the suffering of the poor.

Transforming Te-tsung's Imperial Conduct

All of Lu Chih's reform policies depended on Te-tsung's personal approval for their realization, and many of his suggestions involved changes in imperial attitudes and conduct. His claim that Te-tsung should grant his ministers or generals the necessary powers and responsibilities required trust; his request that Te-tsung should stop accepting provincial "tribute goods," demanded honesty; and his suggestions for Te-tsung to benefit the poor called for benevolence. Thus he consistently attempted to transform Te-tsung's conduct, and his approach to imperial transformation was directly linked to his eventual fall from power.

Let us recall that in the fifth month of 792 Lu urged Te-tsung not to listen to small men's attacks on his recommendation policy, but to conduct a thorough investigation to find out whether the criticisms leveled at him were true.[48] In this way, Te-tsung could reach a just assessment that would be supported by actual evidence instead of by far-fetched accusations. If Te-tsung did not "distinguish whether [the small men's] slander is true or false, nor examine the strong and weak points in their criticism, their gossip will reach everywhere, and cause people like me not to know where we stand" (18: 13b).

Te-tsung did not adopt his advice, but Lu continued to request thorough investigations as a protest against the emperor's own judgment and to defend what he believed to be his or some other official's innocence and correctness. For example, at the beginning of 793, Te-tsung gave Lu Chih confidential instructions secretly to arrange the demotion and banishment of two brothers for rather bizarre reasons. Their late father had once said something offensive to the throne, and Te-tsung believed they had disloyal intentions because their given names were identical to those of the ancient sage kings. He still regarded Lu as his confidant, but his order contradicted Lu's position on the imperial treatment of officials.[49]

To show why these instructions were inappropriate, Lu emphasized that the ancient sage kings constantly insisted on making the rules for rewards and punishments clear to the public:

> Regarding the way of governing the state and educating the people, it lies in rewarding one person's goodness to make all those under Heaven who are doing good works feel encouraged, and in punishing one person's evil doing to give all those under Heaven who are doing evil things a warning. This is why it has to be in the court that ranks are conferred and it has to be in the market-place that punishments are inflicted.[50] This is for fear that the multitude will not see them, and these activities will not be manifested. . . . This is how the sage kings proclaimed and manifested the codes and regulations for rewards and punishments and shared them publicly with all under Heaven. (20: 3b–4a.)

Having established that meting out rewards and punishments in public was prescribed by the ancient sage kings, Lu immediately called for a public investigation of the case of those two brothers. The investigation, moreover, had to be conducted according to the rules recorded in the code of rewards and punishments.[51]

Lu Chih continued to treat rewards and punishments as a necessary means for preventing Te-tsung's arbitrary treatment of officials.[52] He also asserted that "punishments should be light and pardons should be generous [so as] to manifest the principle of benevolence and altruism (*jen shu chih tao*) and to extend the favor of [imperial] virtue and kindness" (22: 4a, 1a–6b).[53] Moreover, in pleading for a public investigation, Lu wanted to warn Te-tsung that secret demotion and banishment violated the way of a benevolent ruler (*wang che chih tao*). A benevolent ruler had to "observe three impartialities." He had to behave as impartially as "Heaven that covers everything, as Earth that bears everything, and as the Sun and Moon that shine on everything" (20: 2b).

Prompting Te-tsung to treat his officials according to the principle of benevolence and altruism was Lu Chih's constant position, and he demanded the same principles be followed in the imperial treatment of the common people. In the summer of 792, the populace of more than forty prefectures suffered from a devastating flood in which twenty thousand people drowned. We mentioned above that Te-tsung ordered a reduction in that year's taxes as a relief measure; this decision resulted primarily from Lu's persuasion.

When the disastrous damage caused by the flood first became known at court, Lu repeatedly urged Te-tsung to provide generous relief to the victims, but the emperor was opposed to the suggestion. Te-tsung said that he heard the flood damage was quite limited, and that giving generous relief would only encourage false reports from local officials trying to make a profit out of flood relief. Lu told Te-tsung quite frankly that his understanding was founded on inaccurate information. Lu had verified the flood reports by comparing them with information obtained from travelers. If Te-tsung had any suspicion, he should send envoys to investigate instead of ignoring the relief plan. Implying that Te-tsung should take the people's welfare as his first priority, Lu cited the paternalistic Confucian ideal that the ruler should be a parent to his people to remind him of his proper role as emperor.[54]

Lu also advised Te-tsung not to allow his unwillingness to spend state revenues on relief to cause him to lose the support of the people. He should either exempt the flood victims from tax levies, or reduce their normal share of the taxes. Lu said "what is required is only the expenditure [of wealth] and what will be won is the people's hearts. If [your majesty] does not lose the support of the people, why worry about a deficiency in revenues?" (18: 16b). Besides, Lu emphasized, the cost of flood relief would not be very great.

Te-tsung eventually followed Lu's suggestion to relieve the flood victims by reducing their tax load, but since the Huai-hsi region had not paid its taxes to the court, he instructed Lu to exclude it from the relief measure.[55] Even though the court had not regained full control over the Huai-hsi region, Lu insisted that it would be unfair to blame the people of the region for their tax delinquency. The ancient sage kings, Lu told Te-tsung, would not have endorsed his idea because "when the people could not preserve their homes, the sage kings felt as if *they* had pushed them into the ditch" (17: 18b).[56] If Te-tsung refused to relieve the Huai-hsi area, Lu warned, it would amount to "deserting the people and strengthening their enmity," plunging them into despair and providing another excuse for revolt.[57]

Lu urged Te-tsung to treat the Huai-hsi people in accordance with the principle of altruism:

> I believe the way of a [benevolent] ruler is quite different from that of opposing states. It is only through virtue [*te*] and rightness [*i*] that he can cherish and pacify ten thousand states. *He would rather allow people to take advantage of him than take advantage of them.* Therefore, he can make hundreds and millions of people give their hearts to him and people from far and near follow and be transformed by him. (18: 19a-b.)[58]

This represents the epitome of Lu Chih's own interpretation of the moralistic aspect of his Confucian approach. By reversing the famous words supposed to have been uttered by Ts'ao Ts'ao, Lu not only advocates the principles of benevolence and altruism as imperatives for winning the people's hearts, but even more significantly, he makes the Mencian conception of "humane government" paramount by requiring the emperor's moral obligation to the people to be absolute.

That Te-tsung finally adopted Lu Chih's advice to provide relief to the Huai-hsi people does not mean he accepted Lu's Confucian principles as the norm of government. As with his behavior in exile, it would seem that his decision to relieve the Huai-hsi people was still related to his fear of causing another revolt rather than to a genuine concern for their plight. In other words, unlike Lu Chih, Te-tsung was probably still manipulating the Confucian teachings as a means to preserve his own rule.

In spite of this small victory in changing the imperial mind regarding the policy of flood relief, Lu's efforts to prevent Te-tsung from accepting provincial "tribute goods" failed completely. At that, the conflict between him and Te-tsung reached the point of no return.

In the sixth month of 792, two months after he became chief minister and one month before the disastrous flood, Lu Chih presented a memorial asking Te-tsung to stop accepting provincial "tribute goods."[59] This is very likely his first memorial as chief minister aimed at restraining Te-tsung's personal greed. The background to this memorial is that the governor of Ling-nan (modern Kwangtung and Kwangsi) requested Te-tsung to send a eunuch and establish him as commissioner for trading with foreign ships (*Shih-po chung-shih*) in An-nan (or Annam, today's Hanoi).[60]

The name of the governor of Ling-nan in 792 is not mentioned in Lu Chih's memorial, but we are quite certain that it was Li Fu (739–797); he had served in this position since the fifth month of 787.[61] He was known for his administrative ability, but he was not exactly an incorruptible official, being criticized by his contemporaries for having accumulated a great amount of wealth during his long service as provincial governor, most likely in the lucrative Ling-nan position.[62]

If Li Fu was intent on accumulating wealth, why would he want a eunuch as imperial commissioner for trading with foreign ships in Annam? The reason Li himself gave implies that the shift of foreign trade from Canton to Annam made him feel it was difficult to control and tax most of the goods coming from abroad.[63] Since Annam was under the jurisdiction of the Ling-nan governor, surely Li Fu could have sent a subordinate either to tax or to buy foreign goods in Annam instead of having a eunuch dispatched from the court, but Li was "truly afraid of being deficient in tribute [goods]" (18: 20a). Thus, he asked Te-tsung to send a eunuch together with his subordinate official to perform these tasks. Li told Te-tsung that this arrangement could avoid any swindle taking place in Annam. With a eunuch present, at least Li would not need to assume direct responsibility for any potential tax loss. We have no other evidence to verify the above inference, but we can be sure of one thing: Te-tsung agreed with Li Fu's request, and instructed Lu Chih to facilitate it right away.[64]

Lu objected to this plan on two grounds. First, he believed the reason foreign ships stopped trading at Canton was either because the official tax imposition at Canton was too heavy, or because officials in Canton failed to treat foreign merchants with due respect. Lu suspected the Ling-nan governor's integrity. Second, Lu maintained that if the court needed money for military defense, it could follow the routine procedures to obtain provincial tribute.

Those who were loyal to the court would certainly provide their tribute without worrying about being remiss in their duties.[65]

Lu cautioned that two evil consequences would result if Te-tsung adopted the governor's suggestion to establish a eunuch at Annam to ensure tax collection. It would mean that the throne agreed that its regular officials had to be supervised by eunuchs when conducting government affairs in the provinces. Worst of all, it would also "display a covetous disposition to all under Heaven and openly invite the use of bribery at court" (18: 21a).[66] Lu asked Te-tsung to abandon the plan. On the surface, Lu was no doubt blaming the governor of Ling-nan for both failing to handle foreign trade properly at Canton and for his intention to corrupt the throne, but Te-tsung was clearly his implied target. If Lu had succeeded, he could have eliminated in one stroke two imperial practices he had opposed ever since the time of exile: the imperial demand for provincial tribute money for personal use, and reliance on eunuchs to oversee regular officials.

We do not know Te-tsung's actual reaction to Lu's plea, but he could not have felt very pleased with his newly appointed chief minister. As mentioned before, when Te-tsung gave Lu secret instructions for the banishment of two brothers, he also gave Lu to know that he was not pleased with his opposition to the acceptance of provincial "tribute."[67] When Te-tsung urged him to accept gifts from local governors, Lu's rationale for not doing so pointedly stated that Te-tsung's acceptance of provincial "tributes" contradicted the imperial policy of punishing officials who committed the crime of bribery.

Lu reminded Te-tsung that whenever he issued a general amnesty, even those who had been sentenced to death were pardoned, but officials who committed bribery never received such grace. This showed that Te-tsung himself considered bribery the most harmful crime. If regular officials were not supposed to take bribes, Lu asked, on what grounds could Te-tsung and his chief minister do so?[68] Imperial acceptance of bribery would certainly lead to a decline of ethical norms:

> If the ruler above likes profits, then officials below will think about amassing wealth. If the ruler on high seeks bribes, then officials below will put forth their energies to grab the common people's wealth. None feel shame in their hearts, but simply indulge their personal desires; one after another they long to imitate each other, [until] the practice

becomes a custom. Day by day, people's families are harmed and rules and regulations are set at naught. This situation [cannot be improved] by exhortation to propriety and rightness or punishment based on rules and regulations because the way of honor and integrity has declined. (20: 9b.)

Clearly Lu Chih's statement was derived from the Confucian doctrine that rulers ought to set themselves up as moral exemplars for their subjects.[69] He believed that because Te-tsung demanded provincial "tributes," a chain of irregular exactions starting from the provinces and reaching down to counties and villages followed. The ultimate source of their "tributes" was nothing less than the "flesh and blood of the exhausted people" (20:8b). He insisted that the main reason provincial officials carried on this practice was because they felt they had to do it to "insure their lives and preserve their offices" (20: 10a). If Te-tsung rectified his conduct, provincial officials could feel secure enough to discontinue their "tributes," and the irregular exactions on the people could come to an end.

Even though Te-tsung again ignored his advice, such repeated frustration did not stop Lu from pursuing what he considered morally correct government.[70] In the fifth month of 794, he set out again to urge Te-tsung to end the practice of provincial "tributes" and, as could be expected, he lost again. By this time, Lu must have realized that all but three of his proposed policies that we know of, whether they concerned affairs in the public domain or the imperial conduct, had been completely rejected by the throne. Meanwhile, P'ei Yen-ling continued to mismanage state finances, mistreat border armies, and use irregular means to feed Te-tsung's personal treasuries.

To Lu, P'ei Yen-ling fully represented his idea of a "small man" who harmed the public well-being and encouraged imperial greed. Toward the end of 794, Lu presented his ill-fated memorial directly attacking P'ei and indirectly pleading with Te-tsung to improve his conduct. Lu reemphasized all his previous admonitions concerning how Te-tsung should treat his officials, care for the people's welfare, and restrain his personal greed. One passage summarizes his position:

As for the person who governs all under Heaven, he should treat rightness [i] as the root and profit [li] as the branches; should treat the people as fundamental and wealth as incidental. If the root flourishes, its branches will naturally become elevated; but if the branches become too large, the tree will fall over and be uprooted. From ancient times to the present, it has never been the case that a ruler came to the point where he did not have abundant resources, nor sufficient wealth and consequently lost his throne and state simply because he had established virtue and rightness, increased the number of [his] people, and made them contented. (24: 17a.)

When he had said everything he felt he had to, Lu directly challenged Te-tsung to conduct a public investigation of his criticisms of P'ei Yen-ling. This time Lu was conscious that he had probably put himself in a precarious position, but he was also certain that he had to speak up because "silently obeying imperial instructions has gradually become the custom" (24: 22b). To assure Te-tsung that his remonstrance was motivated by loyal concern for the state, Lu disclosed his inner struggle in the following words:

I have been raised from my lowly station to occupy the office of chief minister. Since my position is already extremely high, and since I am also greatly beholden for your favor, how could I be unaware that watching the current trends and chiming in with other people's views will be sufficient to maintain your previous favor; following numerous others and drifting with them will avoid severe blame; using illness as a pretext for acquiring relief from my office will bring me a reputation for knowing the right moment; and associating with wicked people, and being accepted by them while perfunctorily discharging my duties will eliminate any worries about being hated by them?

Why should I be in a hurry to look for trouble and be the only one confronting jackals and wolves, and thus defy your eminence's wishes and become a target for those slanderers below? Truly, it is because . . . I have always received your deep understanding that I am simply being honest and straightforward.

It has been twelve years since I started serving intimately in your presence. Since your sagely kindness has tolerated me because of my honesty and straightforwardness, I have also been proud of myself because of this. I was with your

majesty when you experienced the grave danger of leaving
the capital (moving into exile) and I have witnessed your
majesty going through the hardships of restoration. Even
when I think of it now, my heart still beats rapidly. This is
why I am terrified that the carts might be overturned again
and I bemoan sadly that the palaces might be destroyed.
All of these feelings are agitating my heart, and even if I
want to stop them I cannot silence myself. (24: 23a-b.)

Lu Chih's long self-disclosure may contain some exaggeration
of his sense of loyalty and a certain degree of self-righteousness,
but the sober analysis of his chosen position is persuasive. One
might argue that Lu was only manipulating carefully constructed
rhetoric to force Te-tsung to remove his opponent in a power struggle.
He did want to remove P'ei Yen-ling, but on many previous occasions he had rejected imperial instructions to assume much greater
power than he believed he should have. A power-only argument
would also seem insufficient to explain Lu's perfect confidence in
the validity of his indictment of his opponent, or his request for a
public investigation. Lu had no reason to risk his political life save
that he believed both P'ei Yen-ling's and Te-tsung's conduct harmed
the public well-being. He still hoped desperately that he could again
exert some influence on Te-tsung as he had done during his exile.
By this time, though, Te-tsung probably felt just as frustrated by
Lu as Lu was by him. Even though Te-tsung still appreciated Lu
as his long cherished confidant, once Lu's repeated efforts to restrain his personal greed became persistently annoying, and once
Lu's request for the dismissal of P'ei Yen-ling, whom Te-tsung trusted
to acquire money and goods for his personal treasuries, became an
increasingly pressing issue, he was ready without hesitation to
remove Lu from the position of chief minister. Thus ended Lu's
Sisyphean efforts to transform his emperor's conduct.

In our examination of the reform policies Lu Chih proposed
during his tenure as chief minister, we find them to be consistent
with the advice he earlier presented to Te-tsung in exile. What he
advocated earlier remained his primary concern and served as the
perennial frame of reference for his public pursuit of an ideal government in the later stage of his political life.

In our analysis of Lu Chih's memorials, we find that even
though he never presented systematic philosophical discussions
regarding his conception of an ideal government, such a concept is

latent in almost all of them. For Lu, an ideal government was one that was established on the premise that "the people are the foundation of the state." To consolidate that foundation, a frugal government was required in the sense that it would not impose unreasonable tax exactions on the people. Lu maintained that such a government, when dealing with issues touching the people's welfare, should operate according to the principles of "virtue, rightness, altruism and benevolence." Only in this way, could a government treat its people as "the root or the foundation" and "profits" and "wealth" as "branches or incidental elements." Lu Chih's view of "profits" and "wealth" is similar to the Mencian idea that a ruler is responsible for increasing the material abundance of the people's lives, but profit itself should never become his main concern.[71] In short, Lu's ideal government is fundamentally in line with the Confucian idea of a "humane government."

Admittedly, Lu Chih's vision of Confucian government embodied nothing but those basic Confucian principles that most traditional Chinese scholars were familiar with. It contained few innovations to enrich Confucianism as a system of thought. The key element that distinguishes Lu as an unusual Confucian statesman is not the Confucian principles he advocated, but his belief in Confucian political ideals and his commitment to his own beliefs. His conviction and commitment were manifested as much in his frequent employment of the Confucian classics as living guides for conducting government affairs as in his tenacious efforts to realize his ideals.

The Confucian classics cited by Lu Chih ranged from the Five Classics and the *Analects* that T'ang scholar officials were most familiar with, to the much less quoted *Doctrine of the Mean* and the *Book of Mencius*.[72] Lu mentioned that his colleagues also employed the Confucian classics to defend their policies, but this does not mean his perception of the function of the classics was similar to theirs. That Lu criticized his colleagues as being "pedantic" and "reciting platitudes and preserving the dross of the old classics" clearly illustrates his own evaluation of the difference between his attitude toward the classics and theirs. In his view, even though the Confucian classics were appropriated in the current bureaucratic discourse by his colleagues, they failed to see the relevance of the classics to living historical conditions, and their citation of the classics was only a formalistic intellectual exercise.

By contrast, Lu Chih's pursuit of Confucian political ideals never led him to abandon his pragmatist sensibility in designing his reform policies. This again illustrates his seriousness about the Confucian classics, and it equally manifests his pragmatic response to the needs of the time. To establish a fair system for evaluating the bureaucracy, he repeatedly emphasized the necessity of discarding previous precedents to adjust to the present time and circumstances. He arranged a compromise between different views of the system of grain transportation to fill the frontier granaries without allowing the transportation system to fall into desuetude. He worked out a solution to the problem of excess land accumulation that would relieve the poor without intimidating the rich, and would accommodate the present situation while also fulfilling the goals prescribed by the *Chou li*. Even his suggestion to replace cash with goods as the basic unit for the two-tax assessment and collection would later be proven realistic in solving the problem of deflation, a similar suggestion being put into practice during the reign of emperor Mu-tsung (r. 820–824).[73] Lu Chih can be considered extremely practical and farsighted in this regard. All these efforts demonstrate that Lu faithfully observed his own principle of expediency in pursuit of his ideal government.

It should be emphasized that as chief minister Lu Chih paid constant attention to the feasibility of his proposed policies. He also gave careful consideration to the possible results of these policies. This indicates that he still cherished the strong sense of responsibility for political activities that he had acquired during the court's exile. In short, in his pursuit of a better government, his Confucian pragmatist approach continued to exhibit the Weberian concept of the ethics of responsibility.

In spite of constantly upholding the importance of realism in conducting public affairs, Lu Chih seems never to have worried as much about whether his advice for improving Te-tsung's conduct was practical. For him, as for most Confucian scholars, the paramount duty of an emperor was to fulfill his moral obligations to the people as the *Son of Heaven*. They also believed that only by fulfilling these obligations could an emperor preserve a stable state.

Of course, sharing similar beliefs does not necessarily mean that most Confucian scholar officials would, like Lu Chih, persistently attempt to rectify the imperial conduct at the risk of their own interests. As Lu wrote, the general trend among the court officials in his time was simply to obey the imperial will. Lu was unquestionably unusual in that his political behavior was the embodiment of his political beliefs. A person with such a commitment to Confucian political ideals would probably worry less about his own interests than about the results of his political endeavors. When Lu Chih finally challenged the throne to dismiss P'ei Yen-ling, he made it clear that he was conscious of the risks in front of him, but his concern for the public welfare impelled him to speak up for a higher ethical good. He even stated that what he was then doing "is wrong as a plan for consolidating my own position, but as a concern that your majesty will take precautions against calamity, it is nevertheless loyal" (24: 23b).

It is in this readiness to defy the imperial wishes to realize the Confucian Way that we find Lu bringing out what it ultimately means to be a Confucian statesman. To be sure, one might consider Lu a foolish politician on the grounds that he should have drifted with the crowd rather than engage in a hopeless battle against the throne. He would then have "betrayed what [he had] learned in this world"—his Confucian convictions and the goals he had always sought by means of his Confucian pragmatist approach. That he chose to honor his Confucian principles qualifies him to be considered a committed Confucian. From the beginning to the end of his political life at Te-tsung's court, Lu remained consistent in his approach to government. To improve the still far from ideal public well-being, Lu continued his previous efforts to enact his vision of Confucian government, even though they were in complete conflict with the imperial wishes.

Te-tsung had relied heavily on Lu's advice during his exile, but once the historical conditions changed, we see him obsessed with the preservation of what he saw as stability. He was not willing to allow Lu Chih's reformist policies to go against his wishes, not even when Lu repeatedly guaranteed that those policies would not upset the status quo. Lu understood perfectly Te-tsung's opposition, but he was thrust into an inescapable predicament by his sense of duty.

Lu Chih solved his dilemma by following the higher call of the Confucian Way. His dilemma was clearly not created by his failure to design realistic policies in accord with his principle of expediency, nor by any failure to stress the necessity of taking responsibility for the outcome of political action. Even in his repeated efforts to transform the imperial conduct, Lu always presented the possible practical results deriving from Te-tsung's behavior. The fact is that Te-tsung's concept of government was so different from Lu's that it left Lu no room to operate unless he was willing to abandon the pursuit of his Confucian Way—to give up what he felt to be his duty to improve the public welfare. Within this specific context, it is perhaps not inappropriate to compare Lu's commitment to his political beliefs with Weber's depiction of a genuine statesman.

According to Weber, there are times when situations come to a point that a man, after following the ethics of responsibility in every possible way, will still have to stand by his moral principles without further compromise. In Weber's judgment, this sort of political act is "an expression of authentic humanity and stirs one's feelings." When such political action is taken, "the ethics of intention and the ethics of responsibility are not diametrically opposed, but complementary; together they make the true man, the man who can have the 'vocation of politics.' "[74]

Considering the increasingly restricted political space in which Lu Chih was allowed to operate, and considering the compromises he made to design his reformist policies within the limits acceptable to Te-tsung, it does not seem far-fetched to say that Lu's political endeavors came close to Weber's idea of a true statesman who understood the essential meaning of "politics as vocation." Nevertheless, striving within such limited political space, and ultimately refusing to restrain any further his desire to improve the public welfare, Lu's lone pursuit of Confucian political ideals ineluctably transformed him into a quixotic fighter "who [kept] working towards a goal the realization of which he knew to be hopeless (*chih ch'i pu-k'o erh wei-chih che*)."[75] As might be expected, the political life of such a reluctantly quixotic fighter was doomed to come to a sad end.

CHAPTER SEVEN

Mid-T'ang Comparisons

Lu Chih was banished to Chung-chou in the fourth month of 795. Immediately after ascending the throne in 805, Emperor Shun-tsung (r. 805) summoned him and some other exiled officials back to court, but Lu's untimely death forever deprived him of a chance to reappear on the mid-T'ang political stage.

Shun-tsung's recall deserves our attention because his court was dominated by the so-called Wang Shu-wen faction that modern historians generally agree was a Confucian reformist group.[1] The group included eight other idealistic middle-level officials, among whom was the acclaimed *ku-wen* writer Liu Tsung-yüan. The Wang Shu-wen group wanted to correct the bureaucratic corruption and eunuch abuses of power that had accumulated since the latter half of Te-tsung's reign. They also intended to abolish the practice of sending provincial "tributes" to the throne, one of Lu Chih's cherished goals, and they arranged for Lu Chih to be given a chance to return to court in the third month of 805.[2]

Lu Chih's active political life extended from 780 to 795. That the Wang Shu-wen group made his rehabilitation one of their top priorities a decade after his banishment indicates that Lu's political undertakings had gained the respect of these reform-minded officials. It also implies that Lu's political life and work were significant for mid-T'ang history.

The Mid-T'ang Milieu

Mid-T'ang history was markedly different from that of the earlier stages of the dynasty. Politically, provincial powers remained a constant threat to the central government throughout the latter half of T'ang history. Te-tsung's attempts to restore imperial authority only resulted in a series of military uprisings, exile, and a return to the appeasement policies of the past. Emperor Hsientsung managed to establish the so-called Yüan-ho restoration (*Yüanho chung-hsing*) in 817, but it was ephemeral.[3]

Socially, the An Lu-shan rebellion depopulated large areas in Ho-nan, especially in the Lo-yang region, decimated the territorial base of many prestigious clans,[4] and inadvertently contributed to the accelerated bureaucratization of T'ang aristocratic families. Considerable numbers of these dislocated clans escaped and took refuge in the relatively peaceful lands south of the Yangtze, the economic importance of which was underscored by Lu Chih's recommendation to concentrate all the loyalist forces to deal with the Huai-hsi rebels during the second Ho-pei rebellion. The outbreak of this rebellion further impoverished the peasant population that had just survived the An Lu-shan catastrophe. Although the implementation of the two-tax system provided a stable revenue for the state, as Lu's critique revealed, its operation did not relieve the peasants' plight in any substantial way.[5]

The mid-T'ang Confucian revival gradually came into being during this period when the T'ang state was undergoing these violent disruptions. As is well known, it was through this revival that the rise of full-blown neo-Confucianism became possible later during the Sung dynasty.[6]

Previous chapters have presented a detailed record of Lu Chih's political life. It remains now to explore the historical significance of his life's work. A discussion of the mid-T'ang Confucian revival and Lu's possible role in that intellectual development is the most important step in this process. To assess Lu's political life from a more complete perspective, however, I believe it necessary first to compare his political undertakings with those of some renowned chief ministers in his own time. This will help to distinguish even more clearly the main character of Lu's political endeavors and consolidate our subsequent inquiry into Lu's place in the mid-T'ang intellectual milieu. For this comparison, I have chosen Li Mi and Tu Yu, two chief ministers who have not been seriously considered Confucian court officials, but who nevertheless showed concern for the problems of their time.

Li Mi

Li Mi put forth several policies to improve government finances during his tenure as chief minister between 787 and 789. When he was summoned by Te-tsung to serve the throne in exile, Li Mi was already a veteran official. He had served two previous emperors, and, probably due to his Taoist inclinations, survived various power struggles by self-enforced retirement.[7]

Concerned for the state's finances, Li Mi once proposed to abolish supernumerary official posts, especially those in local government created during previous reigns.[8] At the same time, he made it clear that because administrative affairs had increased tenfold, even though there were fewer tax households, the regular official positions still had to be filled.[9]

During his tenure as chief minister between 792 and 794, Lu Chih does not seem to have advocated the elimination of supernumerary official posts. In 780, however, when he served in the local government of Wei-nan county, he did talk about abolishing unnecessary official positions as one of the essential steps toward simplifying bureaucratic operations.[10] Lu's argument for abolishing supernumerary official posts was based more on his concern for administrative efficiency than on the sort of financial concern that troubled Li Mi. On the other hand, when Lu pleaded with Te-tsung not to leave the regular official positions vacant in 794 on the ground that the court needed officials to deal with regular affairs, his request certainly agreed with Li Mi's position.[11]

Li Mi's view of the role of fate in state affairs coincided with Lu Chih's. He too advised Te-tsung not to attribute his exile to a preordained destiny. He told Te-tsung that "as for fate, it is a statement of something that has already happened. Rulers [should] create [their own] destiny; they should not talk about fate. If they talk about fate, then they can no longer reward the good and punish the evil."[12] This exclusion of fate from government is a very Confucian-sounding message. It seems that Li Mi kept his Taoist inclinations strictly confined to his private life. Nevertheless, they may have played a part on one crucial occasion while he served at Te-tsung's court.

Li Mi did not propose any direct measures to improve the people's welfare during his service in Te-tsung's court, but, like Lu Chih, he worried about the imperial demand for provincial tributes. Li Mi's solution to this problem, carried out in 787, was to provide Te-tsung with one million strings of cash annually for his palace expenditure, and request that the throne stop accepting tributes.[13] When Te-tsung violated his own promise and resumed his old practice a few months later, Li Mi was "disconsolate, but [he] did not dare to say anything."[14]

Li Mi's decision not to speak up represents a tacit admission that his earlier arrangement with the emperor was a failure. Why did Li lack the courage to speak up again? There could be many answers to this question, yet the Taoist interest in preserving one's life may have exerted a strong influence on his decision. He had chosen self-imposed retirement in several power struggles to avoid confrontations with other ministers during previous reigns. In a struggle where a chief minister knows his odds of winning over the emperor are near zero, silence would seem to be a natural weapon of self-protection, and Li's Taoist leanings would only reinforce it. In comparison, we have seen how Lu Chih's unrelenting remonstrance against Te-tsung's conduct even at the risk of his own political life exhibited the profound influence of Confucian principles.

Tu Yu

Tu Yu, though much older than Lu Chih, was not appointed as a titular chief minister until near the end of Te-tsung's reign in 803. He was also granted the high honorific rank of *Ssu-k'ung* (minister of works) at about the same time. Before 803, he had spent most of his official life in provincial government, except for a short period in 779 when Yang Yen was chief minister.[15] From 803 to 812, he continued to serve in the court as a senior statesman and held several high honorific ranks with various titles.

Far from having a penchant for Taoism like Li Mi, Tu Yu has been identified as a "neo-legalist," and as a character antithetical to Lu Chih. This is chiefly because Tu Yu's extant work, the encyclopedic *T'ung-tien*, is focused on the history of governmental institutions and displays an appreciation of some aspects of legalist thought.[16] His unreserved support of the two-tax system also contrasts sharply with Lu's position.[17] Yet, Lu Chih does not seem to have regarded Tu Yu as his opposite. We remember that in 792 soon after becoming chief minister, Lu recommended Tu Yu as one of the candidates to head the Department of the Public Revenue, but Te-tsung rejected his suggestion and chose P'ei Yen-ling instead. This incident implies that Lu Chih at least held Tu's ability in financial administration in high regard, and that they seem to have shared some similar views on government.

A comparison of exactly where and how their approaches to government converged and diverged will bring out the similarities in their views as well as the essential differences between them. I begin with their general attitude toward administration.

General Attitude toward Administration

Tu Yu's general attitude toward administration was reflected in his approach to government revenues. To balance the government revenues, Tu Yu, like Li Mi, advocated abolishing the supernumerary official posts, but unlike Lu Chih and Li Mi, Tu does not seem to have ever insisted on filling the regular official positions.[18] Tu argued that since the government revenues in the post–An Lu-shan period decreased drastically, it could no longer afford to keep these supernumerary officials. He understood that when the times change, the bureaucracy needs to adapt to the new conditions: "institutions should be established in accordance with the times; when problems occur, one should make accommodations and adjust [to them] without necessarily following the old customs" (40: 231b). This statement obviously reflects a sense of pragmatism.

As a person whose pragmatist approach to government constantly led him to address the importance of "understanding" and "examining the changes of the times," Lu Chih would have supported Tu's call for accommodation to new circumstances. Lu's criticism of those officials who clung to the ancient classics and refused to adapt to contemporary reality was also in perfect harmony with Tu's assertion that "whenever one consults the books of the ancients, it is because one wishes to discover new meanings and regulate affairs in accordance with the present time [and circumstances]" (12: 68a).[19] As far as adapting to changed times and conditions is concerned, we can see that Lu's once underestimated pragmatist sensibility was as great as, if not greater than, Tu's frequently praised inclination in that direction. The point is that, contrary to the general perception, they both assumed a flexible attitude toward managing government affairs.

On Bureaucratic Efficiency and Civil Recruitment

Tu Yu viewed the elimination of supernumerary posts as a necessary way to reduce the financial burdens of the state, but he suggested that senior officials in provincial governments ought to recommend to the court capable men among the supernumerary officials. Tu believed this would prevent virtuous and talented potential officials from being neglected. He also asserted that if the recommendation was false, the court could punish the provincial sponsors by laying criminal charges.[20]

Tu Yu apparently agreed with Lu Chih in this matter since both of them naturally wanted to select people they considered virtuous and talented to fill the official positions. Tu Yu said rather tautologically that "setting up offices and posts lies in scrutinizing the talent for those offices; scrutinizing the talent for those offices lies in being finely attentive to selection" (1: 9a).[21] It is in the area of how to proceed with the selection that Tu Yu and Lu Chih part company.

Like Lu Chih, Tu Yu was also a member of one of the most eminent aristocratic families in the T'ang. While Lu was from an indigenous southern aristocratic clan, Tu was from the politically more influential Kuan-chung aristocracy. They enjoyed similarly exalted social status, but they entered the bureaucracy through different channels. Unlike Lu , Tu Yu did not enter the bureaucracy through the examination system.[22] It is possible that his personal background led him to regard the examination system, especially the *chin-shih* examination, as an inappropriate channel to recruit officials. Many of Tu's contemporaries shared this view. They all considered a talent for composing poetry and prose, the prerequisite for passing the *chin-shih* examination, irrelevant to practical government affairs.[23] They held several different views of how to improve the situation. Some preferred to maintain the examination system while demanding a change in the subjects examined; others believed the best way was to replace the examination system with the recommendation method practiced in the Han dynasty.[24] Tu Yu embraced the latter position.

As we saw earlier, Lu Chih only intended to apply the recommendation method to the official placement process. He did not propose to abolish the examination system. That Lu himself was a *chin-shih* degree holder may have played a part in his position to preserve the existing system. Judging by his constant emphasis on fairness in official appointment, it is equally possible that Lu considered the examination system a fair channel for candidates to enter the bureaucracy for the first time. This was also the position of those who preferred to change the subjects examined while leaving the system otherwise intact.[25]

Besides these similarities and differences regarding their general attitude toward administration, and their suggestions on the improvement of the bureaucracy, Tu Yu's basic view of the imperial role also seems very close to Lu's. However, it should first be noted that Tu never explicitly discussed the moral transformation of imperial conduct as Lu Chih did.

Relation between Administrative Changes and Moral Leadership

During his service in the court as titular chief minister from 803 to 812, Tu Yu expended very little if any effort on rectifying imperial conduct. His principal concern, as shown in the *T'ung-tien*, was to encourage the throne to apply the relevant governmental policies from previous dynasties to contemporary conditions, but he found that many Confucian classics failed to provide what he regarded as relevant information:

> *The Classic of Filial Piety, The Book of Documents, The Book of Odes, The Book of Changes* and *The Three Commentaries* [to *The Spring and Autumn Annals*] are all essential teachings about the relationship between fathers and sons, and between the ruler and the ministers. . . . However, their contents are almost all recorded words [of the sages]; they rarely include the [previous] laws and regulations. (CTW, 477: 1b.)

In Tu Yu's view, these Confucian classics offered no practical guidance for the conduct of administrative affairs.

When he compiled the *T'ung-tien*, Tu consulted mainly those works from previous dynasties he felt were relevant to administrative improvement. He included in this category the *Analects* and the *Mencius* as well as the works of legalist thinkers such as Shang Yang, and he particularly emphasized that he "still relied on *The Rites of Chou*" as his standard framework of reference.[26] Tu's unreserved respect for *The Rites of Chou*, the specific Confucian classic that has traditionally been associated with institutional reform, indicates that he believed that administrative changes were essential to solve the problems of his time. Tu Yu's interest in administrative changes can be further supported by the fact that he devoted fully half of the *T'ung-tien* to delineating the evolution and function of all the ancient rites as well as other ritual regulations prescribed in the T'ang ritual codes.

This interest in ritual studies is probably related in part to Tu's personal predilection, and partly to his northern aristocratic background. For Tu Yu, rituals were established in order "to set the vulgar trend right." He stated that establishing rituals was one of "the essential governing methods through which the ancient sage kings achieved good order" (1: 9a). Here Tu, unlike Lu Chih, or most traditional Confucian scholar officials, did not emphasize the role of moral leadership in government. Obviously closer to Hsün Tzu than to Mencius, Tu intended to rely on rituals to rectify human behavior. Since rites, in Hsün Tzu's view, referred not just to ceremonial acts and their accouterments, but to all government regulations and institutions, we can say that Tu Yu valued the institutional regulation of human conduct more than moral suasion in government.[27]

Nevertheless, it must be pointed out that Tu Yu apparently took a virtuous ruler for granted. Tu's own words inform us that "the ancient sage kings" served as a given in his idea of state government. Because a virtuous ruler was perceived as the necessary designer of institutional changes, it is not surprising that Tu probably felt no need to address the issue of transforming imperial conduct. What he did not, or perhaps did not intend to, deal with was of course the problem of the ruler's degeneration. The possibility of having an arbitrary ruler invalidating all his proposed administrative measures never seems to have troubled him. This possibility was, of course, the very reality Lu Chih had to confront.

Judging from many of his reform policies, Lu Chih unquestionably also had a strong interest in administrative change. He did not particularly single out *The Rites of Chou* as his model classic, but he did formulate his most innovative rent reduction policy in accord with the ideal prescribed in it. However, unlike Tu Yu, Lu had an equally strong interest in virtuous imperial conduct. He saw both imperial moral cultivation (rightness) *and* administrative change (expediency) as necessary for a good political order.

Lu's intimate relationship with Te-tsung made him deeply aware that his reform measures would be fruitless without imperial support. This caused him to consider the transformation of Te-tsung's conduct a prerequisite for the success of institutional changes. Tu Yu rarely occupied himself with this issue, but his comments on the history of administrative changes do occasionally reveal his perception of the imperial role.[28] This makes possible a comparison between this aspect of his thought and Lu Chih's views.

Similar Views on the Imperial Role

Tu Yu demonstrated that he believed that human effort, not fate, was the key to good government. As Lu Chih advised Te-tsung not to attribute the second Ho-pei rebellion to a predetermined destiny, Tu also commented that the An Lu-shan rebellion "was surely [caused by] human affairs; how could it be just the timing of Heaven?" (12: 71b).[29] While pointing out the government's military policy as the main cause of the rebellion, Tu concurrently implied that Hsüan-tsung's failure to observe his proper imperial role caused "ministers who talked about profits" and "generals who sought rewards" to manage financial and military affairs and subsequently sowed the seeds of the An Lu-shan rebellion.[30]

Many of Tu Yu's comments, like the following, show that he perceived the role of the emperor to be a benevolent one:

> The sage kings in antiquity "considered that rightness was profit, not that profit was profit." They preferred to store up [wealth] among the people, not to hoard [it] in treasuries and depositories. [For] "when the people do not have enough, how can the ruler have enough?" (4: 25a.)[31]

Presented without attribution, this statement could very well be taken for a piece of Lu Chih's typical advice to Te-tsung. Not only is the basic idea of a benevolent ruler manifested in this statement identical to Lu's, but the second quotation from the *Analects* is also the same one Lu cited in 794. Even the issue that both Tu and Lu were discussing when they quoted these lines from the *Analects* was the same—taxation.

Maintaining that the ancient sage kings "considered that rightness was profit" and had regarded the people's welfare as their moral obligation, Tu Yu made it clear that the Confucian principle of light taxation ought to be the guideline for the formulation of contemporary tax policy. As evidence, he cited the position of Confucius and Mencius on light taxation. He also placed the light tax policy proposed in the book of *Kuan tzu*, a work usually considered a forerunner of legalist thought, side by side with similar policies supported by Confucius and Mencius.[32]

Tu Yu's interest in the *Kuan tzu* was so strong that in the introduction to the *T'ung-tien*, where he stresses that a good government ought to take the people's material life as its priority, he again drew a parallel between the views of Confucius and Kuan Tzu on this issue. As Tu Yu saw it:

> The priority in the way of good government lies in implementing moral transformation. The basis of moral transformation lies in having a sufficiency of food and clothes. . . . Kuan Tzu said, "When the granaries are full, [the people] will know propriety and moderation. When their food and clothing is adequate, they will know the [distinction between] honor and shame." Confucius said, "When they (the people) have been made rich, instruct them." This [need for a sufficiency of food and clothes] is what these texts meant. (1: 9a.)[33]

Tu Yu obviously believed that the *Kuan tzu* position on light taxation and on the people's material well-being was synonymous with that of the Confucian thinkers. Tu himself asserted that "Kuan Tzu's wisdom was infinite. Using the small state of Ch'i, [he] set all under Heaven straight. [It] was on the basis of benevolence and rightness that [Kuan Tzu] helped [Ch'i] achieve its hegemony" (12: 68b).

In discussing his own financial proposals, Lu Chih never seems to have relied on the economic policies mentioned in the *Kuan tzu*. Focusing on Kuan Chung's political approach to government, he gave Kuan credit for his advice to Duke Huan of Ch'i to employ and trust capable officials.[34] What is clear, at least up to this point, is that Tu Yu's alleged position regarding the imperial policy on light taxation and the imperial duty to provide a material sufficiency for the people stand as equivalents to Lu Chih's quest to improve the people's welfare.

Conflicting Views on the Imperial Role

Nevertheless, a seemingly contradictory attitude appears in Tu Yu's view of the imperial role. Tu maintained that the emperor's role was a benevolent one, but he followed Kuan Tzu's idea of elevating the ruler. He stated: "when the ruler is exalted, then there will be order and peace; when the subjects (or officials) are powerful, then there will be chaos and danger" (31:177b).[35] During a time when the central government was in decline, one may agree that Tu's call for elevation of the ruler's position was a merely expedient one, and consequently had no bearing on his theoretical position.[36] This view is even more plausible when one discovers that on another occasion Tu asserted that establishing the ruler's position was "to bring good government to the world by means of the one person (the ruler). It was not to offer the world to the one person" (171: 907a).[37]

The fact remains, though, that Tu Yu's willingness to elevate the ruler's position for the sake of consolidating the central power has no parallel in Lu Chih's approach to government. Lu's entire official life was oriented toward the restoration of the T'ang state, but he never mentioned in his extant works that the emperor ought to be exalted. Quite the contrary, he always insisted that humble imperial behavior was a necessary condition for winning popular support. Even when he applied his principle of expediency to political maneuvers, Lu constantly urged Te-tsung to compromise his exalted position for the sake of achieving a higher ethical good, be it for the people or for the state. This crucial difference between Lu Chih and Tu Yu helps to explain the underlying cause of their divergent views on the two-tax system.

Rationale behind Views on the Two-Tax System and Land Policies

Tu Yu's support of the two-tax system was based on two commonly accepted reasons: it could solve the problem of vagrancy, and its implementation had "more than doubled" the state's tax income. "Thus," Tu said, "it gives to taxation a regular rule, and the people know [that there is] a definite regulation. Grasping clerks cannot carry on fraudulent dealings; crafty people are all covered in the household registration. It is indeed a timely system and a good plan for correcting [previous] abuses" (7: 42c). What Tu Yu appreciated most about the two-tax system was that it could stabilize the state revenues by increasing the number of taxpayers.[38] He was not particularly disturbed by the problem that most concerned Lu Chih: the heavy tax burden on the common people created by a situation where they had to pay a fixed quota in terms of greatly depreciated commodity prices.

Surely, having occupied various financial positions himself, Tu Yu could not possibly have failed to notice the problems, such as the shortage of cash and the influence of deflation, involved in the operation of the two-tax system.[39] We can see from this that Tu's concern for the economic well-being of the state was so strong that he did not feel any urgent need to correct the social evils created by implementing the two-tax system. This is not to say that Tu had no sympathy for public suffering; the point is that his practical concerns for accommodation to the "changes of time and circumstances" were primarily oriented toward strengthening the state power, not relieving the people's plight.

Once Tu Yu's paramount concern for the economic well-being of the state is clear, we can then clarify why he had a seemingly contradictory attitude toward Shang Yang's land policy. Indeed, apart from his interest in Kuan Tzu's economic policies, Tu also paid serious attention to the economic policies of Shang Yang, one of the most notable legalists.[40]

On one occasion when Tu Yu was reviewing the land policies of former dynasties, he put Mencius and Shang Yang side by side as if some common ground existed between the land policies of these philosophically opposed thinkers. Tu certainly knew that Shang Yang initiated land reform in the Ch'in state during the Warring States period (403–221 B.C.E.) by abolishing the very well-field (*ching-t'ien*) system that Mencius advocated.[41] Tu specifically quotes Mencius's comments on the well-field system:

> Benevolent government must begin with land demarcation. When boundaries are not properly drawn, the division of land according to the well-field system and the yield of grain used for paying officials cannot be equitable. For this reason, despotic rulers and corrupt officials always neglect the boundaries. Once the boundaries are correctly fixed, there will be no difficulty in settling the distribution of land and the determination of emolument. (1: 10a.)[42]

If Tu Yu appreciated Mencius's view of the well-field system, as the above quotation clearly implies, why did he immediately put forth Shang Yang's policy that was deliberately aimed at abolishing the well-field system? The answer seems to be related to the result of Shang Yang's land reform in the Ch'in state. Tu quotes a passage saying that Shang Yang "abolished the well-field [system] and regulated the pathways [of the land], let [the peasants] cultivate land but not limit its size. Within a few years, the state [became] rich, the army [grew] powerful, and the [Ch'in] was [thus] invincible in all the world" (1: 10a). Evidently, Shang Yang's land reform attracted Tu Yu's attention because it had opened up new land for agricultural cultivation, brought wealth and power to the Ch'in, and made it the most powerful state of its time. It was also due precisely to his emphasis on agricultural cultivation that Tu put Mencius's view of the well-field system together with Shang Yang's antithetical land policy. As is well known both the Confucians and the legalists firmly believed that agriculture was the basis of the economy. Tu's point was that while Mencius's land policy had the merit of leading to a stable agrarian economy, Shang Yang's could make a state invincible throughout the world.

Tu Yu does not seem to have completely approved of Shang Yang's land reform, however. He criticized it for creating certain social ills such as excess land accumulation and the problem of vagrancy.[43] Tu obviously had an ambivalent attitude toward Shang Yang. His principal concern for the state continues to help us understand the rationale behind both his praise *and* criticism of Shang Yang: they were closely related to his view that Shang Yang's land policy simultaneously strengthened *and* damaged the power of the state.

Tu Yu mentioned various efforts to restrict excessive land accumulation in different periods, but he considered that only with the implementation of the two-tax system was the problem of vagrancy solved, and the state's finances finally stabilized.[44] With this accomplished, it seems that he also lost interest in the land accumulation problem. Measured against Lu Chih's efforts to reduce land rents to ameliorate the peasants' suffering, we can see that Tu's sympathy for the peasants paled in comparison to his concern for the economic well-being of the state.

This explains why when Tu Yu specifically singled out Kuan Chung and Shang Yang as "worthy ones [*hsien-che*]," his argument was precisely that they had helped their sovereigns to "enrich the state and strengthen the armies [*fu-kuo ch'iang-ping*]" (12: 71c).[45] Considering the weakened central power in the post–An Lu-shan period, it is possible that Tu's concern for state power again functioned only as an expedient necessity. It differed from that of the legalists, but was similar to Hsün Tzu's position in that theoretically Tu never completely neglected the people's welfare.[46] Of course, Tu's longing for a unified empire in the post-rebellion era was not unique. Such longing was prevalent in the contemporary consciousness. Even Han Yü, the most notable representative of mid-T'ang Confucian revival, gave Shang Yang credit for his ability to strengthen the Ch'in state.[47]

It was also due to this longing for a powerful centralized state that Tu Yu praised the first imperial Ch'in dynasty for its substitution of "the prefectural" or "the commandery and county system

[*chün hsien chih-tu*]" for the ancient "feudal [*feng-chien*] system."
For Tu, one important merit in the establishment of the commandery
system was that it was better than the *feng-chien* system at reducing periods of chaos during dynastic changes.[48]

Tu Yu's comment that "to set up [feudal] states benefits one
house, [but] to establish commanderies benefits ten thousand surnames" makes it seem that he believed such a centralized system
could spare the common people from suffering greater disorder when
dynastic changes took place.[49] His real concern, however, was to
point out that only a centralized system could gather a large population for the state, and with a large population the government
would become safe and stable. "There is security in a multitude of
people and danger in a small number" (31: 177a). In other words, the
stability and security of the state were still his primary concerns.

Even so, because Tu Yu noticed the public misery during dynastic changes, his sympathy for the people in this regard was
consistent with his general position on light taxation and on regulating the government expenditure for the sake of "pacifying the
people." This means that while the search for a powerful state was
unequivocally his primary concern, Tu had no intention of leaving
the people's welfare completely unattended. It is probably from this
perspective that the *Old T'ang History* describes Tu as a man most
concerned with "methods of enriching the state and pacifying the
people."[50]

Against an identical historical background, Lu Chih himself
never said that the state's interests could come before the people's
welfare, not even as an expediency. For Lu, the people were always
the foundation of the state. Only when the people's welfare was
taken care of could the state ensure its stability and prosperity.
That is why Lu repeatedly asked Te-tsung to abolish all the rebellion-
era emergency taxes, and insisted on the reform of the two-tax
system.

Confucian Pragmatist vs. *Utilitarian Confucian*

The key difference between Lu Chih and Tu Yu is precisely
their perception of the relationship between the people and the
state during a time when the center is overshadowed by regional
powers. In spite of the common grounds shared by them, Tu Yu
apparently believed that when the central government was in decline, nothing was more important than "enriching the state."

Because of this overriding concern, Tu showed that he was willing to exalt the ruler and neglect for the time being the suffering inflicted on the common people by the implementation of the two-tax system. If extended to its logical conclusion, Tu's position, however motivated, could lead him to sacrifice everything to establish a powerful state. The potential danger of using political ends to justify whatever means are applied in the process is quite apparent. From this point of view, it is appropriate to consider Tu's views on government to be tinged with legalism.

On the other hand, since Tu Yu's ideal government remains a benevolent one, there is no question that he, like Lu Chih, should be regarded as a Confucian scholar official. To distinguish him from Lu Chih, or a legalist in the true sense, it is perhaps more accurate to identify him as a *utilitarian Confucian*.[51] This term is used here specifically to mean that, although Tu was essentially a Confucian scholar official, his concern for the wealth and power of the state was so great that, during a period of central decline, it often propelled him to put his concern for the people in a subordinate position. This is where he and Lu Chih ultimately part company.

Lu Chih's concern for virtuous imperial conduct usually makes him susceptible of being placed on one end of the Confucian polarity, and thus being categorized as a conservative moralist, or an *idealist* Confucian who appreciated no pragmatism, but only *moral statesmanship*. These terms, as we have demonstrated, portray only one aspect of Lu's approach to government. Lu adopted just as pragmatic an attitude as Tu Yu did in dealing with almost every aspect of government affairs; moreover, he was seriously concerned with the possible practical results of every form of political behavior. It is equally inappropriate to adopt the usual terms, *pragmatist* Confucian, or *practical statesmanship*[52] to label Lu's approach without pointing out that the conventional understanding of these terms is essentially different from the term I have selected in this study—the Confucian pragmatist approach.

The conventional understanding of pragmatist Confucian, or practical statesmanship is functionally equivalent to the above-mentioned definition of utilitarian Confucian. This is because these two terms have been used generally to refer to some Confucian scholar officials who, though believing in the Confucian ideal of benevolent ruler and government, still considered institutional change to strengthen the state their first priority during periods of dynastic decline. Their desire to restore the power of the state could often supersede all their other concerns.

They tended to justify the use of morally dubious and pragmatic means to achieve a stable political order, and they were interested in practical results, but the *pragmatist* Confucians did not necessarily concern themselves with the *ethics of responsibility.* Their political position has only been categorized as "an ethics of social orientation."[53] This implies that the logical result of their overriding concern for the state, just like Tu Yu's utilitarian Confucian approach, could make any realistic estimation of the possible harmful consequences to other domains of public interest totally unnecessary. Thus, I have chosen the term Confucian pragmatist approach instead of the usual term *pragmatist* Confucian in this study to emphasize more precisely the essential features of Lu Chih's approach to government and his dominant concern for the well-being of the people.

To complete our comparison of Lu Chih and Tu Yu, we need to call attention to another major dissimilarity that separates them. As we have noted, due to the fact that he valued institutional change more than moral leadership, as chief minister Tu Yu hardly attempted to transform the emperor's conduct. However, it is also quite probable that Tu did not strive to achieve his ideal of a benevolent ruler because of his concern for self-protection. One source informs us that when he served in the Huai-nan region (between 789 and 803), Tu once mentioned that the great T'ang general Kuo Tzu-i was constantly worried that his high official position would land him in trouble. Tu Yu of course was aware that it was Te-tsung who, right after taking the throne, had elevated this most loyal T'ang general to the post of imperial teacher, and that this elevation was actually granted to relieve Kuo of all his military power.[54] Using Kuo to reflect on the dilemma of a high ranking official, Tu commented that "this (being the highest official in the bureaucracy) was indeed a dangerous matter for the ministers." Tu also mentioned that after he retired he would simply do nothing but amuse himself with variety shows in the market. The implication was that no one would then suspect he had any political ambitions.[55]

Tu Yu's sensitivity to the potential danger involved in a high ranking court position is clear. His cautious attitude was justifiable since he did suffer political injustice in the early 780s. This same cautious attitude may certainly have exerted an equal if not greater influence than his theoretical orientation on his political behavior during his service as chief minister. No matter which element played the dominant role, the impact on Tu's political behavior serves to underscore further the contrast with Lu Chih. Lu's entire career at court was committed to the realization of his Confucian political convictions, even at the risk of his life. His intransigence in the face of imperial resistance did cost him his political life, whereas Tu Yu completed a lengthy tenure as chief minister. It is fair to say that Tu's Confucian consciousness remained largely at the conceptual level in contrast to Lu Chih's actual efforts at practical Confucian reform.

In this chapter, we have singled out Li Mi and especially Tu Yu as the main objects of our comparison. The similarities found between Lu Chih and his two contemporary chief ministers were basically confined to *political* concerns—concerns for bureaucratic efficiency, for a practical attitude toward administrative affairs, or for virtuous rulers. When it comes to their *social* concerns, their concerns for the people's well-being, the essential differences overshadow areas of agreement. Again, this does not mean that Li Mi or Tu Yu had no sympathy for the people, it only means that their sympathy for the people could become secondary when personal interest or raison d'état intervened. It is from this perspective that they cannot be regarded as Lu Chih's closest intellectual counterparts. To discover whether a closer link possibly existed between Lu Chih and other mid-T'ang intellectual characters, we must now examine Lu's significance in the mid-T'ang Confucian revival.

CHAPTER EIGHT

Significance in the Mid-T'ang Confucian Revival

Lu Chih's adult life paralleled the development of the mid-T'ang Confucian revival. His political quest qualifies him to be considered, not just a Confucian bureaucrat, but a Confucian in the mid-T'ang Confucian revival mold—a person seriously committed to the improvement of the public well-being under the guidance of his Confucian convictions.[1] To reach a fair assessment of the significance of Lu's political endeavors, one needs to find out, through a comparison of their approaches to government, whether an essential intellectual link existed between Lu Chih and the leading Confucian revivalists. Such a comparison will help to characterize the political exertions of the representative Confucian revivalists, and provide us with a deeper understanding of the spirit of Lu's time and of his proper place in it.

A brief delineation of the mid-T'ang Confucian revival will serve to historicize our exploration of Lu's significance in this era.

Mid-T'ang Revival of Confucianism

Before the outbreak of the An Lu-shan rebellion, the philosophical sophistication and spiritual consolation offered by Buddhism and Taoism persistently eclipsed the power of Confucianism as a system of thought.[2] Buddhism was the most creative intellectual force throughout the T'ang.[3] Taoism also attracted a huge following among T'ang literary men due to its other-worldly orientation.[4] Confucianism lacked the intellectual vitality to dominate the medieval Chinese mind or the T'ang intellectual scene, but it remained alive as a cultural force and was never completely neglected by the government.[5]

The early T'ang rulers understood the inextricable relation between the teaching of Confucianism and the exercise of imperial government. They strongly supported the establishment of the Confucian canon for use in the civil service examinations. With imperial patronage, the learned tradition of Confucianism was well preserved, though only a limited number of Confucian scholars participated in these activities. These scholars exerted a very slight influence on an intellectual climate where Confucianism held little attraction. Moreover, most of the Confucian scholars in the early T'ang and the first half of the middle T'ang were primarily concerned with classical exegesis and ritual programs; they had neither the intellectual vision nor the intention to reinvigorate an uninspiring Confucianism.[6]

The An Lu-shan rebellion changed the mid-T'ang intellectual landscape. A resurgence of Confucian consciousness led to a categorical change in the mid-T'ang intellectual attitude toward Confucianism. Emphasis on an earnest search for the living relevance of Confucian principles superceded the previous stress on exegetical and ritual studies. This revival of Confucian consciousness went through various stages and expressed itself in different intellectual activities during the mid-eighth and ninth centuries.

In the mid-eighth century, one such activity was the socially conscious verse of poets like Tu Fu (712–770) and Yüan Chieh (719–772). Tu is often regarded as China's greatest poet, and Yüan is also considered "the most adventurous *san-wen* (or prose) writer" at the inception of the *ku-wen* movement. Their poetic efforts to promote Confucian ideals, though celebrated in Chinese literary history, failed to arouse much contemporary attention.[7]

The prose reform campaign initiated by Hsiao Ying-shih, Li Hua (715–766), Chia Chih (718–768), and Tu-ku Chi at this time is generally accepted as the precursor of the *ku-wen* movement that flourished in the early ninth century. The Hsiao group's basic concern was a stylistic reform in prose writing, but they also insisted that the highest goal of literary works was to transmit Confucian moral values. Their interest in studying the Confucian classics for their fundamental meaning and actually regarding them as practical guides for social and political order, establishes this group as one of the representatives of the early mid-T'ang Confucian revival.[8]

This revitalized Confucian consciousness was also reflected in the "critical scholarship" on the *Spring and Autumn Annals* (*Ch'un-ch'iu*) launched by T'an Chu (724–770) and Chao K'uang (fl. 770–780) in 761. They believed that only by examining the *Annals* itself could one grasp the essence of the sage's teaching. Like the Hsiao Ying-shih group, they also intended to erect Confucian principles as the norm for ameliorative social and political action. Their ideas and works were later disseminated in the capital by their follower Lu Ch'un, a member of Lu Chih's clan and also a possible recipient of his patronage.[9]

From 780 to 800, the period of Lu Chih's political rise and fall, the advocates of Confucian revival seem to have remained restricted to carrying forward the ideas of their predecessors. The Confucian revival finally developed into an independent movement when Han Yü and Liu Tsung-yüan together with Li Ao (772?/773?–836?) emerged on the scene near the turn of the ninth century. This new generation of intellectuals was influenced by both their *ku-wen* predecessors and the *Spring and Autumn Annals* school.[10]

Like their predecessors, this new generation of intellectuals continued to regard the Confucian doctrines as guiding principles for social and political action. The major difference between them and their predecessors was that they began to use their own terms to interpret Confucian principles. At this point, the *ku-Tao*, or the *Way in antiquity* was conceptualized as the Confucian moral Way, that is, the way of benevolence and rightness (*jen* and *i*), transmitted from the sage kings Yao, Shun, King Wen, and King Wu to the Duke of Chou and finally down to Confucius and Mencius. Han Yü was of course the one who first established this notion of "the succession of the Way [*Tao-t'ung*]."[11]

Yet, it has been noted that there were some distinctions between Han Yü, Li Ao, and Liu Tsung-yüan. Liu Tsung-yüan primarily perceived the Confucian *Tao* as the Way to improve the public good. By contrast, Han Yü and Li Ao expanded their notion of the *Tao* to include a Way of enhancing the human spiritual world. For Han and Li, the Confucian moral Way was sufficient to sustain a person's inner life, and there was no need for individuals to search for spiritual solace in Buddhism or Taoism.[12]

However, it was Liu Tsung-yüan's perception of Confucianism, not that of Han Yü or Li Ao, which represented the mainstream revivalist consciousness in the mid-T'ang. Han Yü and Li Ao did initiate a new interpretive direction for Confucianism, but it did not flourish until the Sung dynasty.[13] The majority of Confucian revivalists valued primarily the public spiritedness of Confucianism as a political philosophy for the public good. Their private lives, like those of most medieval Chinese intellectuals, were still permeated with Buddhism and Taoism.[14] Their mentality has thus been characterized as "Confucianism without and Taoism and Buddhism within."[15]

Despite the conceptual differences between Liu Tsung-yüan and Han Yü or Li Ao, there was one essential common denominator that impelled them all toward the mid-T'ang Confucian revival: their concern for the social and political challenges of their time. Han Yü and Li Ao expanded their perception of Confucianism as a moral and spiritual guide for human life, but spiritual cultivation per se was not their main concern.[16] The motivating force behind their expansion of Confucianism was less spiritual than social and political. Like Lu Chih, or the other major revivalists, their ultimate concern was to rebuild the T'ang empire. It is precisely within this context that I shall compare Lu Chih with the major Confucian revivalists: Yüan Chieh, Tu-ku Chi, Liu Tsung-yüan, Han Yü, and Li Ao.[17]

This comparison will also include Ch'üan Te-yü's views on government. Ch'üan Te-yü was not a representative Confucian revivalist, but his intellectual disposition as well as his official ascendancy in the late 790s brought him into contact with many of the leading revivalists, such as Liang Su, Liu Tsung-yüan, and Li Ao. He was also the father-in-law of Tu-ku Chi's son. He was clearly sympathetic to the revivalists' cause.[18] He knew Lu Chih's uncle, and his preface to Lu Chih's collected works is the only non-official T'ang source that evinces great respect for Lu Chih. His 792 criticism of P'ei Yen-ling was also partially incorporated into Lu's later critical memorial. To include Ch'üan in our comparison will serve both to help clarify the common ground he and Lu shared, and to discover whether, as chief minister, he played a role in propagating some of Lu's policies in mid-T'ang intellectual circles after Lu's downfall.

Unlike Lu Chih and Ch'üan Te-yü, most of the leading figures of the mid-T'ang Confucian revival never occupied the highest bureaucratic position at court; most of them served a great deal of time in provincial government.[19] Their provincial experience provided them with first-hand understanding of current problems and intensified their social and political concerns. I shall examine Lu Chih's and their concerns under the categories of the state, the bureaucracy, the imperial conduct, and the people's welfare.[20]

On the State

Almost all the representatives of Confucian revival were concerned with the restoration of a unified empire over the powerful provincial governors, and this concern led them to reflect upon basic principles of government.

One essential idea almost all of them shared with Lu Chih was that the state had to be governed by the principles of benevolence and rightness. Both Han Yü and Li Ao agreed that "no way is greater than that of benevolence and rightness."[21] Liu Tsung-yüan equally believed that the way of benevolence and rightness was inseparable from the way of governing.[22] Lü Wen (772–811), Liu's comrade in the Wang Shu-wen group as well as a notable mid-T'ang thinker, also indicated that benevolence and rightness were two necessary foundations for proper polity.[23] Earlier, in a memorial to Tai-tsung around 765, Tu-ku Chi insisted that the emperor should try to "employ the hearts of Yao and Confucius as [his own] heart."[24] Even Yüan Chieh, whose early thinking betrays some elements of Taoist orientation, once asserted that "the way of establishing an ordered government lies first in using benevolence and wisdom."[25] Some of Ch'üan Te-yü's memorials to the throne express a similar view.[26]

Ch'üan Te-yü and all these major representatives of the Confucian revival clearly voiced views on the moral basis of the state that are similar to Lu Chih's, but their position on the principle of expediency does not seem to be as uniformly identical as one might have expected. Both Yüan Chieh and Tu-ku Chi once wrote that to practice expediency was to deviate from the correct way of government. In an earlier essay written in 752, Yüan blamed rulers who intended to save the world by practicing expediency for causing moral degradation. He said that rulers who were anxious to save the world, try to "save it with expediency. Expediency [involves] waste and evil, and the world thus also becomes wasteful and evil."[27] Tu-ku Chi similarly disapproved of applying expediency to government because "the way of expediency is to regard disagreement with the classics as practicality; this deviates even farther from moral virtue."[28]

This antipathy toward expediency probably led Yüan Chieh, unlike Lu Chih and many other Confucian revivalists, to discredit Kuan Chung's contribution to the accomplishments of Duke Huan of Ch'i.[29] Yüan held Kuan Chung responsible for the decline of the Chou feudal system.[30] Yüan was not trying to defend the feudal

system, rather he was worried about maintaining the unity of the
T'ang empire in the midst of the An Lu-shan rebellion. Using Kuan
Chung as a negative example of misplaced loyalty, Yüan made
loyalty an absolute virtue for officials.

Tu-ku Chi's criticism of Chi Cha, an exemplar of the state of Wu
during the Spring and Autumn period, is quite similar.[31] Even though
he emphasized the importance of moral virtue in government, Tu-ku
Chi apparently opposed Chi Cha's preservation of his own personal
integrity at the cost of neglecting his duty to public order, especially
when that order was in peril. Ironically, Tu-ku did not realize that
his critique of Chi Cha amounted to requiring Chi Cha to practice
expediency in different situations. In effect, like Yüan Chieh, Tu-ku
also elevated loyalty to the position of an absolute.

Lu Chih never thought of loyalty the way Yüan and Tu-ku did.
His attitude toward an official accused of treason shows that he
was more willing to judge a person's loyalty in light of the actual
historical situation confronting the person.

I should note that Yüan Chieh agreed with Lu Chih on the
necessity to adapt to new situations to maintain order in the provinces even though he parted company with Lu on the application
of expediency in general.[32] Neither he nor Tu-ku Chi saw expediency as a complementary principle that could help the state pursue
a higher ethical good with minimum losses. Tu-ku Chi was so averse
to expediency that he never seems to have stressed the importance
of adapting to new circumstances. His proclaimed antipathy toward expediency as a means to evil ends thus rendered his political
position closer to that of a pure moralist. Nevertheless, the fact
remains that, like Lu Chih, both he and Yüan Chieh shared a
mutual concern for T'ang stability, and they went on to express this
concern in concrete action.

Han Yü, Li Ao and Liu Tsung-yüan had this same concern.
Because of it, they praised Kuan Chung for the skillful way his
administration helped the Ch'i state to become a hegemon in the
Spring and Autumn period.[33] For this same reason, Han Yü also
commended Shang Yang's legalist methods of strengthening the
Ch'in state. In a manner similar to Lu Chih, their concern for the
state further impelled them all to emphasize the necessity of adapting to changing times and circumstances.

Han Yü, for instance, when discussing the best possible military strategy in 815, stressed the importance of "estimating and
examining the circumstances, and of pursuing benefits by taking
advantage of the times."[34] Han also attributed a colleague's mili-

tary victory to his ability to "adapt to the opportune moment in conducting affairs."[35] When Han recommended a close friend to a provincial governor, he praised this friend as a person who "recognizes the times [and circumstances], knows how to [adapt] to changes, and does not have only one specific talent like the Confucian scholars or literati."[36]

Li Ao likewise wrote that the rulers of the Three Dynasties did not in the beginning intend to elevate one specific way of governing. They ended up doing so because they "adapted to the changed circumstances and practiced expediency."[37] Here Lu Chih would certainly agree.

Liu Tsung-yüan's argument that the establishment of the *feng-chien* system was made necessary by the "conditions and forces [*shih*]" that ancient sages found themselves subject to is well known.[38] What is little known is that Lu Chih had long since viewed changing human organizations as the outcome of accommodation to various new objective circumstances. Liu Tsung-yüan's similar conviction undoubtedly played a part in his emphasis on the importance of expediency in government.

In 814, Liu wrote an essay attacking the Han Confucian theory of interaction that stressed a fixed coordination between one specific season and the execution of punishments. Part of his argument reveals how he considered expediency necessary in government. Contending that what had been the standard of administration was not necessarily an accurate means of carrying out the Confucian moral Way, Liu explained the relation between *Ching* (standard of conduct, norm or classic) and *Ch'üan* (expediency) as follows:

> What is called *ching*, is the norm; what is called *ch'üan*, is to understand the *ching* thoroughly. These are all matters for the benevolent and wise. If [you] separate [*ching* and *ch'üan*] from each other, you will become confused. . . . Those who know *ching*, will not damage my Way (*Tao*) with strange things; those who understand *ch'üan*, will not use [the rule of] ordinary people to oppose my thought; those who combine [the two] into one and have no doubt in doing so, are the ones who truly believe in the Way. (LHTCC, 3: 16b.)

Like the earlier Lu Chih, Liu Tsung-yüan apparently did not think that the application of expediency was analogous to political trickery. He showed that a relation of mutual dependence existed between *Ching* and *Ch'üan*. Their operation, moreover, had to be carried out under the guidance of the *Tao*. When Lu Chih explained his principles of *I* and *Ch'üan*, he seems to have anticipated the understanding Liu later came to.

Ch'üan Te-yü once used the phrase, "*ch'üan heng ch'ing-chung*, or weighing and estimating the seriousness of [affairs]," when asking Te-tsung to replace P'ei Yen-ling as head of the Department of Public Revenues.[39] This was in harmony with Lu Chih's position, as were his views on the duty of government; but contrary to Lu and the majority of the revivalists, Ch'üan did not particularly emphasize the necessity of adapting to changing times and circumstances. His attitude in this respect was closer to that of Tu-ku Chi.

To sum up, with the exception of Tu-ku Chi and Ch'üan Te-yü, all of the above mentioned Confucian revivalists shared with Lu Chih a view of governing the state that was both moralistic and pragmatic. Ch'üan Te-yü and the rest all agreed that the government should operate according to the Confucian principles of benevolence and rightness. Their belief in a moral foundation for the state did not prevent the majority of them from seeing the importance of governmental adaptation to changed times and circumstances. Yüan Chieh still recognized the necessity of accommodation to new situations in local administration even while he expressed a negative view of expediency.

On the Bureaucracy

Appointing capable and virtuous men (*hsien-che* or *hsien-liang*) to government was one of the basic tenets of Confucian political thought, and as one might expect, all the leading revivalists and Ch'üan Te-yü upheld this principle just as Lu Chih did in his service. Around 759, Yüan Chieh pointed out that one principle the Son of Heaven had to observe was "definitely appointing virtuous and outstanding superior men [as his officials]."[40] In his 765 memorial criticizing Tai-tsung's rule, Tu-ku Chi also asked the throne to "seek the capable and the virtuous" as a way of improving the government.[41] When, in his celebrated essay "On Feudalism," Liu Tsung-yüan contended that the commandery system was a better political institution than the ancient *feng-chien* system, one of his arguments focused on the point that the centralized imperial system "causes the capable and virtuous men to remain above, and the unworthy to remain below; then [the world] can [have] order and peace."[42] Liu's main concern in this essay was the stability of the state, but his support for a government run by capable and virtuous men hardly needs emphasis. And the same can be said about Li Ao and Han Yü.[43]

Assessment of Officials

Due to the differences in their official responsibilities, only a few of the major Confucian revivalists, including Yüan Chieh and Liu Tsung-yüan, provided actual plans such as Lu Chih did to deal with the problem of official assessment.

In 764, during his tenure as prefect in Tao-chou, Yüan Chieh presented a memorial to the throne offering his suggestions regarding the assessment of local prefects. He advised the throne to evaluate them in the following manner:

> After one year, ask them how many [people] have returned from exile, and how much land has been reclaimed and cultivated; after two years, ask by how many times the livestock and produce have increased, and by how many times the taxable [households] have increased over the first year; after three years, estimate their merits and faults and precisely distribute rewards and punishments. (YTSC, 8: 124)

Some points in Yüan Chieh's suggestion remind us of Lu Chih's 780 proposal for examining local officials:

> [The court needs] to examine [how local officials] nourish the people by inspecting the growth and decline of the [number of the local] households; to examine [how they] tend to basic agriculture by inspecting the increase and decrease of the reclaimed fields; and to examine [whether they are] honest or greedy by inspecting the weight of the tax [burden] and *corvée* services [they place on the people]. (HTS, 157: 4911)

Yüan Chieh never provided an overall plan for evaluating the entire bureaucracy as Lu did, but both of them undeniably agreed that the evaluation of local officials had to be made on the basis of their actual achievements.

Liu Tsung-yüan did not prescribe specific criteria for official evaluation, but he insisted that the central government should inspect local officials regularly to maintain order in the empire. Like Lu Chih, Liu thought that employing rewards and punishments was a necessary part of the inspection of local officials. This practice could help the government establish a capable and efficient bureaucracy.[44]

Han Yü did not have any plans for official evaluation, but his close friend Li Kuan did. This is interesting because Li Kuan also obtained his *chin-shih* degree along with Han Yü in the spring of 792, the year Lu Chih was responsible for administering the doctoral examinations. Li later claimed to be Lu's "disciple [*men-jen*]."[45]

In the middle of 793, Li Kuan presented a letter to Lu putting forth his views on government.[46] Li pointed out some problems that he found harmful to bureaucratic morale. These problems ranged from a discrepancy between the actual abilities of some officials and their assumed offices to the long waiting period for advancement and transfer. Li wrote that "if one is appointed to an office he is incapable of filling, that office is rendered useless; if the office does not match [the official's] ability, the able [officials] will then complain; quick advancement promotes rash competition, and delayed transfer creates injustice and bias" (LYPWC, 3: 32).

Li Kuan's criticism of official appointment, advancement, and transfer parallels comments presented by Lu Chih both in 792 and 794. Li Kuan could not have influenced the opinions Lu manifested in 792, but it is likely that his letter reinforced Lu's determination to push for bureaucratic reform again in 794. Li Kuan's comments appear general in comparison and contain no concrete proposals for real improvement. Lu's discussion involves detailed suggestions for reform, and even provide what he called a "middle way" to evaluate and regulate officials.[47]

That Lu Chih was always close to the political center, especially to Te-tsung himself, and that he assumed the office of chief minister, undoubtedly contributed to the depth and inclusiveness of his policies on evaluating officials. Had he lacked the necessary knowledge and ability to formulate these policies, however, and if he was not personally preoccupied with the solutions to these problems, his career background alone could not account for his actions. Ch'üan Te-yü also maintained that officials must be assessed according to their real performance, but he did not formulate any specific policies for conducting such evaluations when he was chief minister.[48]

In any event, due to different career backgrounds, most of the representatives of the Confucian revival were unable to communicate directly with the throne as frequently as Lu Chih was. They were not constantly engaged in reforming the bureaucracy with the kind of high intensity that Lu maintained. Consequently, their efforts to transform imperial conduct, though similar to Lu's, were also not as comprehensive or as thorough.

On the Imperial Conduct

The leading representatives of Confucian revival all considered it the emperor's duty to be virtuous, but only some of them explicitly stated that imperial legitimacy depended mainly on the fulfillment of the emperor's moral obligation to the people. That is, only some of them asserted along with Lu Chih the proposition that the ruler's mandate was not predetermined by Heaven, but was rather predicated upon his efforts to improve the public well-being. Some of them went even further than Lu in their attack on the deleterious influence they felt the Han theory of interaction between Heaven and humankind was having on contemporary government.[49]

To downplay supernatural influences on government, Lü Wen once wrote that "Not in Heaven, not in the spirits / Only in the Way should [a minister] put his trust. . . . / Ascendancy and collapse, order and upheaval, depend on virtue, not on cosmic cycles."[50] Tu-ku Chi, though like Lu Chih, still employing the Han Confucian concept of Heaven's warning to remind the emperor of his proper duty, clearly intended to have him focus primarily on human affairs.[51] The same can be said about Ch'üan Te-yü. In 799 when Ch'üan called on the throne to relieve the victims of that year's severe drought, he told Te-tsung that "there is nothing but the rectification of government affairs that can avert natural calamity."[52]

Neither Yüan Chieh nor Han Yü or Li Ao specifically discussed the imperial role from the perspective of the Mandate of Heaven, but both Yüan Chieh and Han Yü occasionally had a fatalistic inclination when facing personal success or failure.[53] This makes them appear less progressive than Lu Chih or the above-mentioned scholar officials, but none of these men ever challenged the fundamental presupposition of the Mandate of Heaven. They all tacitly admitted that Heaven would confer its Mandate on a ruler provided that he was benevolent and virtuous. The only leading revivalist who reached the point of substantially invalidating that presupposition was Liu Tsung-yüan.[54]

Liu argued that "it is not that Heaven takes any part in [the sphere of] men, . . . The affairs of each proceed without interfering with the other."[55] He also maintained that the founding rulers of the T'ang received their mandate not from Heaven but "from the people." Nevertheless, he continued occasionally to claim that Heaven would confer its Mandate upon a ruler if he was benevolent and obtained the support of the people.[56] As with Lu Chih and other contemporary revivalists, Liu's efforts to redefine the Mandate of Heaven were thus confined to urging the throne to concentrate on the improvement of public affairs.[57]

To achieve that goal, these Confucian revivalists each in his own way shared Lu Chih's views on how to improve imperial conduct. They all made one or another of the following suggestions: the ruler should accept remonstrance and reject slander; he should restrain eunuch involvement in government; he should establish himself as sincere and trustworthy, or he should refuse provincial tributes; and finally, he should relieve the people's suffering.

Around 819, right after emperor Hsien-tsung managed to restore dynastic unity, Li Ao presented a memorial that consisted of a six-part discussion of current affairs.[58] His proposals are all of a piece with Lu Chih's. He maintained that "the reason that a state can rise is because its ruler can trust his ministers, and ministers can assist their ruler with loyalty and honesty."[59] He then urged Hsien-tsung to employ loyal and honest ministers to achieve a peaceful and ordered state. Li wrote emphatically that if the deceptive and wicked were trusted by the throne, "the great peace will then definitely not come into being and dangerous dealings will secretly take place." Li Ao defined the deceptive and wicked in terms similar to Lu Chih's "small men": they "do not know the overall situation, do not consider the future, and simply concentrate on benefiting themselves." P'ei Yen-ling was actually on Li Ao's list of deceptive and wicked T'ang ministers.[60]

In a manner almost identical to Lu Chih, Li Ao also pleaded with the throne to stop receiving provincial tributes. He recapitulated Lu Chih's view that frugal imperial conduct would help relieve the economic burden of the local population. To convince the throne of this point, Li argued that "money and goods [sent up by provinces] are neither rain coming from Heaven nor water gushing out of a spring; if they are not extracted from the people, where will they come from?"[61] Not only the intention, but also the grammar and rhetoric of Li's statement all reflect the identical point Lu made in 794. While there is no evidence to establish any direct influence, this surely demonstrates the close affinity between their convictions about imperial conduct and their proposals for realizing those convictions.[62]

As with Lu Chih, or Li Ao, Han Yü and Liu Tsung-yüan also agreed that rulers should rid themselves of slander made by wicked people because slander could cause the decline of the state.[63] The difference was that they expressed their views not directly to the throne, but in personal treatises. Yet, there is no doubt that their intended audience was the ruler.

One specific practice that Liu Tsung-yüan thought necessary to abolish to preserve the ruler's virtue was allowing imperial personal attendants—eunuchs—to meddle in public affairs. He indirectly attacked the employment of eunuchs to manage court affairs in an 809 essay critical of Duke Wen of Chin for seeking a eunuch's advice concerning a minister's administrative ability.[64] Liu warned that this practice would lead to "the ruination of good [ministers] and the failure of government."[65] Such a warning clearly reflects Lu Chih's earlier position.

Han Yü never said that it was the ruler's duty to prevent eunuchs from meddling in court affairs, but he was opposed to their interference with regular bureaucratic operations. When Han served at the Bureau of Sacrifices, also in 809, he was responsible for revoking eunuch control over all the Buddhist and Taoist monasteries in the capital. Because of this, Han admitted in late 810 that he had made enemies of the eunuchs. Later in 811 Han again complained to his provincial superior about the practice of employing eunuchs as army supervisors.[66] Han himself had flattered a eunuch army supervisor during his first official service in Pien-chou, but this did not stop him from opposing eunuch intervention in regular bureaucratic procedures.[67] Even Han Yü's most daring and celebrated act of advising Hsien-tsung not to receive a Buddhist relic in the palace in 819 was partly aimed at cutting the eunuchs off from a major source of revenue.[68]

It should be noted that neither Lu Chih, nor any other leading revivalists would insist, as Han Yü and Li Ao did, that the emperor's inner thoughts were inseparable from his imperial conduct. As is widely acknowledged, Han and Li established the relevance to Confucian government of the *Great Learning* and the *Doctrine of the Mean* sections of the *Record of Rites*. The famous eight-fold progression of the Great Learning, from personal moral cultivation, to regulation of one's household, to bringing order to the state, and, ultimately, to the whole world, led them to regard moral cultivation of the ruler's inner thoughts as the basis for the development of a benevolent government.[69] They especially emphasized "sincerity [*ch'eng*]" as the nucleus of the ruler's moral cultivation.

Before Han Yü and Li Ao, however, sincerity was a virtue that Liang Su, and Ch'üan Te-yü already valued, but they tended to discuss sincerity and other ideas from the *Doctrine of the Mean* in relation to Buddhist concepts rather than the ruler's personal cultivation.[70] We do not know whether Lu Chih ever discussed sincerity in a Buddhist context, but he stressed sincerity more frequently in his memorials than did Liang and Ch'üan and most of the mid-T'ang scholar officials. He also seems to have cited, earlier than they did, passages in the *Doctrine of the Mean* on the necessity of the emperor practicing sincerity.

The point is that Han Yü and Li Ao were not the first ones to emphasize the importance of sincerity, nor were they pioneers in their interest in the *Doctrine of the Mean*. It is undeniable, however, that it was they who argued for an inevitable logical causation between imperial moral cultivation and order in the state. In other words, even though Lu Chih and all the other Confucian revivalists believed that imperial moral cultivation was a necessary condition for an ordered government, it was Han and Li who finally established the causal relationship between the emperor's inner thoughts and public order.

The views of Lu Chih and other Confucian revival intellectuals such as Liu Tsung-yüan also differ from Han Yü's on imperial power. Han was much more inclined than they were to accept as given the actual hierarchical relations between the emperor, the bureaucrats, and the common people.[71] In "On the Origin of the Way," Han wrote:

> The ruler is the one who gives orders; officials are the ones who implement the ruler's orders and bring them to the people, and the people are the ones who provide millet, grain, hemp and silk and make implements and vessels, and circulate goods and money to serve their superiors. . . . If the people do not provide millet, grain, hemp and silk . . . to serve their superiors, they will then be killed. (HCLCC, 11: 3a.)[72]

Han's efforts to defend the hierarchical relationship between the emperor and his subjects may serve as additional evidence of his longing for T'ang unity. Han Yü was not insensitive to public suffering, but his concern for T'ang unity was so intense that he felt impelled to consider a strong monarch a necessary condition for pursuing that goal. Such a willingness to elevate the emperor for the sake of a unified empire found no echoes in either Lu Chih's or Liu Tsung-yüan's perception of the imperial role.

Lu Chih constantly reminded Te-tsung that the relationship between a ruler and his subjects was reciprocal. He shared the paternalistic Confucian attitude toward the people, but he would never have supported Han Yü's suggestion that the state could kill the people if they failed to provide its material necessities. Given Liu Tsung-yüan's radical claim that the ruler's mandate was granted by the people and that "the duty [of the officials] is to be the people's servants, not to make the people serve them,"[73] it is even less likely that Liu would endorse Han Yü's definition of the ruler, the officials, and the people.

Han Yü is justly famous for courting martyrdom by defending Confucianism and challenging the imperial plan to receive a Buddhist relic in his memorial of 819, but such an offensive attitude toward the throne was not characteristic of Han's usual official memorials. The main rationale behind Han's "Memorial on the Buddha Relic" was his disappointment at the throne's indifference to culturally unifying the empire through an exclusive reliance on Confucianism.[74] In other words, unlike Lu Chih, Han Yü never intended to challenge the emperor's power for any other reason as long as he believed that power was the ideal means for the realization of the political and cultural unity of the T'ang. In this regard, Han Yü resembled more the utilitarian Confucian Tu Yu. For the sake of state stability, Tu was also willing to elevate the imperial power, albeit he usually maintained that the imperial role ought to be a benevolent one. It seems that Han Yü, who is sometimes considered a conservative Confucian, actually shared one specific and dominant concern with Tu Yu, a man frequently praised for having progressive views on government.

In sum, although the actual suggestions for improving imperial conduct made by individual Confucian revivalists and Ch'üan Te-yü were not as inclusive as those made by Lu Chih, they all shared Lu's view that the imperial role had to be a benevolent one. It is true that some of them did not particularly emphasize the importance of human striving with regard to the Mandate of Heaven, but none of them refuted the idea that the prerequisite for a ruler to receive the mandate lay in his benevolent and virtuous conduct. Even though Han Yü was more inclined to elevate the emperor's power to an absolute for the sake of T'ang unity, he never betrayed the idea that the emperor had to act benevolently. In short, Lu Chih was in basic agreement with the leading revivalists in their proposals for improving imperial conduct, but he made comparatively more concrete recommendations along those lines to Te-tsung himself.

My final comparison concerns the most important defining characteristic of the mid-T'ang Confucian revivalists: their sympathy for the people and their efforts to improve the people's welfare.

On the People's Welfare

All the leading Confucian revivalists expressed great sympathy for the suffering of the common people. Like Lu Chih, they considered it imperative to reduce the people's heavy tax burdens to improve their living conditions. They tried to relieve local suffering during their provincial service.

The An Lu-shan rebellion made Yüan Chieh deeply aware that "the people are desperate."[75] By 763, when he was appointed prefect of Tao-chou, the area had been devastated in an attack by southern aborigines. He pleaded with the throne to allow the people of Tao-chou an exemption from all back taxes and all the supplementary impositions levied at the time. His advice was accepted and the livelihood of the Tao-chou people was improved through his efforts.[76]

Tu-ku Chi just as strongly memorialized Tai-tsung to take the people's welfare into serious consideration. In 765, he described how the An Lu-shan rebellion devastated the people's lives in this poignantly frank fashion:

> It has been ten years since the ceaseless fighting started. The people produce nothing on their looms. The dwellings of those who command their own soldiers extend throughout the streets and lanes; their servants and maids [already] grow tired of wine and meat, while the poor in weakness and hunger join their armies, become their servants, and suffer terribly. Inside Ch'ang-an city, killing and plundering occur in broad daylight, but the Mayor dares not make inquiries. . . . [The people] are impoverished and have no place to turn. Now their hearts are longing only for [this year's] wheat crop. If the wheat crop fails, they will exchange their children and eat them. (PLC, 4: 21a)[77]

Later, as prefect of Hao-chou and Shu-chou (modern Anhui), Tu-ku Chi also appealed to the throne to reduce the local population's tax burdens to ameliorate their misery.[78]

Although the central government revenues were stabilized through the implementation of the two-tax system, the abuses involved in its operation and the economic difficulties they created for the common people had not been corrected when Li Ao, Han Yü, and Liu Tsung-yüan came on the political scene at the beginning of the ninth century. Between 806 and 819, we see Li Ao expressing his concern for the economic plight of the people by advising emperor Hsien-tsung to stop accepting provincial tribute. Li strongly supported the same general policy of light taxation to reduce the people's tax burdens that Lu Chih had attempted to implement. He even cited those same familiar lines from the *Analects*, "When the people do not have enough, how can the ruler have enough?" to warn the present rulers of their first duty to enhance the people's material well-being.[79] Li's 817 suggestion to abolish the use of cash as the basic unit for tax assessment and payment under the two-tax system also echoed Lu Chih's position.

As with Lu Chih, Li Ao's suggestion was based on the fact that deflation brought economic ruin to the common people.[80] The same two reasons Lu Chih mentioned two decades earlier still held true: the people had to pay their taxes in goods, and deflation had drastically depreciated the cash value of those goods. Li Ao said:

> It has been forty years since [the tax quota of] the two-tax was first fixed at the beginning of the Chien-chung period [of Te-tsung's reign, 780–784]. . . . Compared with the beginning of the Chien-chung period, [the present] tax load has already increased threefold. . . . When tracing the fundamental evil of this [tax system], [I believe] it comes from [the system's continued] demand that the people pay cash while the [value of] the cash remains high. (LWKC, 9: 41a.)

Once the principal cause was identified, Li asked the emperor to allow the people to pay all their taxes in silk cloth. He also advised the government to use silk cloth as the basic unit for accounting. All this is unmistakably reminiscent of Lu Chih's earlier proposal.

Li Ao's sympathy for the poor was expressed not only in words, but equally in deeds. In Lu-chou (modern Anhui) between 825 and 827, he raised twelve thousand strings of cash from rich and powerful local landlords by making them pay taxes on all their previously unreported lands. The poor under his jurisdiction were greatly relieved.[81]

Li Ao was not alone in making the suggestion to replace cash with goods for tax payment.[82] In 794, after Lu Chih's downfall, Ch'üan Te-yü reminded Te-tsung that the problem of deflation had caused the peasants' tax burden to increase fivefold.[83] Probably trying not to offend the throne, Ch'üan never pushed any specific plan to improve the situation. He sympathized with the peasants for the same reason that Lu Chih did, but he somehow lacked Lu's commitment to their cause. It is thus difficult to know to what extent Li Ao formulated his suggestions on the basis of Ch'üan's propagation of Lu Chih's reform proposals.

Li Ao's mentor and close friend Han Yü had earlier supported the same idea. Toward the end of Te-tsung's reign, in the winter of 803 when Han was serving at the Censorate, he presented a memorial in which he proposed several methods to bring down the value of cash. One of his methods was intended to allow the people to pay their taxes in goods, emphasizing that the goods could either be silk cloth, cotton thread, or even grass and grain, depending on the local situation.[84] Not only was Han's prescription for reducing the people's tax burden equivalent to Lu Chih's, but his emphasis on the differences in local production also corresponded to Lu's analysis. With the exception of Ch'üan Te-yü, Han was probably the first scholar official whose proposals for reducing the tax burden closely recapitulated Lu Chih's position.

Han Yü revealed his sympathy for the people on other occasions as well. Just about the time he made the above suggestion, Han and two other colleagues at the Censorate called on Te-tsung to exempt the people of the capital region from their current tax payment due to a crop failure created by that year's severe summer drought and early autumn frost.[85] In the provinces, Han also worked to relieve the misery of local children by bringing an end to the practice of child slavery in the area under his jurisdiction.[86] In 822, toward the end of his life, Han presented a well thought out memorial in opposition to a proposal aimed at reforming the salt monopoly. His main point was that neither the government nor the people would benefit from this reform plan for officials to market salt directly to the consumer without employing merchants as intermediaries.[87] Han took the interests of the rich merchants into consideration, but his concern for the common people is also obvious. This concern persisted throughout his career.

Liu Tsung-yüan was equally concerned for the poor. His high degree of sensitivity to public suffering has already been noted as shaping and characterizing his perception of Confucianism.[88] In

815, a few years before Han Yü ended child slavery, Liu had taken effective measures to free the child slaves in Yung-chou where he served as prefect.[89] However, unlike Han, Liu took more notice of the gap between the rich and the poor. Liu's position is closer to Lu Chih's on this always difficult problem. When discussing the principles of government in a letter to a friend, Liu wrote that contemporary official corruption was so widespread that many rich families could easily escape their tax duties through bribery. The result was that the tax burden for the poor became even more oppressive. Strongly opposed to such an unequal tax distribution, Liu maintained that the rich ought to be taxed more than the poor to make the tax burden equitable and bearable.[90] Liu never intended to overthrow the rich as an economic class; he only hoped to make the tax distribution more equitable to relieve the poor. As he stated: "The rich families are the mother of the poor. They really must not be destroyed. [The government] should also not permit them to enjoy excessive favor and thus make the poor their slaves."[91]

The above discussion demonstrates that, like Lu Chih, both Han Yü and Liu Tsung-yüan took notice of the power of the rich class, but Han and Liu had different views about how to treat the rich, be they merchants or landlords. Liu Tsung-yüan's views were closer to Lu Chih's policy of "pacifying the rich and relieving the poor." While Liu advocated a proper increase in taxes paid by the rich without disturbing their actual financial security, Lu Chih's policy demanded that the rich reasonably reduce land rents in the interest of the poor. They both agreed that the rich had to be pacified, and the poor had to be relieved, but they also insisted that the power of the rich had to be restrained by the government. Social stability would be otherwise impossible. Han Yü worried that rich salt merchants would join the rebellious local governors and revolt against the state if the salt system reforms were to take place.[92] He considered the support of the rich an important element of social stability, just as Lu Chih and Liu Tsung-yüan did. Apparently, for the sake of stability, Han saw no reason to offend the rich merchants, and hence no reason for the government to interfere with the current salt system.

Han Yü's laissez-faire attitude toward both the poor and the rich merchants in this context caused him to ignore the critical problem of how to reduce the economic inequality between rich and poor that both Lu Chih and Liu Tsung-yüan tried to solve. It also made him neglect the need to restrain the abuses of financial power practiced by the rich merchants. In his neglect of these two areas, it seems that Han indirectly supported the idea that the rich and powerful should enjoy certain privileges; at the same time, he unconsciously ignored a very important Confucian principle: that government was obliged to relieve the poor. As a result, even though Han had a genuine concern for the poor, it seems that his concern could be compromised whenever he felt the stability of the state to be at issue; it was apparently not as deeply rooted in his consciousness as in the consciousness of Lu Chih and Liu Tsung-yüan.

Regardless of this difference, during their official lives, Han Yü and the other representatives of the Confucian revival all attempted to relieve the people from their suffering, and their efforts in this respect closely paralleled those of Lu Chih. From this, we can see that the intellectual leaders of the Confucian revival are the closest kindred spirits with whom Lu Chih can be completely identified. It is not only through an affinity between their *political* concerns, but more importantly, it is through the many similarities between their *social* concerns that we can positively affirm a fundamental kinship between Lu Chih and the representatives of Confucian revival.

Such kinship is less obvious between Lu Chih and Ch'üan Te-yü, or between Ch'üan and the leading Confucian revivalists. Ch'üan did share similar political and social concerns with Lu Chih as well as with the revivalists, and he also followed some of Lu's policies for relieving the poor. Unfortunately he left no consistent record to vouch for his commitment to these concerns. Toward the end of his tenure as chief minister, Ch'üan was even criticized for failing to make any suggestions to improve the government. He was removed from this position because of his "silence and perfunctory performance [*hsün-mo*]."[93] It is very likely that Ch'üan Te-yü remained only a distant supporter of Confucian revival, even though he maintained contact with many of the more prominent revival intellectuals.

By contrast, with all his enduring efforts to pursue his Confucian political ideals, and with all the common ground shared between him and the leading figures of the Confucian revival, there is no question that Lu Chih deserves to be granted an equal place of honor in that most significant movement in mid-T'ang intellectual history. Lu Chih strove at court to accomplish what the Confucian revivalists attempted in the provinces, and he tried to put into practice the Confucian Way some of them could only write about.

Lu Chih was intellectually anchored in the same harbor as the major Confucian revivalists. There are close affinities between his *political concerns* and those of the Confucian revival intellectuals.

Because these concerns were also shared by the notable court officials, they have less relevance to Lu's significance in his time. This significance becomes fully apparent when Lu Chih's *social concerns* are discovered to be nearly identical to those of the revival representatives. This does not mean that differences did not exist in their approaches to government, but these differences between Lu and them are differences in degree, not in kind. In short, there is no break in the intellectual chain between Lu and the representatives of Confucian revival.

With the possible exception of Yüan Chieh and Tu-ku Chi, all the representatives of Confucian revival examined here assumed various degrees of pragmatism in their approach to government. Most of them believed that practical considerations were compatible with Confucian moral principles, but, like Lu Chih's, their pragmatist sensibility was different from Tu Yu's sense of pragmatism. Tu's pragmatism was directed first to the pursuit of wealth and power for the state, but theirs, like Lu Chih's, was oriented toward improving the people's welfare or preventing the disintegration of the state due to some clear and present danger. This is the key difference between what I call the Confucian pragmatist approach and the utilitarian Confucian approach. It essentially distinguishes Lu Chih and the revivalists from the other court officials, and thus highlights one of the principal characteristics of the mid-T'ang Confucian revival.

To be sure, Han Yü was very much like Tu Yu in his attitude toward the state and imperial power. Yet, unlike Tu, who exerted no particular effort to relieve the poor during his tenure as chief minister, Han did strive to improve the people's well-being during his official life, even though the people's welfare was not his ultimate concern.

The point is, Lu Chih and the representatives of Confucian revival were all seriously concerned with the people's suffering, but Lu asserted more consistently than most of them that the well-being of the people had to come first before the state, and especially before the emperor. It is precisely because Lu was persistently committed to the improvement of the people's welfare and was driven by a sense of mission to realize his political convictions that we may legitimately claim for him a place in the mid-T'ang Confucian revival. Just what position, then, should Lu occupy in comparison with the leading figures of this revival?

Lu Chih, unlike Yüan Chieh and Tu-ku Chi, was not a member of the early *ku-wen* movement. Most of Lu's political convictions and his efforts to relieve the people's misery had been championed by the early advocates of *ku-wen*, but his reformist policies were more comprehensive and more thorough than theirs. Still, we cannot claim for Lu Chih the role of a forerunner laying the foundations for the later development of the Confucian revival.

Neither did Lu Chih, like Liu Tsung-yüan, Han Yü, and Li Ao, break new ground for the revival by redefining important Confucian concepts such as that of the Confucian *Tao*, or the moral Way. Nevertheless, we should recall that Lu was the first mid-T'ang scholar official to assert the complementary relationship between the principles of rightness and expediency. He was also the first and only one in the mid-T'ang to try consistently to embody this complementary relationship in his political practice. From this perspective, it is reasonable to say that his Confucian pragmatist approach represented a new landmark on the mid-T'ang political landscape even though it was not a conceptual milestone. His political approach also provides a new understanding of the complementary relation between *i* and *ch'üan*, one aspect of the Confucian tradition that has heretofore not received the attention it rightly deserves.

Lu Chih's significance can equally be seen in a different light in the sense that he tried to fulfill the essential vision of the major mid-T'ang Confucian revival intellectuals, for fundamentally the same reasons. To a great extent he was actually more successful than any of the other reform-minded Confucian revivalists. Lu's career background undoubtedly provided him a position where, when he received imperial support, he had much more opportunity to put his political convictions into practice than most of the Confucian revival intellectuals. His early contribution to T'ang stability while serving as a Han-lin scholar offers the best example of the significance of his official position. On the negative side, however, Lu occupied a position where, when the emperor refused to back him up, he risked more to pursue his political ideals than most of his contemporary Confucian revivalists. The result of Lu's service as chief minister is the ultimate example of the dangers inherent in his perseverance.

Lu Chih's political life spanned only a short fifteen years between 780 and 795. This was the time when the major Confucian revivalists merely carried on the cause of their *ku-wen* predecessors. That none of these early representatives of Confucian revival formed a close relationship with Lu during this period indicates that it was through his own observation, and due to his own politi-

cal convictions, that he struggled to effect his Confucian political
ideals. Like the representatives of the revival in this particular
period, Lu forwarded the cause of Confucian revival in his tenacious efforts to advise Te-tsung on how to conduct a benevolent
government. His contribution to the revival of Confucianism did
not then merely lie in his reassertion of Confucian principles in
government. Rather his untiring attempts to realize his convictions
in practice even at a considerable risk to his political life entitle
him to a unique position in comparison to the leading Confucian
revivalists.

All the Confucian revival intellectuals mentioned above tried
to act on their convictions during their provincial tours of office.
Some of their memorials to the throne also contained suggestions
that would not please the throne. The extant records, however, do
not indicate that they continuously expounded their programs with
the full knowledge that their advice was opposed to imperial wishes.
Nor do they indicate that they unceasingly spoke up for the well-
being of the people against the emperor's personal indulgence, or
that they consciously chose to risk their own personal gain for the
sake of the public good. As we have seen, Lu Chih did all three of
these things throughout his fifteen-year career.

None of the leading revivalists had close connections with Lu
Chih, but Lu clearly stood for what they most valued and intended
to put into practice. That is, Lu Chih's political life may be seen to
represent the consummation of their stated ideal type of Confucian
minister. Yüan Chieh exclusively honored those whom he called
"the ministers for the state [she-chi chih ch'en]" on the ground they
were the only officials who would present honest and loyal advice
to the throne.[94] Tu-ku Chi also highly valued officials who could
"employ the way of rightness to improve the contemporary situation."[95] Both Han Yü and Liu Tsung-yüan wrote positive evaluations of Yang Ch'eng, the only official who dared to challenge
Te-tsung's death sentence for Lu Chih. Although their evaluations
were made for different reasons, they both unmistakably respected
officials who remonstrated in accordance with the Confucian moral
Way.[96] Likewise, Li Ao insisted that "a superior man follows the
Way and not the crowd."[97]

It is apparent from these statements what type of official all of
these representative Confucian revivalists held in the utmost respect. Against their criteria, Lu Chih was not only qualified to be
a candidate for their ideal Confucian minister, he was actually a
living exemplar of the type. At the time when all the Confucian

revival intellectuals tried to reinvigorate Confucianism as the guiding principle of government, Lu Chih also brought Confucian political principles to life through his own actions. As a result, a behavior paradigm of the ideal Confucian minister was ultimately established for the mid-T'ang Confucian revival. Having successfully relied upon his Confucian pragmatist approach to restore T'ang stability, and having consistently followed his version of the Way and refused to drift with the crowd, Lu Chih significantly revitalized Confucian governmental principles. His political behavior epitomized the manifestation of a reanimated Confucian consciousness in mid-T'ang history.

Epilogue

The focal points of this study have been Lu Chih's efforts to rebuild the T'ang empire, and the significance of those efforts in the context of the mid-T'ang Confucian revival. I have employed the term *Confucian pragmatist approach* throughout to characterize Lu Chih's responses to his time, and adopted the concept of *behavior paradigm* to define his place in that period of history. That Lu Chih consistently applied a Confucian pragmatist approach during his service at court suggests that he came very close to the Weberian concept of a true statesman. His bittersweet experience with Te-tsung, however, exemplifies the perennially problematic relationship between Chinese emperors and their chief ministers.

My examination of Lu's political life represents another example of how Confucianism was reinvigorated as a viable system of values in the mid-T'ang through the public spiritedness of sensitive intellectuals. It confirms the view that the mid-T'ang Confucian revival was manifest in different activities at different stages, and in Lu's case, was even carried forth by a single individual. My comparison of Lu's political approach and that of the major Confucian revivalists and two notable chief ministers also enables us to identify different intellectual predilections in Lu's time, and to discover that the majority of the leading revivalists all employed a certain degree of Confucian pragmatism in their approaches to government. In closing, it seems proper to discuss the possible implications of the major findings presented in this study.

Lu Chih's Confucian pragmatist approach offers a new perspective from which to characterize the mid-T'ang Confucian revival and distinguish it from Sung Neo-Confucianism. Sung Neo-Confucianism reached its maturity in the middle of the twelfth century. When Chu Hsi began to dominate the intellectual arena, the essential pragmatic feature of Lu Chih and the mid-T'ang Confucian revivalists' approach tended to receive less emphasis among Confucian thinkers who shared similar social concerns with the leading mid-T'ang revivalists. Despite the fact that Chu Hsi paid attention to the complicated relationship between moral principles and expediency, and to the practical needs of his time, in principle he saw the application of expediency to government as a compromise of moral standards. To Chu Hsi, ethics should not be reduced to situational judgments. Nor should social results validate a ruler's virtue. Because of this, Chu Hsi strongly criticized the thought of the Southern Sung utilitarian Confucian Ch'en Liang. Chu Hsi's insistence on a perfect ethical standard in all situations and at all times probably made it difficult for him to accept Lu Chih, or any other mid-T'ang Confucian revivalist, as his ideal type of a quintessential Confucian.[1] It probably also led him to ignore the fact that although he did not believe in fixed historical standards, Lu Chih never asserted that the application of expediency could deviate from the ultimate moral principle of rightness. Lu emphasized the importance of ethical intentions, but he paid equal attention to the possible results of political behavior. Nowhere did he support the idea that the ends could justify the means used in political practice.

With the passage of time, Lu Chih's type of pragmatist sensibility was undervalued. Pragmatism came to be regarded as the hallmark of the utilitarian Confucian political approach. It no longer occupied an equally important place in the approach of non-utilitarian Confucians as had been the case with Lu Chih. As it turned out, it was not his pragmatist sensibility, but rather his commitment to Confucian political principles and his actual efforts to realize those principles, that won Lu great respect in later imperial tradition. Huang Tsung-hsi's selection of him as one of only seven exemplary Confucians in Chinese history is the best testimony to this most obvious aspect of Lu Chih's political approach. Even so, we should not neglect the fact that his balanced application of the principles of rightness and expediency, as he construed them, was just as unique in mid-T'ang history, if not more so in subsequent Chinese history. My reconstruction hopefully restores Lu Chih's Confucian pragmatist approach to its place within the complex Confucian tradition.

The significance of Lu Chih's political life in the mid-T'ang was recognized by the Wang Shu-wen group, but their appreciation does not mean that other contemporary officials necessarily regarded Lu in the same light. Some certainly did not. According to Ch'üan Te-yü, some officials contemporary with Lu commented that the tragic end of his political career was not caused by the fact that he did not serve at the right time, or under the right ruler. They considered that it was rather because Lu's ability to govern was not as great as that of previous notable chief ministers during the reigns of T'ai-tsung and Hsüan-tsung.[2]

Ch'üan Te-yü refuted these criticisms at some length:

> Although the [Confucian] Way resides in oneself, applying it to the fullest depends upon others. When locusts fill the sky, even the Divine Farmer and Lord Millet cannot produce a good harvest. When a run away cart is about to turn over, even Confucius and Mencius [have to] jump off. If the [previous] four gentlemen and Mr. Lu exchanged their times of service [as chief minister], we can not know for certain who would have succeeded and who would have failed. That [Mr. Lu's] service to [Emperor Te-tsung] failed to attain the accomplishments [enjoyed by those previous ministers] in the Chen-kuan and K'ai-yüan reigns (of T'ai-tsung and Hsüan-tsung) is unfortunate for our own time and not only unfortunate for Mr. Lu. Is it not tantamount to a false accusation to suppose that [Lu's failure] was due to the insufficiency of his Way? (CTW, 493: 15a.)[3]

We have no other source to explain why and under what conditions those officials criticized Lu Chih, but Ch'üan Te-yü's reply should be taken seriously. Ch'üan seems to believe, as this present study shows, that the root cause of Lu's political failure was Te-tsung's unwillingness to allow him to utilize his ability to its fullest in those domains where the emperor lacked serious concern. Ch'üan implies that Lu's political downfall had nothing to do with his administrative ability. His statement further helps to flesh out the specific implications of our examination of the relationship between Lu Chih and Te-tsung.

Our exploration of the complex relationship between a chief minister and his emperor touches upon one of the basic flaws of the traditional Chinese political system. In traditional Chinese political reality, when the emperor chose to be autocratic, except for official remonstrances, no other institutional device existed that could effectively balance or restrain imperial power. This was especially the case after the mid-T'ang when the great clans and aristocratic families were in the process of gradually losing their local territorial base and becoming more and more dependent on their bureaucratic positions to preserve their social and political privileges.

It is true that imperial power in traditional China always had to rely on the mechanism of the bureaucracy for its realization, but that power itself was absolute and all-inclusive in theory.[4] Since in reality emperors could employ personal attendants or advisors to bypass any inconvenience imposed upon them by the regular bureaucracy, and since the bureaucracy could not stop such practices except through remonstrances, the power of the bureaucracy as a pressure group vis-à-vis the throne was greatly weakened. In light of this, although the relationship between the emperor and the bureaucracy could not be anything else but symbiotic, it was at best an unbalanced symbiosis. Whenever serious conflicts arose, it was the emperor who had the arbitrary power to replace members of the bureaucracy, but the reverse was rarely if ever the case.

From this perspective, Lu Chih's efforts to transform Te-tsung's conduct in the interests of the public good were inevitably doomed by this inherent flaw in the traditional Chinese imperial system. In order to avoid facing Lu Chih—a constant reminder of his own moral duty to the public well-being—Emperor Te-tsung chose to exercise his arbitrary power to end the political life of his former confidant and advisor whose ability to govern he had once highly appreciated.

Lu Chih emphasized the importance of accommodation to changes in time and circumstances, and he refused mechanically to imitate any historical standard without critical reflection upon its appropriateness. Lu believed only one thing to be forever unchangeable—the moral obligation of the Son of Heaven toward his subjects. It is precisely in this domain that we see Lu's principle of expediency giving way to his principle of rightness. It was also squarely within this sphere that Lu's downfall took shape. It must be noted again that Lu Chih never intended to be a political martyr. In order to improve the public welfare, but, at the same time, not upset the status quo which Te-tsung clung to, we find that he made every reasonable effort to compromise his reformist policies.

The shift in Te-tsung's concern, however, from an urgent need to restore court stability to an obsession with preserving the status quo left little room for Lu to realize his political ideals. It became the essential pre-existent condition under which Lu pursued his political goals. Other factors, such as Lu's power struggle with his chief opponent P'ei Yen-ling, served merely a catalytic function in his political downfall. Just as imperial adoption of Lu's advice was the key to his earlier successful contribution to the restoration of stability during the time of imperial exile, Te-tsung's opposition to Lu's reformist policies in a changed historical setting was also the primary reason for Lu's ultimate failure.

Lu Chih was sure that imperial support was the key to the success of his pursuit of Confucian benevolent government, but except for remonstrating with the throne he had no other means nor did he conceive of any other means to remind Te-tsung of his moral obligation to a suffering public. He was thus impelled to speak up unceasingly for the public interest against the imperial wishes. His political actions undoubtedly enriched the Confucian tradition with another ideal paradigm. Nevertheless, they resulted in no institutional breakthrough to restrain imperial power. Lacking as he was in theoretical possibilities and practical frames of reference, we could hardly expect more from Lu's pursuit of his political ideals.

Despite his emphasis on institutional reform, Tu Yu's political approach does not seem to be an ideal alternative for limiting imperial power either. His overriding concern for the state during a period of decline easily led him to elevate the ruler, leaving the door wide open for autocracy.[5] It is worthwhile to note that in contemporary Chinese political reality, we can still find relevant parallels to both Tu Yu's political views and Lu Chih's political behavior.

Tu Yu's view that the ruler has to be elevated, and that the people's interest have to be subordinated to that of the state when the state is in decline finds its modern Chinese echo in the ideal of a so-called *new authoritarianism*. This term emerged in China around 1988, and has attracted a great following since. It was first used by many concerned young economists to promote economic modernization in China. They affirm that in order to make China rich and powerful, it is necessary to support a strong political leader and increase central control. They argue that this sort of new authoritarianism is different from traditional Chinese authoritarianism because its final goal is to ensure, rather than detract from, individual freedom. They believe that the goal of individual freedom can be achieved only through economic development and prosperity. They state that the new authoritarianism is only "an expediency," and that it will be discarded after China achieves some future level of economic success.[6] Admittedly, the contemporary Chinese historical context is completely different from that of Tu Yu's time, but as far as promoting a strong ruler and placing the people's well-being second to the interest of the state for the sake of expediency is concerned, one can definitely see the parallel between Tu Yu's position and that of many contemporary Chinese scholars.

A relevant parallel can also be discerned between Lu Chih and a different group of Chinese intellectuals. Here Lu Chih's efforts to act as the mouthpiece of the people within a restrained political environment is the point of comparison. The recurrent political campaigns and persecutions in the history of the People's Republic of China are well known. The T'ien-an men massacre of June fourth 1989 is only the most recent example of what abuses of autocratic political power can lead to. What strikes us most is that during each political campaign in recent Chinese history, there have always been a few Chinese intellectuals who, like Lu Chih, or like other Confucian scholar officials in the Ming dynasty, were willing to act as spokesmen for the people.[7] Without denying the vast differences of the two historical contexts, the fact that there is still no effective institutional device to restrain arbitrary abuses of power by one party or one leader, and that any attempt to speak up for the public good or any serious commitment to reform still demands one to take great, even ultimate, personal risks reminds us of the political situation in Lu's day. Thus, we may find that there is an essential link connecting Lu Chih and some modern Chinese intellectuals: their serious concern for the public well-being. Their tenacious efforts to act as the people's spokesmen provides common ground upon which they could carry on a dialogue transcending differences of time and place.

Needless to say, neither Lu Chih's strivings, nor the efforts of such modern intellectuals has so far helped to change the basic power structure in China, be it traditional, or modern. China today seems to be developing in the direction desired most by the supporters of the new authoritarianism. Neither China's recent economic successes nor the problems entailed by these economic reforms have yet led its government to end its authoritarian control, and there is no guarantee that it will do so in the foreseeable future.[8]

These broad parallels between the political behavior of Lu Chih and some post-Mao intellectuals, and between Tu Yu's utilitarian Confucian views and the ideas of the new authoritarians, in the final analysis, provide us with another vantage point from which to reflect upon the fate of Confucianism in contemporary China. Although Confucianism was severely attacked at the beginning of the twentieth century, and although recently many scholars in the West have also committed themselves to evaluating the troubles with Confucianism, the various approaches to government within the Confucian tradition never seem to be completely erased from the political consciousness of contemporary Chinese intellectuals. The fact that scholars continue to debate the relevance of Confucianism to contemporary Chinese political life only confirms further its vigor and resilience.[9] For good or for ill, the diversity of the Confucian tradition continues to produce its modern repercussions.

Appendix 1: A Note on Sources

As Denis Twitchett mentions (Twitchett, "Lu Chih," 1962, 337 note 9), two useful chronicle studies of Lu Chih's life already existed before Yen I-p'ing's *Lu Hsüan-kung nien-p'u*. One is the "Lu Hsüan-kung nien-p'u" composed by the nineteenth-century scholar Ting Yen and is included in the 1768 *Han-yüan chi chu* (Collected works of Lu Chih); the other is the "Nien-p'u chi-lüeh" appended to the Nien Keng-yao edition of Lu Chih's works reprinted in the SPPY edition. Another useful chronicle study was also composed by a nineteenth-century scholar Yang Hsi-min and is entitled *Lu Hsüan-kung nien-p'u*. It is in the *Shih-wu chia nien-p'u ts'ung-shu* collection. Compared with the other two Ch'ing dynasty *nien-p'u*, Yang Hsi-min's study provides more detailed information on Lu's life.

Professor Twitchett gave a detailed description of the various extant editions of the collected works of Lu Chih in his 1962 article. However, as he says, there is a discrepancy concerning the total number of chapters contained in Lu's extant works. In his preface to the *Han-yüan chi* (Collected works of Lu Chih), Ch'üan Te-yü describes Lu's collected works as having twenty-four chapters altogether (CTW: 493: 11–15). He writes that they contained ten chapters of edicts, seven of private memorials (*tsou-ts'ao*), and seven of official memorials (*chung-shu tsou-i*). HTS *I-wen chih* section tells us that there were ten chapters in the *Han-yüan chi*, and also twelve chapters in the *Lu Chih lun-i piao-shu chi*. (HTS, 60: 1616). Obviously, these two volumes together would make twenty-two chapters. The Sung dynasty *Ch'ung-wen tsung-mu* (compiled between 1034 and 1038; Kuo-hsüeh chi-pen ts'ung-shu edition, ch. 5, 377–78) says there were two chapters in the *Lu Chih chih-chi* and ten chapters in the *Han-yüan chi*. The much later *Chih-chai shu-lu chieh-t'i* (probably compiled in the mid-thirteenth century; Kuo-hsüeh chi-pen ts'ung-shu edition, ch. 22, 601) says that there were twenty chapters in the *Lu Hsüan-kung tsou-i*, which is also entitled *Pang-tzu chi*; but on another page (ch. 16, 448) it says that there were ten chapters in the *Han-yüan chi* and twelve chapters in the *Pang-tzu chi*; it combines these two together under the title of *Lu Hsüan-kung chi*. At the same time, the *Chün-chai tu-shu chih* (1151; Kuo-hsüeh chi-pen ts'ung-shu edition, ch. 4A: 363–64) says that there were twelve chapters in the *Lu Chih tsou-i*. It then mentions that previously there were five chapters in Lu Chih's *Pang-tzu chi*, three chapters in the *I-lun chi*, and ten chapters in the *Han-yüan chi*. The author of the *Tu-shu chih* suspects that all these previous works were put together around 1090; the title of the works then became *Lu Chih tsou-i*.

Following the above information, we must agree with Twitchett that the records of Lu Chih's works have become a "bibliographical muddle." However, the *Ssu-k'u ch'üan-shu tsung-mu t'i-yao* (*chi-pu, pieh-chi lei,* 3) tells us that the information in the *Chün-chai tu-shu chih* does not match most of the historical bibliographical descriptions. The *T'i-yao* says that according to other Sung bibliographical records, ever since the Southern Sung all of Lu's works had been put together and placed under the general title of *Han-yüan chi,* a book containing twenty-two chapters. The *T'i-yao* further informs us that the author of *Chün-chai tu-shu chih* must have seen an incomplete edition of Lu's works and thus only listed twelve chapters in *Lu Chih tsou-i*. Because the Sung scholars also refer to Lu's works as the *Lu Hsüan-kung tsou-i,* the *T'i-yao* says, many Ch'ing editions of Lu's works follow this title. Based upon the explanation given by the *T'i-yao,* it seems clear to us that at least by Southern Sung times there were basically only twenty-two chapters in Lu Chih's collected works—the *Han-yüan chi*. It is obvious that this *Han-yüan chi* contained ten chapters of the pre-Southern Sung *Han-yüan chi* and twelve chapters of Lu Chih's other memorials or edicts with a title unclear to us. This explains why almost all the modern editions of Lu Chih's works have twenty-two chapters (ten of edicts, six of private memorials and six of official memorials). The SPTK and SPPY editions apparently also follow the Southern Sung arrangement into twenty-two chapters.

Although there are two twenty-four-chapter editions in existence now—one a late Ming edition by T'ang P'in-yin and Ma Yüan and the other a 1768 edition with extensive commentary by Chang P'ei-fang—as Twitchett points out, the contents of these two editions are identical with the twenty-two chapter Sung edition. When we compare these Ming and Ch'ing editions with the twenty-two-chapter editions, we discover that their editors completely re-grouped Lu Chih's writings into chronological order; there are no new discoveries.

Twitchett's comment of thirty-eight years ago that the best available edition of Lu Chih's works at that time was the 1768 edition by Chang P'ei-fang still applies to the current situation. This is because, like the SPTK and the SPPY editions, this 1768 edition was also compiled on the basis of a Southern Sung edition. However, unlike the SPTK and the SPPY editions which do not give us the exact date of the Southern Sung edition used by them, the 1768 edition used an edition compiled by a Southern Sung official named Lang Yeh (not Lang Hua as the editor of the 1768 edition has it). Lang Yeh presented his edition of Lu Chih's works to the throne in 1132.

This 1132 edition, entitled *Chu Lu Hsüan-kung tsou-i*, includes fifteen chapters of Lu Chih's memorials and Lang Yeh's own commentary. It was reprinted in the *Shih-wan-chüan lou ts'ung-shu* in 1878 and again in the *Pai-pu ts'ung-shu chi-ch'eng* collection. Because the 1768 edition provides the date of the Southern Sung edition (the 1132 edition) which it followed, and moreover, because the 1768 edition preserves not only Sung scholars' comments (though not Lang Yeh's commentary) about Lu's works, but also contains its editor's own commentaries, this edition seems to be preferable. This is why, in this study, I have principally relied upon this 1768 edition. However, I have also compared the 1768 edition with the SPTK and the SPPY editions. In addition, for the sake of comparison, I have also consulted the 1132 edition. The 1768 edition, formerly hard to acquire, is now readily available. In 1982 Taipei's Shih-chieh shu-chü published a reprint of this 1768 edition under the title of *Han-yüan chi chu* (HYCC) edited by Yang Chia-lo as the sixth volume of the Chung-kuo wen-hsüeh ming-chu collection.

Lu Chih's work on medicine, *Lu-shih chi-yen-fang*, his encyclopedic work *Pei-chü wen-yen*, and his fifteen chapters of *Pieh-chi* on literary works were all lost after the Sung dynasty (Twitchett, "Lu Chih," 1962: 86 and 337 note 14). As Twitchett mentions, HTS *I-wen chih* classes *Pei-chü wen-yen* with Tu Yu's *T'ung-tien* and other *Hui-yao*. It also says that it contained twenty chapters (HTS, 59: 1563). The Sung dynasty *Ch'ung-wen tsung-mu* (ch. 3: 178) and the *Chün-chai tu-shu chih* (Hou-chih section, ch. 2: 852) agree with this information. The *Chün-chai tu-shu chih* further mentions that it had more than 450 sections and was similar to the *Po-shih liu-t'ie* (compiled by Po Chü-i), but with more literary polish. The *Wen-hsien t'ung-k'ao* (228: 1828) quotes this passage from *Chün-chai tu-shu chih*. However, both *Sung shih I-wen chih* and *Yü-hai* say that it contained thirty rather than twenty chapters (*Sung shih*, 207: 5293; Wang Ying-lin, ed., *Yü-hai*, Taipei: Hua-wen shu-chü, 1967 reprint, ch. 201: 22). *Yü-hai* informs us that *Pei-chü wen-yen* put passages of a similar nature from the classics and historical works into different categories; altogether it contained 452 sections. Except for the difference in numbers of chapters, all the above sources agree that *Pei-chü wen-yen* is a sort of encyclopedic work. It was probably an administrative encyclopedia, as Twitchett points out. The *Lu-shih chi-yen-fang* is mentioned in HTS, 59: 1572; Ch'üan Te-yü's preface (CTW, 493: 15); SL, 4: 16; and TFYK, 859: 19. HTS says this work on medicine contained fifteen chapters, but all the sources agree that there were fifty chapters in *Lu-shih chi-yen-fang*. It is very likely that fifty chapters is the correct number.

According to the HTS *I-wen chih*, the chief compiler of Lu Chih's works, the *Han-yüan chi*, was Wei Ch'u-hou (773–828). Twitchett suggests that since Wei Ch'u-hou was very likely a maternal relative of Lu Chih, his compilation of Lu Chih's collected works might have been biased though he does not specify biased in what manner. Twitchett's suggestion no doubt deserves our attention, but we also know that it was quite common for a relative or a friend to do such a compilation in T'ang China. It does not follow that their compilation should thus be considered biased. We do not know exactly when Wei compiled the *Han-yüan chi*, but it may very well have been after 806 and before 818. Wei Ch'u-hou was appointed to compile the *Te-tsung shih-lu* around 808 when P'ei Chi was chief minister. Since he had access to all sorts of historical documents, he could have compiled the *Han-yüan chi* without much difficulty. During this time he also worked on the *Shun-tsung shih-lu* until he was demoted to another position in 812. Han Yü took over the compilation in 813. Han completed his version of the *Shun-tsung shih-lu* in 815.

E. G. Pulleyblank has suggested that Han Yü's version of the *Shun-tsung shih-lu* very likely became the text used by Ch'üan Te-yü to write his preface to Lu Chih's collected works, sometime before Ch'üan died in 818. Pulleyblank has further suggested that the present text of the *Shun-tsung shih-lu* is Wei Ch'u-hou's and not Han Yü's version of the work. Whenever material in the present text of the *Shun-tsung shih-lu* about Lu Chih differs from Ch'üan

Te-yü's preface, we often find Ch'üan Te-yü agreeing with the material contained in the *Old T'ang History*. According to Pulleyblank this is because the *Old T'ang History* probably also used Han Yü's version of the *Shun-tsung shih-lu* as the basic text for Lu Chih's biography.

In the early 1980s, Chinese scholars began to debate the authorship of the present *Shun-tsung shih-lu*. Some scholars' arguments support Pulleyblank's point of view, that is, Wei Ch'u-hou should be the compiler of the extant *Shun-tsung shih-lu*. Scholars holding a different point of view, however, argue that it was not possible for Wei Ch'u-hou's version of the *Shun-tsung shih-lu* to be circulated once it was replaced by Han Yü's text of the *Shun-tsung shih-lu*. Although I find the latter group's argument less convincing than that of their opponents, the controversy obviously remains unsettled. Nevertheless, precisely because it is unsettled, the material about Lu Chih contained in the extant *Shun-tsung shih-lu*, Ch'üan Te-yü's preface, and the *Old T'ang History* thus becomes a more useful cross-reference for any reevaluation of Lu Chih's life than we previously thought

On Wei Ch'u-hou's possible connection with Lu Chih, see Twitchett, "Lu Chih," 1962: 85 and 337 note 10 and 11. On the authors of different versions of the *Shun-tsung shih-lu* and the relationship between the *Old T'ang History* and Ch'üan Te-yü's preface, see E. G. Pulleyblank, "The Shun-tsung shih-lu," *Bulletin of the School of Oriental and African Studies*, 19: 2 (1957): 336–44, esp. 340; also see Chang Kuo-kuang, "Chin-pen *Shun-tsung shih-lu* fei Han Yü so tso pien," *Wen-hsüeh p'ing-lun ts'ung-k'an*, vol. 7 (10/1980): 328–40. For scholars holding opposite opinions, see Chiang Fan, "Chin-pen *Shun-tsung shih-lu* tso-che k'ao-pien," *Wen-hsüeh p'ing-lun ts'ung-k'an*, vol. 16 (10/1982): 321–36, and Ch'ü Lin-tung, "Kuan-yü *Shun-tsung shih-lu* te chi-ke wen-t'i," *Pei-ching shih-fan ta-hsüeh hsüeh-pao*, 1 (1982): 45–53.

Appendix 2: Lu Chih's Works Cited in the Text

The following list represents the Chinese titles of all of the works of Lu Chih cited in the text. Chapter and page numbers refer to those in HYCC.

Chapter 1

奉天改元大赦制	1a–14a
平朱泚後車駕還京大赦制	14b–28b

Chapter 2

貞元改元大赦制	1a–9b
冬至大禮大赦制	9b–25a

Chapter 3

貞元九年冬至大禮大赦制	1a–8b
誅李懷光後原宥河中將吏幷招諭淮西詔	11a–18b

Chapter 4

議減鹽價詔	9b–11a
賜京畿及同華等州百姓種子賑給貧人詔	11a–12b

Chapter 5

招諭淮西將吏詔	13b–15b
招諭河中詔	15b–16b

Chapter 23

Chapter 24

Notes

Introduction

1. T'ang China's position in the world is discussed in S. A. M. Adshead, *China in world history*, 2nd edition, (London: MacMillan 1995), ch. 2.

2. I follow Patricia Ebrey's definition of medieval Chinese aristocracy; see chapter one for details.

3. According to Yü Ying-shih, this concern for preserving the rich in the process of creating an economically more equitable society was widespread among Confucian scholars of the sixteenth and seventeenth centuries. He points out that the same concern was already present among Sung dynasty scholars and Han Yü of the mid-T'ang, but Lu Chih's efforts in this area occurred even earlier. Yü Ying-shih, "Hsien-tai ju-hsüeh te hui-ku yü chan-wang," in his *Hsien-tai ju-hsüeh lun*, 1996: 14–18.

4. Prior to the establishment of Han-lin scholars, some eunuchs had already seriously interfered with the regular operation of the bureaucracy. Emperor Su-tsung's (r. 756–762) eunuch Li Fu-kuo is the best example. TCTC, 221: 7073–74 and 222: 7115. For the development of eunuch power in the T'ang, see J. K. Rideout, "The rise of the eunuchs during the T'ang dynasty," AM, 1 (1949–50): 53–72; 2 (1953–54): 42–58; and Wang Shou-nan, *T'ang-tai huan-kuan ch'üan-shih chih yen-chiu*, 1971.

5. For a detailed discussion of polarities of Confucian thought, see Benjamin Schwartz, "Some polarities in Confucian thought," in David Nivison & Arthur Wright, eds., *Confucianism in action*, 1959: 50–62; Howard Wechsler, "The Confucian impact on early T'ang decision-making," *T'oung pao*, 66 (1980): 1–3; note especially how Wechsler distinguishes different types of early T'ang Confucian bureaucrats.

6. Howard Wechsler, *Mirror to the Son of Heaven, Wei Cheng at the court of T'ang T'ai-tsung*, 1974: 4–7, 143–53 and all of chs. 5 and 6. See also Wechsler's "The Confucian impact," 1980: 13–25.

7. See "Sung-ch'ao ming-ch'en chin tsou-i cha-tzu," as included in almost all the editions of Lu Chih's extant works. Robert M. Hartwell, "Historical analogism, public policy, and social science in eleventh- and twelfth-century China," *American historical review*, 76.3 (June 1971): 700, 711, also mentions the popularity of Lu Chih's memorials during the Sung. In my translations, words in parentheses explain the reference of words in the text and words in brackets complete the meaning of the text.

8. Hsüeh Hsüan, "T'ang Lu Hsüan-kung miao-chi," in his *Ching-hsüan wen-chi*, 19: 21b. Chen-kuan of course refers to T'ai-tsung's reign. K'ai-yüan refers to the early reign (712–42) of Hsüan-tsung. For Hsüeh Hsüan's concept of Confucian learning in the early Ming, see William Theodore de Bary, "Neo-Confucian cultivation and the seventeenth-century 'Enlightenment,'" in de Bary, ed., *The unfolding of Neo-Confucianism*, 1975: 141–216, esp., 186 and 200–202.

—9. For Huang Tsung-hsi's critical reflection on Confucianism, see de Bary, "Neo-Confucian cultivation," 1975: 191–99; also see his "Chinese despotism and the Confucian ideal: a seventeenth-century view," in John K. Fairbank, ed., *Chinese thought and institutions*, 1957: 163–203.

10. Huang Tsung-hsi, "Ts'ung-ssu," in the section of his "P'o hsieh lun," in *Huang Tsung-hsi ch'üan-chi*, vol., 1: 193. The English translation is adopted from de Bary, "Neo-Confucian cultivation," 1975: 192.

11. See E. G. Pulleyblank, *The background of the rebellion of An Lu-shan*, 1982 reprint. For post-rebellion regional militarism, see C. A. Peterson, "Court and province in mid- and late T'ang," CHC: 485–560; also see Pulleyblank, "The An Lu-shan rebellion and the origins of chronic militarism in late T'ang China," in John Curtis Perry and Bardwell L. Smith, eds., *Essays on T'ang society*, 1976: 33–60.

12. See Chen Jo-shui, *Liu Tsung-yüan and intellectual change in T'ang China, 773–819*, 1992.

13. Chen Jo-shui's work is one recent study of the mid-T'ang Confucian revival; others are included in my later discussion.

14. Denis Twitchett cites J. B. Du Halde, *Description de la Chine* 1735: 616ff.; S. Balazs, "Beitrage zur Wirtschaftsgeschichte der T'ang-Zeit, Part 3," *Mitteilungen des Seminars für Orientalische Sprachen zu Berlin*, XXXVI (1933): 1–41 in his "Lu Chih (754–805) Imperial adviser and court official," in Arthur Wright and Denis Twitchett, ed., *Confucian personalities*, 1962: 84 and 336, notes 1 and 2.

15. Arthur Waley, *The life and times of Po Chü-i*, 1949: 66.

16. Although this study revises Professor Twitchett's previous study of Lu Chih, it has benefited greatly from his 1962 essay on Lu Chih, and

his lifelong contributions to T'ang studies will be in evidence throughout. For the English translation of Lu Chih's criticism of the two-tax system, see William Theodore de Bary et al., *Sources of Chinese tradition*, 1960: 416–423. For Pulleyblank's essay, see his "Neo-Confucianism and Neo-Legalism in T'ang intellectual life, 755–805," in Arthur F. Wright, ed., *The Confucian persuasion*, 1960: 93–95. Also see Twitchett, "Lu Chih," 1962: 84–122.

17. Fu An-ming, "I-p'ien ts'ung-wei fa-piao kuo te Hu Shih i-kao," in Li Yu-ning, ed., *Hu Shih yü t'a te p'eng-yu*, vol. 2, 1991: 181–92.

18. See a classified document (trial case number 013.11—2110) on file in the Bureau of Historiography of the National Defense Ministry in Taipei. The defendant's name is Liang Hung-chih, and the lawyer's name is Chu Hung-ju. On March 28, 1938, the Japanese occupation forces made Liang Hung-chih the formal leader of their third puppet government at Nanking with jurisdiction over Kiangsu, Chekiang, and Anhwei. See Immanuel C. Y. Hsü, *The rise of modern China*, reprint, 1978: 686.

19. In addition to these short Chinese articles, I have also found one article in Japanese which deals with some limited aspects of Lu Chih's life. All these sources will be consulted in the course of this study. The only lengthy studies of Lu Chih's life and works are Hsieh Wu-hsiung, *Lu Hsüan-kung chih yen-lun chi ch'i wen-hsüan*, 1975, Liu Chao-jen, "Lu Hsüan-kung yen-chiu," *Shih-chien hsüeh-pao*, vol. 9, 1978: 97–125 and vol. 10, 1979: 1–42 and Ch'en Sung-hsiung, *Lu Hsüan-kung chih cheng-shih yü wen-hsüeh*, 1985. A chronicle study of Lu Chih's life (*nien-p'u*), also came out in 1975. See Yen I-p'ing, *Lu Hsüan-kung nien-p'u*, 1975.

20. The important contribution of Twitchett's study of Lu Chih has been widely recognized, and his essay was translated into Chinese and published in Taipei in 1973. See *Chung-kuo li-shih jen-wu lun-chi*, 1973: 104–61.

21. Inaccurate views of Lu Chih's career development include, for example, the length of Lu's first provincial appointment; his later stay in Ch'ang-chou and encounter with his only self-proclaimed close friend; the dates of his following provincial appointment; the date he entered the central government, how he entered, and the position he actually held at that time, and the date when he became a Han-lin scholar.

22. David McMullen, *State and scholars in T'ang China*, 1988: 239.

23. On the matter of the insufficiency of source materials see Twitchett, "Lu Chih," 1962: 84- 87.

24. There are various editions of Lu Chih's extant works. I use the 1768 or *Han-yüan chi-chu* (HYCC) throughout. For a detailed discussion, see Appendix 1.

25. McMullen points out (*State and scholars in T'ang China*, 1988: 8) that philosophical essays written by mid-T'ang scholar officials are much more connected with specific occasions than those by Sung Neo-Confucians. Nevertheless, they still set forth general theoretical themes in a more abstract manner than Lu Chih's extant works do.

26. Benjamin Schwartz, "The intellectual history of China: preliminary reflections," in Fairbank ed., *Chinese thought and institutions*, 1957: 16.

27. For obvious examples of such T'ang memorial rhetoric employed by famous chief ministers prior to Lu Chih, see the memorials of Wei Cheng, Sung Ching (664–738), Chang Yüeh (667–730), Chang Chiu-ling (678–740), and Ch'ang Kun (729–783) to emperors T'ai-tsung, Hsüan-tsung, and Tai-tsung: CTW 140: 7a, 10a, 17a-b; 207: 10a; 223: 18a–19b; 224: 1; 288: 1a–2a; 416: 2a; 417: 12a-b. All the memorials written by these chief ministers are considerably less personal than Lu Chih's.

28. See Pulleyblank, "Neo-Confucianism and Neo-Legalism," 1960.

Chapter One

1. For an earlier and more extensive version of this chapter, see my "The Wu *chün* Lu clan as an example of bureaucratization in the T'ang dynasty," *B.C. Asian Review* 3/4 (1990): 106–52.

2. Denis Twitchett, "The composition of the T'ang ruling class: New evidence from Tunhuang," Arthur F. Wright and Denis Twitchett, eds., *Perspectives on the T'ang*, 1973: 49.

3. Twitchett, "The T'ang ruling class," 1973: 50. I am fully aware of the difference between a "clan" and a "lineage" defined by anthropologists such as Maurice Freedman and Hugh Baker. However, scholars of the T'ang dynasty have pointed out that most prominent medieval lineages were so loosely knit that "clan" and "lineage" are thus used interchangeably for the sake of convenience. In this study, I shall refer to Lu Chih's kinship group and subgroups as the "Lu lineage" or "Lu clan" despite the fact that we can trace the common ancestor of the major Lu subgroups. Hugh D. R. Baker, *Chinese family and kinship*, 1979: 49 and 68. Maurice Freedman, ed., *Family and kinship in Chinese society*, 1970: 13–14; Patricia Buckley Ebrey, *The aristocratic families of early China: A case study of the Po-ling Ts'ui family*, 1978: 22; David Johnson, "The last years of a great clan: The Li family of Chao Chün in late T'ang and early Sung," HJAS 37/1 (June 1977): 98; Chen Jo-shui, *Liu Tsung-yüan*, 1992: 34, note 6.

4. Ebrey, *The aristocratic families*, 1978: 10. For a different view, see David G. Johnson, *The medieval Chinese oligarchy*, 1977.

5. Twitchett, "The T'ang ruling class," *Perspectives*, 1973: 47–48.

6. Ebrey, *The aristocratic families*, 1978: 117 and 28–32. Some scholars believe that education and culture were the most important factors in the earliest stage of the formation of powerful families at the close of the Western Han dynasty (202 B.C.E.–9 C.E.) and in the early period of the Eastern Han (25–220 C.E.). Once having monopolized education and culture, members of these powerful families naturally controlled access to officialdom and economic wealth. In the process, it becomes difficult to distinguish which factor is the cause and which the effect. As a result, these factors mutually influenced each other and constituted a social cycle. See Yü Ying-shih, "Tung-Han cheng-ch'üan chih chien-li yü shih-tsu ta-hsing chih kuan-hsi," in his *Chung-kuo chih-shih chieh-ts'eng shih lun (ku-tai p'ien)*, 1980: 113–15; Etienne Balazs, "Significant aspects of Chinese society," in Arthur F. Wright, ed., *Chinese civilization and bureaucracy*, 1964: 6–7. For social economic and political factors, see Yang Lien-sheng, "Tung Han te hao-tsu," *Ch'ing-hua hsüeh-pao*, 11: 4 (1936): 1007–63, Wang I-t'ung, *Wu-ch'ao men-ti*, 2 vols., Taipei reprint, 1973, vol. 1, chs. 3 and 5; Mao Han-kuang, *Liang-Chin Nan-Pei-Ch'ao shih-tsu cheng-chih chih yen-chiu*, 1966, vol. 1, ch. 3, esp. 63–64., and ch. 7, 230–48; Twitchett, "The T'ang ruling class," *Perspectives*, 1973: 49.

7. Mao Han-kuang, *Shih-tsu cheng-chih*, vol. 1, ch. 4; Wang I-t'ung, *Wu-ch'ao men-ti*, vol., 1, ch. 3; Ebrey, *The aristocratic families*, 1978: 6; Miyazaki Ichisada, *Kyûhin kanjinhô no kenkyû*, 1956, ch. 3, esp. 247.

8. These aristocratic families were known by various terms during the T'ang: *chiu-tsu* (old clans), *shih-tsu* (scholar official clans), *chu-hsing* (famous names), *kuei-tsu* (noble clans), or *ming-tsu* (illustrious clans). Chen Jo-shui, *Liu Tsung-yüan*, 1992: 8; Ch'en Yin-k'o, *T'ang-tai cheng-chih-shih shu-lun kao*, Taipei reprint, n. d.: 56–59, also reprinted in CYKCC, vol. 1: 225–28; Ebrey, *The aristocratic families*, 1978: 3.

9. HTS, 199: 5676–80; CTW, 372: 7a–11b. Liu Fang's classification of aristocratic lineages provides important evidence of what was believed in his own days, and has been widely cited by scholars of T'ang history. See Twitchett, "The T'ang ruling class," *Perspectives*, 1973: 50–51; Ebrey, *The aristocratic families*, 1978: 10–11; Chen Jo-shui, *Liu Tsung-yüan*, 1992: 9–12.

10. Chen Jo-shui, *Liu Tsung-yüan*, 1992: 19–20, especially note 43.

11. The other three native aristocratic groups are the Chu, the Chang and the Ku clans. For details of these four groups, see Ho Ch'i-min, "Chung-ku nan-fang men-ti—Wu chün Chu Chang Ku Lu ssu-hsing chih pi-chiao yen-chiu," in his *Chung-ku men-ti lun-chi*, 1978, ch. 4; Mao, *Liang-Chin Nan-Pei-Ch'ao shih-tsu*, 1966, vol. 1, chs. 1 and 2.

12. To understand how the examination system worked in the T'ang and why its impact on T'ang society should not be overrated, see Denis Twitchett, *The birth of the Chinese meritocracy: bureaucrats and examinations in T'ang China*, 1974. For the transformation of the T'ang aristocracy,

see CHC: 21–22 , and Ebrey, *The aristocratic families*, 1978, esp. her concluding remarks, 118–19.

13. Fan Ch'eng-ta, *Wu Chün-chih*, vol. 1, 1: 2.

14. YHCHTC, vol. 6, 25: 660

15. Lu Shu was a descendant of the twenty-third generation of a major subgroup; his preface to the recompilation of the genealogy of forty-nine Lu branches (812 preface hereafter) is preserved in a Ch'ing dynasty Lu clan genealogy. See *Lu-shih shih-p'u*, 24 vols., compiled by Lu I and Lu Sheng-wu in 1745, Columbia University Rare Books Collection, microfilm # 0876. The author of this preface, Lu Shu, was the surveillance commissioner (*Kuan-ch'a shih*) of the Fu-chien region in 812. This agrees with the information about him contained in HTS, 73: 2972. This 812 preface is also preserved in another Ch'ing dynasty Lu clan genealogy, see *Lu-shih tsung-p'u*, compiled by Lu Chen-chih, 4 vols., Columbia University Rare Books Collection, microfilm # 548; also see Twitchett, "Lu Chih," 1962: 87 and 338, note 22. I rely upon Charles O. Hucker, *A dictionary of official titles in imperial China*, 1985, for translations (where available) of all official titles in this study.

16. HTS, 73: 2965 and 812 preface.

17. HHS, 81: 2682.

18. Hsü Kuo-lin, *Tunhuang shih-shih hsieh-ching t'i-chi yü Tunhuang tsa-lu*, 1937, vol. 2: 154b; also see Twitchett, "Lu Chih," 1962: 87 and Ikeda On, "Tôdai no gumbô hyô," *Tôyô gakuhô*, 42: 3 (1959): 61.

19. Twitchett, "Lu Chih," 1962: 87 and Ikeda On, "Tôdai no gumbô hyô," 1959: 79.

20. HTS, 73: 2965–68.

21. See the 812 preface.

22. HTS, 73: 2965–79.

23. Records of less recognizable branches also exist in dynastic histories both before and during the T'ang. Examples can be found in Lu Kao's biography in *Liang shu*, and in Lu Chih's biography in CTS and HTS. This Lu Chih was a famous scholar of the *Spring and autumn annals*. His original name was Lu Ch'un, but he later changed his name to Chih to avoid a taboo on the name of Emperor T'ang Hsien-tsung. I shall hereafter refer to him by his original name of Ch'un to avoid confusion with Lu Chih, our protagonist. *Liang shu*, 26: 398–99; CTS, 189: 4977–78; HTS, 168: 5127–28. For Lu Ch'un's classical scholarship, see Chang Ch'ün, "T'an Chao Lu san-chia Ch'un-chiu chih shuo," in *Ch'ien Mu hsien-sheng pa-shih sui chi-nien lun-wen-chi*, 1974: 149–59; Pulleyblank, "Neo-Confucianism

and Neo-Legalism," 1960: 89–91; McMullen, *State and scholars*, 1988: 101–3; Inaba Ichirô, "Chûtô ni okeru shinjugaku undô no ichi kosatsu," *Chûgoku chûseishi kenkyû*, 1970: 390–96.

24. *Chin shu*, 54: 1467–68; *Sung shu*, 53: 1510; Ho Ch'i-min, "Chung-ku nan-fang men-ti," in his *Chung-ku men-ti lun-chi*, 1978, ch. 4; Mao, *Liang Chin Nan-pei-ch'ao shih-tsu*, 1966, vol. 1: 140–46; vol. 2: 408, 440, 460, 463, 470, 472, 482–83, 494, 502–5, 507, 509–10.

25. Perhaps, the size of these two branches made a difference. Both before and during the T'ang, the size of these two subgroups bore no comparison with that of the T'ai-wei branch. See HTS, 73: 2966–80; YHHT, 10: 1a–4a.

26. CTS, 189: 4944–45; HTS, 198: 5639–40. As for the Wen-hsüeh-kuan, see Fukusawa Sokichi, "Bungakukan gakushi ni tsuite," *Kumamoto daigaku kyoiku gakubu kiyô*, 1 (1953): 35–41.

27. McMullen, *State and scholars*, 1988: 33 and 72. For the practice of three teachings debates in the T'ang, see Lo Hsiang-lin, "T'ang-tai san-chiao chiang-lun k'ao," in his *T'ang-tai wen-hua-shih*, 1955: 159–76.

28. CTS, 189: 4945 and HTS, 198: 5639–40. For Te-ming's noble status, see CTS, 43: 1821; TT, 19: 110; Wang Shou-nan, *Sui T'ang shih*, 1986: 412–4.

29. Mao Han-kuang thought Lu Te-ming was the only member who served in the early bureaucracy. See his "Wu chün Lu-shih," in *Tao Hsi-sheng hsien-sheng chiu-chih jung-ch'ing chi-nien lun-wen-chi*, 1989: 61. However, Lu Shih-chi also served during T'ai-tsung's reign. See CTS, 188: 4932; HTS, 195: 5584.

30. Of course, very few common people of undistinguished origin could afford the time and money to become a scholar. Twitchett, *Chinese meritocracy*, 1974: 24.

31. Lao Ke and Chao Yüeh, *T'ang Shang-shu-sheng lang-kuan shih-chu t'i-ming k'ao*, Kyoto reprint, 1978: 64–65; HTS, 61: 1643. Like his father, Tun-hsin was also ennobled as Baron of Chia-hsing county. HTS, 61: 1643.

32. Denis Twitchett and Howard Wechsler, "Kao-tsung (reign 649–683) and the Empress Wu: the inheritor and the usurper," in CHC, 1979: 251–55; also see R. W. L. Guisso, *Wu Tse-t'ien and the politics of legitimation in T'ang China*, 1978, ch. 3.

33. CHC, 1979: 251–55.

34. Twitchett, "T'ang ruling class," *Perspectives*, 1973: 51.

35. HTS, 73: 2967; also see Mao Han-kuang, "Wu chün Lu-shih," 1989: 61.

36. HTS, 73: 2967.

37. HTS, 73: 2968–78.

38. See a tomb inscription written during Empress Wu's reign by Chang Yüeh (667–730) to commemorate the Chief Minister Lu Yüan-fang, who died in 701. CTW, 231, 16b. Mao Han-kuang, "Wu chün Lu-shih," 1989: 57, does not include Lu Shan-jen in the first generation of the T'ai-wei branch members who served in T'ang officialdom.

39. CTS, 88: 2875; HTS, 73: 2968 and 116: 4235.

40. CTS, 88: 2875; HTS, 116: 4235; CTW, 231: 16b.

41. CTS, 88: 2875; HTS, 116: 4235; CTW, 231: 16b; TKCK, vol. 3, 27: 1106. According to TKCK, in addition to the *ming-ching* examination, there were eight special subjects decree examinations held in 659. Since Lu Yüan-fang was then about twenty years old, it is very likely that he took the *ming-ching* examination and these special subjects decree examinations in that year.

42. The examination system was also under reform early in Hsüan-tsung's reign, but this does not change the fact that the *chin-shih* examination became the most important channel for acquisition of high office. For the development of the doctoral examinations and Empress Wu's influence on literary composition in the *chin-shih* examination, see Twitchett and Wechsler, "Kao-tsung and the Empress Wu," in CHC: 276–77; Ch'en Yin-k'o, *Shu-lun kao*: 16; also see CYKCC, vol. 1, 1977: 172–73; Cho Tsun-hung, *T'ang-tai chin-shih yü cheng-chih*, 1987: 49–57. Also see Shen Chi-chi's criticism of the *chin-shih* examination contained in *T'ung-tien*. See TT, ch. 15: 84. For the reform of the examination system under Hsüan-tsung's reign, see Twitchett, "Hsüan-tsung (r. 712–756)," in CHC: 405; John Lee, "The dragons and tigers of 792: The examination in T'ang history," in *T'ang Studies*, 6 (1988): 26–27.

43. HTS, 116: 4239, also see TKCK, vol. 3, 27: 1031.

44. Kao-tsung's emphasis on the examination system is demonstrated by his ordering the compilation of the *Hsing-shih lu* (Record of surnames and lineages) in which the criteria for ranking families was strictly based upon office and personal achievement during the reigning dynasty. See Twitchett, "T'ang ruling class," *Perspectives*, 1973: 62–64.

45. Twitchett, *Chinese meritocracy*, 1974: 8–12; also see his introduction in CHC: 21.

46. Twitchett, *Chinese meritocracy*, 1974: 23.

47. For Lu Yüan-fang, see CTS, 88: 2875; HTS, 116: 4235; Lu Yü-ch'ing, see HTS, 116: 4239. Only the HTS biography mentions Lu Yü-ch'ing's achievement in this matter. Since this event took place at the beginning of 697, the pacification of the northwest border area most certainly must refer to the invasion of Ling-chou (modern Ninghsia) by the Turks in 697. See TCTC, 206: 6512–16.

48. Indeed, Lu Yüan-fang was demoted from his position as chief minister when Empress Wu thought he was involved in a factional intrigue, but he was soon reappointed to the same position after she learned of his innocence. See CTS, 88: 2875; HTS, 116: 4235; also see Mao, "Wu chün Lu-shih," 1989: 58.

49. For Lu Yüan-fang's sons, see CTS, 88: 2876–77; HTS, 116: 4236–38. For Lu Yü-ch'ing's descendants, see HTS, 116: 4239–40; CTS, 145: 3937–38. For the *Yin* privilege, see Twitchett, *Chinese meritocracy*, 1974: 9.

50. *Ta-T'ang chuan-tsai*, 1; also see HTS, 196: 5613.

51. HTS, 196: 5613. Also see Wang Tang, *T'ang Yü-lin*, 1978, 4: 147.

52. See Mao Han-kuang, "Ts'ung shih-tsu chi-kuan ch'ien-i k'an T'ang-tai shih-tsu chih chung-yang-hua," in CYYY, 52 (1981): 421–510, esp. see his conclusion; also see Ebrey, *The aristocratic families*, 1978: 28–32; Twitchett, CHC: 22.

53. HTS, 196: 5613.

54. HTS, 116: 4238, 63: 1750–51, 73: 2974.

55. See the biographies of Lu Yüan-fang, Lu Hsiang-hsien, and Lu Kuei-meng of the T'ai-wei branch; Lu Te-ming of the Tan-t'u; and Lu Chih and Lu I of the Shih-lang branch. CTS, 88: 2875–76; HTS, 116: 4235–37 and 196: 5612; CTS, 189: 4944–45; HTS, 198: 5639–40; CTS, 139: 3791 and HTS, 157: 4911; CTS, 179: 4668 and HTS, 183: 5383.

56. As noted above, Lu Tun-hsin, Lu Te-ming's son, was ennobled as Baron of Chia-hsing (HTS, 198: 5640) during Kao-tsung's reign. Both Twitchett and Yen I-p'ing have followed the Ch'ing dynasty *nien-p'u* in writing that Lu Tun-hsin was Lu Chih 's great-grandfather, and thus implying that the Shih-lang branch probably had become established in Chia-hsing at least by Tun-hsin's time. See Twitchett, "Lu Chih," 1962: 88; Yen I-p'ing, *Lu Hsüan-kung nien-p'u*, 1975: 1. However, no T'ang source says that Lu Tun-hsin was Lu Chih's great-grandfather, and neither does the 1745 genealogy entitled *Lu-shih shih-p'u* which I have cited in this study.

57. HTS, 73: 2978.

58. Lu Ch'i-wang's official rank was 3b. YHHT records that Ch'i-wang occupied this position during the K'ai-yüan period. See YHHT, 10: 4a. This

would seem to invalidate Mao Han-kuang's speculation that Lu Ch'i-wang
served during Empress Wu's reign. See his "Wu chün Lu-shih," 1989: 60.
Some sources say that Lu Ch'i-wang's position was vice director instead of
director of the Palace Library (*Pi-shu shao-chien*). See YHHT, 10: 4a and
Twitchett, "Lu Chih," 1962: 88. However, according to a T'ang tomb inscription preserved in a Sung dynasty source, Ch'i-wang's position was Pi-
shu-chien. See Ou-yang Fei, compiled, *Chi-ku lu-mu*, ch. 8, and *Po-k'e
ts'ung-pien*, 14: 388–89. Also see YHHTSCC, vol. 10: 901.

59. Mao, "Wu chün Lu-shih," 1989: 60.

60. HTS, 73: 2979.

61. On Lu Mi's origin, see CTW, 684: 29b; YHHT, 10: 5a.

62. Ts'en Chung-mien, *Lang-kuan shih-chu t'i-ming hsin k'ao-ting*,
1984: 79.

63. The person who mentioned "Lu Feng (or Lu Li) and his younger
brothers Lu Pa, Lu Jun and Lu Huai..." was Fu Tsai. See CTW, 690: 1b.
Moreover, we find that Lu Ch'an must be the youngest son since he still
served in the government toward the end of Yüan-ho era (805–820). See
YHHTSCC, 10: 902. Although we have no information to confirm the age
difference between Lu Wei and Lu Feng, it seems very likely that Lu Wei
was the eldest brother. For while Lu Wei was highly regarded by the
notable *ku-wen* writer Hsiao Ying-shih, Lu Feng (or Lu Li) was a close
friend of Hsiao Ying-shih's son. See CTW, 691: 8b. Of course, it is also
possible that Lu Wei could very well have been the second eldest brother.
Without further information, we can only speculate on their order of seniority. Fu Tsai led a reclusive life on Lu mountain in Kiangsi until around
797. He was then given a post in provincial government by Li Sun, a
notable financial official in Hsien-tsung's reign. See CTW, 688: 1a. For Li
Sun, see CTS, 123: 3522 and HTS, 149: 4805. I shall soon explain why Lu
Feng and Lu Jun had other names.

64. According to the biography of Lu I, Lu Feng was Lu I's great-
grandfather. This contradicts the HTS genealogy. See CTS, 179: 4668;
HTS, 73: 2978–79. Since no other T'ang sources offer any information on
this matter, and since the HTS genealogy is often mistaken, I shall accept
the biographical information contained in the CTS as valid for the time
being.

65. YHHT, 10: 4a.

66. See Ch'üan Te-yü's preface, "T'ang tseng ping-pu shang-shu Hsüan-
kung Lu Chih Han-yüan-chi hsü," in CTW, 493: 11b, or in HYCC: 1–5.

67. Lu Chih's biography in the CTS also says that his father's name
was Lu K'an. See CTS, 139: 3791 and YHHTSCC, 10: 902.

68. CTW, 483: 2b.

69. YHHT, 10: 4a. Also see YHHTSCC, 10: 901–2. YHHT mentions Li-shui while CTS and Ch'üan Te-yü's preface agree that Li-yang was the county where Lu K'an served. See YHHT, 10: 4a; CTS, 139: 3791; CTW, 493: 11b.

70. YHHT, 10: 4a.

71. HTS, 73: 2980.

72. See Chou I-liang, ed., *Hsin T'ang shu tsai-hsiang shih-hsi piao yin-te*, in Harvard-Yenching Index series, no. 16, introduction: i-xvii.

73. When Chief Minister Ts'ui Ch'ün (772–832) administered the 816 doctoral examination, he did not pass Lu Chien-li despite the fact that he himself had acquired the *chin-shih* degree under Lu Chih's administration of the examination in 792. See TKCK, vol. 2, 18: 663–64; *T'ang yü-lin*, 4: 151. Also see CTS, 159: 4187–90.

74. See Fu Tsai's essay in CTW, 690: 1b.

75. HTS, 202: 5769. I have followed Lo Tsung-ch'iang's convincing explanation for Hsiao Ying-shih's dates. See Lo Tsung-ch'iang, *Sui T'ang Wu-tai wen-hsüeh ssu-hsiang shih*, 1986: 271.

76. In the HTS genealogy and YHHT Lu Feng is named Lu Li, but a biography of Lu I says Lu I's great-grandfather was Lu Feng. Except for the difference between Li and Feng, the rest of the data concerning Lu Feng or Lu Li is identical. Besides, many poems addressed to him also did not distinguished between Lu Feng and Lu Li. Thus we know Lu Feng and Lu Li must refer to the same person. See HTS, 73: 2980; YHHTSCC, 10: 902. Poems to Lu Feng include some written by Liu Ch'ang and Huang-fu Jan. Those to Lu Li were written by Li Chia-yu, Yen Wei, and Lu Lun, etc. See CTShih, vol. 3, 3: 1: 853, 856, and 864, vol. 5, 4: 7: 1507, vol. 4, 3: 9: 1173, vol. 5, 4: 9: 1562, vol. 6, 5: 2: 1685. For his friendship with Hsiao Ts'un and Hsiao Ts'un's life, see Hsiao's tomb inscription in CTW, 691: 8a.

77. See the above note and CTShih, vol. 15, 12: 2: 4735 for a poem written to Lu Feng by Chiao-jan.

78. See Lu I's biographies in CTS, 179: 4668; HTS, 183: 5383.

79. In the *New T'ang History* genealogy, Lu Wei was said to have occupied the post of vice minister of the Ministry of Revenue (*Hu-pu shih-lang*) with a rank of 4a. Yen Keng-wang also agrees with this but does not provide any supporting documentation. See HTS, 73: 2980; Yen Keng-wang, *T'ang p'u shang ch'eng-lang piao*, vol. 1, 1956: 148. However, YHHT tells us that Lu Wei's official advancement reached only to the rank of attendant censor (*shih yü-shih*), either 6b2 or 6a. See YHHTSCC, 10, 901.

80. HTS, 202: 5769.

81. Lu Feng's last official post, however, was not attendant censor (*shih-yü-shih*) with a rank of 6b2 or 6a as listed in the *New T'ang History* genealogy, but rather palace censor (*tien-chung shih yü-shih*) with a rank of 7a. CTS, 179: 4668; YHHTSCC, 10: 902; also see CTW, 691: 8b.

82. SKSC, vol. 9, 17: 1a. Lu Jun (or Lu Chien) probably served as vice director of the Bureau of Receptions (*Chu-k'o yüan-wai-lang*) during Te-tsung's reign. For Lu Jun and Lu Chien as the same person, see Ts'en Chung-mien, *Lang-kuan shih-chu t'i-ming hsin k'ao-ting*, 1984: 167 and 190; HTS, 73: 2979, CTW, 690: 1b. Lu Pa enjoyed an equally fine literary reputation, and is listed as director of the Ministry of Personnel (*Li-pu lang-chung*) in the *New T'ang History* genealogy. HTS, 73: 2978. However, except for the HTS, no other T'ang sources mention Lu Pa's official position. Lu Ch'an (*chin-shih* 785) rose to be supervising secretary (*chi-shih-chung*) in 818. TKCK, vol. 2, 12: 428; CTShih, vol. 7, 6:4: 2185; Chi Yu-kung, *T'ang-shih chi-shih*, vol. 2, 59: 904; YHHTSCC, 10: 902; CTW, 663: 17a.

83. Sun Kuo-tung, "Ts'ung Meng-yu-lu k'an T'ang-tai wen-jen ch'ien-kuan te tsui-yu t'u-ching," in his *T'ang Sung shih lun-ts'ung*, 1980: 19 and 30 note 3.

84. CTS, 179: 4668–69; HTS, 183: 5383–84. Also see Mao, "Wu chün Lu-shih," 1989: 60.

85. For Lu Lun's and Ch'ien Ch'i's lives and their achievements in T'ang poetry, see Stephen Owen, *The great age of Chinese poetry: the high T'ang*, 1981: 254–58, 261–64, 275, and 277–80.

86. Lu Chih was then serving as vice minister in the Ministry of War (*Ping-pu shih-lang*). There is a problem concerning the identity of Lu Ch'i-wang's wife. According to the *Chi-ku lu-mu*, his wife's surname was Ho-lan and she was ennobled as Ying-yang hsien chün (district mistress of Ying-yang). This passage is quoted in the *Pao-k'o ts'ung-pien*. However, the *Pao-k'o ts'ung-pien* also quotes another passage from the *Ching-chao chin-shih lu* which says the wife's last name was Cheng and she was ennobled as district mistress of Ying-yang county. From the *Chih-chai shu-lu chieh-t'i* we learn that the *Ching-chao chin-shih lu* was compiled in 1082 while the *Chi-ku lu-mu* was at least ten years earlier than that date since the compiler was a contemporary of Ou-yang Hsiu (1007–1072). The *Pao-k'o ts'ung-pien* was a much later work compiled around 1233.

All this information does not necessary solve our puzzle, although one possibility might be that the compiler of the *Pao-k'o ts'ung-pien* made a mistake when he copied the passage from the *Ching-chao chin-shih lu*; that is, he mistakenly changed Ho-lan-shih into Cheng-shih. This is to say that Lu Chih's granduncle actually married a woman of foreign origin. If this was the case, it confirms the fact that marriages between Chinese and non-Chinese families were not uncommon during the T'ang, especially if the non-Chinese family enjoyed high status in society. See Wang Shou-nan, *Sui T'ang shih*, 1986: 687. After all, the T'ang ruling house was known for its admixture of non-Chinese blood.

It is also equally likely that Lu Ch'i-wang married Cheng-shih because the Ying-yang Cheng was one of the most illustrious lineages in the T'ang. Such a marriage would have enhanced the prestige of the two families. Besides, the title of the ennoblement—"Ying-yang hsien chün"—also seems to indicate the origin of the receiver's family. Whatever the case may be, we can only leave it as it is due to the lack of further information. See *Chi-ku lu-mu*, ch. 8; *Pao-k'o ts'ung-pien*, 14: 388–89 and 7: 182; *Chih-chai shu-lu chieh-t'i*, vol. 2, 8: 225 and 230. For the Ho-lan family, see YHHTSCC, 9: 838–40.

In the extant passage of the tomb inscription composed for Lu Ch'i-wang's wife, Lu Chih refers to himself as the great-grandnephew rather than grandnephew of Lu Ch'i-wang. As Ts'en Chung-mien points out, this must be a copyist's mistake. Since all of Lu Ch'i-wang's sons were still alive at the beginning of Yüan-ho era (805–820), the age differences between Lu Chih and them could not have made him their grandnephew. (See YHHTSCC, 10: 902.) This study of Lu Chih and Lu Ch'i-wang's families has also demonstrated the real relationship between them.

87. HYCC, 20: 6b. Unless otherwise noted, all quotations from Lu Chih are from the 1768 editions of his works, the *Han-yüan chi-chu* (HYCC), and references are to chapter: page number with *a* for recto and *b* for verso.

Chapter Two

1. CTS, 139: 3791; HTS, 157: 4911; YHHT, 10: 4a. Other sources such as Ch'üan Te-yü's preface and ch. 4 of SL only mention Lu Chih's choronym as Wu *chün*. For Ch'üan Te-yü's preface, CTW, 493: 11b; SL, 4: 14.

2. CTS, 139: 3791.

3. CTS, 189a: 4939. Ch'en Jo-shui also discusses this *"chung-wen ch'ing-ju"* phenomenon in his *Liu Tsung-yüan*, 1992: 18.

4. See Lu Chih's "Hung-chien fu," CTW, 460:8b. All of his seven extant rhapsodies are preserved in CTW. Although most of them are occasional pieces, some of the passages do reveal his inner thoughts. See CTW, 460: 1b–8b.

5. CTW, 460: 7b. I have followed Hoyt Tillman's translation of *chün-tzu* as *superior person*, instead of the conventional translation of *gentleman*.

See Tillman, *Confucian discourse and Chu Hsi's ascendancy*, 1992: 13. William Theodore de Bary, *The trouble with Confucianism*, 1991, explains in detail the virtues of a genuine *chün-tzu* and translates it as *noble man*.

6. HYCC, 13: 8a.

7. McMullen, *State and scholars*, 1988, chs. 3 and 4. Lu Chih of course understood the political function of Confucian rituals, see McMullen, ibid., 325 note 158.

8. I follow the convention of translating *jen* as *benevolence*, but to avoid the possible religious connotation of the Western term *righteousness*, I follow Tillman in using *rightness* to translate *i*. See Tillman's comments in his *Confucian discourse*, 1992: 12.

9. Ch'üan Te-yü's preface says Lu Chih obtained this degree at age 18, that is, in 771. Both SL and CTS contain the same message. Based upon TKCK, Twitchett has explained why the date of Lu Chih's degree conferment should have been in 773. Yen I-p'ing, following TKCK and the passage in *T'ang-shih chi-shih*, also agrees that 773 should be the correct date. See Twitchett, "Lu Chih," 1962: 88 and 338 note 28; Yen I-p'ing, *Nien-p'u*, 1975: 9–10. Also see TKCK, 10: 380; *T'ang-shih chi-shih*, 32: 504.

10. The four steps of assessment in the usual placement process include tests on deportment (*shen*), speech (*yen*), calligraphy (*shu*), and judgment on administrative affairs (*p'an*). See HTS, 45: 1171; TT, 15: 84; Twitchett, *Chinese meritocracy*, 1974: 17.

11. See HTS, 45: 1172; TT, 15: 85; TFYK, 639: 7662; Waley, *Po Chü-i*, 1949: 27–28; Robert des Rotours, *Le Traité des examens*, Paris: 1932: 219–22; Charles Hartman, *Han Yü and the T'ang search for unity*, 1986: 29; Chen, *Liu Tsung-yüan*, 1992: 51 note 67; Liu Po-chi, *T'ang-tai cheng-chiao shih*, 1974: 159. The English for *po-hsüeh hung-tz'u* is Charles Hartman's translation. Unless otherwise indicated, all the English translations are mine.

12. A poem entitled "Seeing Lu Chih Off for Su-chou after acquiring a degree," written by Ch'ien Ch'i (CTShih, vol. 5, 4: 5: 1419) seems to suggest that Lu Chih did not take this examination in 773:

> Why are you returning home so early,
> For joy in Yun-chien at your success?
> Long thinking of your family, the kumquats have ripened;
> All washed with rain, the sojourner's sails are swift.
> By night fires, you'll pass the ford;
> At morning bell, you'll face P'u-ch'eng.
> Rest your transcendent wings at Hua-t'ing,
> And plan another time to soar again.

Yun-chien is the ancient name of Hua-t'ing county (*hsien*). Ch'ien Ch'i's use of Hua-t'ing here is obviously an allusion to the phrase "the cry of the crane at Hua-t'ing" (*Hua-t'ing he-li*) by Lu Chi, the famous literary talent of the Lu lineage during the Western Chin dynasty. Hua-t'ing had also been the traditional residence of the Lus before the T'ang. See YHCHTC, 25: 661. However, the *Wu-ti chi* says that it was in 746 that Hua-t'ing county was established, see Lu Kuang-wei, *Wu-ti chi*, 7–8. During the T'ang, P'u-cheng was one of the counties of Chien-chou (north of modern Fu-chou, Fukien), see YHCHTC, 29: 801; *Chung-kuo li-shih ti-t'u chi*, vol. 5: 55–56.

The title of this poem does not specifically mention the *chin-shih* degree, but it is obviously assumed by the author; passing the *po-hsüeh hung-tz'u* would have been indicated by subject (*k'o*) instead of by degree (*ti*). The encouragement and expectation expressed in the last two couplets seems further to imply that Lu Chih might not have passed the placement examination, but was already on his way to Su-chou or Wu *chün*. Had he passed the examination and then been given a position but rejected it, the content of the poem should be different. Meanwhile, since the purpose of taking such an examination was to acquire an immediate appointment, it would have been pointless for him to delay the examination for another two or three years. Thus, the year which Lu Chih took the *po-hsüeh hung-tz'u* examination was most likely 774.

13. CTS, 139: 3791; HTS, 157: 4911; SL, 4: 14; Ch'üan Te-yü, preface, CTW, 493: 12a.

14. CTS, 139: 3791; HTS, 157: 4911; SL, 4: 14; Ch'üan Te-yü, preface, CTW, 493: 12a.

15. Lu Chih could not have visited Chang I at Shou-chou in 774 because Chang I was not appointed prefect of Shou-chou until at least 777. By the time Te-tsung ascended the throne in 779, Chang I was promoted to another position and no longer served in Shou-chou. Yü Hsien-hao, *T'ang tz'u-shih k'ao*, vol., 3, 1987: 1554–55; CTS, 125: 3545–46; HTS, 152: 4829–30.

Lu Chih himself also mentioned that he had spent two years in Ch'ang-chou (in modern Kiangsu) where Hsiao Fu was serving as prefect. Hsiao Fu's appointment in Ch'ang-chou did not begin until after the fourth month of 777, and he had to leave for another position by 779. Lu Chih's residence in Ch'ang-chou must, then, have been two years before 779, and his visit to Chang I could only have taken place in the early months 777. See HYCC, 14: 7b; CTS, 125: 3551.

A passage contained in the collated edition of *T'ang Yü-lin* by Ch'ien Hsi-tso says that Lu Chih was once appointed to be "Huai-nan wei," but was denied the position by the vice director of the Ministry of Personnel (*Li-pu shih-lang*); Ku Shao-lien (741–803) later received the position. Since Ku

Shao-lien was only appointed as "Teng-feng chu-pu" (assistant magistrate of Teng-feng) and since Teng-feng was in Honan, Yen I-p'ing argues that Lu Chih was originally given the office in Honan after he had resigned from the Cheng county office; "Huai-nan wei" must have been a mistake for "Honan wei." Because Lu Chih was denied the appointment in Honan, he then left for Su-chou. See Yen I-p'ing, *Nien-p'u*, 1975: 16; also see Chien Hsi-tso, "*T'ang Yü-lin* chiao-k'an chi'" in *T'ang Yü-lin*, 312. For Ku Shao-lien, see HTS, 162: 4994; CTW, 478: 3b.

16. CTS, 125: 3545; HTS, 152: 4829.

17. Yü Hsien-hao, *T'ang tz'u-shih k'ao*, vol. 3, 1987: 1515.

18. McMullen, *State and scholars*, 1988: 105–12 and his references. For Chang I's work on *Mencius*, see CTS, 125: 3546; on his government, see Ch'üan Te-yü's comments on him, Ch'üan Te-yü, "T'ang ku Chung-shu shih-lang t'ung Chung-shu men-hsia p'ing-chang shih T'ai-tzu pin-k'o tseng Hu-pu shang-shu Ch'i Cheng-kung shen-tao pei-ming," CTW, 499: 5b.

19. The other two best provincial administrators are said to be Hsiao Fu—Lu Chih's close friend as shall be shown soon—and Hsiao Ting. See CTS, 185: 4826.

20. CTS, 139: 3791 and HTS, 157: 4911. The Japanese scholar Kitô Yûichi noticed the close relationship between Lu Chih and Chang I, but he mistakenly dated the visit as 771. See Kitô Yûichi, "Lu Hsüan-kung tsou-i cha-chi," *Kôgakkan Ronsô*, vol. 18: 6 (1985): 16–35, esp. 24–25.

21. CTS, 139: 3791 and HTS, 157: 4911; Ch'üan Te-yü's preface, CTW, 493: 12a.

22. Hsiao Fu only took the position of prefect in Ch'ang-chou after the fourth month of 777. Before that time, Tu-ku Chi, an early advocate of *ku-wen*, had governed Ch'ang-chou for at least four years and was also known for his excellent administration based upon Confucian principles. Unable to employ Lu Chih himself, it is likely that Chang I might have recommended the youthful Lu, who also considered himself a follower of Confucian principles, to visit Tu-ku Chi. See the life accounts (*hsing-chuang*) of Tu-ku Chi given by his disciple Liang Su (753–793), CTW, 522: 3b–7b.

23. HYCC, 14: 7b–8a.

24. Ibid.: 8a.

25. CTS, 99: 3093–96; HTS, 101: 3953–55.

26. CTS, 125: 3550; HTS, 101: 3955.

27. CTS, 125: 3552; HTS, 101: 3957. Hsiao Fu died in 788 at age 57.

28. CTS, 125: 3552; HTS, 101: 3957. Chang I is also said not to have made friends lightly. CTS, 125: 3545; HTS, 152: 4829.

29. For eunuchs appointed as army supervisors, see TCTC, 223: 7151 and 7158; 224: 7210–13; 228: 7353; Wang Shou-nan, *T'ang-tai huan-kuan*, 1971: 30–32; Yano Chikara, "Tô-dai kangunshi-sei no kakuritsu ni tsuite," *Nishi-nibon shigaku*, 14 (1953): 16–32; C. A. Peterson, "Court and province," CHC: 512–14. For Hsiao Fu, see CTS, 125: 3551; TCTC, 229: 7397.

30. HYCC, 14: 8a.

31. None of the traditional sources tell us when exactly Lu Chih took his *shu-p'an pa-ts'ui* examination. Yen I-p'ing assumes that Lu went to the capital in 778 and took the examination that year, but this could only have taken place at the end of 778, otherwise it would contradict Lu Chih's own account that he had stayed in Ch'ang-chou for exactly two years. If this was the case, Lu Chih then must have arrived at Ch'ang-chou before Hsiao Fu became prefect in that region; that is, Lu must have had a chance to know Tu-ku Chi. If Lu Chih arrived at Ch'ang-chou after Hsiao Fu became prefect in the fourth month of 777, this would then put Lu's departure date for the capital right before the fifth month of 779, otherwise it would also contradict the fact that he had stayed in Ch'ang-chou for exactly two years. Moreover, the placement examination usually began in the late months of the year and ended in late spring of the next year, and this matches with the two possible dates of Lu's departure for the capital. It also seems reasonable that Lu had to seek a new appointment since he must have learned that Hsiao Fu was no longer able to keep him there. Yen I-p'ing, *Nien-p'u*, 1975: 17. For the placement examination, see TT, 15: 84. For Hsiao Fu's new post see CTS, 11: 320 and 125: 3551. For Lu Chih, see CTS, 139: 3791 and HTS, 157: 4911; SL, ch. 4: 14 and Ch'üan Te-yü's preface in CTW, 493: 12a.

32. CTShih, vol. 6, 5: 2: 1681.

33. Ch'ien Ch'i came from the southeast region and obtained his *chin-shih* in 752, two years before Lu Chih was born. (CTS, 168: 4382–83; HTS, 203: 5786.) Lu Lun, on the other hand, was not a native Southerner. His early ancestors belonged to the most prominent Lu clan of Fan-yang in the Shan-tung area. He originally intended to take the *chin-shih* examination at the end of the T'ien-pao era (742–756), but the An Lu-shan rebellion forced him, like so many other scholar official families, to take refuge in the south with his parents. (CTS, 163: 4268; HTS, 203: 5785.) For the intellectual migration during the An Lu-shan rebellion see Pulleyblank, "Neo-Confucianism and Neo-Legalism," 1960: 83.

34. We shall discuss the two-tax system in ch. 6.

35. Te-tsung's order is preserved in TFYK, 162: 1957–58, a short version is also in TTCLC, 104: 534. Twitchett has translated this edict in his *Financial administration under the T'ang dynasty*, 1970: 161–62. Also see TCTC, 226: 7277; HTS, 157: 4911.

36. HTS, 157: 4911; YHCHTC, 1: 1. Except for HTS, none of the other traditional sources mention this discussion. Yen I-p'ing notices this information, but since he believes that Lu Chih already served in the central government, he does not see the connection of this information to Lu Chih's career development. See Yen I-p'ing, *Nien-p'u*, 1975: 18. Twitchett does discuss this information, but because he assumes that Lu Chih's suggestion to the commissioner at this time was actually one of his memorials to the throne as Han-lin scholar, he does not make the connection either. See Twitchett, "Lu Chih," 1962: 89–90.

37. We do not know exactly when he was promoted to this new position, but since his suggestions were presented to the commissioner in the second month of 780, his promotion could not have been earlier than that. Yen I-p'ing assumes that Lu Chih took this new service in 779, but I believe this is incorrect. See HTS, 157: 4911–12; Yen I-p'ing, *Nien-p'u*, 1975: 17.

38. HYCC, 12: 23b.

39. The position of investigating censor was a major channel through which an official could be further selected to assume those prestigious and important offices designated as *pure official (ch'ing-kuan)*. See Sun Kuo-tung, "Meng-yu-lu," in his *T'ang Sung shih lun-ts'ung*, 1980: 20; Twitchett, "Lu Chih," 1962: 89.

40. For details concerning Han-lin scholars, see Li Chao, "Han-lin chih" and Wei Chih-i, "Han-lin yüan ku-shih" in *Han-yüan ch'ün-shu*; TCTC, 228: 7347; HTS, 46: 1183–84; Yano Chikara, "Tôdai ni okeru kanrin gakushiin ni tsuite," *Shigaku kenkyû*, 50 (1953): 63–70; Yamamoto Tatsuyoshi, "Tô-Sô jidai ni okeru kanrin gakushi ni tsuite," *Tôhôgaku*, 4 (1952): 28–38; Twitchett, "Hsüan-tsung," CHC: 450.

41. On the contention between "inner" and "outer" court in the Former Han dynasty, see Wang Yü-ch'üan, "An outline of the central government of the Former Han dynasty," HJAS, 12 (June 1949): 134–87, esp. 166–73; in T'ang, see Michael Dalby, "Court politics," CHC: 587. The *Old T'ang History* mentions that after 805, the most respected Han-lin scholars would eventually become chief ministers, see CTS, 43: 1853–54.

42. See Ting Chü-hui, "Ch'ung-hsiu Ch'eng-chih hsüeh-shih pi-chi," in *Han-yüan ch'ün-shu*; Ts'en Chung-mien, "Han-lin hsüeh-shih," *Hsin k'ao-ting*, 1984: 221. Most other sources state that Te-tsung heard Lu Chih's name when he was still heir apparent, and after he ascended the throne, he made Lu a Han-lin scholar. (CTS, 139: 3791; HTS, 157:4912; TCTC, 228: 7347; Ch'üan Te-yü's preface, CTW, 493: 12a.) This has led modern historians to date Lu Chih's appointment to that position at 779. (Twitchett, "Lu Chih," 1962: 89; McMullen, *State and scholars*, 1988: 239; Liu Chao-jen, "Lu Hsüan-kung yen chiu," *Shih-chien hsüeh-pao*, 9, 1978: 97; Hsieh

Wu-hsiung, *Lu Hsüan-kung*, 1975: 2.) Yen I-p'ing does not accept 779 as the date of Lu Chih's appointment, but neither does he offer any reasons for choosing 781 as the date. See his *Nien-p'u*, 1975: 18–19.

The details of this determination concerning Lu Chih's Han-lin appointment are rather complicated. We must recall that in 779 Lu was still serving in Wei-nan county, and could only assume his duties in the Censorate after his conference with the personnel evaluation commissioner in the second month of 780. Besides, right after his enthronement in 779 Te-tsung asked his former classics tutor, Chang She, to remain in his previously acquired position of Han-lin scholar. Chang enjoyed the imperial favor until the third month of 780 when his involvement in a bribery scandal was discovered. After Chang She's fall from grace, Te-tsung did not seem to have any favorite Han-lin scholar though he did keep a few of them at the court. Up to 783, he seems to have favored only one particular minister, Lu Ch'i, whose protégé was going to be Lu Chih's nemesis.

Chang She was appointed as Han-lin scholar after 766, in Tai-tsung's reign. Although he had already acquired this position before Te-tsung ascended the throne, he was very likely the first Han-lin scholar Te-tsung kept in his private court. The other Han-lin scholars in Te-tsung's court during this time included men like Chiang Kung-fu whom we shall discuss soon. Ts'en Chung-mien has carefully dealt with the problem of when Chang She was appointed as Han-lin scholar and who the Han-lin scholars were at the beginning of Te-tsung's reign. See his "Han-lin hsüeh-shih pi-chi chu pu," in his *Hsin k'ao-ting*, 1984: 215–21. For Chang's life see CTS, 127: 3577–78; TCTC, 226: 7278.

We are certain that Lu Chih remained as investigating censor for some time, but we do not know the exact length of his service in this office. The *Old T'ang History* attributes his appointment as Han-lin scholar to Chang I's influence. (CTS, 139: 3799.) This implies that he probably acquired this post after the seventh month of 781 when Chang I became chief minister. However, Ting Chü-hui unmistakably wrote in 837 that Lu Chih was appointed to be Han-lin scholar in the third month of 783 while he was serving concurrently as vice director of the Bureau of Sacrifices (*Tz'u-pu yüan-wai-lang*), a subordinate section of the Ministry of Rites (*Li pu*).

As Ts'en Chung-mien points out, Lu Chih, according to "Ch'ung-hsiu ch'eng-chih," seems to have been appointed as *Tz'u-pu yüan-wai lang* first and to the Han-lin scholar position later. The TFYK (99: 1187) also accepts 783 as the date Lu was established in this position. This date seems convincing. For one thing, if Lu Chih was appointed in the third month of 783, this would explain why he did not present any memorials to the throne before 783, not even when his patron Chang I was sent away from the capital in the fourth month of 782. He was probably not so much afraid to make a protest as he was unable to gain access to the emperor. It is thus quite reasonable to accept that Lu Chih assumed the position of Han-lin scholar in the third month of 783.

43. CTS, 139: 3817.

44. On the Confucian concept of music, see *Lun yü* IX.14; XV.10; XVII. 18; *Hsün tzu*, "Yüeh-lun"; *Li chi*, "Yüeh-chi."

45. Translation from Twitchett, "Lu Chih," 1962: 96, with minor modifications.

46. Su Shih, "Ta Yü kua feng-i shu," in *Tung-p'o ch'i chi*, SPPY, vol. 2, 14: 8. Chu Hsi commented: "Lu Hsüan-kung's memorials were extremely well written. . . . People said that Lu Hsüan-kung could not express himself orally, but could only write things out, . . . I suspect that this is probably true." We have no way to prove whether Lu Chih had a speech impediment, but what is clear is that Chu Hsi admired Lu Chih's writing style. Li Ching-te, ed., *Chu-tzu yü-lei*, vol. 8, 136: 3248.

47. See Lo Tsung-ch'iang, *Sui T'ang Wu-tai wen-hsüeh ssu-hsiang-shih*, 1986: 220–21; Hsieh Wu-hsiung, *Lu Hsüan-kung*, 1975: 92–103; also see Langley's entry on Lu Chih in William Nienhauser, Jr. ed., *The Indiana companion to traditional Chinese literature*, 1986: 603–4. By Lu's time, *p'ien-wen* had dominated Chinese literary writing for more than five centuries. For differences between ancient and parallel prose styles, see Liu Wu-chi, *An introduction to Chinese literature*, 1966: 125–26; for the nature and development of parallel prose, see James Hightower, "Some characteristics of parallel prose," in John Bishop, ed., *Studies in Chinese literature*, 1966: 108–38.

48. CTS, 139: 3817.

49. This passage also appears in TCTC, 229: 7385–86. Twitchett, "Lu Chih," 1962: 98.

50. TCTC, 228: 7360 and 229: 7372; Li Sheng's biography, CTS, 133:3661–76; Li Huai-kuang, CTS, 121: 3491–95.

51. On Lu Chih's promotion see CTS, 12: 343 and 347; SL, 4,: 14; Ch'üan Te-yü, preface, CTW, 493: 12b. On the importance of the position of *Chung-shu she-jen*, see Sun Kuo-tung, "Meng-yu-lu," *T'ang Sung shih lun-ts'ung*, 1980: 24 and his references.

52. CTS, 125: 3549; TCTC, 228: 7359.

53. HYCC, 14: 8b–9a.

54. HYCC, 20: 6b.

55. Twitchett, "Lu Chih," 1962: 86.

56. CTS, 12: 337 and 138: 3787. Chiang Kung-fu became Han-lin scholar in 780, see Ting Chü-hui, "Ch'ung-hsiu ch'eng-chih," in *Han-yüan ch'ün-shu*; Ts'en Chung-mien, "Han-lin hsüeh-shih," in his *Hsin k'ao-ting*, 1984: 219–20.

57. CTS does not even give his family origin, it is listed in HTS, 152: 4831. For Ai-chou, see HTS, 43a: 1113.

58. CTS, 138: 3787; HTS, 152: 4831.

59. CTS, 12: 341; TCTC, 230: 7422–23; CTS, 138: 3787–88; HTS, 152: 4832.

60. HYCC, 15: 4a.

61. HYCC, 7: 18a–9b.

62. CTS, 138: 3788 and 139: 3816–17; HTS, 152: 4833. While Ch'üan Te-yü's preface does not mention this incident at all, the *Shun-tsung shih-lu* says that Lu Chih was criticized by current opinion as being responsible for Tou Shen's subsequent death. However, the *Shih-lu* also mentions that it was Tou Shen, rather than Lu Chih, who divulged the secret to Chiang Kung-fu. See SL, 4: 15. Since the authorship of SL is still an unsettled question, there is not much significance in determining who divulged this secret at this point. For the authorship of SL, see appendix 1.

63. HYCC, 14: 9b–10b.The thirteen candidates include Yüan Kao, see CTS, 153: 4086; HTS, 120: 4324; Yang Hsü, see CTS, 190: 5059; Sun Ch'eng, see CTS, 190: 5044; HTS, 118: 3423; Chou Hao, CTS, 136: 3746; HTS, 207: 5865–66; P'ei Hsü, CTS, 126: 3567; HTS, 130: 4490; P'ei Chou, CTS, 122: 3507; HTS, 130: 4491; Tsui Tsao, CTS, 130: 3625; HTS, 150: 4813; Yin Liang, HTS, 199: 5683; Li Chou, CTS, 118: 3423 and 121: 3490; Ho Shih-kan, CTS, 13: 365 and 185: 4830; Yao Nan-chung, CTS, 153: 4081; HTS, 162: 4989; Lu Ch'un, CTS, 189: 4977; HTS, 168: 5127; Shen Chi-chi, CTS, 149: 4034; HTS, 132: 4538. None of these men ever wrote anything about Lu Chih.

64. See the above note.

65. CTS, 130: 3626; HTS, 150: 4813. On the *Four K'uei* group, see Pulleyblank, "Neo-Confucianism and Neo-Legalism," 1960: 84–85; Hartman, *Han Yü*, 1986: 21.

66. For Lu Ch'un's and Shen's biographies, see note 63. Also see McMullen, *State and scholars*, 1988: 101–4. On Yang Yen's life, see CTS, 118: 3418–26; HTS, 145: 4722–27.

67. CTS, 118: 3423. The date of Li Chou's banishment is unclear. See David McMullen, "Li Chou, a forgotten agnostic of the late-eighth century," AM 8, part 2 (1995): 82. I am grateful to Professor McMullen for calling my attention to Li Chou.

68. For details about Lu Ch'un's career development and related information, see McMullen, *State and scholars*, 1988: 307 note 169.

69. Li Chou was obviously known to Lu Chih, but, no record survives in which Li mentions Lu. See McMullen, "Li Chou," 57–105.

70. Ch'üan Te-yü, preface, CTW, 493: 12b; HTS, 157: 4931. "Lu Chiu" refers to his rank among all the cousins of his generation. For the manner in which family seniority was determined in the T'ang dynasty, see Ts'en Chung-mien, *T'ang-jen hang-ti lu*, 1978: 5–13.

71. HTS, 157: 4931.

72. Ch'üan Te-yü, preface, CTW, 493: 12b–13a; Twitchett, "Lu Chih," 1962: 341.

73. The only memorial presented by Lu between 785 and 787 was around the eighth month of 785. See HYCC, 17: 10a–21b; also see TCTC, 232: 7463–65.

74. Twitchett, "Lu Chih," 1962: 102.

75. For the reforms of Li Mi and Ts'ui Ts'ao, see Dalby, "Court politics," CHC: 589–94. Also see TCTC, 232: 7467–68, 7475, 7489–95; CTS, 130: 3620–23, 3625–27.

76. HYCC, 11: 14a.

77. None of the sources tell us exactly when his mother died. However, as we shall see, Lu Chih was appointed to a new position at the beginning of 790 after finishing the mourning ritual. Moreover, since the three-year mourning ritual generally only lasted twenty-five months, Lu Chih's mother must have passed away in the winter of 787. For Lu Chih's appointment, see CTS, 13: 369; for the three-year mourning ritual, see *Li-chi*, "San-nien wen"; *Hsün Tzu*, "Li-lun p'ien."

78. CTS, 139: 3800; HTS, 157: 4923; Ch'üan Te-yü's preface, CTW, 493: 13a. It is possible that Lu Chih's continuing intimacy with the emperor was due to an affined relation on his mother's side with Te-tsung's favorite new consort, who also belonged to the prominent Wei clan of the Kuan-chung region. Since we do not know in what way Consort Wei's family was connected to Lu Chih's mother, or whether they were really connected, we still do not know how close their relationship was; we really do not have enough evidence to substantiate this connection. Moreover, T'ang lineages were often rather loosely knit groups, and simply having the same surname does not guarantee any real connection.

79. Mao Han-kuang, "Wu chün Lu-shih," 1989: 66, also points out Lu Chih's re-interment of his father represents another example of aristocratic centralization.

80. Ch'üan Te-yü's preface, CTW, 493: 13a; CTS, 139: 3800; HTS, 157: 4923. Wei Kao's biography, see CTS, 140: 3822–26.

81. Twitchett, "Lu Chih," 1962: 88 and 104.

82. Lu Chih's observance of the mourning rituals at Feng-lo Ssu reflected the custom among the T'ang literati of pursuing studies and intellectual discussions at scenic Buddhist temples on famous mountains. See Yen Keng-wang, "T'ang-jen hsi-yeh shan-lin ssu-yüan chih feng-shang," in his *T'ang shih yen-chiu ts'ung-kao*, 1969: 367–424, esp. 381–83 for the popularity of Sung-shan.

83. For details of *Pei-chü wen-yen* see appendix 1. Lu Chih's other works include *Ch'ien-shih lu* and *Ch'ing-nang shu*. Only the *Sung-shih I-wen chih* lists *Hsüan-tsung pien-i lu* and *Ch'ing-nang shu*, it also says that there were two chapters in the former work and ten chapters in the latter. *Ch'ing-nang shu* seems to have been a kind of literary encyclopedia since it is placed in the *Lei-shu* section of the *Sung-shih I-wen chih*. Both HTS and *Sung-shih* agree that there was only one chapter in *Ch'ien-shih lu*, it probably dealt with dispatches from various envoys. See HTS, 58: 1485; SS, 203: 5113 and 5115, 207: 5295. Also see Twitchett, "Lu Chih," 1962: 86 and 337 notes 13 and 14.

84. TFYK, 859: 19.

85. CTS, 125: 3552.

86. Ch'üan Te-yü's preface mentions that Lu wrote fifteen chapters of *Pieh-chi*.

Chapter Three

1. Twitchett, "Varied patterns of provincial autonomy," in *Essays on T'ang society*, 1976: 103–4; Wang Shou-nan, *T'ang-tai fan-chen yü chung-yang kuan-hsi chih yen-chiu*, 1978: 311–57.

2. Wang, *T'ang-tai fan-chen*, 1978: 65–66 and 207–9.

3. CTS, 13: 369 and 139: 3800; HTS, 157: 4923; SL, 4: 15; CTW, 493: 13a.

4. CTS, 139: 3800; CTW, 493: 13a; HTS, 157: 4923.

5. Li Chao, *T'ang kuo-shih pu*, Yang Chia-lo, ed., vol. 1: 50; Yen Keng-wang, *T'ang p'u shang ch'eng-lang piao*, 1956: vol. 1: 7–12, esp. 11.

6. A year later, in 791, Lu Chih composed the tomb inscription for his grandaunt, that is, for Lu Ch'i-wang's wife. If he had not received this new position, he probably would not have been asked to do so.

7. We often find Lu writing to Te-tsung that he was "greatly beholden to Your Majesty for taking me as an intimate friend." See HYCC,

12: 13a and 20: 12b for the similar passage. Considering Lu Chih's career development and his personal relationship with Te-tsung up to this point, his words would appear to convey more genuine appreciation than perfunctory rhetoric.

8. According to the biographies of the Wu brothers in CTS, Wu T'ung-wei became a Han-lin scholar in 783 while T'ung-hsüan took that office in 785, but the CTS Annals say that Wu T'ung-hsüan also started this service in 783. See CTS, 12: 338 and 190b: 5057–58; Ts'en Chung-mien, "Han-lin hsüeh-shih," in his *Hsin k'ao-ting*, 1984: 223–24.

9. CTS, 190b: 5057–58; HTS, 145: 4732.

10. CTS, 139: 3800.

11. The *Old T'ang History* says here that Lu Chih's "narrow and impetuous temperament" (*hsing pien-chi*) motivated his haughty treatment of the Wu brothers. CTS, 190b: 5057.

12. THY: 57: 979 dates the memorial at 788. The biography of Wu T'ung-hsüan in CTS, 190b: 5057 also contains a similar but undated passage. We know that Lu Chih's mother died toward the end of 787. Considering all the necessary procedures he had to go through before he resigned from office it is most likely that he did not leave the capital until the beginning of 788. Moreover, since the "three years mourning period" generally corresponds to twenty-five months, and since Lu Chih returned to the capital around the second month of 790, he must have left the capital around the first month of 788. It would thus have been possible for him to present this memorial right before he left for Mt. Sung.

13. CTS, 190b: 5057.

14. CTS, 139: 3818.

15. According to Wu T'ung-hsüan's biography in CTS, he was hoping to receive the position of drafter in the Secretariat. His biography in HTS says that he was appointed to this post in 794 which is definitely a mistake. As we shall see, he had already been banished to the south by 792. CTS, 190b: 5057–58; HTS, 145: 4732.

16. TCTC, 233: 7517–18.

17. CTS, 136: 3745–46; HTS, 145: 4730; Michael Dalby, "Court politics," CHC: 594.

18. CTS, 136: 3745–46; HTS, 145: 4730.

19. CTS, 136: 3747–48; HTS, 145: 4731.

20. CTS, 136: 3748 and 190b: 5058.

21. CTS, 190b: 5057 and 139: 3800; TCTC, 233: 7524.

22. TKCK, 13: 463–70; THY, 76: 1384; CTS, 139: 3800; Twitchett, "Lu Chih," 1962: 104. For Li Kuan's birth date, see Ts'en Chung-mien, *T'ang-jen hang-ti lu*, 1962: 430–34.

23. HTS, 203: 5787; Twitchett, "Lu Chih," 1962: 104.

24. Wang Ting-pao, *T'ang chih-yen*, 8: 82; also see CTS, 139: 3800; and 159: 4190; Pulleyblank, "Neo-Confucianism and Neo-Legalism," 1960: 94.

25. In 802, when Ch'üan Te-yü was in charge of the administration of the doctoral examinations, Lu Shen, the Vice Director of the Ministry of Sacrifices, was his assistant. Han Yü then wrote a letter to Lu Shen and made his comments on that unusual 792 examination. See Han Yü, "Yü Tz'u-pu Lu Yüan-wai shu," CTW, 553: 6a. Also see TKCK, 15: 556; Lo Lian-t'ien, *Han Yü yen-chiu*, 1977: 59.

26. HTS, 202: 5774; CTW, 523: 26b. For a biographical study of Liang Su, see Kanda Kiichiro, "Ryô Shuku nempu," in *Tôhô Gakkai sôritsu nijûgo shûnen kinen tôhôgaku ronshû*, 1972: 259–74.

27. On Tu-Ku Chi, see David McMullen, " Historical and literary history in the mid-eighth century," *Perspectives*, 1973: 308–12. On Liang Su's interest in Buddhism, see McMullen, *State and scholars*, 1988: 107. Liang Su's essay, see his "Chih-kuan t'ung-li," CTW, 517: 15b–20a.

28. See Ts'ui Yüan-han's biography, CTS, 137: 3766–67; HTS, 203: 5783–84.

29. See CTW, 521: 12b. This is a tomb inscription written for Hsiao Fu's late sister.

30. Liang Su's own account is in his "Chi Tu-ku Ch'ang-chou wen," CTW, 522: 11a; also see Kanda Kiichiro, "Ryô Shuku nempu," in *Tôhô Gakkai sôritsu nijûgo shûnen kinen tôhôgaku ronshû*, 1972: 259–74. However, Kanda Kiichiro was not aware of Liang Su's close connection with Hsiao Fu.

31. Liang Su's wife, like Lu Chih's mother, also came from the eminent Wei clan, but whether this had any influence on Lu Chih's trust in Liang Su remains unclear to us. For Liang Su's wife, see CTW, 523: 27a; Kanda Kiichiro, "nempu," 1972: 15.

32. For Liang's circle of friends see Kanda Kiichiro, "nempu," 1972: 15; also see Liang's extant work in CTW: ch. 517–22.

33. For the responsibility of the chief examiner in the *chin-shih* examination, see Fu Hsüan-tsung's study on *T'ang-tai k'o-chü yü wen-hsüeh*,1986: 226–28.

34. John Lee compares the background of these twenty-three graduates in his "The dragons and tigers of 792," *T'ang Studies*, 6 (1988): 33–36.

35. For the *hsing-chüan* practice and the problem of fairness it created for the administration of the examinations, see Fu Hsüan-tsung, *T'ang-tai k'o-chü*, 1986, esp. chs. 9 and 10; also see Victor Mair, "Scroll presentation in the T'ang dynasty," HJAS, 38 (1978): 35–60;

36. TCTC, 234: 7527–28; CTS, 190b: 5058 and 136: 3748.

37. On Tou Shen's taking money see CTS, 136: 3747; TCTC, 234: 7542; on Li Sun, CTS, 123: 3521–22, 13: 375 and 386. On Lu Chih's recommendation, see HYCC, 18: 21b.

38. CTS, 139: 3817, 138: 3788; SL, 4: 15. The title of this story by Liu Ch'eng is "Shang Ch'ing." It is collected in Li Fang, et al., *T'ai-p'ing kuang-chi*, 275: 2168–69. We do not know Liu Ch'eng's actual dates, but Pien Hsiao-hsüan tells us that he was a grandson of the famous genealogist Liu Fang and was probably active during emperor Wu-tsung's reign (840–846). See Pien Hsiao-hsüan, "T'ang-tai hsiao-shuo yü cheng-chih," *Chung-hua wen shih lun-ts'ung* (1985), vol. 1: 180–86.

39. HYCC, 19: 19b–20a.

40. CTS, 138: 3748.

41. HYCC, 19: 22a. On the confiscation law, see HTS, 46: 1200; *Ta T'ang liu-tien*, 6: 40.

It would certainly seem that if Lu Chih had intended to have Tou Shen killed, he would not have wasted so much time and energy in preventing the emperor from carrying out his will. Moreover, as Ssu-ma Kuang (1019–1086) pointed out, even if Chiang Kung-fu learned a secret from Lu Chih, Lu Chih still should not have taken the blame because it was Chiang Kung-fu's own initiative, not Lu Chih's, to resign from office and thus be forced to reveal Tou Shen's name to the emperor. (TCTC *K'ao-i* section, TCTC, 234: 7537.)

In this *K'ao-i* section Ssu-ma Kuang first quotes the *Te-tsung shih-lu* to show that it was Tou Shen, not Lu Chih, who told Chiang Kung-fu the "secret." Probably knowing that Wei Ch'u-hou, a possible relative of Lu Chih, was the compiler of the *Te-tsung shih-lu*, Ssu-ma then presented the fact that it was Lu Chih who tried to save Tou Shen and the argument given in our discussion. In his conclusion, Ssu-ma further pointed out that the contemporary criticism of Lu Chih was pure speculation. Because they knew Lu Chih and Tou Shen were already in disagreement, any disaster befalling Tou Shen then had to have been caused by Lu Chih. In addition, Ssu-ma believed, the official historian who disliked Lu Chih would thus attribute the fall of Tou Shen to him. Here "the official historian" must refer to Li Chi-fu since Ssu-ma Kuang knew Han Yü's version of *Shun-tsung shih-lu* was compiled under Li's supervision. From this point of view, the fact that the extant *Shun-tsung shih-lu* does not hide the contemporary criticism of Lu Chih seems to make it a more objective text for our evaluation of Lu Chih's life.

Since Lu's contemporaries did not necessarily have access to his memorials, it is not surprising that some of them blamed him for Tou Shen's death. On the other hand, given Lu's historically verifiable actions, it seems more reasonable to agree with Ssu-ma Kuang's judgment that the T'ang short story's accusation of murder against Lu Chih is completely unfounded. TCTC, 234: 7529–30. Pien Hsiao-hsüan also takes a similar point of view in "T'ang-tai hsiao-shuo," *Chung-hua wen-shih lun-ts'ung*, 1 (1985): 179–86.

42. CTS, 183: 4747; TCTC, 233: 7525.

43. Yü Kung-i acquired the *chin-shih* degree in 781, but he may have failed the earlier examination in 773 when Lu Chih acquired his degree. See TKCK, 11: 418; CTS, 137: 3767.

44. CTS, 137: 3767–68.

45. Ibid.; HTS, 203: 5784.

46. Chao ling-chih, ed., *Hou ch'ing lu*, 6: 55.

47. Yü Shao's biography see CTS, 137: 3766; HTS, 203: 5783. Except that Lu Chih and Yü Shao were not on good terms, we have no information to explain why Lu Chih banished Yü to the south.

48. Yü Ying-shih, "Han-Chin chih-chi shih chih hsin tzu-chüeh yü hsin ssu-ch'ao," in his *Chung-kuo chih-shih chieh-ts'eng shih-lun*, 1980: 324–27, esp. 327.

49. For details on the T'ang promotion of filial piety, see McMullen, *State and scholars*, 1988: 88 and 300 notes 90 and 91.

50. See Yang Wan's memorial to Tai-tsung in 763; there were other suggestions for the improvement of the doctoral examinations in the post-rebellion period. See McMullen, *State and scholars*, 1988: 88–97 and 303 note 124; on the criticisms of the examinations see TT, 17: 93–99.

51. The crimes known as *ten abominations* had been established before the Sui dynasty, the T'ang only inherited and revised them. See *Ta T'ang liu-tien*, 6: 22–23. Also see *The T'ang code*, translated with an introduction by Wallace Johnson, 1979: 17 and 74–77.

52. CTS, 123: 3519; HTS, 149: 4803.

53. I shall use Twitchett's translation "Department of Public Revenues" instead of Hucker's "the Bureau of General Account" to refer to *Tu-chih ssu*. For the development of dual financial authorities, see Twitchett, *Financial administration*, 1970: 111–13; Twitchett, "The Salt Commissioners after An Lu-shan's rebellion," AM, n. s. IV (1959): 65–67.

54. See TCTC, 226: 7273–74; Twitchett, *Financial administration*, 1970: 113; also see Twitchett, "The Salt Commissioners," 1959: 64–74; Twitchett, "Lu Chih," 1962: 113.

55. CTS, 136: 3747 and 123: 3519.

56. CTS, 123: 3519; HTS, 149: 4803. *P'an Tu-chih* or *Ling Tu-chih* refer to the practice of appointing officials holding other offices to be in charge of the business of the Public Revenue Department. This was the result of shifting power from the Ministry of Revenue to the Department of Public Revenue. For details, see Twitchett, "The Salt Commissioners," 1959: 65–66 and 72–73; Twitchett, *Financial administration*, 1970: 100–101 and 111–13; THY, 59: 1018.

57. CTS, 123: 3519–20 and 13: 373–74; TCTC, 234: 7530; Twitchett, "The Salt Commissioners," 1959: 73; Twitchett, "Lu Chih," 1962: 115–16.

58. HYCC, 18: 21b.

59. Tu Yu's biography, CTS, 147: 3978–83; HTS, 166: 5085–90; Lu Cheng, CTS, 146: 3966–67; HTS, 149: 4799; Li Sun, CTS, 123: 3521–23; HTS, 149: 4805–6; there is no official biography for Li Heng, but information about his career can be found in CTS, 13: 371 and 373 and in Ts'en Chung-mien's *Lang-kuan shih-chu hsin k'ao-ting*, 1982: 94; also see T. H. Barrett, *Li Ao: Buddhist, Taoist or Neo-Confucian?* 1992: 35, note 9. On Li Heng's service under Liu Yen, see CTS, 123: 3515.

60. On Tu Yu's treatment see CTS, 147: 3978 and 12: 333. For Lu Ch'i, see CTS, 135: 3713–18; HTS, 223: 6351–54.

61. CTS, 146: 3967.

62. HYCC, 18: 22a.

63. HYCC, 18: 22a.

64. See CTS, 135: 3720; HTS, 167: 5106.

65. CTS, 135: 3720; HTS, 167: 5106.

66. Li Sun, with Tu Yu's support, became one of the most powerful financial experts during Hsien-tsung's reign (805–820); his subordinates even continued to dominate the financial administration until 830. CTS, 123: 3522; Twitchett, "Lu Chih," 1962: 120.

67. CTS, 135: 3720; TCTC, 234: 7533.

68. Yano Chikara, "Haishi kenkyu," *Shakai Kagaku Ronsô*, 14 (1965): 43; CTS, 135: 3719. Twitchett, "Lu Chih," 1962: 90.

69. According to CTS, it was through the recommendation of the Personnel Evaluation Commissioner in Hua-chou that P'ei Yen-ling, then serving in that area, gained a post as erudite at the Court of Imperial Sacrifices (*T'ai-ch'ang po-shih*). He was later appointed to be a *Chi-hsien* scholar. All the sources that I have consulted agree that it was Lu Ch'i who placed P'ei Yen-ling in the Chi-hsien yüan while concurrently promoting

him to be director of the Catering Bureau (*Shan-pu lang-chung*) after he became chief minister in the second month of 781. When Te-tsung sent eleven personnel evaluation commissioners to the provinces in the second month of 780, the commissioner who was sent to the Hua-chou area was Liu Wan. It seems that it was Liu Wan who recommended P'ei Yen-ling for a post in the Court of Imperial Sacrifices before Lu Ch'i assumed the post of chief minister. On P'ei Yen-ling's career and Lu Ch'i's recommendation, see CTS, 135: 3720; HTS, 167: 5106; TCTC, 226: 7297; Twitchett, "Lu Chih," 1962: 90, 339 note 46 and 47. On regions where Liu Wan was dispatched at the beginning of 780, see TFYK, 162: 1957. For the nature and history of the Chi-hsien yüan, see Fu Shi-chen, *T'ang-tai Chi-hsien yüan chih yen-chiu*, 1977; Ikeda On, "Sei Tô no Shukenin," *Hokkaidô daigaku Bungakubu kiyô*, 19, no. 2 (1971): 45–98; Twitchett, "Hsüan-tsung," in CHC: 378; McMullen, *State and scholars*, 1988: 15–16;

70. CTS, 135: 3720; HTS, 167: 5106. On the functions of these financial offices, see Chü Ch'ing-yüan, *T'ang-tai ts'ai-cheng shih*, 1940: 137–38; Twitchett, *Financial administration*, 1970: 102–3.

71. CTS, 135: 3720; HTS, 167: 5106.

72. Twitchett, "Lu Chih," 1962: 120.

73. HYCC, 18: 23a. Also see TCTC, 234: 7533. HYCC, 18: 23a and 23b.

74. CTS, 135: 3720; HTS, 167: 5106; TCTC, 234: 7548; Twitchett, "Lu Chih," 1962: 120.

75. CTS, 135: 3721; TCTC, 234: 7548.

76. CTS, 135: 3722; HTS, 167: 5107.

77. See CTS, 148: 4002; HTS, 165: 5076.

78. CTS, 148: 4002; HTS, 165: 5076; TCTC, 234: 7549; CTW, 486: 5a–7a; *Ch'üan Tsai-chih wen-chi*, SPTK edition, 47: 280–81.

79. Ch'üan's friendship with Lu Chih's uncle probably led to his acquaintance with Lu Chih.

80. Twitchett, "Lu Chih," 1962: 120. For the Tibetan invasion of Kansu, see Twitchett, "Hsüan-tsung," in CHC: 430–33.

81. HYCC, 20: 21a–4b; Twitchett, "Lu Chih," 1962: 120.

82. CTS, 135: 3721; HTS, 167: 5106; TCTC, 234: 7548–49.

83. HYCC, 24: 1a–24a.

84. HYCC, 24: 9a.

85. HYCC, 24: 22a.

86. SL, 4: 15. The TCTC authors (235: 7565) obviously believe that Lu Chih did recommend Chao Ching to be chief minister. Neither biography of Chao Ching in CTS and HTS mentions such a recommendation. Chao Ching had a reputation for learning. His eloquence pleased Te-tsung and he was promoted to be supervising secretary (*Chi-shih chung*) in 787. He had also served in various provincial offices. It is recorded that he had "deep knowledge of the way of government" (*shen yü li-tao*). CTS, 138: 3775–76 and 12: 358; HTS, 150: 4811;

87. CTS, 138: 3779; TCTC, 234: 7543. Originally the official title of chief minister for both Lu Chih and Chao Ching was "Vice Minister of the Secretariat, Jointly Manager of Affairs with the Secretariat-Chancellery" (*Chung-shu shih-lang, T'ung Chung-shu Men-hsia p'ing chang shih*). Chao Ching later was given the title of "Vice Minister of the Chancellery" (*Men-hsia shih-lang*) which implied that his position as chief minister was second to that of Lu Chih. However, the power of the *Men-hsia shih-lang* sometimes superseded that of the *Chung-shu shih-lang*, but this was not the general case. On the development of the different titles and their power status for the T'ang chief minister, see Sun Kuo-tung, "T'ang-tai san-sheng chih chih fa-chan yen-chiu," in his *T'ang Sung shih lun-ts'ung*, 1980: 83–185, esp. 117–23, 129, and 147. Also see 157 for examples of the higher status accorded to *Men-hsia shih-lang*.

88. HYCC, 20: 1b. Also see TCTC, 234: 7540.

89. HYCC, 20: 2b–3a; TCTC, 234: 7541. Despite the evidence to the contrary, the *Old T'ang History* says that Lu Chih transferred Chao Ching to the position of second chief minister because Lu "relied upon his long service in the palace, . . . received special benevolence and favor, [and thus] regarded the administration of the state as his own responsibility." CTS, 138: 3779.

90. SL, 4: 15; TCTC, 235: 7565.

91. CTS, 138: 3778; HTS, 150: 4811. CTS (138: 3789) comments that since Chao Ching deliberately failed Lu Chih, his noble efforts to save some officials are suspect.

92. CTS, 138: 3779; HTS, 150: 4811; TCTC, 235: 7565.

93. CTS, 139: 3817 and 13: 380; TCTC, 235: 7565; SL, 4: 15; CTS, 139: 3817 and 13: 380. Since most of Lu Chih's uncles were also serving in the court then, "relatives" here must have referred to them.

94. CTS, 149: 4022; HTS, 203: 5784.

95. SL, 4: 15; CTS, 139: 3817; 135: 3727; TCTC, 235: 7566.

96. CTS, 192: 5133; HTS, 194: 5570; TCTC, 235: 7567.

97. SL, 4: 16; CTW, 493: 14a; CTS, 139: 3818; HTS, 157: 4932.

98. Twitchett, "Lu Chih," 1962: 121, believes Wei Kao's contribution to the improvement of the border situation with the Tibetans must have influenced the imperial decision on Lu Chih's sentence. For Wei Kao's appeal, see CTS, 139:.3818; CTW, 493: 14a; TCTC, 236: 7611. For Wei Kao's contribution, see CTS, 140: 3822–24; TCTC, 233: 7515–17, 7519–20, 7525; 234: 7534, 7537, 7540, 7547–48. Since Lu Chih knew that Te-tsung's reason for finally executing Tou Shen in his banishment was that Tou had some connection with a provincial governor, it is doubtful that Lu himself would have asked Wei Kao to make a case for him.

99. Both TCTC and CTS mention that Lu Chih met Li Chi-fu in Chung-chou. Lu Chih originally was afraid that Li would take some revenge on him because he had banished him to the south due to his close connection with Tou Shen in 792. However, Li is said not to have resented Lu Chih at all; he still treated him as if he were chief minister. Thus they became close friends and visited each other every day. See TCTC, 236: 7611; CTS, 139: 3818 and 148: 3992–93. The fact that neither Ch'üan Te-yü's preface nor the extant SL mentions this episode makes us tend to agree with Pulleyblank's suggestion that this episode "may have been reported to the History Office by Li Chi-fu during the time that he had the supervision of [the Han Yü version of the SL], that is, during Han Yü's tenure of office." This is to say that the validity of the "friendship" between Li Chi-fu and Lu Chih cultivated in Chung-chou is questionable. See Pulleyblank, "The Shun-tsung shih-lu," BSOAS, 19 (1957): 342. Since neither the extant SL nor Ch'üan Te-yü's preface record such an episode, the authors of these two works either did not know about it or did not accept its authenticity. From this point of view, we also have to question whether or not Ch'üan Te-yü used Han Yü's version of the SL to write his preface, as Pulleyblank suggested (see Appendix 1 for the authorship of the SL). If he did, he should have mentioned this episode in his preface. Perhaps, on this particular episode, Ch'üan Te-yü did not follow Han Yü's version of the shih-lu since he and Li Chi-fu were colleagues during Hsien-tsung's reign and he probably knew Li Chi-fu was not very generous toward his opponents. Or perhaps knowing that Lu Chih was basically an unsociable person he did not believe Lu Chih would have made "close friends" with Li Chi-fu. For Li Chi-fu's attitude toward his opponents, see TCTC, 237: 7649, 7654 and 7687. Without any further evidence, we can only leave this matter as it is.

100. CTS, 139: 3818.

101. SL, 4: 16; Ch'üan Te-yü, preface, CTW, 493: 14a; CTS, 139: 3818; HTS, 59: 1572; Twitchett, "Lu Chih," 1962: 121. For Te-tsung's interest in medicine see HTS, 59: 1572.

102. Lu Yu-jen, ed., *Wu-chung chiu-shih*, 11b–12a. This Yüan dynasty (1264–1368) source provides our only information concerning Lu Chih's

burial and possible re-interment. It says that there was a place named "Lu cemetery" (*Lu-mu*) which up to the Yüan was believed to be the location where Lu Chih had been buried. This cemetery was five or six miles north of the Wu *chün* city wall. Between 1174 and 1189, some residents of Wu *chün* are said to have discovered some information that confirmed that Lu Chih's tomb was in Lu cemetery. However, because the same source also presents material that claims that Lu Chih was buried in Chung-chou near a certain Yü-hsü temple (*Kuan*), it concludes that Lu Chih was probably buried in Chung-chou first and re-interred in Wu *chün* later.

103. CTS, 139: 3818; SL, 4: 16; Twitchett, "Lu Chih," 1962: 121.

104. CTW, 493: 13b; CTS, 139: 3817; HTS, 157: 4932.

Chapter Four

1. Chao-i was an area occupying a part of present-day southern Hopei and northern Honan provinces. On Li Pao-chen. See CTS, 139: 3800; HTS, 157: 4932; TCTC, 229: 7392.

2. HYCC, 17: 13a. Also see TCTC, 232: 7464.

3. CTW, 493: 12b; also see HTS, 157: 4932.

4. Peterson, "Court and province in mid- and late T'ang," CHC: 484.

5. My summary here is based on Twitchett's detailed analytical study of these regional forces: "Varied patterns of provincial autonomy in the T'ang dynasty," in *Essays on T'ang society*, 1976: 90–109. Also see Wang, *T'ang-tai fan-chen*, 1978; Peterson, "Court and province," CHC, 1979: 485–560; Pulleyblank, "The An Lu-shan rebellion," *Essays on T'ang society*, 33–60.

6. Michael Dalby, "Court politics in late T'ang times," CHC: 500–501; TCTC, 226: 7277–81.

7. TCTC, 227: 7302.

8. Twitchett, *Financial administration*, 1970: 91–93; also see his "Varied patterns," *Essays on T'ang society*, 1976: 100–103; Ch'üan Han-sheng, *T'ang Sung ti-kuo yü yün-ho*, CYYY chuan-k'an, 1946: 42–76. On the development of the second Ho-pei rebellion, see Dalby, "Court politics," 501–55; Twitchett, "Lu Chih," 1962: 91–94. Also see TCTC, 226: 7291–96, 227: 7316–21, 7335–37 and 228: 7341.

9. TCTC, 227: 7336–37 and 228: 7344–45; Twitchett, "Lu Chih," 1962: 94–95.

10. TCTC, 228: 7351–54; Twitchett, "Lu Chih," 1962: 95–96; Jen Yü-ts'ai, *T'ang Te-tsung*, 29–31. When Te-tsung refused to accept Liu Wen-hsi

as the governor of Ching-yüan in the second month of 780, Chu Tz'u was appointed governor of that region to suppress Liu Wen-hsi. Liu was killed by his subordinate generals in the fifth month of that year; Chu Tz'u later was given the title of chief minister as a concurrent position in addition to his actual position as military governor in various provinces, but his governorship in Ching-yüan was given to a royal prince. See TCTC, 226: 7278 and 7281 and 7288–89. When his younger brother Chu T'ao rebelled in 782, he invited Chu Tz'u to join him, but his secret letter to Chu Tz'u was discovered by the court before it reached him. Te-tsung did not charge Tz'u with any crime. However, the emperor did make him stay in the capital and thus took away his military power. See TCTC, 227: 7328; CTS, 200b: 5386. By the time he was established as the leader at the capital by his former troops, he was obviously ready to join the rebellion. This has led one modern historian to suspect that Chu Tz'u's rebellion was a premeditated one. See Jen Yü-ts'ai, *T'ang Te-tsung Feng-t'ien ting-nan chi ch'i shih-liao chih yen-chiu*, 1970: 10–12. Also see Chao Yüan-i, *Feng-t'ien lu*, 2.

11. For example, Lu Ch'i engineered the death of Yang Yen. CTS, 135: 3713–18; HTS, 223: 6351–54; TCTC, 226: 7297 and 227: 7301, 7304, 7308–9, 7334–35 and 228: 7339.

12. Twitchett, "Lu Chih," 1962: 101. For Li Huai-kuang's resentment, see TCTC, 230: 7402–3;.CTS, 133: 3664–65. For the different imperial treatment of the Shen-ts'e armies compared with other local forces during Te-tsung's reign, see HTS, 50: 1334. The Shen-ts'e Army was originally established to defend the northwest frontier in 754. It was sent east when the An Lu-shan rebellion broke out and later stationed in Shan-chou (in modern Honan) as an inner defense line of the capital. In 763 when Te-tsung's father, Tai-tsung, fled from the Tibetans to Shan-chou the Shen-ts'e Army there protected him well. After his return to the capital, Tai-tsung incorporated the Shen-ts'e Army into the palace guards, and thus established its importance in the T'ang military system as the Palace Army. Its importance to the throne became even more obvious when Te-tsung also had to rely upon its protection when he escaped to Feng-t'ien. The preferential treatment accorded the Shen-ts'e army was in part a reflection of Te-tsung's gratitude to this army. For the history of the Shen-ts'e Army, see HTS, 50: 1332–36; THY, 72: 1294; Dalby, "Court politics," CHC: 573–74 and 586–87; Obata Tatsuo, "Shinsakugun no seiritsu," *Tôyôshi kenkyû*, 18:2 (1959): 35–56.

13. TCTC, 229: 7377–78; CTS, 121: 3493–94.

14. TCTC, 229: 7385 and 230: 7402–10.

15. TCTC, 228: 7359–60; CTS, 125: 3548–49.

16. TCTC, 230: 7419–20.

17. Ibid.; HYCC, 16: 1b; 17: 6b.

18. For the quote, see *Lun yü*, ch., 15 (*Wei Ling-kung*): 26, in D. C. Lau, trans., *Confucius, the analects*, 1979: 135. Compare James Legge's translation, "Want of forbearance in small matters confounds great plans," in his *The four books*, Taipei reprint, n. d., 352.

19. Duke Huan's appointment of Kuan Chung as chief minister is recorded in "Chuang kung," the ninth year, in the *Tso chuan*, see Yang Po-chün, ed., *Chun-ch'iu Tso chuan chu*, vol. 1, 1981:180.

20. HYCC, 17: 7a.

21. See the *Lun yü*, ch., 9 (*Tzu-han*): 29. For the English translation, see D. C. Lau, *Confucius, the analects*, 1979, 9/30: 100. Emphasis added. Lu Chih did not quote other classical philosophers' ideas about *ch'üan* to support his own definition, but we can find similar explanations of *ch'üan* in *Mencius*, in *Hsün tzu,* and in *Mo tzu*. One common feature shared by Lu Chih and these philosophers' interpretation of *ch'üan* is their agreement concerning the importance of discarding small gains for the sake of reaching an ethically higher good. Hsün Tzu even stated that "the Way is the correct weighing standard, or the right balance, from ancient times to the present [*Tao che, ku-chin chih cheng-ch'üan ye*]." For Mencius's notion of *ch'üan*, see D. C. Lau, trans., *Mencius*, 1970: 1A/ 7, 4A/ 17, and 6A/ 14 and 15. My translation of Hsün tzu combines those of Dubs and Knoblock. See Homer H. Dubs, trans., *The works of Hsuntze*, ch. 22: 514–515, and John Knoblock, *Xunzi: A translation and study of the complete works*, vol. 3, 1994: 137 (section 22.6b). For Mo tzu's, see A. C. Graham, *Later Mohist logic, ethics and science*, 1978: 46 and 252–53.

22. Lu did not explicate the meaning of *chi*, but in an earlier memorial (HYCC 12: 15a) he briefly mentioned that "*chi* is the slight beginning of things [*chi che, shih chih wei ye*]." In *The Book of Changes* (or *I ching*), we find *chi* defined as "the infinitesimally small beginning of action, the point at which the precognition of good fortune can occur. The superior man [*chün-tzu*] acts upon something as soon as he becomes aware of its incipience and does not wait for the day to run its course." This passage is from the second "Hsi-tz'u" section of the *I ching*. *The classic of changes: a new translation of the I Ching as interpreted by Wang bi*, translated by Richard John Lynn, 1994: 84, with *superior man* rather than Lynn's *noble man*. Scholars have translated *chi* in many ways. Lynn consistently uses *incipience;* James Legge renders it *springs of things;* Richard Wilhelm translates it as *seeds;* Joseph Needham as *germ*. For other translations, see Raymond Van Over, ed., *I ching*, based upon Legge's translation, 1971, section on "The Great Treatise," ch. 5: 407; Richard Wilhelm trans., *The i ching*, rendered into English by Cary F. Baynes, 1950: 342; and Joseph Needham, *Science and civilization in China*, vol. 2, *History of scientific thought*, 1962: 43 and 80.

23. HYCC, 17: 8a.

24. TCTC, 231: 7443.

25. McMullen, *State and scholars*, 1988: 239.

26. On the establishment and development of the institution of emperor in Chinese imperial history, see Hsing I-t'ien's study, "Chung-kuo huang-ti chih-tu te chien-li yü fa-chan," originally published in 1982, but now included in his *Ch'in Han shih lun-kao*, 1987: 43–84, esp. note 65. On the nature of rulership, see Huang Chün-chieh, "Some observations and reflections," in Huang Chün-chieh and Frederick P. Brandauer, eds., *Imperial rulership and cultural change in traditional China*, 1994: 120 and 281–89.

27. For a discussion of the origin of the Mandate of Heaven, see H. G. Creel, *The origins of statecraft in China*, 1970: 501–6.

28. Hsing I-t'ien, "Huang-ti chih-tu," *Ch'in Han shih lun-kao*, 1987: 59.

29. HYCC, 12: 1b. On Te-tsung and Lu Ch'i, see TCTC, 228: 7357 and 229: 7385; CTS, 12: 338.

30. A soothsayer named Sang Tao-mao told Te-tsung in 780 that he would have to escape from the palace to Feng-t'ien within a few years. Te-tsung followed his advice and constructed a high city wall around Feng-t'ien at that time. See TCTC, 226: 7355; Sang Tao-mao's biography, CTS, 191: 5113; HTS, 204: 5812.

31. HYCC, 12: 4a-b.

32. These two passages do not appear in the present edition of the *Shu ching* (*Book of documents* or *Book of History*). They appear in the chapters called "The Great declaration (*T'ai-shih*), section 2" and "The Common possession of pure virtue (*Hsien yu i-te*)" in the forged ancient text of the *Book of documents*. The first passage also appears in book 5A/ 5 of *Mencius*. Since the authenticity of this forged part of the *Book of documents* was not seriously dealt with until the Ch'ing dynasty (1644–1911), Lu Chih and other T'ang literati naturally believed it to be authentic. On the problem of the forged *book of documents*, see Ch'ü Wan-li, *Shang-shu chi-shih*, 1983: 21–31. For the English translation, see James Legge, trans., *The shu king*, in F. Max Müller, ed., *The sacred books of the east* (2nd edition), vol. 3, 1899: 128 and 101. I have modified Legge's version slightly.

33. Also see Hsieh Wu-hsiung, *Lu Hsüan-kung*, 1975: 38–39.

34. Lynn, tr., *Changes*, 1994: 67, retaining Wade-Giles romanization. From the first "Hsi-tz'u" section of the *I ching*.

35. HYCC, 12: 7a.

36. Ibid.: 8b.

37. HYCC, 18: 17a.

38. Chen, *Liu Tsung-Yüan*, 1992: 108.

39. HYCC, 12: 8b and 18: 17a. A modern historian also notices Lu's emphasis on the primacy of virtuous rule in this regard, see H. G. Lamont, "An early ninth century debate on Heaven: Liu Tsung-yüan's T'ien shuo and Liu Yü-hsi's T'ien lun," AM, n. s., 18 (1973): 195 note 53.

40. HYCC, 12: 8a.

41. For the English translation, see Legge, *The li ki*, in Müller ed., *The sacred books of the east*, vol. 27, reprinted, 1966: 389. The original Chinese is from *"Li yün"* section of the *Li chi*.

42. HYCC, 12: 10b–11a.

43. Also see TCTC, 229: 7381; HTS, 157: 4916.

44. HYCC, 13: 10a.

45. Ibid.: 10b

46. Ibid. For an alternative translation, see Legge, *The four books*, Taipei reprint, 96.

47. I have modified Legge's translation of this passage from the *Chung yung*. See Legge, *The four books*, 92.

48. See Lau, *Confucius, the analects*, 1979, 12/11: 114; and his translations of *Mencius*, 1970, 4b/3: 128.

49. Lu's statement does logically imply tacit approval of the Mencian idea of removing a tyrannical ruler. See Lau, trans., *Mencius*, 1970, 1b/8: 68.

50. HYCC, 12: 15b.

51. Ibid.: 16b–18a.

52. HYCC, 15: 13a-b; also see TCTC, 230: 7425.

53. To explain how the people, not the ruler, were the main body of the state, Lu Chih also cited a frequently used ancient boat and water metaphor (HYCC, 12: 14b). The origin of this metaphor is not clear, but it seems to appear first in *Hsün tzu*, ch. 9, "Wang chih" (On the regulations of a king), see Knoblock, *Xunzi*, vol. 2, 1990: 97, 293.

54. HYCC, 11: 13a. Lu Chih's main argument is that the state should protect its *roots*—the people. See HYCC, 11: 19b–20a.

55. Perhaps the earlier suggestion was presented to the throne at the beginning of 780, see TCTC, 226: 7275. The translation of the title is Twitchett's, see his "Lu Chih," 1962: 98.

56. CTS, 139: 3792; HTS, 157: 4919; TCTC, 229: 7389.

57. HYCC, 13: 1b.

58. Ibid.: 2b–5a translation in D. C. Lau, trans., *Lao Tzu tao te ching* 1963, 39: 100.

59. Partly because Li, the supposed surname of Lao Tzu, was the same as that of the T'ang ruling house, T'ang rulers, more out of political than religious needs, claimed that they were his descendants. For the imperial promotion of, and its relationship with the Taoist religion, see THY, 50: 865–69. Also see Wang Shou-nan, *Sui T'ang shih*, 1986: 708–10; Kubo Noritaka, *Dokyoshi*, 1977: 219–36; Chen, *Liu Tsung-Yüan*, 1992: 16.

60. HYCC, 14: 1a–6b.

61. CTS, 139: 3793; HTS, 157: 4920.

62. At the very beginning of his reign, Te-tsung's policies showed that he intended to put into effect clean and honest government. see CTS, 12: 320–22.

63. CTS, 139: 3793–94; HTS, 157: 4919–20; TCTC, 229: 7389, 7397.

64. HYCC, 1: 1b, 5a, and 13a-b.

65. Hsü Fu-kuan, "Chung-kuo te chih-tao—tu Lu Hsüan-kung chuang chi shu hou," first published in *Min-chu p'ing-lun* (1953): 4: 9, later collected in his *Hsüeh-shu yü cheng-chih chih-chien*, 1980: 120.

66. HYCC, 11: 20a. In this memorial Lu Chih quoted the passage "the people are the root of a country [*min wei pang pen*]" from the *Book of documents*. This passage, however, only appears in the chapter entitled "The Songs of the five sons [*wu-tzu chih ke*]" in the forged ancient text of the *Book of documents*. For the English translation, see Legge, *The shu king*, in *The sacred books of China*, vol. 3, 1899: 79.

67. See Lu Chih's earliest memorials presented in the eighth month of 783 (HYCC, 11: 1a–26b), to be dealt with in the following section.

68. HYCC, 13: 6a–7a.

69. HYCC, 11: 1a–26b.

70. Ibid.: 21b–23a; Twitchett, "Lu Chih," 1962: 100.

71. External invasion refers to the possibility of a Tibetan attack. Twitchett mentions that Lu Chih was involved in the treaty negotiations during the early month of 783 due to the fact that some state correspondence with the Tibetans was drafted by him at that time. However, the minister who negotiated with the Tibetans was Chao Yü, and Chao Yü was designated to this mission in 786, the year the state correspondence was

actually drafted. See, Twitchett, "Lu Chih," 1962: 95. On state correspondence, see HYCC, 10: 9b–17b. On Chao Yü, or Chao Chien as given in HTS, see CTS, 196b: 5249; HTS, 216: 6094.

72. HYCC, 11: 1b.

73. Ibid.: 15b–16a.

74. HYCC, 1: 1a–13b, Twitchett, "Lu Chih," 1962: 99.

75. TCTC, 228: 7360.

76. Except Chu T'ao in Yu-chou, Wang Wu-chün from Ch'eng-te, T'ien Yüeh from Wei-po, and Li Na from P'ing-lu, all expressed their repentance to the throne. See TCTC, 229: 7392–93.

77. Issued in the seventh month of 784, after Chu Tz'u was defeated and the capital was recovered; in the first month of 785 when amnesty was offered to Li Huai-kuang and Li Hsi-lieh; and in the eleventh month of the same year, after the court suppressed Li Huai-kuang and again offered amnesty to the remaining rebel forces under Li Hsi-lieh. See HYCC, 1: 14b–28b; 2: 1a–25a.

78. See the two imperial edicts to recruit the rebel forces under the command of Li Huai-kuang and Li Hsi-lieh in HYCC, 5: 13b–16b. The weakened will to fight of Li Huai-kuang and Li Hsi-lieh's troops is reflected in the death of these two rebel governors: Knowing that his followers were reluctant to fight the loyalist troops any longer, Li Huai-kuang committed suicide while Li Hsi-lieh was murdered by a subordinate general. In Li Huai-kuang's biography, it is said that he was murdered by a subordinate general, but the *K'ao-i* section in TCTC disregards this record, see CTS, 121: 3494; TCTC, 232: 7460–61, esp. the *K'ao-i* section, and 7468.

79. HYCC, 17: 3b–6a.

80. TCTC, 231: 7434–37; CTS, 200b: 5389–90; CTS, 133: 3668–70; Twitchett, "Lu Chih," 1962: 98.

81. Lu Chih's explanation of Chao Kui-hsien's case contradicts the information recorded in the two T'ang dynastic histories and in the TCTC. According to these records, Chao Kuei-hsien originally served under Li Huai-kuang. When Huai-kuang revolted in the beginning of 784, he had already sent Chao to T'ung-chou (in the east of modern Shensi) to establish a foothold for him. However, P'ei Hsiang (751–830), the local official in charge, successfully persuaded Kui-hsien not to betray the court. See CTS, 113: 3356; HTS, 140: 4647; TCTC, 230: 7417. Since P'ei Hsiang was only in charge of T'ung-chou affairs near the end of 783, if Kui-hsien was indeed sent there by Li Huai-kuang, this must have taken place around that time. For the date of P'ei Hsiang's service in T'ung-chou, see Yü Hsien-hao, *T'ang tz'u-shih k'ao*, vol. 1, 1987: 115. This is clearly in conflict

with what Lu Chih explained in his memorial. However, Lu Chih's accounts do not contradict the fact that Te-tsung did summon troops to relieve Hsiang-ch'eng from Li Hsi-lieh's attack in the ninth month of 783. See TCTC, 228: 7351. Moreover, Lu Chih's statement indicated that Te-tsung and his court officials were all aware of Chao Kui-hsien's surrender to Chu Tz'u. Thus, it seems strange that Lu Chih's account would be false. Since we do not have sufficient information to conduct further investigation about Chao Kui-hsien's case, and even if Chao did serve under Li Huai-kuang, it would not change the nature of Lu Chih's advice to the emperor, I shall leave this issue unsettled.

82. At this point Lu also drew a parallel between the trial of those ministers who had fallen under An Lu-shan's rule during Su-tsung's reign and Te-tsung's intended sentence for Chao Kuei-hsien. He reminded Te-tsung that when Su-tsung went back on his original promise of amnesty, those T'ang subjects still in the rebel camp ceased to regret their submission to An Lu-shan, and this imperial bad faith served to prolong the war. Su-tsung, Lu said, had managed only to "trust the legal officials but miss the expediency principle." See HYCC, 17: 4a–5b. Lu Chih's accounts of Su-tsung's sentence of those ministers is similar to the historical records, see TCTC, 220: 7043–50.

83. HYCC, 1: 15b.

84. HYCC, 17: 10a–21b.

85. Ibid.: 18a-b, 19a and 20b. Also see TCTC, 232: 7463–65.

86. On Li's murder, see TCTC, 232: 7468–69.

87. HYCC, 3: 11a–18a. Also see, TCTC, 232: 7465–66.

88. TCTC, 230: 7402–03; Twitchett, "Lu Chih," 1962: 101.

89. HYCC, 14: 10b–12b. Also see TCTC, 230: 7403–4.

90. HYCC, 14: 13a–15a; TCTC, 230: 7404–6 and 7409.

91. Li Sheng's armies played a major role in suppressing the rebel forces. For Li Sheng's military deeds and his contribution to the court, see CTS, 3661–87; also see HYCC, 8: 11b–14a. This is the imperial edict drafted by Lu Chih that showed Te-tsung's acknowledgment of Li Sheng's meritorious deeds; Tung K'e-ch'ang, "Lun Li Sheng," *Liao-tung ta-hsüeh hsüeh-pao*, 3 (1980): 49–52.

92. TCTC, 230: 7412.

93. HYCC, 16: 13b.

94. Ibid.: 13b–16a. Part of this memorial also appears in TCTC, 231: 7430–31.

95. Unlike his intimate friend Hsiao Fu's attack on this practice, Lu's criticism was directed more at the actual disadvantages it created than at the resulting abuse of power. Even though their points of emphasis are different, these two friends advocated essentially the same principle, but Hsiao Fu's recent banishment to the south left Lu to present a solitary protest at court. For Hsiao Fu's attack, see CTS, 125: 3551; TCTC, 229: 7397.

96. As far as I know, no particular historical records indicate otherwise. The fact that later on Lu Chih would again oppose this practice shows that Te-tsung probably did not adopt his present advice at all. We shall discuss his later suggestion in due course.

97. HYCC, 16: 6b. Also see CTS, 139: 3797.

98. HYCC, 15: 9b–10b.

99. CTS, 122: 3502.

100. HYCC, 14: 15b–16a and 16b–20a.

101. Lu Chih must be referring here to the practice during Su-tsung's reign; for details see TCTC, 219: 7023–24.

102. HYCC, 14: 18a–20a. Also see TCTC, 230: 7418.

103. These palace maids had become lost in the chaos of exile and rebellion. See HYCC, 16: 16b. Also see CTS, 139: 3788–89; TCTC, 231: 7437.

104. CTS, 139: 3799; TCTC, 231: 7438.

105. See Kung-ch'üan Hsiao, translated by F. W. Mote, *A history of Chinese political thought*, 1979: 148–66, esp. 155–56.

106. Studies of Lu Chih in Chinese or studies in English that discuss him neglect Lu Chih's concept of expediency (*ch'üan*). For example, Hsieh Wu-hsiung devotes half of his book to a discussion of Lu Chih's memorials. He deals with Lu Chih's emphasis on the importance of "sincerity" and "people's welfare" in governance; he also mentions that Lu talked about grasping an opportunity in military maneuvers, but he never notices or discusses Lu Chih's emphasis on expediency . See Hsieh Wu-hsiung, *Lu Hsüan-kung*, 1975: 36–63. Liu Chao-jen's study of Lu Chih briefly mentions that Lu Chih was "good at applying the method of expediency [*shan-yung ch'üan-pien chih-shu*]" to military operations, but does not give any analysis of Lu Chih's conception of expediency nor the role of expediency in Lu Chih's approach to government. See Liu Chao-jen, "Lu Hsüan-kung yen-chiu," *Shih-chien hsüeh-pao*, 10 (1979): 11. Pulleyblank's article on Neo-Confucianism in mid-T'ang intellectual life treats Lu Chih primarily as a conservative statesman with a realistic view of practical matters, but does not take Lu's prag-

matism into further consideration. See Pulleyblank, "Neo-Confucianism and neo-Legalism," 1960: 94. On the other hand, as mentioned above, McMullen (*State and scholars* 1988: 239) maintains that Lu Chih condemned expediency. Although Twitchett's study emphasizes Lu's practical concerns, it does not discuss Lu's concept of expediency; it tends to treat Lu Chih as a pure pragmatist whose theoretical belief in orthodox Confucianism was only secondary. See Twitchett, "Lu Chih," 1962: 118.

107. Lu's definition of expediency subsequently won him the accolade of being the one who corrected the mistake made by the Han Confucians's explanation of expediency as "that which is at variance with the standard and complies with the Tao is the expedient." See the comments in TCTC, 231: 7439. Also see Tillman, *Confucian discourse*, 1992: 168 for the Han Confucians's definition of expediency.

108. As far as I know, Feng Yung-chih who served as a middle-level official around 752 actually wrote the first systematic essay on expediency in the post–An Lu-shan rebellion era. We do not have much information about Feng's life, nor do we know whether or not his essay had any impact on Lu Chih, or on mid-T'ang intellectual circles. Suffice it to say that a major difference between Lu Chih's explanation of expediency and that of Feng Yung-chih seems to be that Feng was more a pure pragmatist who was primarily concerned with achieving beneficial ends. For Feng's life, see CTW, 404: 1a; also see *T'ang shang-shu-sheng lang-kuan shih-chu t'i-ming k'ao*, 16: 9. For his essay, see "Ch'üan lun," in CTW, 404: 4b–8a.

109. I have followed W. G. Runciman's translation of Weber's terms. For Max Weber's concept of political ethics, see his "Politics as vocation," in W. G. Runciman, ed., *Weber selections in translation*, 1978: 212–25.

110. Ibid.: 217.

Chapter Five

1. The SPTK and SPPY editions have a one word textual difference. Unless such differences change the basic meaning of passages quoted, I shall make no further mention of them and simply follow the 1768 edition.

2. TCTC, 232: 7469; 235: 7572; CTS, 48: 2087–88.

3. Michael Dalby, "Court politics," CHC: 607–11; Twitchett, "Lu Chih," 1962: 108, esp. notes 168 and 169.

4. Twitchett, "Lu Chih," 1962: 106.

5. For Ts'ui Tsao's and Li Mi's reforms, see Dalby, "Court politics," CHC: 589–94; TCTC, 232: 7467–68, 7475, 7489–95; CTS, 130: 3620–23, 3625–27.

6. HYCC, 18: 1a–13b. For Lu Chih, "secondary heads" included vice directors of the Three Departments (i.e., the vice director of the Department of State Affairs, *Shang-shu p'u-yeh*; vice director of the Secretariat, *Chung-shu shih-lang*; and vice director of the Chancellery, *Men-hsia shih-lang*); assistant directors of the Left and the Right in the Department of State Affairs (*Shang-shu tso yu ch'eng*); attendant censors (*Shih yü-shih*); grand masters (*Ta-fu*) who occupied mid-level head posts in all bureaus (*ssu*) or in the Nine Courts (*chiu-ssu*) and the palace aid to the censor-in-chief (*Chung-ch'eng*).

7. TCTC, 234: 7531. Also see CTS, 13: 374.

8. HYCC, 18: 1b; also see TCTC, 234: 7531.

9. For Confucius's saying, see Lau, *Confucius, the analects*, Book II/10, 1979: 64. The system of recommendation Lu Chih advocated was supposed to involve the official placement process only; it does not mean that Lu was opposed to the examination system as a whole. Lu seems to have endorsed such a policy in an imperial edict drafted as early as 785 when still a Han-lin scholar. That Lu is again pushing for a similar recommendation system in 792 indicates that the 785 policy was probably never carried out. This further implies that this 792 policy recommendation may actually represent a continuing effort to pursue an earlier position (HYCC, 2: 4b–5a).

10. HYCC, 18: 3b–4a; on this issue, also see TT, 15: 84; Twitchett, "Chinese meritocracy," 1974: 17.

11. HYCC, 18: 5a-b, 6a, and 10a-b.

12. HYCC, 18: 9b, 10b.

13. Wang Shou-nan, "Lu Chih te shih-kung chi ch'i cheng-chih ssu-hsiang," *Yu-shih yüeh-k'an*, vol. 47: 5 (1978): 59; also see Sa Meng-wu, *Chung-kuo cheng-chih ssu-hsiang shih*, 1969: 308–9.

14. Mote, trans., Hsiao, *Chinese political thought*, 1979: 190–94, and chs. 6 and 7, esp. 423–24. Hsün Tzu's attitude toward "rewards and punishments" can be found in the chapter entitled "Fu-kuo (On enriching the state)." For English translation, see Knoblock, *Xunzi* vol. 2 book 10, 1990: 128–29. H. G. Creel also discusses this attitude of Hsün Tzu in *Shen Pu-hai, A Chinese political philosopher of the fourth century B. C.*, 1974: 135–36.

15. HYCC, 18: 11b–12a. As we recall, the Lu clan's rise in the T'ang bureaucracy corresponded exactly with the period of Empress Wu's ascendance. This perhaps answers in part the question why Lu Chih may have been the first T'ang chief minister to praise Empress Wu's rule. Guisso, *Wu Tse-t'ien*, 1978: 201.

16. TCTC, 234: 7532. As Twitchett points out, (see his "Lu Chih," 1962: 105) in the eleventh month of 793, an Act of Grace drafted by Lu Chih did urge the provincial governors to recommend talented and virtuous scholars to the throne, but this was not intended to institute Lu Chih's recommendation measure as a regular practice. This only referred to a special decree examination which was supposed to take place in the seventh month of 794, and in fact did take place in the tenth month of that year, see HYCC, 3: 6b; TKCK, vol., 2, 13: 488.

17. It was P'ei Yen-ling who suggested not filling vacant offices. See chapter 3, in the section "On the decline."

18. The first passage Lu quotes is from the "Wen wang" chapter of the "Ta-ya" section of the *Shih ching (The book of odes)*; the second is from the "Kao-yao mo" chapter of the *Shang shu*. For the English translations, see Bernhard Karlgren, trans., *The book of odes*, 1950: 186; Legge, *The shu king*, vol. 3, 1899: 55, with two changes.

19. HYCC, 22: 9a–15b.

20. Ibid.: 10b.

21. HYCC, 18: 8b. Lu quotes Book 13/21 of the *Analects*, for the English translation, see Legge, *The four books*, Taipei reprint, 309.

22. HYCC 22: 16b–18a.

23. Twitchett, "Lu Chih," 1962: 118.

24. Italics added. The powerful chief minister in Tai-tsung's reign refers to Yüan Tsai (d. 777); for his abuse of the power of official appointment, see TCTC, 225: 7257–58; also for his rise and fall, see Dalby, "Court politics," in CHC: 577–79.

25. TCTC, 234: 7555.

26. CTS, 139: 3803–4; HTS, 157: 4924; also see Twitchett, "Lu Chih," 1962: 105.

27. HYCC, 19: 1a–17a.

28. Twitchett, "Lu Chih," 1962: 107.

29. HYCC, 19: 6a.

30. Traveling scholars refer to those scholars, with or without doctoral degrees, who obtained their first service in provincial governments not through regular channels of official appointment by the court, but through personal recruitment by local governors (*pi-chao*). They provided administrative expertise and clerical advice to local government. In middle and late T'ang, a great number of scholar officials entered the bureaucracy in this manner. Han Yü's initial career is a case in point. For more

information on the rise of this practice, see CHC: 20–21 and 648; for Han Yü's first service, see Hartman, *Han Yü*, 1986: 28 and 35–36.

31. Lu mentioned that due to past practices and official abuses, the capital population and the people of more than forty prefectures in the Honan and Huai-nan regions suffered a terrible flood in the summer of 792. See HYCC, 19: 14b; TCTC, 234: 7533.

32. For details on the background and operation of the T'ang grain transportation system, see HYCC, 19: 10a–14b; CTS, 12: 348; TCTC, 231: 7453; Twitchett, *Financial administration*, 1970:87–89; 327 note 78; Twitchett, "Hsüan-tsung," in CHC: 395–96; Pulleyblank, *Background*, 1982 reprint, 34–35.

33. HYCC, 19: 14b–15b; Twitchett, *Financial administration*, 1970: 94 and 327 note 79.

34. HYCC, 19: 15b–16a, 17b.

35. Ibid.: 9b. One *shih* corresponds roughly to 132 pounds.

36. TCTC, 234: 7536.

37. CTS, 49: 2125; also see ibid., especially the *K'ao-i* section.

38. The "Shih-huo chih" section of the HTS is the only source I know of which says Te-tsung did not completely follow Lu's policy. See, HTS, 43: 1374. Lu himself made it clear that Te-tsung had listened to his suggestion regarding the grain reserves in the frontier provinces. It was with a sense of pride that he said his policy had enabled those provinces to store more than one million *shih* of grain. HYCC, 21: 3a.

39. HYCC, 21: 1a–2b.

40. I have reversed the order of Lu's conditional clauses.

41. HYCC, 21: 12b.

42. HYCC, 19: 4b–5a.

43. In 779, when Te-tsung began his reign, he was afraid that Kuo Tzu-i (695–781), one of the most notable generals of the mid-T'ang, would become hard to control due to his accumulated military power. The emperor thus elevated the general to the rank of imperial teacher while actually taking away all of Kuo's military power. In order to prevent any one military governor from having too much concentrated power again, three new military governors were also appointed to be stationed in Kuo's original province, in the Shuo-fang region (in the southwest and northern area near Ling-wu county of modern Ning-hsia). TCTC, 234: 7545; 225: 7259; for Kuo Tzu-i's life and contribution to the T'ang, see CTS, 120: 3449–66.

44. HYCC, 21: 22a.

45. On inland forces from the Ho-nan and Chiang-huai regions, see CTS, 139: 3804.

46. HYCC, 21: 14a–15a.

47. Ibid.: 21a-b.

48. Ibid.: 24b–25b. Lu Chih was not the first chief minister who intended to carry out this sort of *t'un-t'ien* policy in the border provinces. Li Mi made a similar suggestion in 787. As early as 781 such a policy was widely discussed among some officials. Later, after the Ho-pei rebellion had been gradually settled, the court even encouraged the policy in some inland provinces. These previous suggestions for colonizing the frontier provinces were mainly oriented toward reducing the cost of maintaining the border armies. Twitchett, "Lu Chih," 1962: 106, 107; THY, 89: 1619; TFYK, 503: 22–23; HYCC, 2: 21a; Dalby, "Court politics," in CHC: 593; TCTC, 232: 7493–94.

49. TCTC, 234: 7547.

50. CTS, 145: 3933–34; TCTC, 234: 7549–50; HYCC, 20: 13a and 14a–20a. The Hsüan-wu troops, not the court, established Liu Shih-ning as governor. See TCTC, 234: 7528 and 235: 7582; CTS, 145: 3937–38.

Chapter Six

1. This edict to relieve the poor in the capital region by distributing seeds was issued in 786; the same concern can be detected in a 785 edict. See HYCC, 4: 10b; HTS, 54: 1379; Twitchett, *Financial administration*, 1970: 49–58, and "Lu Chih," 1962: 114.

2. HYCC, 23: 1a–49b; one of the six parts of this memorial is translated in de Bary et al., *Sources*, 1960: 416–23.

3. Twitchett's translation of the title of "Chün-chieh fu-shui hsü pai-hsing," in "Lu Chih," 1962: 116.

4. For details on the relationship between the *tsu-yung-tiao* system and the *chün-t'ien* system and how the *tsu-yung-tiao* system worked, see Twitchett, *Financial administration*, 1970: 1–39; Han Kuo-p'an, *Pei-ch'ao Sui T'ang te chün-t'ien chih-tu*, 1984: 142–64; Ho Ch'ang-ch'ün, *Han T'ang chien feng-chien te kuo-yu t'u-ti-chih yü chün-t'ien chih*, 1958, chs. 9 and 10; Hori Toshikazu, *Kindensei no kenkyû— Chûgoku kodai kokka no tochi seisaku to tochi shoyû-sei*, 1975, chs. 1–4.

5. For more information on the problem of land accumulation, see Han Kuo-p'an, *Chün-t'ien chih-tu*, 1984: 229–31. I am fully aware that the terms vagrant and vagrancy reflect the point of view of the T'ang state. However, I have used these terms because it is the common practice in T'ang studies to translate the Chinese terms *fu-hu* and *liu-jen* as vagrant. See, for example, Twitchett's usage of these terms. Twitchett points out that there were complex reasons for this migration, such as a search for fertile land in the south, official oppression, and escape from military service. The T'ang government's failure to provide an adequate law to punish offenders against the *chün-t'ien* system also contributed to its break-down. See Twitchett, *Financial administration*, 1970: 9–11 and 12–14, 371, 374; see also Hori Toshikazu, *Kindensei no kenkyû*, 1975: 315–16. Han Kuo-p'an and Wang Chung-lo, however, believe that the problem of land shortage created by land accumulation was a very basic cause for migration. See Han Kuo-p'an, *Chün-t'ien chih-tu*, 1984: 232; Wang Chung-lo, "T'ang-tai liang-shui-fa yen-chiu," *Li-shih yen-chiu*, 6 (1963): 117–18.

6. See chapter 3, "Tenure as Chief Minister," and chapter 4, "The Second Ho-pei Rebellion."

7. The main practices and policies of the two-tax system were developed long before 780, and it is generally agreed that this system was not a revolutionary invention. It is commonly regarded as a system that was designed to rationalize and unify the multifarious existing taxes into a simpler tax structure. Twitchett, *Financial administration*, 1970: 39. My summary of this system is mainly based upon Twitchett and the following studies: Ch'ü Ch'ing-yüan, *T'ang-tai ts'ai-cheng shih*, 1940: 28–55. Also see Wang Chung-lo, "T'ang-tai liang-shui fa yen-chiu," *Li-shih yen-chiu*, 6 (1963): 117–34; Hino Kaisaburô, "Ryôzeihô no kihonteki yon gensoku," *Hôseshi kenkyû*, 11 (1960): 40–77; idem, "Yô En no ryôzeihô no genkyo gensoku to sensû; sennô gensoku," *Shien*, 84 (1961): 1–37; idem, "Yo En no ryozeiho ni okeru zeigaku no mondai, *Tôyô gakuhô*, 38, 4 (1956): 370–410; idem, "Ryozeiho to bukka," *Tôyô shigaku*, 12 (1950): 1–54; 13 (1955): 1–60. These four articles are now in Hino Kaisaburô's collected works, *Tôyô shigaku ronshu*, vol. 4, 1982, part 1, ch. 1: 17–56, ch. 2: 57–94, ch. 4: 119–58 and part 2, ch. 4: 335–483. Also see his "Ryôzeihô," 1982: 21–54 and "Yô En no ryôzeihô no genkyo gensoku to sensû; sennô gensoku," *Tôyô shigaku ronshu*, vol. 1, 1982: 57–94.

8. C. A. Peterson, "Court and province," CHC: 498–99.

9. See chapter 2, "First Appointment in the Central Government."

10. This translation is a modified version of Twitchett's, see his "Lu Chih," 1962: 114.

11. HYCC, 2: 20a.

12. Twitchett, "Lu Chih," 1962: 113; CTS,48: 2093; THY, 83: 1537.

13. Ch'üan Han-sheng, "T'ang-tai wu-chia te pien-tung," originally published in CYYY, vol. 11; it is now in his *Chung-kuo ching-chi shih yen-chiu*, vol. 1; 1976: 159–78 and 188–92; also see P'eng Hsin-wei, *Chung-kuo ho-pi shih*, 1958: 216–17; Twitchett, *Financial administration*, 1970: 77–80. Twitchett puts more weight on other factors, but both Ch'üan Han-sheng and P'eng Hsin-wei assert that the launching of the two-tax system was the major reason for the deflation. Although both Ch'üan and P'eng fail to mention that under the two-tax system, grain, instead of cash, was the unit of assessment and payment for the land levy, their explanation of why the two-tax system was the main cause of this long period of deflation is quite convincing. For one thing, in order to pay cash for the household levy, it seems that most of the rural population had to use their grain or other agricultural products for the exchange of cash money. This itself seems to have been sufficient to cause the prices of their grain and other products to fall. Moreover, while the government required cash payment for the household levy, it nonetheless stored the cash in state treasuries without circulating it back to the market. This apparently worsened the problem of cash demand in the market. It also led opportunistic merchants and powerful families to store cash money as well. Consequently, the inflation was replaced by a prolonged period of deflation. Ch'üan Han-sheng, "T'ang-tai wu-chia," 1976: 188–92; P'eng Hsin-wei, *Ho-pi shih*, 1958: 216–17.

14. Twitchett, "Lu Chih," 1962: 113; idem., *Financial administration*, 1970: 46–47.

15. Twitchett, "Lu Chih," 1962: 112; TFYK, 488: 5833; HTS, 52: 1351–52.

16. HYCC, 23: 4a.

17. Twitchett, *Financial administration*, 1970: 24–28.

18. In the "Liang Hui Wang" chapter of *Mencius*, we see that Mencius insisted "that the people [should] always have sufficient food in good years and escape starvation in bad." See, Lau, trans., *Mencius*, 1/A, 1970: 58–59.

19. The translation of these three passages is a modified version of de Bary et al., *Sources*, 1960: 418, 419.

20. HYCC, 23: 7b–8a; Twitchett, "Lu Chih," 1962: 118.

21. Translation modified from de Bary, et al., *Sources*: 420.

22. HYCC, 23: 9a.

23. For a summary of these abuses, see de Bary, et al., *Sources*, 1960: 421–22.

24. Twitchett, *Financial administration*, 1970: 44; also see his "Lu Chih," 1962: 118.

25. The translation is modified from Lau, *Confucius, the analects,* 1979, 12: 114.

26. HYCC, 23: 13a.

27. HYCC, 23: 20a–34b. One major reason for using cash as the unit of tax assessment for the household levy was the growth of trade after the beginning of the eighth century. Ch'üan Han-sheng, "Chung-ku tzu-jan ching-chi," in his *Chung-kuo ching-chi shih,* 1976: 101–6; for the growth of trade during this time, also see idem., "T'ang Sung shih-tai Yang-chou ching-chi ching-k'uang ti fan-jung yü shuai-lo," CYYY, 11 (1947): 149–76; Twitchett, "Merchant, trade and government in late T'ang," AM, 2nd series, 14 (1968): 63–95, esp., 77–79. From this perspective, Lu's suggestion to replace cash with goods as the basic unit for assessing taxes seems to be regressing toward a more primitive economic situation. Nevertheless, because there was not enough cash circulating in the mid-T'ang market, cash-assessed taxation did not necessarily reflect substantial progress in the economy. See Twitchett, *Financial administration,* 1970: 42, especially see his modification of the view that the two-tax system represented the beginning of money taxation in China.

28. Li Hsüeh-hua, "Kuan-yü Lu Chih lun liang-shui-fa te chi-ko wen-t'i," *Chung-kuo she-hui ching-chi shih yen-chiu,* 3 (1982): 78; Chou Yen-pin, "Ch'ien-p'ing Lu Chih te ching-chi ssu-hsiang," *Ching-chi k'o-hsüeh,* 3 (1982): 57; Hu Chi-ch'uang, *Chung-kuo ching-chi ssu-hsiang shih,* vol., 2, 1963: 433.

29. HYCC, 23: 23a.

30. Ibid.: 26a–27b.

31. Ibid.: 29a-b.

32. HTS, 145: 4724; THY, 83: 1536.

33. Two smaller final suggestions accompanied Lu's proposition to abolish cash-assessed taxation. See HYCC, 23: 35a–41a.

34. HYCC, 23: 41a–46a.

35. Ibid.: 45a.

36. CTS, 13: 376 and 49: 2128; TCTC, 234: 7539–40; THY, 84: 1546; also see Twitchett, *Financial administration,* 1970: 63.

37. CTS, 49: 2128; TCTC, 234: 7539–40.

38. HYCC, 18: 16b.

39. HYCC, 23: 45a.

40. Ibid.: 46a–49b.

41. Ibid.: 46b–47a. On the discussion of the accumulation of land by officials and great aristocratic families at the end of the Later Han dynasty (25–220), see Etienne Balazs, *Chinese civilization and bureaucracy*, 1964: 220–21; for information about this problem in T'ang China, see Twitchett, *Financial administration*, 1970: 1–23.

42. Although Lu Chih seems to imply that the *chün-t'ien* system only worked in ancient times, he still believed its collapse caused the problem of land accumulation to go out of control. He probably never considered the possibility that the reverse might have been the case. Even so, what he intended here was not to restore the *chün-t'ien* system, but to restrict land accumulation and reduce its deleterious effect on the poor. HYCC, 23: 47b–48b.

43. One *shih* = 1.75 bushels = 300 *sheng*, see Twitchett, *Financial administration*, 1970: xiii.

44. HYCC, 23: 48b.

45. The goals of "an-fu hsü-p'in" appear in the "Ti-kuan, or Earthly officers" chapter of the *Chou li*. See, *Chou li*, with the commentary by Lin Yin, 1974: 99.

46. Some officials before the T'ang tried to solve the problem of excess land accumulation, but their solutions were primarily aimed at having the government limit the actual land holdings of rich land owners. Hu Chi-ch'uang, *Chung-kuo ching-chi ssu-hsiang shih*, vol., 2, 1963: 426–27; Chou Yen-pin, "Ch'ien-p'ing Lu Chih te ching-chi ssu-hsiang," *Ching-chi k'o-hsüeh*, 3 (1982): 55–56; Li Chin-pao, "Lu Chih ching-chi ssu-hsiang yen-chiu," *Che-chiang hsüeh-k'an*, 3 (1983): 68–69. Tung Chung-shu (179–104 B.C.E.) in the Former Han dynasty and Hsün Yüeh (148–209) in the Later Han are the two famous examples.

47. Twitchett, *Financial administration*, 1970: 22.

48. See Chapter 5, "Reforming the bureaucracy" and HYCC, 18: 8a and 13a.

49. HYCC, 20: 1b–2a, 2b.

50. These two ideas appear in the "Wang-chih " (Royal regulations) chapter of *The records of rites*. The English translation is a modified version of Legge, *The li ki*, vol. 27, 1966: 215.

51. HYCC, 20: 4b.

52. As discussed in chapter 5, see HYCC, 18: 5b.

53. I have adopted Wing-tsit Chan's translation "altruism" for *shu*. See, Wing-tsit Chan, *Source book*, 1963: 785.

54. HYCC, 18: 15a-b; Lu cited a passage in the "K'ung-tzu hsien chü, or Confucius at home at leisure" chapter of *The records of rites.*

55. HYCC, 18: 17b.

56. Emphasis added. On the contemporary situation in Huai-hsi, see TCTC, 232: 7470, 235: 7583–84 and 7591–92, 238: 7668, 239: 7705ff. and 240: 7737–45. Also see Wang, *T'ang-tai fan-chen,* 1978: 68.

57. HYCC, 18: 18a.

58. Some officials were encouraging Te-tsung to take advantage of this flooding of 792 and send a punitive force to bring Huai-hsi under complete control, but Lu disagreed because such action would violate the principle of benevolent government (ibid.: 19a).

One might argue that Lu's opposition to sending a punitive expedition to Huai-hsi in 792 may be responsible for the damaging Huai-hsi revolt twenty-two year later (814–817), but this seems quite problematical. Lu Chih's advice to relieve Huai-hsi does not directly concern military matters. In 792, Lu advised the emperor to provide flood relief to Huai-hsi on both humanitarian and utilitarian grounds—to alleviate suffering and to avoid giving reasons for revolt. The emperor agreed, primarily because he feared another revolt and apparently had no reason to believe his forces could win a war with Huai-hsi. The emperor's decision was based on a military assessment, Lu Chih's advice was not. The Huai-hsi region was peaceful throughout the rest of Emperor Te-tsung's reign. When Huai-hsi rebelled in 814, during Emperor Hsien-tsung's reign, the historical situation was very different. The empire was stronger and had a better chance of winning, which they did after a three-year campaign. In 792, however, the empire had not completely recovered from the second Ho-pei rebellion and more than forty prefectures were suffering from a disastrous flood. In my opinion, even if Lu Chih had advised Emperor Te-tsung to use force against Huai-hsi, it is doubtful that the emperor could have carried out a successful campaign at that time; in any case, having already decided on an appeasement policy toward recalcitrant provinces (completely independent of Lu Chih's advice), he very likely had no stomach for war with Huai-hsi.

As we have seen in chapter 5, Lu Chih did not always caution against policies that might lead to war. In 793, he advised the emperor to take action to restore central control over Pien-chou. The emperor rejected his advice; six years later, a revolt broke out in that area.

59. HYCC, 18: 19b–21a.

60. The Chinese term *shih-po chung-shih,* or *shih-po shih,* is usually translated as commissioner for overseas trade, or commissioner for foreign shipping. See Twitchett, "The T'ang market system," AM, n. s., 12–2 (1966): 222 and his "Lu Chih," 1962: 119. The term adopted here is used by Wang Zhenping in his study of this particular post. For details on this commis-

sioner, see his "T'ang maritime trade administration," AM, 3rd series, 4, part 1 (1991): 7–38. Canton in Ling-nan and Annam in An-nan were the two most prosperous T'ang sea ports and were often rivals when trade in one port became threatening to the other. In the post–An Lu-shan era, eunuchs were occasionally appointed as commissioner for trading with foreign ships to conduct or supervise official purchasing in those ports, but the regular procedure was to have the Ling-nan governor (usually also serving as prefect of Kwang-chou) assume the responsibility of this position. In other words, they had both to administer the routine maritime trade and acquire foreign goods for the court. Because of this concurrent responsibility, the post of Ling-nan governor was a very lucrative one, and many of them are said to have accumulated a great deal of wealth through inappropriate means. For further information, see K'ung Pao-k'ang, "Wo-kuo ku-tai shih-po-chih-tu ch'u-t'an," and Lu Jen, "Lun shih-po-ssu hsing-chih he li-shih tso-yung te pien-hua," both of these articles are in Hai-chiao shih yen-chiu, vol. 13 (1988): 1–13, esp. 2 and 5; Lü Ssu-mien, Sui T'ang Wu-tai shih, 1984, 909; Fang Hao, Chung hsi chiao-t'ung shih, 1953: 28–29; Wang Gung-wu, "The Nanhai trade," Journal of the Malayan Branch of the Royal Asiatic Society, 31, part 2 (1958): 72–84; Shen Fu-wei, "Lun T'ang-tai tui-wai mao-i te ssu-ta hai-kang," in Hai-chiao-shih yen-chiu, vol. 10, 2 (1986): 20–25; CTS, 8: 174; THY, 62: 1078; TFYK, 546: 6548.

61. Yü Hsien-hao, T'ang tz'u-shih k'ao, vol. 5, 1987: 2761. Also see CTS, 12: 356.

62. CTS, 112: 3337–38; HTS, 78: 3533. Li Fu's service in Ling-nan lasted till at least the eighth month of 792. In the ninth month of that year, new governor was appointed. See Yü, T'ang tz'u-shih k'ao, vol. 5, 1987: 2761–62; also CTS, 13: 375.

63. HYCC, 18: 20b.

64. Ibid.

65. Ibid.: 20b–21a.

66. I have slightly modified Twitchett's translation, see Twitchett, "Lu Chih," 1962: 119.

67. HYCC, 20: 6a-b and the discussion in chapter 2, "Limited Circle of Friends."

68. Ibid.: 7a.

69. See Confucius's famous analogy of "wind and grass." See the "Yen Yüan" chapter of Lun yü.

70. Two months after this confrontation with the throne about provincial tributes, Lu again remonstrated unsuccessfully with Te-tsung, urging him not to confiscate Tou Shen's property and slaves as personal imperial

possessions. About this same time, Lu also skillfully extricated himself from a difficult situation involving a request to write a tomb inscription for a former rebel governor. See HYCC, 19: 23b–24b.

71. See Kung-ch'üan Hsiao's discussion on Mencius's idea of nourishing the people, in Mote, trans., Hsiao, *A history of Chinese political thought*, 1979: 152–53.

72. Throughout his memorials, as far as I can trace, Lu Chih cited *The book of documents* twenty-nine times, *The analects* twenty-eight times, *The book of rites* twenty-three times, *The book of odes* seventeen times, *The book of changes* ten times, *The Spring and autumn annals* eleven times, *The Mencius* seven times, and *The Chou li* (*The rites of Chou*) once.

73. I shall discuss in chapter 8 those who made similar suggestions about using goods as the basic unit of taxation. It is sufficient to point out here that it was due to Yang Yü-ling's (753–830) efforts that this suggestion was finally put into practice. For Yang Yü-ling's proposal and its result, see HTS, 52: 1360–61. Also see, Hu Chi-ch'uang, *Chung-kuo ching-chi ssu-hsiang shih*, vol., 2, 1963: 441, 460, and 477.

74. Weber, "Politics," in Runciman, ed., *Weber: Selections*, 1978: 224.

75. See the well-known description of Confucius by the gatekeeper at the Stone Gate. The passage is in the "Hsien wen" chapter of *Lun yü*. For the English translation, see Lau, *Confucius, the analects*, XIV/38, 1979: 130.

Chapter Seven

1. TCTC, 236: 7606–10; SL, 1: 2–4; also see Bernard S. Solomon, tr., *The veritable record of the T'ang emperor Shun-tsung*, 1955: 3–4. For modern historians' evaluations of the Wang Shu-wen group, and for details about the reformist nature and policies of this group and the reasons for its rise and fall, see Chen, *Liu Tsung-yüan*, 1992, ch. 3: 66–80; Pulleyblank, "Neo-Confucianism and neo-legalism," 1960: 107–10; Dalby, "Court politics," CHC: 601–7; also see Wang Yün-sheng, "Lun erh Wang pa ssu-ma cheng-chih ko-hsin ti li-shih i-i," *Li-shih yen-chiu*, 3 (1963): 105–30; Sun Ch'ang-wu, *Liu Tsung-yüan chuan lun*, 1982: 118–25; Wu Wen-chih, *Liu Tsung-yüan p'ing-chuan*, 1962: 35–44; Chen K'e-ming, *Han Yü shu-p'ing*, 1985: 58–60.

2. Solomon, tr., *Veritable record*, 1955: 18; SL, 2: 6; TCTC, 236: 7611.

3. Peterson, "Court and province," CHC: 523–39; also see his "The restoration completed; Emperor Hsien-tsung and the provinces," in *Perspectives*, 1973: 159–68; Wang, *T'ang-tai fan-chen*, 1978: 66–70.

4. See Peterson, CHC: 485; also see a widely cited letter composed by Liu Yen (715–780) to Yüan Tsai, the former being a famous financial expert and the latter the most powerful chief minister during Tai-tsung's reign. See CTS, 123: 3512–13.

5. See Wu Chang-ch'üan, *T'ang-tai nung-min wen-t'i yen-chiu*, 1963: 94–132 and 162–82.

6. Several impressive studies in English which deal with mid-eighth-century T'ang intellectuals and the mid-T'ang Confucian revival movement are David McMullen, "Yüan Chieh (719–772) and the early *ku-wen* movement," Ph.D. dissertation, 1968; idem., *State and scholars*, 1988; Barrett, *Li Ao*, 1992; Hartman, *Han Yü*, 1986; Chen, *Liu Tsung-yüan*, 1992. Peter Bol's "*This culture of ours*," 1992, a study of T'ang Sung intellectual change, partly deals with this issue from the point of view of the self-interest of the *shih* class. Most scholars, however, agree that the revivalists' public concerns are crucial to our understanding of the mid-T'ang Confucian revival.

7. It is said that Li Mi liked to talk about Taoist lore and had a strong interest in self-cultivation and the search for immortality. For Li Mi's life and his Taoist inclinations, see CTS, 130: 3620–23; HTS, 139: 4631–38; also see Li Fan, "Yeh-hou wai-chuan," in *Wu Ch'ao hsiao-shuo ta-kuan*, 40: 319–26; Dalby, "Court politics," CHC: 592–93.

8. CTS, 130: 3622; HTS, 139; 4635.

9. CTS, 130; 3622; HTS, 139: 4635.

10. HTS, 157: 4911–12.

11. See chapter 5, "Establishing a Capable and Just Bureaucracy."

12. HTS, 139: 4637. For a similar passage, see TCTC: 233: 7512.

13. HTS, 139: 4637; TCTC, 233.; 7501.

14. TCTC, 233: 7510.

15. For Tu Yu's life, see CTS, 147: 3978–84; HTS, 166: 5085–90; also see Cheng Ho-sheng, *T'ang Tu Chün-ch'ing hsien-sheng Yu nien-p'u*, 1980; Pulleyblank, "Neo-Confucianism and neo-Legalism," 1960: 100–01.

16. On a discussion of the nature of Tu's *T'ung-tien*, see Ch'ü Lin-tung, "Lun '*T'ung-tien*' te fang-fa he chih-ch'ü," *Li-shih yen-chiu*, 5 (1984): 112–28; Pulleyblank, "Neo-Confucianism and neo-legalism," 1960: 98–101; McMullen, *State and scholars*, 1988: 203.

17. Pulleyblank, "Neo-Confucianism and neo-legalism," 1960: 105–6.

18. TT, 40: 231a; or see the CTW version entitled "Sheng kuan i," CTW, 477: 8b–9a. Unless otherwise noted, all quotations from Tu Yu are from TT, and references are to chapter: page number.

19. My translation is a modified version of Pulleyblank, "Neo-Confucianism and neo-legalism," 1960: 101.

20. TT, 40: 231a.

21. Translation is from McMullen "Views of the state in Du You and Liu Zongyuan," in S. R. Schram, ed., *Foundations and limits of state power in China*, 1987: 68.

22. Tu Yu entered the officialdom through the protective *yin* privilege. See CTS, 147: 3978; HTS, 166: 5085.

23. TT, 17: 97–99, 18: 104a; Pulleyblank, "Neo-Confucianism and neo-legalism," 1960: 104.

24. For example, Chao K'uang, one of the leading figures of the critical study of Confucian classics, proposed to use classical studies instead of poetry and prose writings as the subject of the examinations. TT, 17: 97–99; 18: 101–4; also see HTS, 45: 1178–79; Pulleyblank, "Neo-Confucianism and neo-legalism," 1960: 104; McMullen, *State and scholars*, 1988: 241–43.

25. Chao K'uang is a case in point. See TT, 17: 97–99.; Pulleyblank, "Neo-Confucianism and neo-legalism," 1960: 104.

26. CTW, 477: 1b.

27. On Hsün Tzu's view of rites, see Mote, trans., Hsiao, *A history of Chinese political thought*, 1979: 182–83.

28. McMullen, *State and scholars*, 1988: 261; also see his "Views of the state," 1987: 72–74.

29. Translation from McMullen, "Views of the state," 1987: 69.

30. TT, 148: 773b and 12: 71b; also see McMullen, "Views of the state," 1987: 69.

31. Translation modified from McMullen, "Views of the state," 1987: 73. McMullen locates the first quotation from the *Li-chi chu-shu*, 60: 6a–7b; the second is from the *Analects*, 12: 9.

32. TT, 4: 25a. It has been pointed out that Tu Yu suspected that Kuan Tzu, the person, or rather Kuan Chung, was not the author of the *Kuan tzu*. For the sake of convenience, whenever the name of Kuan Tzu is used here, it refers to the person so named in the book *Kuan tzu*, not the real historical person Kuan Chung. For a discussion of whether or not Kuan Chung was the author of the *Kuan tzu*, and why Kuan Chung has been regarded as the pioneer of the legalist school, see Allyn Rickett, tr., *Guanzi, political, economic, and philosophical essays from early China*, 1985: 8–24. For Kuan Tzu's economic policy, see Mote, tr., Hsiao, *A history of Chinese political thought*, 1979: 355–61.

33. Translation from McMullen, "Views of state," 1987: 68. I have replaced his version of Kuan Tzu's famous lines with Allyn Rickett's translation (Rickett, tr., *Guanzi*, 1985: 51). Kuan Tzu's lines are from the "Mu-min or On shepherding the people" chapter of the *Kuan tzu* . See *Kuan tzu chiao-cheng*, 1: 1. Confucius's saying is from the "Tzu Lu" chapter of the *Analects*, the line quoted here was a paraphrase by Tu Yu.

34. HYCC, 18: 8a.

35. Also see McMullen, "Views of the state," 1987: 73. For Kuan Tzu's concept of elevating the ruler, see Mote, tr., Hsiao, *A history of Chinese political thought*, 1979: 325–26.

36. See McMullen's interpretation of Tu Yu's inconsistent view on the ruler's position, "Views of the state," 1987: 73.

37. Translation from McMullen, "Views of the state," 1987: 74.

38. Both Ch'ü Ch'ing-yüan and Wang Shou-nan agree that Tu Yu's support of the two-tax system was based upon his concern with the financial stability of the state. See Ch'ü Ch'ing-yüan, *Ts'ai-cheng shih*, 1943: 37; Wang Shou-nan, *Sui T'ang shih*, 1986: 591.

39. CTS, 147: 3978; HTS, 166: 5086.

40. J. J. L. Duyvendak, tr., *The book of Lord Shang*, 1928: 41–55. Li Yu-ning, *Shang Yang's reforms and state control in China*, 1977: chs. 3 and 4.

41. For Shang Yang's land reform and the nature of the well-field system, see Duyvendak, *The book of Lord Shang*, 1928: 175–84; also see Li Yu-ning, *Shang Yang's reforms*, 1977: ch. 4, esp. 51–58.

42. Also see the first part of the "T'eng Wen-kung" chapter in the *Mencius*. For the translation, see Lau, *Mencius*, 3/A, 1970: 99.

43. TT, 1: 9b.

44. TT, 1: 10c–13a.

45. Besides Kuan Chung and Shang Yang, Tu Yu also included as worthy ones four other ministers from previous dynasties, all famous for their administrative abilities. On Kuan Chung's and Shang Yang's contributions to the Ch'i and Ch'in states, see Charles Hucker, *China's imperial past: An introduction to Chinese history and culture*, 1975: 35–42, and Li Yu-ning, *Shang Yang's reforms*, 1977.

46. For Hsün Tzu's well-known position, see Mote, tr., Hsiao, *A history of Chinese political thought*, 1979: 193 and 322–23.

47. Hartman, *Han Yü*, 1986: 130; for Han Yü's comments on Shang Yang, see his "Chin-shih ts'e-wen shih-san shou," HCLCC, 14: 6a.

48. McMullen, "Views of the state," 1987: 79–80. For Tu Yu's own comments on the prefectural system in relation to the feudal system, see TT, 31: 177a-b.

49. TT, 31: 177b. Also see McMullen, "Views of the state," 1987: 79–80, and Pulleyblank, "Neo-Confucianism and neo-legalism," 1960: 103.

50. TT, 12: 71c; CTS, 147: 3982.

51. I agree with Chen Jo-shui in adopting Hoyt Tillman's term of *utilitarian Confucian* to demarcate Tu Yu's approach to government. Tillman, *Utilitarian Confucianism*, 1982; Chen, *Liu Tsung-yüan*, 1992: 120, note 84.

52. The term *moral statesman* is used by Chang Hao in "On the *Ching-shih* ideal in neo-Confucianism," in *Ch'ing-shih wen-t'i*, 3, (Nov., 1974): 36–61; part of my argument follows his.

53. Ibid.

54. For Te-tsung's policy and Kuo's life, see chapter 5, note 43.

55. Liu Yü-hsi, *Liu Pin-k'o chia-hua lu*, 6b–7a.

Chapter Eight

1. Wechsler, "The Confucian impact," *T'oung pao*, 66 (1980): 1–3. The term *Confucian bureaucrat* is used here to describe those court officials who applied Confucian teachings one way or another in the performance of their duty, but who were not necessarily committed to them. Liu Tsung-yüan described the actions of his ideal Confucian as follows: "[When] one acquires office, one [should] carry out in actual affairs the ways of the *Book of Poetry*, the *Classics of Rites*, and the *Spring and Autumn Annals*, benefiting the people, [always] keeping in mind [the necessity] to live up to Confucius' pen and tongue. Only by doing that, is one entitled to be called a Confucian" ("Sung Hsü Ts'ung-shih pei-yu hsü," LHTCC, 25: 5a). Translated in Chen, *Liu Tsung-yüan*, 1992: 92.

2. Chen, *Liu Tsung-yüan*, 1992, ch. 1.

3. For the development of T'ang Buddhism, see Stanley Weinstein, *Buddhism under the T'ang*, 1987; Peter N. Gregory, *Tsung-mi and the signification of Buddhism*, 1991; Peter N. Gregory and Patricia Buckley Ebrey, "The religious and historical landscape," in Ebrey and Gregory, eds., *Religion and society in T'ang and Sung China*, 1993: 1–44; T'ang Yung-t'ung, *Sui T'ang fo-chiao shih kao*, 1982; Chang Tsun-liu, "Sui T'ang Wu-tai fo-chiao ta-shih nien-piao," in Fan Wen-lan, *T'ang-tai fo-chiao*, 1979: 116–292.

4. Chen, *Liu Tsung-yüan*, 1992: 13–17; Barrett, *Li Ao*, 1992: 15–17; for examples of poems that express a longing for a Taoist spiritual world, see Stephen Owen, *The great age of Chinese poetry: the High T'ang*, 1981: 41–46. For a detailed account of the general development of Taoism in the T'ang, see Jen Chi-yü, ed., *Chung-kuo tao-chiao shih*, 1990: 249–457, and Sunayama Minoru, *Zui Tô dokyô shisoshi kenkyû*, 1990, section two.

5. Chen, *Liu Tsung-yüan*, 1992: 19–20. Confucianism was also alive in the official education, see Kao Ming-shih, "T'ang-tai chiao-yü te te-se," *Yu-shih yüeh-k'an*, vol. 47, 5 (1978): 63–64.

6. McMullen, *State and scholars*, 1988: chs., 3, 4, and 5, esp. 71–85 and 114; Chen, *Liu Tsung-yüan*, 1992: 17–18; Kao Ming-shih, "T'ang-tai chiao-yü te te-se," *Yu-shih yüeh-k'an*, vol. 47, 5 (1978): 63–64. Also see CTS, 189a: 4941–42; HTS, 198a: 5636–37.

7. A. R. Davis, *Tu Fu*, 1971: 45–46 and 100–101; Shan Chou, "Tu Fu's social conscience: compassion and topicality in his poetry," HJAS, 51: 1 (6, 1991): 5–53. Also see, Fang Yü, "Chi-mo yü ch'ao-yüeh—shih lun Tu Fu Ch'ang-an ch'u-yu shih ssu-shou," in *Ti-i chieh kuo-chi T'ang-tai hsüeh-shu hui-i lun-wen chi*, 1989: 398–413. William Hung, *Tu Fu, China's greatest poet*, 1952. McMullen, "Historical and literary theory," *Perspectives*, 1973: 340. Chen, *Liu Tsung-yüan*, 1992: 26.

8. Modern historians generally agree that the social and political crises caused by the An Lu-shan rebellion led directly to the *ku-wen* movement. See Ch'en Yin-k'o, "Lun Han Yü," *Li-shih yen-chiu*, 2 (1954): 111; Pulleyblank, "Neo-Confucianism and neo-Legalism," 1960: 83–84; Hayashida Shinnosuke, "Tôdai kobun undô no keisei katei," *Nippon Chûgoku gakkai hô*, 29 (1977): 107; Chen, *Liu Tsung-yüan*, 1992: 25–29. Of course, the fundamental reasons for the rise of the Confucian revival movement were complicated. For example, the origin of this revival was also connected with the poetic movement initiated by Ch'en Tzu-ang (661–702) in the seventh century. The poetic movement exerted a great influence on the *ku-wen* movement; the *ku-wen* movement nonetheless had a more distinct Confucian outlook. For Ch'en Tzu-ang's influence, see Ch'ien Mu, "Tsa-lun T'ang-tai ku-wen yün-tung," *Hsin-ya hsüeh-pao*, 3, no. 1 (1957): 123–25; Lo Ken-tse, *Chung-kuo wen-hsüan p'i-p'ing shih*, vol. 2, 1957: 113 and 120–22; Sun Ch'ang-wu, *T'ang-tai ku-wen yün-tung t'ung-lun*, 1984: 3–4 and 19; Chen, *Liu Tsung-yüan*, 1992: 30 note 76. See also Chen, *Liu Tsung-yüan*, 1992: 26–30; Peter Bol, *"This culture of ours,"* 1992: 108–47; McMullen, "Historical and literary theory" 1973: 307–42, esp., 339–41; Pulleyblank, "Neo-Confucianism and neo-legalism," 1960: 85–88; Hayashida Shinnosuke, "Tôdai kobun undô no keisei katei," *Nippon Chûgoku gakkai hô*, 29 (1977): 106–23; Sun Ch'ang-wu, *Ku-wen t'ung-lun*, 1984: 57–99.

9. Chen, *Liu Tsung-yüan*, 1992: 28–9; Sun, *Ku-wen t'ung-lun*, 1984: 23–25; Chang Ch'ün, "T'an-Chao-Lu san-chia Ch'un-ch'iu chih shuo," in

Ch'ien Mu hsien-sheng pa-shih-sui chi-nien lun-wen-chi, 1974: 149–59; McMullen, *State and scholars* 1988: 101–5; Pulleyblank, "Neo-Confucianism and neo-legalism," 1960: 88–91; Inaba Ichiro, "Chûtô ni okeru shinjugaku undô no ichi kosatsu: Ryû Chike no keisho hihan to Ta-Chô-Riki shi no Shunjû gaku," Chûgoku chûseishi kenkyûkai ed., *Chûgoku chûseishi kenkyû,* 1970: 377–403, esp. 390–96; Tozaki Tetsuhiko, "Liu-ch'uan Jih-pen te yu-kuan Lu Chih (i.e., Lu Ch'un) te shih-liao chi jo-kan k'ao-cheng," in *Chung-kuo che-hsüeh shih yen-chiu,* 1 (1985): 49–58.

10. There are different views regarding Li Ao's dates. Here I have adopted the dates provided by Barrett. For reasons, see his *Li Ao,* 1992: 156–57; for a different view, see Lo Lien-t'ien, "Li Ao yen-chiu," *Kuo-li pien-i-kuan kuan-k'an,* 2: 3 (Dec., 1973): 58–60; CTS, 160: 4205–09; HTS, 177: 5280–82; . For Han Yü's life, see Hartman, *Han Yü,* 1986; Ch'ien Chi-po, *Han Yü chih,* 1958; Lo Lien-t'ien, *Han Yü yen-chiu,* 1977; also see CTS, 160: 4195–4204; HTS, 176: 5255–65. For Liu Tsung-yüan's life, see Chen, *Liu Tsung-yüan,* 1992: 30; Shih Tzu-yü, *Liu Tsung-yüan nien-p'u,* 1958; also see CTS, 160: 4213–14; HTS, 168: 5132–42. Liu Tsung-yüan was influenced by the critical approach to the Confucian classics advocated by Lu Ch'un of the *Spring and autumn annals* school around 804. See Lamont, "An early ninth century debate on Heaven, part I," 1973: 196–97; Chen, *Liu Tsung-yüan,* 1992, chs. 4 and 5.

11. Lo Ken-tse, *P'i-p'ing shih,* 1957: 139–41; Sun, *Ku-wen t'ung-lun,* 1984: 89–90. For Han Yü's definition of the Way, see his "Yüan Tao," in HCLCC, 11: 4a–4b. Also see Hartman, *Han Yü,* 1986: 149–60.

12. Chen, *Liu Tsung-yüan,* 1992: ch. 4; also see McMullen, *State and scholars,* 1988: 261; for Han Yü's conception of the Confucian *Tao,* see Hartman's discussion on Han Yü's famous essay "Yüan Tao, or On the origin of the Way," in *Han Yü,* 1986: 149–60, esp. 150. Han Yü's anti-Buddhist and anti-Taoist mentality is a well-known fact, and Hartman also has dealt with it carefully, see his *Han Yü,* 1986: 149–60. Barrett's study of Li Ao has also established Li as a true defender of Confucianism in the face of the challenge of Buddhism and Taoism. See Barrett, *Li Ao,* 1992: chs. 2 and 3.

13. McMullen, *State and scholars,* 1988: 261 and 105–12; Chen, *Liu Tsung-yüan,* 1992: 126.

14. In their private lives, both Liu Tsung-yüan and Po Chü-i were seriously involved with Buddhism or Taoism. For examples and details see Chen, *Liu Tsung-yüan,* 1992: 120 and 172–80; McMullen, "Historical and literary theory," 1973: 311–13; Waley, *Po Chü-i,* 1949; Lo Lien-t'ien, "Po Chü-i yü fo tao kuan-hsi ch'ung-t'an," *T'ang-tai hsüeh-shu,* 1989: 25–76; Sun Ch'ang-wu, "Han Liu i-ch'ien te 'ku-wen' lun," *Wen-hsüeh p'ing-lun ts'ung-k'an,* 16 (1982): 284; this article was recollected in his *T'ang-tai ku-wen yün-tung t'ung-lun,* 1984, ch. 4. It is interesting to note that although

Han Yü and Li Ao were famous for their anti-Buddhist attitudes, Buddhist monks were not excluded from their social circle. Han Yü's contact with the Ch'an Buddhist monk Ta Tien is well known. Li Ao's relationship with Buddhist monks is difficult to prove, but it is also likely that he met with some of them. See Hartman, *Han Yü*, 1986: 93–99; Barrett, *Li Ao*, 1992: 51–53.

15. Chen, *Liu Tsung-yüan*, 1992: 21. This phrase has also been used to describe Ke Hung's (283–343) thought. See Lin Li-hsüeh, *Pao-p'u tzu nei-wai p'ian ssu-hsiang hsi-lun*, 1980: 177. Peter Bol takes issue with Chen's characterization. See his review of Chen, *Liu Tsung-yuan*, in HJAS, Vol. 56, no. 1 (June 1996): 181.

16. McMullen comments that the principle theme of Han Yü's most important treatise on social and political thought, "On the Origin of the Way," is actually "the re-assertion of the Confucian view of the world, of hierarchy and morality, in the face of what Han characterized as Buddhist and Taoist denial of the value of social and moral activity." McMullen, "Han Yü: An alternative picture," a review article in HJAS, vol. 49, 2 (Dec. 1989): 638.

17. Although he will not be discussed in this study, Po Chü-i is well known for his conscientious performance as a censor and his compassion for the people's suffering. See, Waley, *Po Chü-i*, 1949.

18. McMullen, *State and scholars*, 1988: 107–8; also see Barrett, *Li Ao*, 1992: 83–84.

19. The careers of Yüan Chieh, Liu Tsung-yüan, and Han Yü are three well-known examples. Yüan Chieh started his official career around 759 at the age of forty. He spent almost the entire thirteen years of his official life in the provinces. Han Yü served nearly fourteen years in provincial governments out of his thirty-two years in official life. Liu Tsung-yüan also spent sixteen years in local services out of his twenty-two years in official life. See Sun Wang, *Yüan Tz'u-shan nien-p'u*, 1962; Shih Tzu-yü, *Liu Tsung-yüan nien-p'u*, 1958; Lo Lien-t'ien, *Han Yü yen-chiu*, 1977:396–404.

20. The state in our context means "an all embracing socio-political order" centering on the Son of Heaven. It is distinctly different from the Western idea of a "sovereign state." Benjamin Schwartz, "The primacy of the political order in East Asian societies: some preliminary generalizations," in Schram, ed., *Foundations and limits of state power in China*, 1987: 1. See also Jacques Gernet's definition of the traditional Chinese concept of state in his introduction to S. R. Schram, ed., *The scope of state power in China*, 1985: xxxii. For a brief summary of the history of the Western concept of the *sovereign state*, see David L. Silk, ed., *International encyclopedia of the social sciences*, 1968: 150–56.

21. "Sung fu-t'u Wen-ch'ang shih hsü," HCLCC, 20: 4a. The translation follows Hartman with minor changes, and I have used "benevolence and rightness (*jen i*)" to replace his "humanity and justice." See Hartman, *Han Yü*, 1986: 148–49. For Li Ao's view, see his "Ta Hou Kao ti erh shu," LWKC, SPTK edition, 7: 31a.

22. See "Shou Tao lun," LHTCC, vol. 1, 3: 10a; Chen, *Liu Tsung-yüan*, 1992: 89.

23. For Lü Wen's life and his relationship with Liu Tsung-yüan during their participation in the Wang Shu-wen group, see Ma Ch'eng-su, *Lü Ho-shu hsüeh-p'u*, 1977: 19–86; CTS, 137: 3769–70; HTS, 160: 4967; CTS, 135: 3734; also see, Liu Tsung-yüan, "Chi Lü Heng-chou Wen," in LHTCC, 40: 4a–5b; "Jen-wen hua-ch'eng lun," LHSWC, 10: 54b.

24. "Chien piao," PLC, 4: 21a. The same essay also appears in CTW, but under the title of "Chih-chien piao," see CTW, 384: 20a–22b. Tu-ku Chi mentioned in this memorial that it had been ten years since the An Lu-shan rebellion broke out, thus I believe that this memorial was presented around 765.

25. "Er feng shih-lun," YTSC, Sun Wang, ed., 1960: 10. For Yüan's life and his role in the *ku-wen* movement, see McMullen, "Yüan Chieh," 1968; Sun Wang, *Yüan Tz'u-shan nien-p'u*, 1962; HTS, 143: 4681–86.

26. See Ch'üan Te-yü, "Lun Chiang Huai shui-tsai shang-shu," and "Lun han-tsai piao," in CTW, 486: 1a–2b and 488: 4b–7b.

27. "Shu ming," YTSC, 5: 76.

28. "Ta Yang Pen ch'u-shih shu," PLC, 18: 114b.

29. See Yüan Chieh's 757 essay, "Lun Kuan Chung," YTSC, 6: 87–88; also see McMullen, "Historical and literary theory," 1973: 328; McMullen, "Yüan Chieh," 1968: 73.

30. McMullen, "Historical and literary theory," 1973: 329.

31. For details, see ibid.: 329–30.

32. Up to 757, Yüan Chieh disagreed on moral grounds with practicing expediency in government, but he understood the importance of accommodation to changing times and circumstances. In 764, during his service as prefect in Tao-chou (in modern Hunan), Yüan said that "if [a prefect] does not accommodate to changes to satisfy the needs of the time, ... it will lead to a revolt" ("Hsieh Shang piao," YTSC, 8: 124).

33. Han Yü, "Chin-shih ts'e-wen shih-san shou," HCLCC, 14: 6a; Li Ao, "Chien so chih yü Hsü-chou Chang P'u-yeh shu," LWKC, 8: 32, and his "Tsa shuo," op. cit., 5: 22; Liu Tsung-yüan, "Chin Wen-kung wen shou Yüan i," LHTCC, 4: 1b. Also see Hartman, *Han Yü*, 1986: 130.

34. "Lun Huai-hsi shih-i chuang," HCLCC, 40: 8b.

35. "Yü E-chou Liu Chung-ch'en shu yu i-shou," HCLCC, 19: 3b. Han's colleague was Liu Kung-ch'o (768–832) who voluntarily pleaded with the court to let him fight against the rebellious Huai-hsi governor in 815. See TCTC, 239: 7708; CTS, 165: 4302; also see Lo, *Han Yü yen-chiu*, 1977: 88.

36. "Yü Yüan hsiang-kung shu," HCLCC, 19: 2a. Han Yü's close friend was Fan Tsung-shih (d. 824). For their relationship, see Ch'ien Chi-po, *Han Yü chih*, 1958: 73–74. Han Yü's resistance to change in one occasion was taken as an example of his conservative side. See McMullen, "Han Yü," 1989: 621–23. However, the above quoted passages show that Han also had a pragmatic side. He was not opposed to change per se.

37. "Ti-wang so shang wen," LWKC, 4: 18b.

38. Wu Wen-chih, *Liu Tsung-yüan p'ing-chuan*, 1962: 98–100; Sun Ch'ang-wu, *Liu Tsung-yüan chuan-lun*, 1982: 264–66; Pulleyblank, "Neo-Confucianism and neo-legalism," 1960: 103; McMullen, "Views of the state," 1987: 80; Chen, *Liu Tsung-yüan*, 1992: 95–96.

39. "Lun tu-chih shu," CTW, 486: 5b.

40. "Shih-i hsia-p'ien," YTSC, 6: 96.

41. "Chien piao," PLC, 4: 21a.

42. Liu Tsung-yüan, "Feng-chien lun," LHTCC, 3: 6b. Also see Wu Wen-chih, *Liu Tsung-yüan p'ing-chuan*, 1962: 95; Sun, *Liu Tsung-yüan chuan-lun*, 1982: 273–74.

43. Li Ao's view is expressed in his "Chien so-chih yü Hsü-chou Chang p'u-yeh shu," LWKC, 8: 33a. Han Yü's support for appointing capable and virtuous men to office has been carefully dealt with elsewhere, see Hartman, *Han Yü*, 1986: 171–72.

44. "Feng-chien lun," LHTCC, 3: 5b.

45. For Li Kuan's life, see HTS, 203: 5779. For Han Yü and Li Kuan's friendship, see Han Yü, "Li Yüan-pin mu-ming," HCLCC, 24: 1a-b; Lo Lien-t'ien, Han Yü yen-chiu, 1977: 138–40. Li Kuan's claim to be Lu Chih's disciple is in "Shang Lu hsiang-kung shu," LYPWC, 3: 29. It is well known that there were various ways to form teacher-disciple relationships in the mid-T'ang, and for a young graduate like Li Kuan to claim a connection with a former examination administrator like Lu Chih was indeed a very common practice. For the rise of such relationship and why it was a common practice in the mid-T'ang, see McMullen, *State and scholars*, 1988: 62.

46. "Shang Lu hsiang-kung shu," LYPWC, 3: 29–33. We know the date of this letter because it mentions that Lu Chih had just recommended Chia Tan (730–805) and Lu Mai (739–798) to be chief ministers. See,

"Shang Lu hsiang-kung shu," ibid.: 32. Also see Yen I-p'ing, *Nien-p'u*, 1975: 152. These two became chief minister in the fifth month of 793; Li's letter could only have been written after that date. For Lu Mai's life, see CTS, 136: 3753–54; for Chia Tan's, see CTS, 138: 3783–87; for the date of their tenure as chief ministers, see HTS, 62: 1706.

47. We have no evidence, however, to make a case for Li Kuan's influence on Lu Chih. See Yen I-p'ing, *Nien-p'u*, 1975: 3. Also see chapter 5 above, "Establishing a capable and just bureaucracy."

48. Ch'üan Te-yü, "Ch'ing chih liang-sheng kuan piao," CTW, 486: 4a.

49. Lamont, "An early ninth century debate on Heaven, part I," 1973: 195–200.

50. "Tung ku-Chou ch'eng ming," LHSWC, 8: 43b as translated in Chen, *Liu Tsung-yüan*, 1992: 117. Also see Lamont's translation of the same passage in "On Heaven, part I," 1973: 198.

51. "Chien piao," PLC, 4: 21a.

52. Ch'üan Te-yü, "Lun han-tsai piao," CTW, 488: 4b. For another example, see his "Ho Ts'ui Hsiang-kuo shu," CTW, 489: 10b.

53. See Yüan Chieh, "Shu ming," YTSC, 5: 76; Han Yü, "Yüan kuei," HCLCC, 11: 10a-b. Also see Chen K'e-ming, *Han Yü shu-p'ing*, 1985: 131–32.

54. Chen, *Liu Tsung-yüan*, 1992: 154–55; Lamont, "On Heaven, part I," 1973: 200–202. Also see Sun Ch'ang-wu, *Liu Tsung-yüan chuan-lun*, 1982: 237–53 and 261–64; Wu Wen-chih, *Liu Tsung-yüan p'ing-chuan*, 1962: 100–118.

55. "Ta Liu Yü-hsi t'ie-lun," LHTCC, 31: 4b and 5a. The translation of the first line is from Chen, *Liu Tsung-yüan*, 1992: 108, the second line is from Lamont, "An early ninth century debate on Heaven, part II," 1974: 81. Lamont also translates the entire text of this debate, see Lamont, "On Heaven," parts 1 and 2.

56. "Chen fu," LHTCC, 1: 20a; Chen, *Liu Tsung-yüan*, 1992: 105–6; Lamont, "On Heaven, part II," 1974: 201.

57. For an extended analysis of Liu's unusual ideas on Heaven and the Mandate of Heaven, see Chen, *Liu Tsung-yüan*, 1992: 99–118.

58. "Lun shih shu piao," LWKC, 9: 38b–42b. Also see Lo Lien-t'ien's explanation of why Li Ao presented this memorial in 819 in his "Li Ao yen-chiu," 1973: 71–72.

59. "Shu yung chung cheng," LWKC, 9: 40a.

60. "Shu ping-ch'ih chien-ning," LWKC, 9: 40b.

61. "Shu chüeh chin-hsien," LWKC, 9: 41b.

62. The only possible evidence that I can reasonably speculate about is that Li Ao's "uncle," Li Heng, was recommended by Lu Chih in 792 as one of the candidates to head the Department of Public Revenue. Li Heng may have known about Lu Chih's memorials and later told his "nephew." See, Barrett, *Li Ao*, 1992, 35.

63. Han Yü, "Yüan hui," HCLCC, 11: 8b; Liu Tsung-yüan, "Tu Chien tui," LHTCC, 14: 6b–7b.

64. Liu Tsung-yüan, "Chin Wen-kung wen shou Yüan i," LHTCC, 4: 1a–2b. For the background of this event which took place in the Spring and Autumn era, see Legge, *The Chinese classics*, vol. 5, 2 parts, *The Ch'un Ts'ew with the Tso chuen*, 1872: 194–96. Chen, Liu *Tsung-yüan*, 1992: 138, has pointed out that Liu's real purpose in writing this essay was to attack the political situation of his day.

65. LHTCC, 4: 1b.

66. "Shang Cheng shang-shu hsiang-kung ch'i," HCLCC, 15: 8a-b; "Shang liu-shou Cheng hsiang-kung ch'i," ibid., 8b–10a. For more details, see Hartman, *Han Yü*, 1986: 74–76.

67. The eunuch Han Yü flattered was Chü Wen-chen (d. 812), the main force responsible for establishing the future Emperor Hsien-tsung in 805 when the Wang Shu-wen group was attempting their reform. In 797, when Han Yü served in Pien-chou, he wrote a poem for Chü, the then army supervisor in Pien-chou. Because this poem and its preface gave Chü unusual praise, Han Yü thus appeared quite flattering. See Han Yü, "Sung Pien-chou chien-chün Chü Wen-chen hsü," in his *Wai-chi*, 3: 1a-b as included in HCLCC. Also see, CTW, 556: 10a. For Chü Wen-chen's life, see CTS, 184; 4767; HTS, 207: 5868. On the other hand, on the grounds that Han Yü was probably instructed to write this poem to Chü, and that Han also had some familial relations with Chü, Lo Lien-t'ien has explained why Han's connection with this eunuch was not necessarily the flattering behavior some traditional and modern historians have criticized it for being. See Lo, *Han Yü yen-chiu*, 1977: 52–53.

68. Hartman, *Han Yü*, 1986: 85–86.

69. "Yüan Tao," HCLCC, 11: 3b; Li Ao, "Fu-hsing shu chung," LWKC, 2: 10a. Hartman provides a thorough discussion of Han Yü's perception and application of the *Great learning*, see his *Han Yü*, 1986, chs. 2 and 3. Also see Barrett's study of the formation of Li Ao's thought in his *Li Ao*, 1992: chs. 3 and 4.

70. Liang Su took an interest in the *Doctrine of the mean* in a passage concerning "exhausting one's nature" in his famous essay "Chih-kuan t'ung-li i" and in other essays such as "Shu ch'u fu." For "Chih-kuan t'ung-li i,"

see CTW, 517: 15b–20a, esp. 15b–17a; for "Shu ch'u fu," see CTW, 517: 6a. As pointed out by McMullen, Ch'üan Te-yü had already paid serious attention to the *Doctrine of the mean* in 781. See McMullen, "Han Yü," 1989: 647. Barrett also discusses Ch'üan's interest in this regard, see his *Li Ao*, 1992: 83–85, 105, and 137. For Ch'üan Te-yü's own interest, see his "Hsin-chou Nan-yen ts'ao-i ch'an-shih yen-tso chi," and "Li-pu ts'e-wen wu-tao," in CTW, 494: 13a, and 483: 15b–16a.

71. One modern Chinese historian even castigates Han Yü for "ardently worshipping the imperial power." See Wang Yün-sheng, "Han Yü he Liu Tsung-yüan," *Hsin chien-she* (Feb., 1963): 56.

72. Hsiao Kung-ch'uan also noticed this interesting aspect of Han Yü's thought, see his "Legalism and autocracy in traditional China," *Ch'ing-hua hsüeh-pao*, N.S., 4: 2 (1964): 111–12.

73. "Sung Hsüeh Ts'un-i chih jen hsü," LHTCC, 23: 3a as translated in Chen, *Liu Tsung-yüan*, 1992: 153.

74. Hartman, *Han Yü*, 1986: 84–85, 90–91, and 132–35. Also see Han Yü, "Lun fo-ku piao," HCLCC, 39: 3a–5b.

75. Yüan Chieh went on to say, "Those who bear the [burden of] taxes and *corvée* are mostly widows and children, the poor and the helpless. They live and die in vagrancy, worrying and suffering on the road" ("Shih i chung-p'ien," YTSC, 6: 95).

76. Yüan described what the Tao-chou people's living conditions were like after he arrived: "They breakfast on grasses and roots / And dine on the bark of trees / Their breath is exhausted by speaking / Their words are swift but their feet are slow." "Ch'ung-ling hsing," YTSC, 3: 34. For more details on the background of this attack, see McMullen, "Yüan Chieh," 1968: 164. Also see "Tsou mien k'e-shuai chuang," YTSC, 8: 125–26, and McMullen, "Yüan Chieh," 1968: 172–75.

77. Also see HTS, 162: 4991–92.

78. "Hsieh Shu-chou Tz'u-shih chien chia Ch'ao-san ta-fu piao," PLC, 5: 30b.

79. "P'ing-fu shu," LWKC, 3: 12b.

80. Po Chü-i's like-minded sympathy for the poor is well known, see for example his "Lun ho-ti chuang," PCIC, 58: 1234–36; also see Waley, *Po Chü-i*, 1949: 60.

81. HTS, 177: 5282. For the date of Li's service in Lu-chou, see Yü Hsien-hao, *T'ang tz'u-shih k'ao*, vol. 3, 1987: 1543.

82. Po Chü-i also favored goods for tax payment.

83. "Lun han-tsai piao," CTW, 488: 6b.

84. "Ch'ien-chung wu-ch'ing chuang," HCLCC, 37: 13b. Also see HCLCC, 37: 3A and Lo, *Han Yü yen-chiu*, 1977: 63–64.

85. See "Yü-shih t'ai shang lun t'ien-han jen-chi chuang," HCLCC, 37: 8b–9a.

86. Ibid.: 93 and 103. Also see CTS, 160: 4203.

87. "Lun pien yen-fa shih-i chuang," HCLCC, 40: 10a–15a. This entire memorial in opposition to reform of the salt monopoly is translated in Twitchett, *Financial administration*, 1970: 165–72. Han contended that if the people had to buy salt with cash directly from the officials, it would force the officials not to sell salt to those who had no cash and thus only bring misery to the poor.

88. Chen, *Liu Tsung-yüan*, 1992, ch. 7.

89. CTS, 166: 4214; HTS, 168: 5142.

90. "Ta Yüan Jao-chou lun cheng-li shu," LHTCC, 32: 1a–3a. Also see, Sun Ch'ang-wu, *Liu Tsung-yüan p'ing-chuan*, 1982: 278–80.

91. LHTCC, 32: 2a.

92. See HCLCC, 40: 15a and Twitchett, *Financial administration*, 1970: 172.

93. CTS, 148: 4004–5.

94. "Ch'u kuei," YTSC, 5: 66.

95. "Ku yü-shih chung-ch'eng Lu I shih i," PLC, 6: 34b.

96. Han Yü, "Cheng ch'en lun," HCLCC, 14: 9a–12a; Liu Tsung-yüan, "Kuo-tzu ssu-yeh Yang Ch'eng i-ai chieh," LHTCC, 14: 2b–4b. I have quoted Liu Tsung-yüan's portrait of an ideal Confucian in footnote 1.

97. "Ts'ung Tao lun," LWKC, 4: 15b.

Epilogue

1. Tillman, *Utilitarian Confucianism*, 1982, ch. 4, esp. 142–45; also see his *Confucian discourse*, 1992. For Chu Hsi's view of expediency, see *Chu Tzu yü-lei*, vol. 3, 37: 987–95.

2. CTW, 493: 14b–15a. The other chief ministers mentioned by these officials included T'ai-tsung's confidant Fang Hsüan-ling, and Yao Ch'ung and Sung Ching who served at the beginning of Hsüan-tsung's reign. For Fang Hsüan-ling's life, see CTS, 66: 2459–67; HTS, 96: 3853–59; for Yao Ch'ung's and Sung Ching's life, see CTS, 96: 3021–36; HTS, 124: 4381–94.

3. The Divine Farmer, or Shen Nung, is a legendary sage ruler said to have invented the plow. This is recorded in the second "Hsi-tz'u" section of the *I ching*. Lord Millet, or Hou Chi, half human and half divine, was claimed as ancestor by the ruling house of the Chou dynasty (1122?–256 B.C.). The legend of Hou Chi can be found in the "Sheng-ming" chapter in the "Ta-ya" section of the *Shih ching*.

4. See Jacques Gernet, Introduction, in S. R. Schram, ed., *Foundations and limits of state power in China*, 1987: xx–xxii. Also see Yü Ying-shih, " 'Chün tsun ch'en pei' hsia te chün-ch'üan yü hsiang-ch'üan," in his *Li-shi yü ssu-hsiang*, 1976: 52–53.

5. Tu Yu's position is not completely the same as some Northern Sung Neo-Confucians, such as Sun Fu, or Ch'eng I. While just as much concerned with dynastic stability as Tu Yu was, these Northern Sung Neo-Confucians, unlike Tu Yu, were also very conscious of the problem of autocracy. See a perceptive study of these Neo-Confucians in Alan Wood, *Limits to Autocracy, from Sung Neo-Confucianism to a doctrine of political rights*, 1995.

6. For a concise analysis of this new authoritarianism, see Ch'iu Ch'ui-liang, "Lun hsin ch'üan-wei chu-i te wei-hsien-hsing," in *The Chinese intellectual*, (Spring, 1994): 16–20.

7. For Ming dynasty examples of intellectuals who opposed autocratic political powers, see Charles Hucker, "The Tung-lin movement of the late Ming period," and de Bary, "Chinese despotism and the Confucian ideal," in Fairbank, ed., *Chinese thought and institutions*, 1957: 132–62 and 163–203. For modern examples, see Liu Pin-yen, *A higher kind of loyalty: a memoir by China's foremost journalist*, tr. by Chu Hung, 1990; Perry Link, ed., *People or monsters and other stories and reportage from China after Mao*, 1983; and Michael S. Duke, *Blooming and contending: Chinese literature in the post-Mao era*, 1985, ch. 4. Also see Wei Ching-sheng, *The courage to stand alone, letters from prison and other writings*, edited and translated by Kristina M. Torgeson, 1997.

8. China's economic openness combined with political repression is the main theme of Nicholas D. Kristof and Sheryl WuDunn, *China wakes: the struggle for the soul of a rising power*, 1994; much of this material is summarized in Sheryl WuDunn and Nicholas D. Kristof, "China's rush to riches," *New York times magazine*, September 4, 1994: 38–41, 46, 48, 54. For a critique of the Deng era reforms as authoritarian and inequitable, see Liu Binyan and Perry Link's review of the economist He Qinglian's book *Zhongguo de xianjing* [China's Pitfalls] in *The New York review of books* (October 8, 1998), 19–23.

9. For early-twentieth-century attacks on Confucianism, see Chou Ts'e-tsung, *The May Fourth Movement: intellectual revolution in modern*

China, 1960, and Lin Yü-sheng, *The crisis of Chinese consciousness: radical antitraditionalism in the May Fourth era*, 1979. For some recent discussions of Confucianism, see William Theodore de Bary, *The trouble with Confucianism*, 1991, and various responses to his book in a "Roundtable discussion," in *China review international*, vol. 1, no. 4, (1994): 9–47. See also Yü Ying-shih, *Hsien-tai ju-hsüeh lun*, 1996, and a critical review of it by Yang Nien-ch'ün, "Ju-hsüeh nei-tsai p'i-p'an te hsien-shih k'un-ching," in *Twenty-first century bimonthly*, 40, (4/1997): 94–99.

Glossary

Ai-chou 愛州
an-fu hsü-p'in 安富恤貧
An Lu-shan 安祿山

chan-suan mi-shu 占算秘術
Chang I 張鎰
Chang P'ang 張滂
Chang She 張涉
Chang Yen-shang 張延賞
Ch'ang-an 長安
Ch'ang-chou 常州
Chao Ching 趙憬
Chao-i 昭義
Chao Kuei-hsien 趙貴先
Chao K'uang 趙匡
Chao-tsung 昭宗
Chen-kuan chih-chih 貞觀之治
Ch'en 陳
Ch'en-chou 辰州
ch'eng 誠
Ch'eng-te 成德
chi 幾
chi che, shih chih wei ye 幾者, 事之微也
Chi-hsien yüan 集賢院
Chi-shih-chung 給事中
Ch'i 齊
Chia Chih 賈至
Chiang-huai 江淮

Chiang Kung-fu 姜公輔
Chiao-jan 皎然
Chien-chung 建中
chih-hsing 志行
Chia-hsing 嘉興
Chien-ch'a yü-shih 監察御史
Chien-i ta-fu 諫議大夫
Chien-nan 劍南
Ch'ien Ch'i 錢起
chih chi chih nan ye 知幾之難也
chih ch'i pu-k'o erh wei-chih che 知其不可而爲之者
chin-chung 盡忠
chin-shih 進士
Ch'in 秦
Ch'in-fu wen-hsüeh-kuan hsüeh-shih 秦府文學館學士
ching 經
ching-t'ien 井田
ching-yü li-chih 精於吏治
Ching-yüan 涇原
ch'ing-miao-ch'ien 青苗錢
chiu-pi 九弊
chiu-tsu 舊族
Chou 周
Chou-li 周禮
Chu Hsi 朱熹
chu-hsing 著姓

275

Chu-k'o yüan-wai-lang　主客員外郎

Chu-pu　主簿

Chu T'ao　朱滔

Chu Tz'u　朱泚

Ch'u-chih shih　黜陟使

ch'u-hsin　初心

Ch'ü Huan　曲環

Ch'üan　權

ch'üan-ling Tu-chih　權領度支

ch'üan-shu　權術

Ch'üan Te-yü　權德與

Ch'un-chiu　春秋

chün hsien chih-tu　郡縣制度

chün-t'ien　均田

chün-tzu　君子

Chung-chou　忠州

Chung-shu she-jen　中書舍人

Chung-shu sheng　中書省

Chung-shu shih-lang　中書侍郎

chung-wen ch'ing-ju　重文輕儒

Chung yung　中庸

fei yü jen-shih chih wai, pieh yu T'ien-ming ye　非於人事之外別有天命也

feng-chien　封建

Feng-hsiang　鳳翔

Feng-lo Ssu　豐樂寺

Feng-t'ien　奉天

fu　賦

"Fu-hsing shu"　"復性書"

fu-kuo ch'iang-ping　富國强兵

Han-lin hsüeh-shih　翰林學士

Han-lin yüan　翰林院

Han Yü　韓愈

Hao-chou　濠州

Heng　衡

Ho-chung　河中

Ho-nan　河南

Ho-pei　河北

Ho-shuo　河朔

ho-ti　和糴

ho-t'iao　和糴

Ho-tung　河東

Ho-yin　河陰

Hsiao ching　孝經

Hsiang-yang　襄陽

Hsiao Fu　蕭復

Hsiao Heng　蕭衡

hsiao-jen　小人

Hsiao Sheng　蕭升

Hsiao Sung　蕭嵩

Hsiao Ts'un　蕭存

Hsiao Ying-shih　蕭穎士

hsien-che　賢者

hsien-liang　賢良

Hsien-tsung　憲宗

Hsien-yang　咸陽

Hsin-ch'ang　新昌

Hsin T'ang-shu tsai-hsiang shih-hsi piao　新唐書宰相世系表

hsing-chüan　行卷

hsing pien-chi　性褊急

Hsü-chou　徐州

Hsüan　宣

Hsüan-fu　宣撫

Hsüan-tsung　玄宗

Hsüan-wu　宣武

Hsüeh Hsüan　薛瑄

Hsün tzu　荀子

Hu-pu　戶部

Hu-pu shih-lang　戶部侍郎

hu-shui　戶稅

Hua-t'ing　華亭

Huai-hsi　淮西

Huai-nan　淮南

Huang Tsung-hsi　黃宗曦

hui　惠

I　義

I ching　易經

jen-hsin　人心

jen-shu chih tao　仁恕之道

Jih-nan 日南

K'ai-yüan 開元
Kao-tsung 高宗
k'ao 考
K'ao-kung lang-chung 考功郎中
k'o 科
k'o-chü chih-tu 科舉制度
kou-ch'ieh 苟且
ku-Tao 古道
ku-wen 古文
Kuan Chung 管仲
Kuan-lung 關隴
Kuan-chung 關中
Kuan tzu 管子
kuei-tsu 貴族
Kun 鯀
Kuo-tzu po-shih 國子博士

li 利
Li Ao 李翱
Li chi 禮記
Li Chi-fu 李吉甫
Li Chiang 李絳
Li Ch'u-lin 李楚琳
Li Ch'ung 李充
Li Fu 李復
Li Heng 李衡
Li Hsi-lieh 李希烈
Li Hua 李華
Li Huai-kuang 李懷光
Li Kuan 李觀
Li Ling-yao 李靈曜
Li Mi 李泌
Li Pao-chen 李抱眞
Li Pao-ch'en 李寶臣
Li-pu 吏部
Li-pu 禮部
Li-pu lang-chung 禮部郎中
Li Sheng 李晟
Li Sun 李巽
Li Wan-jung 李萬榮
Li Wei-yüeh 李惟岳
Liang-chou 梁州
Liang Su 梁肅
liang-shui 兩稅
liang-shui fa 兩稅法
Ling-nan 嶺南
ling Tu-chih 領度支
Liu Fang 柳芳
Liu-hou 留後
liu-shih 六失
Liu Shih-ning 劉士寧
liu-su 流俗
Liu Tsung-yüan 柳宗元
Liu Wen-hsi 劉文喜
Liu Yü-hsi 劉禹錫
Lo-yang 洛陽
Lu Ch'an 陸滻
Lu Cheng 盧徵
Lu Ch'i 盧杞
Lu Ch'i-cheng 陸齊政
Lu Ch'i-wang 陸齊望
Lu Chien-chih 陸柬之
Lu Chien-li 陸簡禮
Lu Chih 陸贄
Lu Ching-yü 陸敬輿
Lu Chiu 陸九
Lu-chou 盧州
Lu Ch'un 陸淳
Lu Feng (or Lu Li) 陸灃 (陸澧)
Lu Hsi-sheng 陸希聲
Lu Hsiang-hsien 陸象先
Lu Hsüan-kung 陸宣公
Lu Hsün 陸潯
Lu Huai 陸淮
Lu I 陸扆
Lu Jun (or Lu Chien) 陸潤 (陸澗)
Lu K'an 陸侃
Lu K'an-ju 陸侃如
Lu Keng 陸賡
Lu Kuan 陸瓘
Lu Kuei-meng 陸龜蒙
Lu Lun 盧綸

Lu-lung　盧龍

Lu Mi　陸泌

Lu Pa　陸灞

Lu Shan-jen　陸山仁

Lu Shang　陸賞

Lu-shih chi-yen fang　陸氏集驗方

Lu Shu　陸庶

Lu Te-ming　陸德明

Lu Tun-hsin　陸敦信

Lu Wei　陸渭

Lu Yü-ch'ing　陸餘慶

Lu Yüan-fang　陸元方

Lu Yüan-lang　陸元朗

Lü Wen　呂溫

"Lun fo-ku piao"　"論佛骨表"

lung-hu pang　龍虎榜

Men-hsia sheng　門下省

men-jen　門人

Meng Tzu　孟子

min wei kuei　民爲貴

ming-ching　明經

ming-tsu　名族

mo　末

mo-i　末議

Mo tzu　墨子

mou　畝

Mu-tsung　穆宗

Nan-kung　南宮

nei-hsiang　內相

Ou-yang Chan　歐陽詹

Pan Hung　班宏

p'an-ni　叛逆

p'an Tu-chih　判度支

Pei-chü wen-yen　備舉文言

P'ei Yao-ch'ing　裴耀卿

P'ei Yen-ling　裴延齡

pen　本

Pi-pu lang-chung　比部郎中

Pi-shu-chien　秘書監

Pi-shu sheng chiao-shu-lang　秘書省校書郎

Pieh-chi　別集

Pieh-chia　別駕

Pien-chou　汴州

p'ien-wen　駢文

p'in　品

Ping-pu shang-shu　兵部尙書

Ping-pu shih-lang　兵部侍郎

P'ing-liang　平涼

P'ing-lu　平盧

p'o ch'in ju-hsüeh　頗勤儒學

po-hsüeh hung-tz'u　博學宏詞

P'u-ch'eng　蒲城

san-wen　散文

Shan　禪

Shan-chou　陝州

Shan-tung　山東

Shang　商

Shang shu　尙書

Shang Yang　商鞅

she-chi chih ch'en　社稷之臣

shen-ch'a ch'ün-ch'ing　審察群情

Shen-ts'e　神策

sheng　升

shih　石

shih　勢

Shih chi　史記

shih-e　十惡

shih-i　時議

Shih-lang　侍郎

Shih-po chung-shih　市舶中使

shih-shih　時勢

shih ta-fu　士大夫

shih-tsu　士族

shih wei tsu-hsing　世爲族姓

Shih-yü-shih　侍御史

Shou-chou　壽州

shu　術

Shu-chou　舒州

Shu-ju hsiao-chung 豎儒小忠
shu-min 庶民
shu-p'an pa-ts'ui 書判拔萃
shu-shih 術士
Shun 舜
Shun-tsung 順宗
Ssu-K'ung 司空
Ssu-ma Kuang 司馬光
Ssu-nung shao-ch'ing 司農少卿
Su-chou 蘇州
Su Shih 蘇軾
su so an-chih 素所諳知
Su-tsung 肅宗
Sui 隋
Sung 宋
Sung-shan 嵩山

Ta hsüeh 大學
Ta-li 大曆
Ta-li shih ts'ai-tzu 大曆十才子
Tai-pei 岱北
Tai-tsung 代宗
T'ai-fu shao-ch'ing 太府少卿
T'ai-fu ssu 太府寺
T'ai-tsung 太宗
T'ai-wei 太尉
T'ai-tzu pin-k'o 太子賓客
Tan-t'u 丹徒
T'an Chu 啖助
tang 黨
T'ang 湯
T'ang-an 唐安
Tao 道
Tao che, ku-chin chih cheng-ch'üan ye 道者, 古今之正權也
Tao-chou 道州
Tao-t'ung 道統
te 德
t'e-li pu-ch'ün 特立不群
te-chung tse te-kuo 得眾則得國

Te-tsung 德宗
ti 第
ti-shui 地稅
T'ien-an men 天安門
Tien-chung shih-yü-shih 殿中侍御使
t'ien-chieh 天戒
t'ien-ch'ien 天譴
t'ien-hsia 天下
t'ien-ming 天命
t'ien-ming yu-jen 天命由人
T'ien-pao 天寶
t'ien-tzu 天子
T'ien Yüeh 田悅
tou 斗
Tou Shen 竇參
Tso pu-chüeh 左補闕
Tso-tsang k'u 左藏庫
tsu-yung-tiao 租庸調
Ts'ui Ch'ün 崔群
Ts'ui Tsao 崔造
Ts'ui Yüan-han 崔元翰
tsun-mu jen i 遵慕仁義
tsun Tao 遵道
tu-chih 度支
tu-fu 獨夫
Tu Fu 杜甫
Tu-ku Chi 獨孤及
Tu Yu 杜佑
t'ui-ch'eng 推誠
t'un-t'ien 屯田
T'ung-tien 通典
t'ung yü tao che shih wei chün-tzu 通於道者是爲君子
Tzu-hsia 子夏
Tzu-kung 子貢
Tz'u-pu yüan-wai-lang 祠部員外郎

wang che chih tao 王者之道
wang-nien chiao 忘年交
wang-shih 望氏
Wang Shih-ch'ung 王世充

Wang shu-wen　王叔文
Wang Wu-chün　王武俊
wei　威
Wei Cheng　魏徵
Wei Kao　韋皋
Wei-nan　渭南
Wei-po　魏博
Wu chün　吳郡
Wu hsien　吳縣
Wu-hsien nan　吳縣男
Wu shang pu-fu T'ien-tzu, hsia
　pu-fu wu so-hsüeh, pu hsü
　ch'i-t'a　吾上不負天子下不
　負吾所學, 不恤其它
Wu Tse-t'ien　武則天
Wu Ts'ou　吳湊
Wu T'ung-hsüan　吳通玄
Wu T'ung-wei　吳通微
wu-wei　無爲

Yang Ch'eng　陽城
Yang Yen　楊炎

Yao　堯
Yen-chou　鹽州
yin　蔭
yin-pao　淫暴
ying-t'ien　營田
Yu　佑
Yu Jo　有若
Yu Pu-ch'üeh　右補闕
Yü　禹
Yü Ho　庚何
Yü Kung-i　于公異
Yü Shao　于邵
Yüan Chieh　元結
yüan-ch'ing　原情
Yüan-ho chün-hsien t'u-
　chih　元和郡縣圖志
Yüan-ho chung-hsing　元和中
　興
Yüan-ho hsing-tsuan　元和姓纂
"Yüan Tao"　"原道"
Yün-chien　雲間
Yung-chou　永州

Bibliography

Pre-modern Sources

Chi-ku lu-mu 集古錄目, compiled by Ou-yang Fei 歐陽棐, Miao Ch'üan-sun 繆荃孫 edited in Yün tzu-tsai k'an ts'ung-shu 雲自在龕叢書 edition.

Chih-chai shu-lu chieh-t'i 直齋書錄解題, Ch'en Chen-sun 陳振孫, ed., Kuo-hsüeh chi-pen ts'ung-shu 國學基本叢書 edition. Taipei: Commercial Press, 1968.

Chin shu 晉書, compiled by Fang Hsüan-ling 房玄齡 et al. Peking: Chung-hua shu-chü 中華書局 edition, 1974.

Ching-hsüan wen-chi 敬軒文集, by Hsüeh Hsüan 薛瑄, Ssu-k'u ch'üan-shu chen-pen 四庫全書珍本 edition.

Chiu T'ang-shu 舊唐書, Liu Hsü 劉煦 et al., eds. Peking: Chung-hua shu-chü edition, 1975.

Chou li 周禮, with the commentary by Lin Yin 林尹. Taipei: Commercial Press edition, 1974.

Ch'üan T'ang-shih 全唐詩, compiled by Ts'ao Yin 曹寅, P'eng Ting-ch'iu 彭定球 et al. Taipei: Fu-hsing shu-chü 復興書局 reprint, 1961

Ch'üan T'ang-wen 全唐文, compiled by Tung Kao 董誥 et al. Peking: Chung-hua shu-chü reprint, 1982.

Ch'üan Tsai-chih wen-chi 權載之文集, by Ch'üan Te-yü 權德與, SPTK edition.

Chu Lu Hsüan-kung tsou-i 註陸宣公奏議 (1132 edition), Lang Yeh 郎曄 ed., and with a commentary, reprinted in the Pai-pu ts'ung-shu chi-ch'eng 百部叢書集成 collection.

Chu-tzu yü-lei 朱子語類, Li Ching-te 黎靖德, ed. 8 vols. Peking: Chung-hua shu-chü edition 1986.

Chün-chai tu-shu chih 郡齋讀書志, compiled by Ch'ao Kung-wu 晁公武, Kuo-hsüeh chi-pen ts'ung-shu edition.

Ch'un-ch'iu Tsuo chuan chu 春秋左傳注, Yang Po-chün 楊伯竣, ed. 4 vols. Beijing: Chung-hua shu-chü, 1981.

281

Ch'ung-hsiu Ch'eng-chih hsüeh-shih pi-chi 重修承旨學士壁記, compiled by Ting Chü-hui 丁居晦, in *Han-yüan ch'ün-shu* 翰苑群書, Chih pu-tsu chai ts'ung-shu 知不足齋叢書 edition.

Ch'ung-wen tsung-mu 崇文總目, compiled by Wang Yao-ch'en 王堯臣 et al., Kuo-hsüeh chi-pen ts'ung-shu edition.

Feng-t'ien lu 奉天錄, by Chao Yüan-i 趙元一, Ts'ung-shu chi-ch'eng ch'u-pien 叢書集成初編 edition, Commercial Press, 1937.

Han-lin chih 翰林志, by Li Chao 李肇, in *Han-yüan ch'ün-shu*, Chih pu-tsu chai ts'ung-shu edition.

Han-lin yüan ku-shih 翰林院故事, by Wei Chih-i 韋執誼, in *Han-yüan ch'ün-shu*, Chih pu-tsu chai ts'ung-shu edition.

Han-yüan chi-chu 翰苑集注 (1768 edition), by Lu Chih 陸贄, edited by Chang P'ei-fang 張佩芳 with collected commentaries, reprinted in Yang Chia-lo 楊家駱, ed., Chung-kuo wen-hsüeh ming-chu 中國文學名著. Vol. 6. Taipei: Shih-chieh shu-chü 世界書局, 1982.

Han-yüan chi 翰苑集, by Lu Chih 陸贄, SPTK edition.

Han Ch'ang-li ch'üan-chi 韓昌黎全集, by Han Yü 韓愈, SPPY edition. Taipei: Chung-hua shu-chü reprint, 1970.

Hou ch'ing lu 侯靖錄, compiled by Chao Ling-chih 趙令畤, Ts'ung-shu chi-ch'eng edition, Commercial Press, 1939.

Hou-Han shu 後漢書, by Fan Yeh 范曄, Peking: Chung-hua shu-chü edition, 1965.

Hsin T'ang-shu 新唐書, Ou-yang Hsiu 歐陽修 et al., eds. Peking: Chung-hua shu-chü edition, 1975.

Huang Tsung-hsi ch'üan-chi 黃宗羲全集, by Huang Tsung-hsi 黃宗羲. Vol. 1. Chekiang: Ku-chi ch'u-pan-she 古籍出版社, 1985 edition.

Kai-yü ts'ung-k'ao 陔餘叢考, by Chao I 趙翼, Chan-I tang 湛貽堂 edition. Taipei: Hsin-wen-feng ch'u-pan 新文豐出版 reprint, 1975.

Kuan tzu chiao-cheng 管子校証, Chu tzu chi-ch'eng 諸子集成 edition.

Li chi chu-shu 禮記注疏, with commentary by Cheng Hsüan 鄭玄, SPPY edition.

Li Wen-kung chi 李文公集, by Li Ao 李翱, SPTK edition.

Li Yüan-pin wen-chi 李元賓文集, by Li Kuan 李觀, Ts'ung-shu chi-ch'eng ch'u-pien edition, 1936.

Liang shu 梁書, compiled by Yao Ssu-lien 姚思廉 et al., Chung-hua shu-chü edition, 1973.

Liu Ho-tung ch'üan-chi 柳河東全集, by Liu Tsung-yüan 柳宗元, SPPY edition. Taipei: Chung-hua shu-chü reprint, 1970.

Liu Pin-k'o chia-hua lu 劉賓客佳話錄, by Liu Yü-hsi 劉禹錫, Pai-pu ts'ung-shu chi-ch'eng edition. Taipei: I-wen 藝文.

Lu Hsüan-kung chi 陸宣公集, SPPY edition. Taipei: Chung-hua shu-chü, 1970.

Lü Ho-shu wen-chi 呂和叔文集, by Lü Wen 呂溫, SPTK edition.

Lu-shih shih-p'u 陸氏世譜, 24 vols., Lu I 陸逸 and Lu Sheng-wu 陸繩武, eds., compiled in 1745, Ch'ien-lung shan-te-t'ang 乾隆山德堂 edition. Columbia University Rare Books Collection, microfilm #0876.

Lu-shih tsung-p'u 陸氏宗譜, 4 vols., Lu Chen-chih 陸振之, ed. Columbia University Rare Books Collection, microfilm #548.

Pao-k'e ts'ung-pien 寶刻叢編 (1233), compiled by Ch'en Ssu 陳思, Ts'ung-shu chi-ch'eng edition, 1937.

P'i ling chi 毘陵集, by Tu-ku Chi 獨孤及, SPTK edition.

Po Chü-i chi 白居易集, by Po Chü-i 白居易, Chung-kuo ku-tien wen-hsüeh chi-pen ts'ung-shu 中國古典文學基本叢書 edition. Peking: Chung-hua, 1979.

Po-K'ung liu-t'ie 白孔六帖, Po Chü-i 白居易 and K'ung Ch'uan 孔傳, eds., P'u-pan 蒲版 edition.

San kuo chih 三國志, Ch'en Shou 陳壽, ed. Peking: Chung-hua shu-chü edition, 1959.

Shun-tsung shih-lu 順宗實錄, compiled by Han Yü 韓愈, Ts'ung-shu chi-ch'eng edition, Commercial Press, 1936.

Ssu-k'u ch'üan-shu tsung-mu t'i-yao 四庫全書總目提要, Kuo-hsüeh chi-pen ts'ung-shu edition.

"Sung-ch'ao ming-ch'en chin tsou-i cha-tzu 宋朝名臣進奏議箚子," by Su Shih 蘇軾 et al., as included in HYCC and in most editions of Lu Chih's extant works.

Sung kao-seng chuan 宋高僧傳, compiled by Tsan-ning 贊寧, 14 vols., Ssu-k'u ch'üan-shu chen-pen edition.

Sung shih 宋史, compiled by T'uo-t'uo 脫脫 et al. Peking: Chung-hua shu-chü edition, 1977.

Sung shu 宋書, compiled by Shen Yüeh 沈約. Peking: Chung-hua shu-chü edition, 1974.

Ta T'ang chuan-tsai 大唐傳載, Shou-shan-ke ts'ung-shu 守山閣叢書. Taipei: I-wen reprinted in 1968.

Ta T'ang liu-tien 大唐六典, compiled by Chang Yüeh 張說 et al. Taipei: Wen-hai ch'u-pan-she 文海出版社 reprint, 1962.

T'ai-p'ing kuang-chi 太平廣記, Li Fang 李昉 et al., eds. Peking: Chung-hua shu-chü edition, 1961.

T'ang chih-yen 唐摭言, by Wang Ting-pao 王定保, Chung-kuo wen-hsüeh tsan-k'ao tzu-liao hsiao ts'ung-shu 中國文學參考資料小叢書, Shanghai ku-chi ch'u-pan-she, 1957.

T'ang Hui-yao 唐會要, by Wang P'u 王溥. Taipei: Shih-chieh shu-chü edition, 1982.

T'ang kuo-shih pu 唐國史補, by Li Chao 李肇. Taipei: Shih-chieh shu-chü edition, 1962.

T'ang shang-shu-sheng lang-kuan shih-chu t'i-ming-k'ao 唐尚書省郎官石柱題名考, Lao Ke 勞格 and Chao Yüeh 趙鉞, eds., Yüeh-he ching-she ts'ung-shu 月河精舍叢書. Kyoto: Chung-wen ch'u-pan-she 中文出版社 reprint, 1978.

T'ang-shih chi-shih 唐詩記事, compiled by Chi Yu-kung 計有功. Peking: Chung-hua shu-chü edition, 1965.

T'ang ta-chao-ling chi 唐大詔令集. Peking: Commercial Press edition, 1959.

T'ang Yü-lin 唐語林, compiled by Wang Tang 王讜. Shanghai: Ku-chi ch'u-pan-she edition, 1978.

Teng-k'o chi-k'ao 登科記考, compiled by Hsü Sung 徐松. Peking: Chung-hua shu-chü edition, 1984.

Ts'e-fu yüan-kuei 冊府元龜, compiled by Wang Ch'in-jo 王欽若 et al. Peking: Chung-hua shu-chü reprint, 1960.

Tung-p'o ch'i chi 東坡七集, by Su Shih 蘇軾, SPPY edition. Taipei: Chung-hua shu-chü reprint, 1970.

T'ung-tien 通典, by Tu Yu 杜佑. Peking: Chung-hua shu-chü edition, 1984.

Tzu-chih t'ung-chien 資治通鑑, by Ssu-ma Kuang 司馬光, with commentary by Hu San-hsing 胡三省. Peking: Chung-hua shu-chü edition, 1956.

Wen-yüan ying-hua 文苑英華, Li Fang 李昉 et al., eds. Peking: Chung-hua shu-chü reprint, 1966.

Wu Chün-chih 吳郡志, compiled by Fan Ch'eng-ta 范成大. 6 vols. Ts'ung-shu chi-ch'eng ch'u-pien edition. Shanghai: Commercial Press reprint, 1939.

Wu-chung chiu-shih 吳中舊事, Lu Yu-jen 陸友仁, ed., Ssu-k'u ch'üan-shu chen-pen pieh-chi edition.

Wu-ti chi 吳地記, compiled by Lu Kuang-wei 陸廣微, Ts'ung-shu chi-ch'eng edition, 1939.

Yeh-hou wai-chuan 鄴侯外傳, compiled by Li Fan 李繁, collected in Wu Ch'ao hsiao-shuo ta-kuan 五朝小說大觀. Taipei: Hsin-hsing shu-chü 新興書局 reprint, 1960.

Yü-hai 玉海, Wang Ying-lin 王應麟, ed. Taipei: Hua-wen shu-chü 華文書局 reprint, 1967.

Yüan-ho chün-hsien t'u-chih 元和郡縣圖志, by Li Chi-fu 李吉甫, Kuo-hsüeh chi-pen ts'ung-shu edition. Taipei: Commercial Press, 1968.

Yüan-ho hsing-tsuan 元和姓纂, compiled by Lin Pao 林寶, Ssu-k'u ch'üan-shu chen-pen pieh-chi edition.

Yüan Tz'u-shan chi 元次山集, by Yüan Chieh 元結, edited by Sun Wang 孫望. Shanghai: Chung-hua shu-chü, 1960.

Modern Sources

Baker, Hugh D. R. *Chinese family and kinship*. New York: Columbia University Press, 1979.

Balazs, Etienne. *Chinese civilization and bureaucracy*. Edited by Arthur F. Wright. New Haven: Yale University Press, 1964.

Balazs, S. "Beitrage zur Wirtschaftsgeschichte der T'ang-Zeit, part 3. *Mitteilungen des Seminars für Orientalische Sprachen zu Berlin*, 36 (1933): 1–41.

Barrett, Timothy Hugh. "Buddhism, Taoism and Confucianism in the thought of Li Ao." Ph.D. dissertation, Yale University, 1978.

———. *Li Ao: Buddhist, Taoist, or Neo-Confucian?* New York: Oxford University Press, 1992.

Bol, Peter, *"This culture of ours": Intellectual transitions in T'ang and Sung China*. Stanford: Stanford University Press, 1992.

———. Review of Chen Jo-shui, *Liu Tsung-yüan and the intellectual change in T'ang China, 773–819*, 1992. HJAS 56, no. 1 (June 1996): 165–81.

Chan, Wing-tsit. *A source book in Chinese philosophy*. Princeton, N.J.: Princeton University Press, 1963.

Chang Ch'ün 章群. "T'an Chao Lu san-chia Ch'un-chiu chih shuo 啖趙陸三家春秋之說." in *Ch'ien Mu hsien-sheng pa-shih sui chi-nien lun-wen-chi* 錢穆先生八十歲紀念論文集. Hong Kong: Hsin ya yen-chiu-so 新亞研究所. 1974.

Chang Hao. "On the ching-shih ideal in Neo-Confucianism." *Ch'ing-shih wen-t'i* 3: 1 (Nov., 1974): 36–61.

Chang Hsing-lang 張星烺. *Chung hsi chiao-t'ung shih-liao hui-pien* 中西交通史料彙編. 6 vols. Shanghai: Fu-jen ta-hsüeh ch'u-pan 輔仁大學出版, 1930.

Chang Kuo-kuang 張國光. "Chin-pen Shun-tsung shih-lu fei Han Yü so tso pien 今本《順宗實錄》非韓愈所作辯." *Wen-hsüeh p'ing-lun ts'ung-k'an* 文學評論叢刊 7 (10/1980): 328–40.

Chang Ta-jen 張達人. *Liu Yü-hsi nien-p'u* 劉禹錫年譜. Taipei: Commercial Press, 1982.

Chen Jo-shui. *Liu Tsung-yüan and the intellectual change in T'ang China, 773–819*. Cambridge: Cambridge University Press, 1992.

Chen K'e-ming 陳克明. *Han Yü shu-p'ing* 韓愈述評. Peking: Chung-kuo she-hui k'e-hsüeh ch'u-pan-she 中國社會科學出版社, 1985.

Chen Sung-hsiung 陳松雄. *Lu Hsüeh-kung chih cheng-shih yü wen-hsüeh* 陸宣公之政事與文學. Taipei, Wen-shih-che, 1985.

Ch'en Yin-k'o 陳寅恪. *Ch'en Yin-k'o hsien-sheng ch'üan-chi* 陳寅恪先生全集. Taipei: Chiu-ssu ch'u-pan-she 九思出版社, 1977.

———. *T'ang-tai cheng-chih-shih shu-lun-kao* 唐代政治史述論稿, CYYY chuan-k'an. Taipei reprint, n. d., also reprinted in CYKCC.

———. "Lun Han Yü 論韓愈." *Li-shih yen-chiu* 歷史研究, 2 (1954): 105–114.

Cheng Ho-sheng 鄭鶴聲. *T'ang Tu Chün-ch'ing hsien-sheng Yu nien-p'u* 唐杜君卿先生佑年譜. Taipei: Commercial Press, 1980.

Chiang Fan 蔣凡. "Chin-pen Shun-tsung shih-lu tso-che k'ao-pien 今本《順宗實錄》作者考辯." *Wen-hsüeh p'ing-lun ts'ung-k'an* 16 (10/1982): 321–36.

Ch'ien Chi-po 錢基博. *Han Yü chih* 韓愈志. Shanghai: Commercial Press, 1958.

Ch'ien Mu 錢穆. "Tsa-lun T'ang-tai ku-wen yün-tung 雜論唐代古文運動." *Hsin-ya hsüeh-pao* 新亞學報 3, no. 1 (1957): 123–68.

Ch'iu Ch'ui-liang 邱垂亮. "Lun hsin ch'üan-wei chu-i te wei-hsien-hsing 論新權威主義的危險性." *Zhishi fenzi* 知識份子 (The Chinese intellectual) (Spring, 1994): 16–20.

Chiu-Duke, Josephine. "The Wu *chün* Lu clan as an example of bureaucratization in the T'ang." *B. C. Asian Review* 3/4 (1990): 106–52.

Cho Tsun-hung 卓遵宏. *T'ang-tai chin-shih yü cheng-chih* 唐代進士與政治. Taipei: Kuo-li pien-i-kuan 國立編譯館, 1987.

Chou I-liang, ed. *Hsin T'ang shu tsai-hsiang shih-hsi piao yin-te*, Harvard-Yenching Institute Sinological Index Series, No. 16. Taipei: Chinese Materials and Research Aids Service Center reprint, 1966.

Chou, Shan, "Tu Fu's social conscience: compassion and topicality in his poetry." HJAS, 51: 1 (June, 1991): 5–53.

Chou Ts'e-tsung. *The May Fourth Movement: intellectual revolution in modern China*. Cambridge: Harvard University Press, 1960.

Chou Yen-pin 周彥彬. "Ch'ien-p'ing Lu Chih te ching-chi ssu-hsiang 淺評陸贄的經濟思想." *Ching-chi k'o-hsüeh* 經濟科學 3 (1982): 54–60.

Chü Ch'ing-yüan 鞠清遠. *T'ang-tai ts'ai-cheng shih* 唐代財政史. Ch'ang-sha: Commercial Press, 1943.

Ch'ü Lin-tung 瞿林東. "Kuan-yü <Shun-tsung shih-lu> te chi-ke wen-t'i 關於《順宗實錄》的幾個問題." *Pei-ching shih-fan ta-hsüeh hsüeh-pao* 北京師範大學學報 1 (1982): 45–53.

———. "Lun T'ung-tien te fang-fa he chih-ch'ü 論《通典》的方法和旨趣." *Li-shih yen-chiu* 5 (1984): 112–28.

Ch'ü Wan-li 屈萬里. *Shang-shu chi-shih* 尚書集釋. Taipei: Lien-ching ch'u-pan 聯經出版, 1983.

Ch'üan Han-sheng 全漢昇. *T'ang Sung ti-kuo yü yün-ho* 唐宋帝國與運河. Shanghai: Commercial Press, 1946.

———. "T'ang Sung shih-tai Yang-chou ching-chi ching-k'uang ti fan-jung yü shuai-lo 唐宋時代揚州經濟情況的繁榮與衰落." CYYY, 11 (1947): 149–76.

———. "T'ang-tai wu-chia te pien-tung 唐代物價的變動." Originally published in CYYY 11; it is now in his *Chung-kuo ching-chi shih yen-chiu* 中國經濟史研究. Vol. 1. Hong Kong: Hsin-ya yen-chiu-so, 1976.

———. "Chung-ku tzu-jan ching-chi 中古自然經濟." In his *Chung-kuo ching-chi shih*. Vol. 1. Hong Kong: Hsin-ya yen-chiu-so, 1976.

Chung-kuo li-shih jen-wu lun-chi 中國歷史人物論集. Translated and edited by Chung-yang yen-chiu-yüan Chung-mei jen-wen k'e-hsüeh he-tso wei-yüan-hui 中央研究院中美人文科學合作委員會. Taipei: Chung-shan hsüeh-shu wen-hua tung-shih-hui 中山學術文化董事會, 1973.

Chung-kuo li-shih ti-t'u chi 中國歷史地圖集. Sui T'ang Wu-tai Shih-kuo shih-ch'i 隋唐五代十國時期. Shanghai: Ti-t'u ch'u-pan-she 地圖出版社, 1982.

Creel, H.G. *The origins of statecraft in China*. Chicago: University of Chicago Press, 1970.

———. *Shen Pu-hai: A Chinese political philosopher of the fourth century B.C.* Chicago: University of Chicago Press, 1974.

Dalby, Michael. "Court politics in late T'ang times." *CHC*. Vol. 3, *Sui and T'ang China, 589–906, Part 1*. Cambridge: Cambridge University Press, 1979.

Davis, A. R. *Tu Fu*, New York: Twayne Publishers, 1971.

de Bary, William Theodore et al. *Sources of Chinese tradition*. New York: Columbia University Press, 1960.

———. "Chinese despotism and the Confucian ideal: a seventeenth-century view." In *Chinese thought and institutions*. Edited by John K. Fairbank. Chicago: University of Chicago Press, 1957.

———. "Neo-Confucian cultivation and the seventeenth-century 'Enlightenment.'" In *The unfolding of Neo-Confucianism*. Edited by William Theodore de Bary. New York: Columbia University Press, 1975.

des Rotours, Robert. *Le Traité des examens*. Paris: Ernest Leroux, 1932.

Dubs, Homer, tr. *The works of Hsuntze*. Taipei: Wen-chih ch'u-pan she reprint, n. d.

Duke, Michael S. *Blooming and contending: Chinese literature in the post-Mao era*. Bloomington: Indiana University Press, 1985.

Duyvendak, J. J. L., tr. *The book of Lord Shang*. Chicago: University of Chicago Press, 1928.

Ebrey, Patricia Buckley. *The aristocratic families of early China: A case study of the Po-ling Ts'ui family*. Cambridge: Cambridge University Press, 1978.

Fang Hao 方豪. *Chung hsi chiao-t'ung shih* 中西交通史. Taipei: Hsien-tai kuo-min chih-shih chi-pen ts'ung-shu 現代國民知識基本叢書, 1953.

Fang Yü 方瑜. "Chi-mo yü ch'ao-yüeh—shi lun Tu Fu Ch'ang-an ch'u-yu shih ssu-shou 寂寞與超越——試論杜甫長安出遊詩四首." In *Ti-i chieh kuo-chi T'ang-tai hsüeh-shu hui-i lun-wen chi* 第一屆國際唐代學術會議論文集. Taipei, Hsüeh-sheng shu-chü 學生書局, 1989.

Freedman, Maurice, ed. *Family and kinship in Chinese Society*. Stanford: Stanford University Press, 1970.

Fu An-ming 傅安明. "I-p'ien ts'ung-wei fa-piao kuo te Hu Shih i-kao 一篇從未發表過的胡適遺稿." In Li Yu-ning 李又寧, ed. *Hu Shih yü ta te p'eng-yu* 胡適與他的朋友. New York: T'ien-wai ch'u-pan-she 天外出版社, 1991.

Fu Hsüan-tsung 傅璇琮. *T'ang-tai k'o-chü yü wen-hsüeh* 唐代科舉與文學. Shensi: Jen-min ch'u-pan-she 人民出版社, 1986.

Fu Shi-chen 傅士眞. *T'ang-tai Chi-hsien yüan chih yen-chiu* 唐代集賢院之研究. Taipei: Ming-hsiung ch'u-pan-she 明雄出版社, 1977.

Fukusawa Sokichi 福澤宗吉. "Bungakukan gakushi ni tsuite 文學館學士につ いて." *Kumamoto daigaku kyoiku gakubu kiyo* 熊本大學教育學部紀要 1 (1953): 35–41.

Graham, A.C. *Later Mohist logic, ethics and science.* Hong Kong: Chinese University Press, 1978.

Gregory, Peter N. *Tsung-mi and the sinification of Buddhism.* Princeton: Princeton University Press, 1991.

——. and Patricia Buckley Ebrey. "The religious and historical landscape." In *Religion and society in T'ang and Sung China.* Edited by Patricia Buckley Ebrey and Peter N. Gregory. Honolulu: University of Hawaii Press, 1993.

Guisso, R.W.L. *Wu Tse-t'ien and the politics of legitimation in T'ang China.* Bellingham, Washington: Western Washington University Program in East Asian Studies, 1978.

Han Kuo-p'an 韓國磐. *Pei-ch'ao Sui T'ang te chün-t'ien chih-tu* 北朝隋唐的 均田制度. Shanghai: Jen-min ch'u-pan-she, 1984.

Hartman, Charles. *Han Yü and the T'ang search for unity.* Princeton: Princeton University Press, 1986.

Hartwell, Robert M. "Historical analogism, public policy, and social science in eleventh- and twelfth-century China." *American Historical Review* 76, 3 (June 1971): 690–727.

Hayashida Shinnosuke 林田慎之助. "Tōdai kobun undō no keisei katei 唐代 古文運動の形成過程." *Nippon Chūgoku gakkai hō* 日本中國學會報 29 (1977): 106–23.

Hightower, James. "Some characteristics of parallel prose." In *Studies in Chinese literature.* Edited by John Bishop. Cambridge: Harvard University Press, 1966.

Hino Kaisaburō 日野開三郎. "Ryozeiho to bukka 兩稅法と物價." *Tōyō shigaku* 東洋史學 12 (1950): 1–54; 13 (1955): 1–60.

——. "Yo En no ryozeiho ni okeru zeigaku no mondai 楊炎の兩稅法にお ける稅額の問題." *Tōyō gakuhō* 東洋學報 38, 4 (1956): 370–410.

——. "Ryōzeihō no kihonteki yon gensoku 兩稅法の基本的四原則." *Hōseshi kenkyū* 法制史研究. 11 (1960): 40–77; also in his *Tōyō shigaku ronshu* 東洋史學論叢. vol. 4. Tokyo: San'ichi shobō 三一書房, 1982.

——. "Yō En no ryōzeihō no genkyo gensoku to sensū; sennō gensoku 楊 炎の兩稅法の見居原則と錢數錢納原則." *Shien* 史淵 84 (1961): 1–37; also in his *Tōyō shigaku ronshu*, vol. 4. 1982.

——. "Government monopoly on salt in T'ang in the period before the enforcement of the liang-shui fa." *Memoirs of the Research Department of the Tōyō Bunko* 22 (1963): 1–55.

Ho Ch'ang-ch'ün 賀昌群. *Han T'ang chien feng-chien te kuo-yu t'u-ti-chih yü chün-t'ien chih* 漢唐間封建的國有土地制與均田制. Shanghai: Jen-min ch'u-pan-she, 1958.

Ho Ch'i-min 何啓民. *Chung-ku men-ti lun-chi* 中古門第論集. Taipei: Hsüeh-sheng shu-chü, 1978.

Hori Toshikazu 堀敏一. *Kindensei no kenkyū — Chūgoku kodai kokka no tochi seisaku to tochi shoyū-sei* 均田制の研究──中國古代國家の土地政策と土地所有制. Tokyo: Iwanami Shūten 岩波書店, 1975.

Hsiao Kung-ch'üan. *A history of Chinese political thought.* Translated by F. W. Mote. Princeton University Press, 1979.

———. "Legalism and autocracy in traditional China." *Ch'ing-hua hsüeh-pao* N.S. 4: 2 (1964): 108–21.

Hsieh Wu-hsiung 謝武雄. *Lu Hsüan-kung chih yen-lun chi ch'i wen-hsüeh* 陸宣公之言論及其文學. Taipei: Chia-hsin shui-ni corporation 嘉興水泥, 1975.

Hsü, Immanuel C. Y. *The rise of modern China*, reprinted edition. Taipei: Hung-ch'iao shu-tien, 1978.

Hsing I-t'ien 邢義田. *Ch'in Han shih lun-kao* 秦漢史論稿. Taipei: Tung-ta t'u-shu kung-ssu 東大圖書公司, 1987.

Hsü Fu-kuan 徐復觀. "Chung-kuo te chih-tao — tu Lu Hsüan-kung chuan chi shu hou 中國的治道 ── 讀陸宣公傳集書後." In his *Hsüeh-shu yü cheng-chih chih-chien* 學術與政治之間. Taipei: Hsüeh-sheng shu-chü, new edition, 1980.

Hsü Kuo-lin 許國霖. *Tunhuang shih-shih hsieh-ching t'i-chi yü Tunhuang tsa-lu* 敦煌石室寫經題記與敦煌雜錄. 2 vols. 1937.

Hu Chi-ch'uang 胡寄窗. *Chung-kuo ching-chi ssu-hsiang shih* 中國經濟思想史. 2 vols. Shanghai: Jen-min ch'u-pan-she, 1963.

Huang, Chün-chieh, "Some observations and reflections." In *Imperial rulership and cultural change in traditional China.* Edited by Frederick P. Brandauer and Chün-chieh Huang. Seattle: University of Washington Press, 1994: 281–89.

Hucker, Charles O. "The Tung-lin movement of the late Ming period." In *Chinese thought and institutions.* Edited by John K. Fairbank. Chicago: University of Chicago Press, 1957.

———. *China's imperial past: An introduction to Chinese history and culture.* Stanford: Stanford University Press, 1975.

———. *A dictionary of official titles in imperial China.* Stanford: Stanford University Press, 1985.

Hung, William. *Tu Fu: China's greatest poet.* New York: Russell & Russell, 1969 [1952].

Ikeda On 池田溫. "Tōdai no gumbō hyō 唐代の郡望表." *Tōyō gakuhō* 42 (1959): 293–331, and 42 (1960): 412–30.

———. "Sei Tō no Shukenin 盛唐の集賢院," *Hokkaidō daigaku Bungakubu kiyō* 北海道大學文學部紀要 19, no. 2 (1971): 45–98

Inaba Ichiro 稻葉一郎, "Chūtō ni okeru shinjugaku undō no ichi kosatsu: Ryū Chike no keisho hihan to Ta-Chō-Riki shi no Shunjū gaku 中唐にお

ける新儒學運動の一考察 —— 劉知幾の經書批判と啖趙陸氏の春秋學."
In *Chūgoku chūseishi kenkyū—Rikuchō Zui Tō no shakai to bunka* 中國
中世史研究 —— 六朝隋唐の社會と文化, Tokyo: Tōkai Daigaku Shuppan-
kai 東海大學出版會, 1970.

Jen Chi-yü 任繼育, ed. *Chung-kuo tao-chiao shih* 中國道教史. Shanghai: Jen-
min ch'u-pan-she, 1990.

Jen Yü-ts'ai 任育才. *T'ang Te-tsung Feng-t'ien ting-nan chi ch'i shih-liao
chih yen-chiu* 唐德宗奉天定難及其史料之研究. Taipei: Commercial Press,
1970.

Johnson, David. *The medieval Chinese oligarchy*. Boulder: Westview Press,
1977.

———. "The last years of a great clan: The Li family of Chao Chün in late
T'ang and early Sung." HJAS, 37 / 1 (June, 1977): 5–102.

Johnson, Wallace, tr. *The T'ang code*. Vol. 1, *General principles*. Princeton:
Princeton University Press, 1979.

Kanda Kiichiro 神田喜一郎. "Ryō Shuku nempu 梁肅年譜." In *Tōhō Gakkai
sōritsu nijūgo shūnen kinen tōhōgaku ronshū* 東方學會二十五週年紀念
東方學論集. Tokyo: Toho Gakkai, 1972.

Kao Ming-shih 高明士. "T'ang-tai chiao-yü te te-se 唐代教育的特色." *Yu-
shih yüeh-k'an* 幼獅月刊 47, 5 (1978): 63–65.

Karlgren, Bernhard, tr. *The book of odes*. Stockholm: Museum of Far Eastern Antiquities, 1950.

Kitō Yūichi 鬼頭有一. "Lu Hsüan-kung tsou-i cha-chi 陸宣公奏議箚記."
Kōgakkan ronsō 皇學館論叢 18, 6 (1985): 16–35.

Knoblock, John, tr. *Xunzi*. 3 vols. Stanford: Stanford University Press, 1988,
1990, 1994.

Kubo Noritaka 窪德忠. *Dokyōshi* 道教史. Tokyo: Yamakawa Shuppan-sha 山
川出版社, 1977.

Kristof, Nicholas D. and Sheryl WuDunn. *China wakes: the struggle for the
soul of a rising power*. New York: Times Books, 1994.

———. "China's rush to riches." *New York times magazine*. September 4,
1994: 38–41, 46, 48, 54.

K'ung Pao-k'ang 孔寶康. "Wo-kuo ku-tai shih-po chih-tu ch'u-t'an 我國古代
市舶制度初探." *Hai-chiao shih yen-chiu* 海交史研究 13 (1988): 1–4.

Kuwabara Jitsuzō 桑原騭藏. *T'ang Sung mao-i-kang yen-chiu* 唐宋貿易港
研究. Translated by Yang Lien 楊鍊. Taipei: Commercial Press, 1963.

Lamont, H. G. "An early ninth century debate on Heaven: Liu Tsung-yüan's
T'ien shuo and Liu Yü-hsi's T'ien lun." *Asia Major* (n. s.) 18 (1973): 181–
208, and 19 (1974): 37–85.

Lau, D. C., tr. *Lao Tzu Tao Te Ching*. Penguin Books, 1963.

———, tr. *Mencius*. Harmondsworth, England: Penguin Books, 1970.

———, tr. *Confucius: the Analects*. Harmondsworth, England: Penguin Books,
1979.

Lee, John. "The dragons and tigers of 792: the examination in T'ang history." *T'ang Studies* 6 (1988): 25–48.

Legge, James, tr. *The Chinese classics*. Vol. 5, *The Ch'un Ts'ew with the Tso chuen*, London: Trübner & Co.1872.

———, tr. *The four books*. Taipei: Wen-hua t'u-shu reprint, n. d.

———, tr., *The shu king*. In *The sacred books of the east*. Edited by F. Max Müller. 2nd edition. Vol. 3. Oxford: Clarendon Press, 1899.

———, tr. *The li ki*, part IV. In *The sacred books of the east*. Edited by F. Max Müller. Vol. 28, reprinted by Motilal Banarsidass, 1966.

Li Chin-pao 李金寶. "Lu Chih ching-chi ssu-hsiang yen-chiu 陸贄經濟思想研究." *Che-chiang hsüeh-k'an* 浙江學刊 3 (1983): 68–71.

Li Hsüeh-hua 李雪華. "Kuan-yü Lu Chih lun liang-shui-fa te chi-ko wen-t'i 關於陸贄論兩稅法的幾個問題." *Chung-kuo she-hui ching-chi shih yen-chiu* 中國社會經濟史研究. 3 (1982): 74–81.

Li Yu-ning. *Shang Yang's reforms and state control in China*. New York: M. E. Sharpe, 1977.

———, ed. *Hu Shih yü ta te p'eng-yu*. 2 vols. New York: T'ien-wai ch'u-pan she, 1990, 1991.

Lin Li-hsüeh 林麗雪. *Pao-p'u tzu nei-wai p'ien ssu-hsiang hsi-lun* 抱朴子內外篇思想析論. Taipei: Hsüeh-sheng shu-chü, 1980.

Lin Yü-sheng. *The crisis of Chinese consciousness: radical antitraditionalism in the May Fourth era*. Madison: University of Wisconsin Press, 1979.

Liu Chao-jen 劉昭仁. "Lu Hsüan-kung yen-chiu 陸宣公研究." *Shih-chien hsüeh-pao* 實踐學報 9 (1978): 97–125, and 10 (1979):1–42.

Liu Pin-yen. *People or monsters and other stories and reportage from China after Mao*. Edited by Perry Link. Bloomington: Indiana University Press, 1983.

———. *A higher kind of loyalty: a memoir by China's foremost journalist*. Translated by Chu Hung. New York: Pantheon Books, 1990.

——— and Perry Link. "A Great Leap Backward?" Review of He Qinglian, *Zhongguo de xianjing* [China's Pitfall], Beijing, 1998. *New York Review of Books*. October 8, 1998, 19–23.

Liu Po-chi 劉伯驥. *T'ang-tai cheng-chiao shih* 唐代政教史. Taipei: Chung-hua shu-chü, 1974.

Liu Wu-chi. *An introduction to Chinese literature*. Bloomington: Indiana University Press, 1966.

Lo Hsiang-lin 羅香林. "T'ang-tai san-chiao chiang-lun k'ao 唐代三教講論稿." In his *T'ang-tai wen-hua-shih* 唐代文化史. Taipei: Commercial Press, 1955.

Lo Lien-t'ien 羅聯添. *Han Yü yen-chiu* 韓愈研究. Taipei: Hsüeh-sheng shu-chü, 1977.

———. "Li Ao yen-chiu 李翱研究." *Kuo-li pien-i-kuan kuan-k'an* 國立編譯館館刊 2, 3 (Dec., 1973): 55–89.

Lo Tsung-ch'iang 羅宗強. *Sui T'ang Wu-tai wen-hsüeh ssu-hsiang-shih* 隋唐五代文學思想史. Shanghai: Ku-chi ch'u-pan-she, 1986.

Lu Jen 陸靭. "Lun shih-po-ssu hsing-chih he li-shih tso-yung te pien-hua 論市舶司性質和歷史作用的變化." *Hai-chiao shih yen-chiu* 13 (1988): 5–13.

Lü Ssu-mien 呂思勉. *Sui T'ang Wu-tai shih* 隋唐五代史. Shanghai: Ku-chi ch'u-pan-she edition, 1984.

Lynn, Richard John. *The classic of Changes: a new translation of the I Ching as interpreted by Wang Bi*. New York: Columbia University Press, 1994.

Mair, Victor. "Scroll presentation in the T'ang dynasty." HJAS, 38 (1978): 35–60.

Ma Ch'eng-su 馬承驌. *Lü Ho-shu hsüeh-p'u* 呂和叔學譜. Taipei: 1977.

Mao Han-kuang 毛漢光. *Liang-Chin Nan-Pei-Ch'ao shih-tsu cheng-chih chih yen-chiu* 兩晉南北朝士族政治之研究. 2 vols. Taipei: Chung-kuo hsüeh-shu chu-tso chiang-chu wei-yüan-hui 中國學術著作獎助委員會, 1966.

———. "Ts'ung shih-tsu chi-kuan ch'ien-i k'an T'ang-tai shih-tsu chih chung-yang-hua 從士族籍貫遷移看唐代士族之中央化." CYYY, 52 (1981): 421–510.

———. "Wu chün Lu-shih 吳郡陸氏." In his *Tao Hsi-sheng hsien-sheng chiu-chih jung-ch'ing chi-nien lun-wen-chi* 陶希聖先生九秩榮慶紀念論文集. Taipei: Shih-huo 食貨, 1989.

McMullen, David, "Yüan Chieh (719–772) and the early ku-wen movement." Ph.D. dissertation. Cambridge: Cambridge University, 1968.

———. "Historical and literary theory in the mid-eighth century," In *Perspectives on the T'ang*. Edited by Arthur F. Wright and Denis Twitchett. New Haven: Yale University Press, 1973.

———. "Views of the state in Du yu and Liu Zongyuan." In *Foundations and limits of state power in China*. Edited by S. R. Schram. Hong Kong: Chinese University Press of Hong Kong, 1987.

———. *State and Scholars in T'ang China*. Cambridge: Cambridge University Press, 1988.

———. "Han Yü: An alternative picture." Review article in HJAS, 49, 2 (Dec. 1989): 603–57.

———. "Li Chou, a forgotten agnostic of the late-eighth century," AM, 8, 2 (1995): 57–105.

Miyazaki Ichisada 宮崎市定. *Kyūhin kanjinhō no kenkyū* 九品官人法の研究. Kyoto: Tōyōshi Kenkyūkai 東洋史研究會, 1956.

Needham, Joseph. *Science and civilization in China*. Vol. 2, *History of scientific thought*. Cambridge: Cambridge University Press, 1962.

Nienhauser, William H., Jr., ed. *The Indiana companion to traditional Chinese literature*. Bloomington: Indiana University Press, 1986.

Obata Tatsuo 小畑龍雄. "Shinsakugun no seiritsu 神策軍の成立." *Tōyōshi kenkyū* 東洋史研究 18, 2 (1959): 35–56.

Owen, Stephen. *The great age of Chinese poetry: the high T'ang*. New Haven: Yale University Press, 1981.

P'eng Hsin-wei 彭信威. *Chung-kuo huo-pi shih* 中國貨幣史. Shanghai: Jen-min ch'u-pan-she, 1958.

Peterson, C. A. "Court and province in mid- and late T'ang." In *CHC*. Edited by Denis Twitchett. Vol. 3. *Sui and T'ang China, 589–906, Part 1.* Cambridge: Cambridge University Press, 1979.

Pien Hsiao-hsüan 汴孝萱. "T'ang-tai hsiao-shuo yü cheng-chih 唐代小說與政治." *Chung-hua wen shih lun-ts'ung* 中華文史論叢 1 (1985): 179–208.

Pulleyblank, E.G. *The background of the rebellion of An Lu-shan.* London: Greenwood Press reprint, 1982 [1955].

———. "The Shun-tsung shih-lu," BSOAS, 19, 2 (1957): 336–44.

———. "Neo-Confucianism and neo-legalism in T'ang intellectual life, 755–805." In *The Confucian persuasion.* Edited by Arthur F. Wright. Stanford: Stanford University Press, 1960.

———. "The An Lu-shan rebellion and the origins of chronic militarism in late T'ang China." In *Essays on T'ang society.* Edited by John Curtis Perry and Bardwell L. Smith. Leiden: E. J. Brill, 1976.

Rickett, Allyn, tr. *Guanzi, political, economic, and philosophical essays from early China.* Princeton: University Press, 1985.

Rideout, J. K. "The rise of the eunuchs during the T'ang dynasty." AM, 1 (1949–50): 53–72 and 2 (1953–54): 42–58.

Runciman, W.G., ed. *Weber selections in translation.* Cambridge: Cambridge University Press, 1978.

Sa Meng-wu 薩孟武. *Chung-kuo cheng-chih ssu-hsiang shih* 中國政治思想史. Taipei: San-min shu-chü 三民書局. 1969.

Schram, S. R., ed. *The scope of state power in China.* Hong Kong: Chinese University Press, 1985.

———, ed. *Foundations and limits of state power in China.* Hong Kong: Chinese University Press, 1987.

Schwartz, Benjamin, "The Intellectual history of China: preliminary reflections." In *Chinese thought and institutions.* Edited by John K. Fairbank. Chicago: University of Chicago Press, 1957.

———. "Some polarities in Confucian thought." In *Confucianism in action.* Edited by David S. Nivison and Arthur F. Wright. Stanford: Stanford University Press, 1959.

Shen Fu-wei 沈福偉. "Lun T'ang-tai tui-wai mao-i te ssu-ta hai-kang 論唐代對外貿易的四大海港." *Hai-chiao-shih yen-chiu* 10, 2 (1986): 19–32.

Silk, David L., ed. *International encyclopedia of the social sciences.* New York: Macmillan, 1968.

Soloman, Bernard S., tr. *The veritable record of the T'ang emperor Shun-tsung.* Cambridge: Harvard University Press, 1955.

Strickmann, Michel. "The Mao Shan revelations, Taoism and the aristocracy." *T'oung Pao* 43, 1 (1977): 1–62.

Sun Ch'ang-wu 孫昌武. *Liu Tsung-yüan chuan-lun* 柳宗元傳論. Peking: Jen-min wen-hsüeh ch'u-pan-she 人民文學出版社, 1982.

———. *T'ang-tai ku-wen yün-tung t'ung-lun* 唐代古文運動通論. Tientsin: Pai-hua wen-i chu-pan-she 百花文藝出版社, 1984.

Sun Kuo-tung 孫國棟. *T'ang Sung shih lun-ts'ung* 唐宋史論叢. Hong Kong: Lung-men shu-chü 龍門書局, 1980.

Sun Wang 孫望. *Yüan Tz'u-shan nien-p'u* 元次山年譜. Shanghai: Chung-hua shu-chü, 1962.

Sunayama Minoru 砂山稔. *Zui Tō dokyō shisoshi kenkyū* 隋唐道教思想史研究. Tokyo, Hirakawa Shuppan 平川出版, 1990.

T'ang Ch'ang-ju 唐長孺. "Tu Pao-p'u tzu t'ui-lun nan-pei hsüeh-feng te i-t'ung 讀抱朴子推論南北學風的異同." In his *Wei-Chin Nan-pei-ch'ao shih lun-ts'ung* 魏晉南北朝史論叢. Peking: San-lien shu-tien, 1955: 351–81.

T'ang Yung-t'ung 湯用彤. *Sui T'ang fo-chiao shih kao* 隋唐佛教史稿. Peking: Chung-hua shu-chü, 1982.

Tillman, Hoyt Cleveland. *Utilitarian Confucianism: Ch'en Liang's challenge to Chu Hsi*. Cambridge: Council on East Asian Studies. Cambridge: Harvard University, 1982.

———. *Confucian discourse and Chu Hsi's ascendancy*. Honolulu: University of Hawaii Press, 1992.

Tozaki Tetsuhiko 戸崎哲彦, "Liu-ch'uan Jih-pen te yu-kuan Lu Chih (i.e. Lu Ch'ün) te shih-liao chi jo-kan k'ao-cheng 流傳日本的有關陸質 (即陸淳) 的史料及若干考証." *Chung-kuo che-hsüeh shih yen-chiu* 中國哲學史研究 1 (1985): 49–58.

Ts'en Chung-mien 岑仲勉. *Yüan-ho hsing-tsuan ssu-chiao chi* 元和姓纂四校記. 3 vols. Shanghai: Commercial Press, 1948.

———. *T'ang-jen hang-ti lu* 唐人行第錄. Shanghai: Ku-chi ch'u-pan-she, 2nd edition, 1978.

———. *Lang-kuan shih-chu t'i-ming hsin k'ao-ting (wai san-chung)* 郎官石柱題名新考訂 (外三種). Shanghai: Ku-chi ch'u-pan-she, 1984.

Tung K'e-ch'ang 董克昌. "Lun Li Sheng 論李晟." *Liang-tung ta-hsüeh hsüeh-pao* 遼東大學學報 3 (1980): 49–52.

Twitchett, Denis. "The Salt Commissioners after An Lu-shan's rebellion." *Asia Major*, N. S. 4, 1 (1959): 60–89.

———. "Lu Chih (754–805): Imperial adviser and court official." In *Confucian personalities*. Edited by Arthur F. Wright and Denis Twitchett. Stanford: Stanford University Press, 1962.

———. "The T'ang market system." *Asia Major*, N. S. 12–2 (1966): 202–48.

———. "Merchant, trade and government in late T'ang." *Asia Major*, 2, 14 (1968): 63–95.

———. *Financial administration under the T'ang dynasty*. Cambridge: Cambridge University Press, 2nd edition, 1970.

———. "The composition of the T'ang ruling class: new evidence from Tunhuang." In *Perspectives on the T'ang*. Edited by Arthur F. Wright and Denis Twitchett. New Haven: Yale University Press, 1973.

————. *The birth of the Chinese meritocracy: bureaucrats and examinations in T'ang China*. A lecture delivered to the China Society in London on December 17, 1974 and printed by Bendles (Torquay) Ltd.

————. "Varied patterns of provincial autonomy in the T'ang dynasty." In *Essays on T'ang society*. Edited by John Curtis Perry and Bardwell L. Smith. Leiden: E. J. Brill, 1976.

————. Introduction to *CHC*. Vol. 3, *Sui and T'ang China, 589–906*, Part 1. Cambridge: Cambridge University Press, 1979.

———— and Howard Wechsler. "Kao-tsung (reign 649–83) and the Empress Wu: the inheritor and the usurper." In *CHC*. Vol. 3, *Sui and T'ang China, 589–906*, Part 1, 1979.

————. "Hsüan-tsung (reign 712–56)." In *CHC*. Vol. 3, *Sui and T'ang China, 589–906*. Part 1, 1979.

————, ed. *The Cambridge history of China* Vol. 3, *Sui and T'ang China, 589–906*, Part 1. 1979.

Van Over, Raymond, ed. and tr. *I ching*. New York: New American Library, 1971.

Waley, Arthur. *The life and times of Po Chü-i*. London: George Allen & Unwin, 1949.

Wang Chung-lo 王仲犖. "T'ang-tai liang-shui fa yen-chiu 唐代兩稅法研究." *Li-shih yen-chiu* 6 (1963): 117–34.

Wang Gung-wu. "The Nanhai trade." *Journal of the Malayan Branch of the Royal Asiatic Society* 31, 2 (1958): 3–127.

Wang I-t'ung 王伊同. *Wu-ch'ao men-ti* 五朝門第. 2 vols. Taipei: Wen-hai ch'u-pan-she, reprint, 1973.

Wang Meng-ou 王夢鷗. *Li chi chin-chu chin-i* 禮記今註今譯. Vol. 1. Taipei: Commercial Press, 2nd edition, 1971.

Wang Shou-nan 王壽南. *T'ang-tai huan-kuan ch'üan-shih chih yen-chiu* 唐代宦官權勢之研究. Taipei: Cheng-chung shu-chü 正中書局, 1971.

————. *T'ang-tai fan-chen yü chung-yang kuan-hsi chih yen-chiu* 唐代藩鎮與中央關係之研究. Taipei: Ta-hua shu-chü 大華書局, revised edition, 1978.

————. "Lu Chih te shih-kung chi ch'i cheng-chih ssu-hsiang 陸贄的事功及其政治思想." *Yu-shih yüeh-k'an* 47, 5 (1978): 57–62.

————. *Sui T'ang shih* 隋唐史. Taipei: San-min shu-chü, 1986.

Wang Yü-ch'üan. "An outline of the central government of the Former Han dynasty." *HJAS*, 12 (June, 1949): 134–87.

Wang Yün-sheng 王芸生. "Lun erh Wang pa ssu-ma cheng-chih ko-hsin ti li-shih i-i 論二王八司馬政治革新的歷史意義." *Li-shih yen-chiu* 3 (1963): 105–30.

Wang, Zhenping. "T'ang maritime trade administration," *Asia Major*, 3rd series, 4, 1, (1991): 7–38.

Weber, Max. "Politics as a vocation." In *Max Weber: Selections in transla-*

tion. Edited by W. G. Runciman. Cambridge: Cambridge University Press, 1978.

Wechsler, Howard. *Mirror to the Son of Heaven*. New Haven: Yale University Press, 1974.

———. "The Confucian impact on early T'ang decision-making." *T'oung pao* 66 (1980): 1–40.

———. *Offerings of jade and silk: ritual and symbol in the legitimation of the T'ang dynasty*. New Haven: Yale University Press, 1985.

Wei Ching-sheng, *The courage to stand alone, letters from prison and other writings*, edited and translated by Kristina M. Torgeson. New York: Viking, 1997.

Weinstein, Stanley. *Buddhism under the T'ang*. Cambridge: Cambridge University Press, 1987.

Wilhelm, Richard, tr. *The i ching*. Rendered into English by Cary F. Baynes. Princeton: Princeton University Press, 1950.

Wong Kwok-yiu. "Liu Yü-hsi (772–842): a study of his thought." M. A. thesis, University of British Columbia, 1993.

Wood, Alan T. *Limits to autocracy: from Sung neo-Confucianism to a doctrine of political rights*. Honolulu: University of Hawai'i Press, 1995.

Wu Chang-ch'üan 吳章銓. *T'ang-tai nung-min wen-t'i yen-chiu* 唐代農民問題研究. Taipei: Chung-kuo hsüeh-shu chu-tso chiang-chu wei-yüan-hui, 1963.

Wu Wen-chih 吳文治. *Liu Tsung-yüan p'ing-chuan* 柳宗元評傳. Peking: Chung-hua shu-chü, 1962.

Yamamoto Tatsuyoshi 山本隆義. "Tō-Sō jidai ni okeru kanrin gakushi ni tsuite 唐宋時代における翰林學士について." *Tōhōgaku* 東方學 4 (1952): 28–38.

Yang Lien-sheng 楊聯陞. "Tung Han te hao-tsu 東漢的豪族." *Ch'ing-hua hsüeh-pao* 清華學報 11, 4 (1936): 1007–63.

Yang Nien-ch'ün 楊念群. "Ju-hsüeh nei-tsai p'i-p'an te hsien-shih k'un-ching 儒學內在批判的現實困境: 余英時《現代儒學論》簡評." In 二十一世紀 40, 4 (1997): 94–99.

Yano Chikara 矢野主稅. "Tō-dai kangunshi-sei no kakuritsu ni tsuite 唐代監軍使制の確立について." *Nishi-nibon shigaku* 西日本史學 14 (1953): 16–32.

———. "Tōdai ni okeru kanrin gakushiin ni tsuite 唐代における翰林學士院について." *Shigaku kenkyū* 史學研究 50 (1953): 63–70.

———. "Haishi kenkyu 裴氏研究." *Shakai kagaku ronsō* 社會科學論叢 14 (1965): 17–48.

Yen I-p'ing 嚴一萍. *Lu Hsüan-kung nien-p'u* 陸宣公年譜. Taipei: I-wen, 1975.

Yen Keng-wang 嚴耕望. "T'ang-jen hsi-yeh shan-lin ssu-yüan chih feng-shang 唐人習業山林寺院之風尚." In his *T'ang shih yen-chiu ts'ung-kao* 唐史研究叢稿. Hong Kong: Hsin-ya yen-chiu-so, 1969.

———. *T'ang p'u shang ch'eng-lang piao* 唐僕尙丞郎表. 4 vols. Taipei: CYYY, 1956.

Yü Hsien-hao 郁賢皓. *T'ang tz'u-shih k'ao* 唐刺史考. 5 vols. Hong Kong: Chung-hua shu-chü fen-chü, 1987.

Yü Ying-shih 余英時. "'Chün tsun ch'en pei' hsia te chün-ch'üan yü hsiang-ch'üan — fan-chih lun yü Chung-kuo cheng-chih ch'uan-t'ung yü-lun '君尊臣卑' 下的君權與相權 —— 反智論與中國政治傳統餘論." In his *Li-shi yü ssu-hsiang* 歷史與思想. Taipei: Lien ching, 1976.

———. *Chung-kuo chih-shih chieh-ts'eng shih lun (ku-tai p'ien)* 中國知識階層史論 (古代篇). Taipei: Lien-ching, 1980.

———. "Hsien-tai ju-hsüeh te hui-ku yü chan-wang — ts'ung Ming-Ch'ing ssu-hsiang chi-tiao te chuan-huan k'an ju-hsüeh te hsien-tai fa-chan 現代儒學的回顧與展望 —— 從明清思想基調的轉換看儒學的現代發展." In his *Hsien-tai ju-hsüh lun* 現代儒學論. Hong Kong: Global Publishing Co., 1996.

Index